Strategies for Personality Research

The Observation Versus
Interpretation of Behavior

Donald W. Fiske

Strategies for Personality Research

Jossey-Bass Publishers
San Francisco • Washington • London • 1978

STRATEGIES FOR PERSONALITY RESEARCH
The Observation Versus Interpretation of Behavior
by Donald W. Fiske

Library of Congress Catalogue Card Number LC 78-1150

International Standard Book Number ISBN 0-87589-373-2

Manufactured in the United States of America

JACKET DESIGN BY WILLI BAUM

FIRST EDITION

Code 7810

The Jossey-Bass
Social and Behavioral Science Series

Special Advisor,
Methodology of Social and Behavioral Research
Donald W. Fiske
University of Chicago

Preface

Strategies for Personality Research is intended for persons who are concerned with behavioral science and who are convinced that it is a domain of critical importance, both as a science and as a discipline that may provide guidance for attacking the pressing problems that confront mankind today. More particularly, this book is intended for those who are troubled by the current state of the several behavioral sciences. Although the chapters of this volume concentrate on the discipline of personality, the potential ramifications or extensions of its arguments for other areas in behavioral science are examined as well. The book is divided into two parts. Part One is critical; Part Two is more positive in its proposed reorientations and strategies.

Investigators and practitioners who are satisfied with the current state of their specialty within behavioral science—be it personality or some other discipline—and who are content with the rate of progress they perceive in their field will find little of interest in this book. The audience to whom this book is primarily directed includes journeymen in the behavioral sciences who are already active scholars and investigators as well as apprentices in training. In addition, the book is intended for applied scientists and practitioners who are willing to reflect on their basic procedures for gathering information about people. The book's intended audience does not include philosophers of science. I have not had the presumption to join in the debates now current in the philosophy of science. Since any writing on the subject matter of this volume, however, of necessity involves an implicit philosophical position, I have sketched mine below.

The argument developed in this volume is directed primarily at the domain of personality, including experimental investigations of psychodynamics and clinical judgment. It is also pertinent to the classical topic of individual differences, to clinical assessment, and to personnel psychology—selection, classification, and the evaluation of performance. Beyond personality, this volume has relevance for much of social and organizational psychology and for much of developmental psychology insofar as these areas use data that are judgments made by observers about other people. The argument is especially applicable to studies of the whole person or of characteristics attributed to persons. Hence, it applies to studies of group differences where each group has been formed on the basis of someone's judgment concerning the property (schizophrenia, sociopathy, or whatever) common to its members. Outside of psychology, the argument in this book seems relevant to those parts of anthropology, education, sociology, political science, and economics that are concerned with judged attributes of persons.

The exposition focuses on personality for two reasons. First, the concentration on one discipline simplifies the presentation and examination of the argument. Second, as a psychologist who has worked primarily on measurement and research methodology in personality, I can state the critique and the argument most easily for that substantive area. Although I am convinced that they also apply to some other parts of psychology, I cannot judge with confidence the extent to which the critique and argument aimed at personality research are pertinent to other social sciences; the possibilities of extending the argument, however, are considered in Chapter Fifteen.

To keep this volume within reasonable size, I have not attempted a comprehensive critique of the whole field of personality, nor have I tried to evaluate current practices in measuring personality. Analyses of difficulties with these practices can be found in Mischel (1968), Fiske (1971), and Wiggins (1973). The persisting relevance of articles collected a decade ago by Jackson and Messick (1967) is itself a commentary on the state of the field. Furthermore, although I emphasize methodology, my coverage of that orientation is not complete. In particular, I do not examine closely the matter of studying behavior as interaction with immediate environment. Instead, I have focused on the major obstacle to scientific progress in personality—the basic role of interpretive, attributive judgments as the phenomena to be understood and as the data now used in empirical research.

Although the argument of this book can be stated in a few hundred words, such a presentation would not enable the reader to see its full implications and ramifications. Since my viewpoint is sharply different from the standard orientation, which is so generally and uncritically accepted, the exposition is intentionally discursive or conversational in many places in order to give readers an opportunity to consider at length their own implicit, unstated assumptions and to contrast them with the assumptions and arguments presented here. Where readers find the discussion obvious, they are invited to assess its compatibility with their own unstated premises.

The argument is based on a number of propositions and generalizations that are interdependent. As a consequence, the examination of one thesis often requires mention of others and the same point may need to be made in more than one place. I hope that such interweaving of themes helps to clarify and to bring out implications. The primary assertions of this book can be found in the summaries of the several chapters. Definitions of basic terms are given in the Glossary at the end of this volume.

Many of the propositions and theses examined in this book are not new. In some instances, I have adapted or taken them from earlier writers. In other cases, after formulating a proposition, I found a similar statement in the literature and was gratified by the convergence of views. For many of the assertions, there is more than one similar statement in the literature. For others, I have undoubtedly forgotten the original stimulus. I have not attempted to provide references for these borrowed assertions. Writers who influenced my arguments or who unwittingly supported them include D'Andrade (1965, 1974), Hanson (1958), Koch (1974), Kuhn (1970b), Lachenmeyer (1973), Mandler and Kessen (1959), Mischel (1968), Nagel (1961), Popper (1959), Skinner (1950), Weick (1969), and Wigner (1964).

It may seem to the reader that there is an inconsistency in my thinking, especially in the first part of this book. Although I question the current orientation and substance of personality conceptualizations as a basis for a science of the behavioral phenomena usually subsumed under the rubric of personality, I write from that orientation in many places. For example, I refer to needs, traits, expectancies, dispositions, and values, as in the prevalent mode of writing in this area. I have written from that orientation in order to provide examples that would be useful for the reader. Moreover, it seemed wise to start from the contemporary conceptual orientation in developing the critique, rather than expecting the reader to plunge immediately into a new style of thinking about the phenomena. And I must admit that I continue from time to time to think in the conventional terms, especially when I am talking to colleagues or when I am not working within the proposed new viewpoint. Indeed, contemporary concepts may be useful in research directed at problems formulated in terms of the human world outside psychology buildings. In this volume, such thinking in the contemporary mode is not rejected but rather is reinterpreted. Hence, the apparent inconsistency is, I hope, more an appearance than a fact.

This book presents my most recent work on the problem that has occupied my attention for many years: How can measurement in the area of personality be improved so as to facilitate more productive research and to enable substantial progress to be made in our empirical understanding of behavior? I began by investigating the variability over time in the behavior of individuals, to see what that factor contributed to the problem. Later, I explored the low degree of homogeneity in personality measurements. That topic led to investigating the heterogeneity in each personality concept and the nature of the processes that produce the responses to items in personality tests.

All of that earlier work is brought into *Measuring the Concepts of Personality* (Fiske, 1971), where the major theme is the need to analyze the concepts at which personality measurements are aimed. While writing that book, I was troubled by some vaguely recognized issues. Since they seemed to fall outside the scope of that book, I put them aside until that manuscript was completed. Later I returned to confront those issues and resolve them in my own mind. The outcome was a conversion experience leading to the present book.

Reexamining what we have been doing in studying personality, I have come to the conclusion that we have tried to build on shifting sands and that we must seek a more solid foundation for our efforts to understand behavior and to contribute to human welfare. I have lived with my present convictions for several years, testing my perspective in dialogue with colleagues and in reading the literature. My reorientation appears to me to be internally consistent. It has given me an understanding of the confusing agglomeration of published work in personality and in related fields. My recurring periods of depression and pessimism about the study of behaving people have been replaced by a steady optimism. Readers who are depressed and discouraged by the critique in Part One are urged to turn to Part Two before giving up hope.

Let me sketch my present position. The natural sciences have made marked progress, some more than others. In contrast, progress in the behavioral sciences has been very limited and spotty. While there have been advances in some parts of some fields, other fields have little to show for many decades of work. Writers have argued that the natural sciences are inherently different from the behavioral sciences and that, as a consequence, a different scientific approach is needed for the behavioral sciences. No one, however, has come up with an alternative approach that is convincing to me. I therefore believe that the behavioral sciences should adhere to the same standards and criteria for scientific knowledge that are used in the natural sciences. Just as each natural science employs methods of making observations that are appropriate to its phenomena, so should each behavioral science. But differences in phenomena do not require differences in basic methodological principles.

Our concern must be with Reichenbach's (1938) context of justification, or context of confirmation, as I prefer to call it. I am not concerned here with his context of discovery, with how we get our ideas; this is the crucial part of any science, to be sure. But those who are creative have found their own ways of being so and do not need guidance from others. I am convinced, however, that creativity in the behavioral sciences does not come from sitting in an armchair and devising still another construal of people and their behavior. Rather, it comes from sitting at a desk and confronting empirical data, searching for the ideas suggested by the data and the findings.

An established science has consensus among the members of its own community. Although lively disagreement and debate always exist at the frontiers, it is the accepted foundations that concern us here. In the well-known terms of Kuhn (1970b), an established science has a paradigm shared by those working in that field. For me, such a paradigm includes agreement on some basic concepts and their definitions, on some basic operations for measuring some of those concepts, and on some basic observations or empirically replicable phenomena. It is taken for granted, for example, that two persons will read the dial of a recording instrument and record the same value, with any discrepancies being small relative to the range of values being determined. As one psychologist has put it, "Forming as it does the verification basis of all the scientist's statements, it is essential that this class of basic observables display a high degree of intersubjective agreement among different observers and in the same observer from one occasion to another" (Spence, 1956, p. 14). I would suggest that the principle of interchangeability of observers is a major axiom that behavioral science should take over from natural science. However, agreement between observers with the same orientation and expectations is clearly not enough. And even fairly general agreement among observers from diverse orientations may be a product of expectations and perceptual habits common to the discipline as a whole.

Behavioral science should also adopt the axiom that low-order empirical concepts linked to these common observations are a necessary foundation for a science. On these concepts conceptual schemes that are fruitful can be built, since higher-order concepts can be explicitly linked to concepts at the next order below them, and so on down to those concepts linked to observations. In this statement of belief, I follow the scheme stated by Feigl (1970, p. 7): "The meaning of theoretical concepts can be specified only by their place in the entire theoretical system involving the postulates, definitions, correspondence rules, and finally the operational definitions." Note that operational definitions are needed only for the lowest order, the empirical concepts. Note also that meaning is given not only by relationships to concepts at the same level of abstraction but also by relationships to higher-order and to lower-order concepts. A complete nomological net is hierarchical as well as horizontal.

These, then, are the crucial aspects of the approach in the natural sciences that I believe should be used in the behavioral sciences. They involve standards, norms, and ways of thinking. Other aspects, such as the role of time, are less central. And, although knowledge of the observational setting is always important, experimental manipulation may be significant only in some areas.

How can we move toward this approach? Some argue that conceptualizations and tentative theorizing should precede empirical observation in order to provide explicit guidance. This view recognizes that no observation, especially of behavior, is completely fresh and concept-free. Others argue that one should start with naturalistic observations and generate tentative concepts from them. In principle, the starting point should not be important, since scientific work involves repeated cycling between observations and concepts, observations serving only to modify concepts and concepts influencing the subsequent observations. In the study of behavior, however, it is dangerous to start with preconceptions from everyday experience because the observations guided by them are not likely to be accepted as demonstrating the need for modifying the prior notions. It is wiser to begin with the examination and reexamination of observational protocols, devising concepts for the regularities we observe there.

The scientific approach is not the only route to knowledge. I recognize that there are other ways of knowing and understanding the world, ways that I use in much of my life away from the office. These ways have methodologies of their own. Since science studies regularities in phenomena observed from a shared perspective, the scientific approach is not directly helpful to me when trying to understand my personal experience or to you when you try to understand your experience. I doubt that it will ever explain the private experience of a particular individual. But there are many other interesting human phenomena for us to understand, phenomena that you and I can observe together and can try to comprehend from a scientific perspective that we can share with each other and with many fellow scientists.

I am indebted to the Division of Social Psychology within the National Science Foundation for Grants GS-399, GS-1060, GS-3127, and GS-3127 A No. 1 supporting the conceptual and empirical work that led to this book. The University of Chicago provided me with the atmosphere and the facilities that fostered this work and with resources for producing the manuscript. Most of the drafting was done under a visiting professorship at the University of British Columbia (1975–76). I am grateful to its department of psychology for freeing me from departmental business during that period.

The work of Edmund Bourne, Richard Perline, and Patrick Shrout contributed to particular topics discussed in these chapters. Special thanks must be expressed to Jacob V. Getzels for his friendly, persistent, and goading queries about "what is really *new* in personality and its measurement?" I am very grateful to Lewis R. Goldberg for reacting to a prepublication copy of my first statement of the arguments in this book in a way that gave me the positive reinforcement I badly needed in a period of doubt. Barbara Page Fiske contributed invaluable help in pursuing references and in making the writing intelligible.

Many people have, in one way or another, helped me in writing this book. Colleagues, students, and other friends have discussed the content, contributed suggestions, and raised important questions. A large number of people have read part or all of some draft of this book, and their comments and reactions have helped to clarify issues and to improve the exposition. For their contributions, the reader and I are indebted to Abraham Bookstein, Edmund Bourne, Susan Butt-Finn, Lee J. Cronbach, Starkey Duncan, Jr., Hillel Einhorn, Alan Page Fiske, Barbara Page Fiske, Susan Tufts Fiske, Charles Hulin, Eric Klinger, Paula Leven, Richard Perline, Karlene Roberts, James Russell, Stephanie Scharf, Patrick Shrout, Richard Shweder, Nella Weiner, and Jerry Wiggins.

The lengthy task of cutting stencils for drafts has been shared by several conscientious people: Carol Delaney, Mabel Frazier, Lilly Lam, Lucia Luk, Merri Monks, Brenda Spiga, and Florence Stuart; Dorothy Ford typed and retyped drafts and later prepared the final copy. My thanks to each of them.

Chicago, Illinois DONALD W. FISKE
February 1978

Contents

xix

The Author

DONALD W. FISKE is professor of psychology at the University of
Chicago and chairman of the Committee on Methodology of Behavioral Research in the Department of Behavioral Sciences. Currently
president of the American Psychological Association's Division on
Evaluation and Measurement, he has been president of the Midwestern Psychological Association (1962–1963) and of the Society for
Multivariate Experimental Psychology (1968–1969); for two years he
edited the latter's journal, *Multivariate Behavioral Research* (1971–
1973).

    A college course with Henry A. Murray (1936–1937) led to his
initially entering the field of personality at the Harvard Psychological

Clinic. During World War II, Fiske worked on pilot selection for the U.S. Navy and then entered the Office of Strategic Services (OSS) and contributed to the *Assessment of Men* (1948), written by the OSS Assessment Staff. He was awarded his Ph.D. degree in psychology in 1948 from the University of Michigan, where, with Lowell Kelly, he did research leading to *The Prediction of Performance in Clinical Psychology* (1951). He joined the psychology department at the University of Chicago in 1948, where his curiosity about variation in individuals' behavior led to *The Functions of Varied Experience* (with S. Maddi, 1961). A continuing preoccupation with the weaknesses of the personality discipline resulted in *Measuring the Concepts of Personality* (1971). When that work did not resolve his concerns, he started on this present volume while a visiting professor at the University of British Columbia (1975–1976). He worked with Starkey Duncan, Jr., on *Face-to-Face Interaction: Research, Methods, and Theory* (1977), and he is currently working with Duncan on people's strategies in these interactions. Earlier research interests have included psychotherapy and psychosomatic specificity.

With his wife, Barbara, Fiske gets away from professional work by acting in a play-reading group, sailing on Lake Michigan, and cruising in the Aegean.

To my children, Alan and Susan, and to their peers—
a generation that will contribute to a much-needed science
about people and human interaction

Strategies for Personality Research

The Observation Versus Interpretation of Behavior

Part One

Inadequacies
of Interpretive
Judgments

I

State of the
Personality Field

A thorough reexamination of the personality field is imperative. The need is evident not only from consideration of the current substantive state of the field but also from an unprejudiced appraisal of the limited progress made in recent decades and of the nature of that progress. The assumptions underlying the study of personality must be made explicit and critically reviewed. What have we been doing? Where are we? What can we do about our situation?

A wide range of people are studying personality. In addition to those whose psychological field is personality, there are clinical psychologists, many investigators working on problems in social psychology, and people in such other disciplines as cultural anthropology. All of them need to reexamine the area of personality.

Laymen and scientists have frequently contrasted the social or behavioral sciences with the natural sciences. The very rapid rate of progress in the physical sciences has been described as an accelerating, even exponential, function. The rate of advance in the biological sciences has also been increasing, perhaps as a consequence of their developing ties with basic areas of physics and chemistry. In contrast, the accretion of established knowledge in the behavioral sciences proceeds at a snail's pace. Straggling along behind the others are personality and the fields closely related to it. Something fundamental must happen if these domains are ever going to become sciences.

This book reexamines the personality field, although some applications and extensions to other fields are suggested. It emphasizes the nature of the data utilized in the study of personality and points out the consequences for empirical statements and conceptual propositions that follow from the properties of these data. My call for reexamination is, fortunately, not an isolated one. Confessions of discomfort are numerous (see Chapter Fourteen). Commentaries have included both comprehensive critiques and focused attacks. Most of the critics have offered their cures for the malaise they perceive and usually have turned their own investigations in the directions they have proposed. Others have concluded, quite understandably, that their own line of research and their own experimental paradigms and procedures are the correct route toward progress, if only everyone else would follow their path instead of being misguided and going off in some other direction.

Each of the proposed solutions for the unsatisfactory state of the personality field should be tried by some investigators, because no one can now tell for sure which paths will lead to progress. Some proposals, however, suggest alterations in contemporary practices too minor to make much difference. Although others urge more substantial changes, even these often do not go far enough. The reexamination of research in personality and related fields must be intensive. We must look again at our premises and basic assumptions. It has been said that science progresses by questioning its assumptions— and finding that they must be replaced.

Great personal effort is required for reexamining our ways of looking at people. We are very familiar with these ways because they have become as automatic as the way we scan the road ahead while driving a car. We have had much experience with these ways, and we have practiced them constantly in our daily interactions with other people. This familiarity makes it all the more difficult to force ourselves to reevaluate our assumptions. Yet those of us concerned with personality and other disciplines close to everyday experience are in the greatest danger of deceiving ourselves, of believing that we are working objectively within the scope of the scientific method when in fact much subjectivity enters.

Some observers say that it is much easier to study phenomena more distant from everyday experience, phenomena such as physical particles and the back side of the moon, because the investigator in those areas is not burdened by preconceptions and presuppositions carried over from daily experience. In contrast, investigators of personality have felt it quite natural to obtain subjective data by asking people to report their perceptions and judgments of other people or of themselves, even though the setting was highly contrived. It is now time to examine the processes leading to these judgments, to determine when and how these judgments are formed. Especially important, and yet particularly difficult, is the task of discovering how perceptions and judgments are formed in the natural world. The contrived laboratory simulations of natural conditions are inadequate representations of the actual phenomena we wish to understand; and, inevitably, they introduce factors associated solely with the context of the laboratory.

The Lack of Consensus

An established science can be differentiated from other scholarly disciplines by the degree of consensus among those working within it. As Kuhn puts it, an established field has a *paradigm*, that term referring to "the entire constellation of beliefs, values, techniques, and so on shared by members of a given [scientific] community" (1970b, p. 175). The lack of consensus among workers is characteristic of a prescientific field.

On what do investigators in the personality field agree? They have in common their self-identification as psychologists who spe-

cialize in personality. Beyond that superficial consensus, it is difficult
to find areas of essentially universal agreement. There is only limited
agreement on appropriate methods for collecting observations. What
exists is more a tolerance for the methods used by others than a firm
endorsement. It is generally recognized that each kind of data-
gathering procedure has its serious inherent limitations, and yet each
investigator must adopt some method. There is qualified acceptance
of those methods with scoring that give the appearance of objectivity,
such as questionnaires and other paper and pencil instruments for
obtaining self-reports. Also generally acceptable are observer ratings
and laboratory measurements. Less acceptable are interviews, projective techniques, and other procedures requiring heavy reliance on
someone's personal judgments and inferences.

Some observers argue that, since each single method is fallible,
the use of two or more independent methods in each investigation is
valuable and perhaps necessary. Campbell and Fiske (1959) have
shown the need for demonstrating convergent validation. Garner
(1974) goes even further, urging the strategy of convergent research
operations. Yet the use of multiple methods is no panacea. Separate
methods may share the same limitations.

In estimating the developmental stage of a discipline, the
degree of consensus on substantive matters is particularly crucial.
Here the primitive state of personality as a scientific field is most
apparent. Considerable overlapping does exist in the labels for concepts that are investigated: *Anxiety, achievement, creativity,* and
aggression are but a few of the labels that are employed by numbers of
investigators. But even in terms of labels for topics, there is only fair
agreement on which ones are basic.

Although generally shared technical terms are a prerequisite
for building a scientific discipline, even more critical is consensus on
the definitions of these common words. The lack of agreed-on definitions has been recognized for decades (for example, Arrington, 1943;
Blumer, 1940). Yet there is still no standard definition for any concept
in the personality field, even for the term *personality.* If a definition of
personality were required for this book, I would define it as the way a
person is construed as interacting with his external environment and
with his intrapsychic world (Fiske, 1971, Chap. 3). That definition is
fairly close to one given by McClelland, "[personality is] the most

adequate conceptualization of a person's behavior in all its detail that the scientist can give at a moment in time" (1951, p. 69). The notion of personality as a conceptual interpretation of a person's behavior by someone else fits easily into the argument of this book. My argument, however, does not presuppose a particular definition of personality. It is directed toward the research activities of persons working in the personality domain and of persons in related domains who work with similar types of concepts and methods.

Ordinarily, each writer who discusses a particular concept, such as anxiety, gives it a personal definition. Several of these definitions may overlap to a large extent, but partial agreement is not sufficient for an established, advancing science. Even when several investigators state that they are studying the same concept (for example, one of Murray's needs), their formulations of brief definitions for it show areas of disagreement about what is to be subsumed by the technical term.

Compare the first two definitions given by Jackson (1967, p. 6) for scales in the Personality Research Form with those used by Gough and Heilbrun (1965, pp. 7, 9) for their Adjective Check List:

Jackson	**Gough and Heilbrun**
Abasement	
"Shows a high degree of humility; accepts blame and criticism even when not deserved; exposes himself to situations. where he is in an inferior position; tends to be self-effacing."	"To express feelings of inferiority through self-criticism, guilt, or social impotence."
Achievement	
"Aspires to accomplish difficult tasks; maintains high standards and is willing to work toward distant goals; responds positively to competition; willing to put forth effort to attain excellence."	"To strive to be outstanding in pursuits of socially recognized significance."

There is, to be sure, considerable similarity of general meaning between the pair of definitions for each need. Yet the "feelings of inferiority" and the "guilt" in the Gough and Heilbrun definition for Abasement are only implicit in Jackson's definition. The major emphasis on "socially recognized significance" does not appear in Jackson's definition of Achievement.

In both theoretical writing and reports of research, the absence of explicit definitions is common, if not prevalent. Writers do not heed Brodbeck's statement that "a concept means what its definition says it means. If it does not say this clearly, so that we know when we do and when we do not have an instance of it, then the concept may be criticized as being inadequately defined" (1968, p. 5). In publications on personality today, the reader is expected to determine what the author means by his conceptual terms on the basis of the discussion of each concept, a clearly unsatisfactory condition in scientific work. The author's meaning is indicated more or less by the procedures that the writer employs for measuring the concept. Inspection of the procedures chosen by those investigating a given concept reveals a variety of apparent interpretations. In his review of techniques for assessing anxiety, McReynolds (1968) finds at least eight potential types of anxiety scores. Variation among interpretations of dominance, as operationalized in the content of questionnaire scales, produces scores that have different patterns of correlations with other variables (Butt and Fiske, 1969). (The failure to define central concepts is not peculiar to personality. In discussing a set of papers on *Forms of Symbolic Action*, Spiro (1969) notes that none of the authors define the term *symbol*.)

Investigators in a discipline might agree on statements relating two or more concepts even when they do not agree exactly on the definitions of those concepts. That kind of agreement is, however, also lacking in the personality domain. There are no laws of personality on which there is consensus. Frustration leads to aggression? Sometimes. Aggression begets aggression? In some people. Men are more aggressive than women? Perhaps they are, but under what conditions? Statements of generalizations in the personality area rarely include the circumstances under which they are presumed to hold.

Investigators in the personality field do not have a consensus on other matters involved in Kuhn's concept of paradigm. They do not have classic, exemplary experiments that typify the field for all of them. At the most, they can claim that certain variables are usually found to covary to some extent, although the extent of such relationships is not consistent from one set of observations to the next. Furthermore, many empirical relationships that appear with some regularity cannot be accepted as necessarily indicating a relationship between the concepts that the empirical measurements are presumed to reflect. There may be common components of the measuring procedures that can account for the observed correlations. And if these procedures involve verbal reports, such as ratings, there is always the possibility that the relationship is largely a product of semantic associations (friendliness and cheerfulness, achievement and persistence) rather than psychological reality.

The absence of agreed-on and established empirical findings can be looked at in another way. Personality does not have replicable observational data. Investigators cannot produce a given set of observations at will, in the way that chemists can demonstrate simple chemical reactions and teachers of physics can illustrate basic mechanical phenomena. More general and more disturbing is the consequence of not having replicable phenomena; investigators have no common sets of observational data. The observations and measurements analyzed and interpreted by one investigator are not those studied by other researchers. Even when two investigators try to carry out the same measurement operations, their two samples of organisms yield data that at best have similar, rather than essentially congruent, descriptive statistics.

We have, to be sure, accumulated a few rules of thumb. The more similar the content and other aspects of two measuring procedures, the larger the correlation is likely to be between them. A related generalization is that the best prediction of future performance is obtained from a work sample. This statement is a particular form of the more general proposition that, to predict what a person will do in a situation, see what she did the last time she was in that situation. Although these generalizations have empirical support, they are little more than folk maxims; note that they are more methodological than substantive.

Science progresses by disagreements and opposition. In Kuhn's terms (1970b), what is normal science for one period is overthrown when advocates of a different paradigm have been able to win enough converts. One explanatory hypothesis becomes more plausible when empirical research has demonstrated flaws in all alternative hypotheses (Platt, 1964) and the advanced state of the field compels other scientists to accept those disproofs. Békésy (1960) writes that a scientist needs a capable enemy to criticize his work competently. As Feyerabend (1975) says, differing opinions are necessary to advance our knowledge. But criticisms and disproofs are effective only when there is agreement on the basic rules for conducting research and on some fundamental substantive knowledge. There can be no important disagreements or opposition unless the two protagonists can speak the same basic scientific language and can agree on the pertinent observations and data. When different conceptualizers use different words or use the same words differently, when different investigators have no common empirical demonstrations, each is trying to create a science in a solipsistic fashion.

Apparent Agreement

Personality investigators are under the impression that they agree with each other more than is actually the case. One reason for that impression is that they can readily agree on the protocol from which a particular researcher obtains his measurements. He has the answer sheets from the self-report inventories or the rating scales completed by his observers, and his colleagues accept these as the responses of his subjects or observers. These records are objective and enduring; there is no question about the locus of the checkmarks. With the response records in front of them, the investigator and his colleagues concentrate on these protocols and on the scores derived from them, paying too little attention to the unknown and largely unknowable processes that eventuated in the checkmarks. Although they have no objective records showing the phases of those processes, they occasionally speculate about the nature of these internal events.

At the level of personality descriptions, there is also the appearance of agreement. When a friend describes to you a person you both know, you consider the description and check it against your recollections of that person, and usually you can retrieve perceptions that are consistent with the description offered. Even if you do not see the person in exactly the same way, you are inclined to tolerate the proposed description, knowing that perceptions of people do tend to be influenced by the perceiver. In addition, it typically makes no difference whether you and your friend perceive and interpret the other person in partially dissimilar ways. As a consequence, your friend may have the impression that you agree with her much more closely than you actually do.

Another source of apparent agreement is the use of descriptive terms that apply to a large proportion of the group being described. A study by Bourne (1977) illustrates this point. Within each of three groups of friends, each member described each of the others. The level of agreement between descriptions of one friend (Joe and Bill describing Tom, for example) varied from low to high, as a function of the descriptive task given to the raters. But the level of correspondence between two persons' descriptions of *different* persons (Joe's description of Tom and Bill's description of Jim) rose in parallel fashion, the means falling just a little below those for concurrences on the same person. Thus, high agreement on descriptions of a person is produced in large part by agreement on characteristics common to many members of the group. There can be quite sizable agreement on the stereotype, on the average characteristics attributed to a group. Such communality in attributions can contribute to an exaggerated estimate of the levels of agreement on differentiations among individuals.

Tolerance for individual meanings and interpretations is also found in conceptual discussions, and it contributes to the impression of higher levels of consensus than actually exist. In everyday verbal interactions, people communicate with others in a fairly effective way. Although meanings and connotations for words are not exactly the same for each person, a listener understands the speaker's usages of words on the basis of the context in which they are embedded. Similarly, in conceptual writing within personality, the reader ordinarily can grasp the writer's meaning and associations for a concept. The reader is greatly aided by considerable overlap between her own connotations for the word labeling the concept and those of the writer. Even when the writer invents a new conceptual dimension, her colleague can usually recognize instances in her own experience where the concept might apply to someone.

Each personality investigator holds onto his set of concepts for describing a person. In spite of technical looseness, the concepts make sense to him and are applicable to other people as he perceives them. He encounters no reason for giving up any of them. No empirical findings refute them. If his attempt to measure one of his concepts is unsuccessful by psychometric criteria, he usually decides that it was the design of his measuring procedure that was unsatisfactory, not the concept. Especially when his label for a concept is a label also used by others, he experiences some reinforcements for his interpretation of that label. Finally, looking at the matter in broader terms, he shares with his colleagues a common cultural socialization.

This common socialization influences many professional concepts derived from the lay language, concepts that have been taken over with a burden of assorted connotations. In addition, in activities outside the office, the investigator meets terms that were developed or given special meaning in professional writing but have become a part of the lay person's vocabulary. The notions of complexes, defenses, unconscious motives, and many others are encountered often in everyday conversation and reading matter. These usages add to the load of diverse connotations that increase the investigator's difficulties in dealing with his specialized concepts in a rigorous way.

There are other bases for our belief that we agree more on our impressions of people and on our meanings for lay and technical concepts than we actually do. One source is the fact that our everyday knowledge about human behavior is probabilistic, not deterministic. We know that, in a certain set of circumstances, people are very likely to act in a given way, but with exceptions. Hence, when your impressions about other people do not agree exactly with mine, I am quite ready to overlook the discrepancy, attributing it to differences in our meanings for terms like *usually* and *generally,* and also to the likelihood of your sample of observations involving somewhat different conditions than mine.

Our impression of agreement is also promoted by the way human beings make choices and decisions. Herbert Simon (1955, 1967) has pointed out that, in considering alternative solutions to a problem, a person will often try each in turn against his criteria for an adequate solution and accept the first alternative he encounters that meets his criteria at a minimal level. Simon says that the alternative "satisfices" the person, who prefers to accept it rather than spend the unknown amounts of time and energy required to find an optimal solution.

Just as descriptive terms, even if a bit ambiguous, serve their purpose in everyday life, so do trait names and other concepts satisfy investigators in the study of personality. And each of us as investigators is easily satisfied. We read theoretical statements or empirical findings, check them against our experience, and tend to accept them if they fit our experience. The nature of personality phenomena, the utilization of everyday experience in our thinking about personality, and the plethora of research papers lead us to accept solutions that, although plausible, are far from ideal.

A similar process may occur in each of us when we attribute intentions. "The perceiver seeks to find *sufficient reason* why the person acted and why the act took on a particular form. Instead of the potentially infinite regress of cause and effect which characterizes an impersonal, scientific analysis, the perceiver's explanation comes to a stop when an intention or motive is assigned that has the quality of being reason enough. 'He eats because he is hungry' would not ordinarily bring a request for further explanation" (Jones and Davis, 1965, p. 220).

Progress in Negative Knowledge

Some readers may not be discouraged by the preceding pessimistic account of the personality field. They may grant that personality has no shared paradigm, no generally accepted theory or concepts, and very little on which there is any substantial consensus. They may argue that we should not feel depressed about the present condition of personality because the field is still in its infancy, and it is developing in a healthy fashion.

What would these optimistic readers cite to support their diagnosis? What positive progress has been made in the last thirty years? Are there any signs that some theory or some set of concepts is gaining more general and lasting acceptance than any of the older theories that were once fashionable? Will behavior theory, with its emphasis on manifest actions, acquire such status? What about the conceptualizations of social learning theory? Will one of these lead to a conceptual orientation endorsed by a substantial majority of workers in the discipline? Although their adherents have that hope or expectation, most of us are unwilling to predict that outcome.

On the side of empirical methods, there is little evidence of progress. We have known for years that agreement among observers is higher when they are asked to observe simple overt acts as opposed to making judgments requiring interpretation and inference. And yet the typical levels of observer agreement are not rising over the years, because most investigators are willing to work with observations on which observers have only limited agreement. Our instruments continue to be just as particular as they have been. The covariation of independent measures of the same variable continues to be modest (the correlations usually being in the neighborhood of .30). Although we have developed sophisticated techniques for constructing questionnaires, the practical value of these techniques appears to be limited. For example, empirical studies (Ashton and Goldberg, 1973; Jackson, 1975) indicate that items written by amateurs may do as well as items developed by refined technical methods.

For the field of personality, the real puzzle is: How does it happen that, after decades of hard work by many investigators, we have gained so little and have made such limited scientific progress? Have we failed to ask the right question? Certainly we have failed to specify our question. We have not explicitly identified what we want to understand. We seem to have felt such explicit identification was not necessary—the phenomena of personality are right there in front of us. We have been trying to understand our experience with people, while telling ourselves that we were trying to understand people. We have neglected the contribution of the mediator, ourselves or other observers.

We have been seeking propositions about people that fit in with our experience and construal of people's behavior. But such propositions are stated in terms of concepts that are familiar to us, the concepts acquired from everyday experience or refined from such origins. It is time to turn to more consensual ways of observing people as they behave, to identify significant elements in behavior and determine their interrelationships. This major recommendation will be developed in later sections of this book.

The accumulation of negative knowledge may well be the

main achievement of personality research to date and may also be the area in which there is the highest degree of consensus. There seems to be more agreement that certain propositions are not true than agreement that some statements are true. Some things that the general public has taken for granted have not been demonstrated in systematic research or have been found to be true only under highly circumscribed conditions. For example, it is obvious that both members of certain pairs of antithetical maxims cannot be generally true. Compare "birds of a feather flock together" and "opposites attract each other"; consider "a bird in the hand is worth two in the bush" and "the grass on the other side of the fence is greener." Each maxim expresses a bit of folk wisdom applicable under certain circumstances. Antithetical maxims imply contrasting contexts for their applicability.

There is a widespread conviction that human judgments about other persons provide the best means for predicting their behavior—a viewpoint that is quite understandable when we consider the extent to which each of us relies on his own judgments, predictions, and expectations in the everyday business of living with others. Yet careful investigations have established that statistical or actuarial predictions of human behavior are as good as or better than those extrapolated from integrative human judgments (Meehl, 1954; Sawyer, 1966).

Hyman notes that "progress in psychology as a science goes hand in hand with the course of its rejection of 'facts' that come from everyday forms of observation and experience" (1964, p. 33). Perhaps the field of personality is progressing by becoming more skeptical about its ways of observing and collecting data. As more and more studies demonstrate the difficulties in objective research on personality, an attitude of questioning may be replacing a naive overconfidence. For example, it is clear that subjects actively interact with the materials and the context in which measurement takes place, rather than passively and automatically responding to each presented stimulus. Again, we know that the covariation of two procedures for measuring a concept depends primarily on the degree to which the procedures are similar with respect to content of stimulus items, response formats provided, the task set for the respondents, and the general setting within which they work on that task.

Perhaps the most important generalization that has emerged in recent decades of research is that personality data have a high degree of specificity. At one level, this specificity is apparent in the modest levels of correlation between measurements derived from separate procedures for assessing a single concept. It is becoming notorious that two such procedures will typically correlate about .30 with each other; most such correlations are above .20, but few exceed .45. The proportion of common variance between such a pair of measures is far too low to permit them to be considered as equivalent alternatives, as interchangeable. And even these correlational values may reflect in part some common component in the measuring procedures.

A crucial kind of specificity in personality measurements is that associated with the role and perspective of the observer producing the data. We know that self-ratings may or may not agree with ratings by peers. We know that judgments by other people vary with the kind of information available to those people and with their relationship to the person observed. For example, descriptions of patients before and after psychotherapy, as well as estimates of their changes during treatment, depend in large part on the viewpoint of the observer (Cartwright, Kirtner, and Fiske, 1963; Fiske, 1975).

The production of negative knowledge may not be restricted to the domain of personality. Sigmund Koch has stated that the history of psychology does not show that it has been a cumulative or progressive discipline. "Throughout its history as 'science,' the *hard* knowledge which it has deposited has usually been *negative* knowledge!" (1974, p. 19).

The Source of the Problem

The preceding material has stressed the necessity for a reexamination of the personality field, pointed out the lack of consensus among workers in that field, and noted the absence of positive progress. The subsequent chapters in Part One develop the critique of standard personality research and examine its implications. At this point, the critique is stated in bald terms so that the reader can see the direction being taken.

1. Investigators in the field of personality have not been clear

about what they are trying to understand. While they see themselves as seeking to understand persons and the behavior of persons, *investigators have unwittingly been seeking to understand their own impressions and attributions about behaving persons, other people, and themselves.* White (1972) has noted that a distinctive and complicating feature of personality is the inclusion of one's own self as part of the subject matter. In addition, each investigator enters the discipline not only with his past experiences of other people but also with his impressions about them and with words to describe those impressions. As a consequence, he has personal construals for his subject matter even before he studies the conceptual work of others and before he undertakes his own investigations.

The biologist Stent has recently phrased the problem for the human sciences in broader terms. "In contrast to the clearly definable research aims of physical science, it is often impossible to state explicitly just what it really *is* about human behavior that one wants to explain. This in turn makes it quite difficult to set forth clearly the conditions under which any postulated causal nexus linking the observed facts could be verified" (1975, p. 1052).

1a. In his effort to understand, *an investigator uses concepts derived from everyday and clinical experience.* Some are labeled by words from lay language. Others are common words given a special meaning; a few are invented by a theorist. Most of the concepts are at the same broad and global level. All of the concepts verbalize impressions from everyday or professional interactions with people.

2. In their efforts to understand impressions about people, *investigators use, as their research data, observers' explicit judgments based on these observers' impressions.* For each datum, there is an observer who has perceived some behavior and then has cognized and interpreted it to arrive at a judgment. These reported judgments are themselves behaviors, the responding behaviors of the observers. They are not the behaviors or the behavioral processes of the people described, the phenomena that many investigators may say are the phenomena they are studying. Thus, the specific responses of observers are treated as though they represented the behavior of the subjects per se. Instead, these judgments are interpretations of the subjects' behavior. Each datum is an observer-observed entity.

2a. *A judgment by an observer in a research study can be*

viewed as an appendage extending a natural process. In interacting with others, a person perceives the stream of behaving in others and in herself. She forms impressions leading to expectations about future behaviors. Although most of these are not verbalized, the person at a later time may summarize some impressions in verbal form, either in reviewing and reflecting on her personal perceptions or in communicating them to someone else. However, when an observer produces a judgment in response to the instructions of an investigator, she formulates her judgment in the words and format specified by the investigator. The production of that judgment includes a separate phase added onto the normal process, a phase affected by the research conditions. The judgment is an artifactual product constructed for the special purpose of the research. It has no function in human behavior other than in the interaction between observer and investigator and in the subsequent vocational behavior of the investigator. One consequence of the complex process preceding an observer's judgment is that the judgment is, to a degree, relative to the time when it was made. When an observer is asked at two separate times to make independent judgments about a person, her judgments will often differ, especially if she has had new experiences with the person in the interim.

2b. *Judgments by observers are attributed to persons typically without restriction as to time or situation.* Even though the observer's experience with the person judged has been limited to some small segment of the whole of the person's behavior, the attribution is made to the person without reference to a setting or settings and without reference to a period in chronological time.

2c. *There is considerable individuality in the perceptions of each observer, as well as in the process by which these perceptions are converted into impressions and ultimately into attributive judgments.* This individuality stems from several sources. Different observers may observe different segments of the person's behavior, and the reactions of the person observed to the observer and the observer's reactions to the person have individual if not idiosyncratic aspects. Whether or not the person is able to perceive and to react to the observer, the observer uses her personal cognitive style in her observing.

2d. The observers' judgments are expressed in words, either words of their own choosing or verbal response alternatives provided by the investigator. Words are also essential in the instructions and in the stimuli that form the instruments. *The meanings of the words used by the observers for their judgments, as well as the meanings of the words used by the investigator in eliciting those judgments and in forming his own conceptualizations, are to a crucial degree specific for each user.* Neither observers nor investigators agree among themselves on the explicit meanings of the words used to identify the attributes being studied. Measurement in personality and related fields has depended almost totally on words because it has not been possible to identify and specify unequivocally each of the phenomena of interest.

2e. *As a consequence, the judgments of independent observers have significant degrees of specificity and are not interchangeable.* Therefore, we cannot generalize with high confidence from results for one observer to expected results for other observers. Yet consensus among observers and the resulting interchangeability of observers are necessary conditions for developing a science.

3. *Each datum, score, and descriptive statistic in personality research is synthesized from heterogeneous elements.* An attributive judgment is typically based on an assortment of experiences with the person judged. A score from a questionnaire is compiled from responses to separate items that have minimal intercorrelations. A mean for a person or a group is derived from a distribution with considerable variance around that central tendency. Moreover, it is often not possible even to specify the elements that have been included in a datum. Agglomeration, not integration, is the prevailing practice. Hence, there is little replication of observations, limited reproducibility of findings, and poor generalizability.

4. *Relying on particularistic judgments and casual syntheses, investigators make unwarranted extrapolations and unsystematic generalizations.* Investigators treat data as comparable, in spite of the complex and often dissimilar origins of the several judgments. Scores with the same numerical value are considered identical regardless of the degree of overlap in the units contributing to them. Investigators place little emphasis on the setting in which each observation is made, even though the setting is typically a particular instance unrepresentative of the conditions they wish to generalize about. Settings affect observations and data. And, within a given setting, the method of obtaining measurements affects the data obtained. Finally,

the generalizability of findings from an empirical study cannot be established on rational grounds and is rarely supported by clear-cut empirical demonstration. Most of the time, generalizations from both data and findings are intuitive and premature.

5. *Investigators of personality have failed to locate conceptually useful units in the stream of behavioral phenomena.* The general practice is to allow the observer to determine the complex segment of behavior on which a judgment is based. Frequently, that segment is not even identified, and when it is, it is not described in specific terms. The investigator's unit has been the response reporting a judgment made in accordance with his instructions. His subsequent analyses are based on the assignment of attributes to persons. The focus has been on measuring the person and only minimally on categorizing the stream of behaving into readily identifiable homogeneous acts.

6. *The conceptualization and investigation of personality have neglected the fundamental status of the temporal dimension in the flow of behaving.* Investigators seem to view people as having characteristics that are there to be measured, just as a desk has its height, weight, color, and shape. Judgments about observed segments of behavior summarize a flow of activity by neglecting the time dimension, thereby losing essential information. Behaving is immediate, almost instantaneous, and actions are related to preceding actions by the same or different actors. In work on personality and related fields, there is a blurring of the temporal dimension.

The major thesis of this book, based on several of the preceding propositions, is this: *The discipline of personality as currently studied is and will remain prescientific.* It does not have the several kinds of consensus that are found among the practitioners of an established science: consensus on fundamental constructs and their definitions; consensus on empirically confirmed relationships among constructs; consensus on linkages between constructs and observables; and consensus on the basic observations on which all else is built. There have been no signs of movement toward consensus on any of these topics and nothing in current practice suggests that there will be movement in the near future.

The preceding propositions provide a critique of investigation in the domain of personality. A final assertion concerns the extension of this critique. *Most of the propositions can be applied to one or more other parts of the behavioral sciences.*

Many of these propositions are assertions, the accuracy of which has not and perhaps cannot be established by systematic inquiry (for example, Proposition 1). Others can be readily supported by examination of published papers and measuring procedures (for example, Proposition 2b). Some propositions merit detailed examination of their soundness and of their implications. The several subsequent chapters of Part One will discuss particular propositions (for example, aggregations and generalizations are considered in Chapter Six). There is not, however, a one-to-one correspondence between propositions and chapters. Some propositions enter into several chapters.

The several propositions are not coordinate. They are at different levels of abstraction—and necessarily so, because they pertain to research procedures, psychological processes in observers, the concepts and the orientations of investigators, and the nature of behavior. The propositions are, however, interrelated and interdependent. In explicating any one argument in subsequent chapters, I have often found it necessary to consider other parts of the critique that are more intensively examined elsewhere. Some repetition of themes has been unavoidable.

Summary

There is considerable dissatisfaction with the state of personality as a scientific discipline. At no level, from observations to theory, is there the extent of consensus among the students of personality so necessary to a science. There are no signs of progress toward sufficient consensus, although some negative knowledge has accumulated. The nature of the subject matter has contributed to the appearance of more agreement than actually exists.

A major source of the difficulties in the personality field is the reliance on interpretive judgments that are determined by the observer as well as by the observed and that are produced for the special purposes of the research. The judgments also involve words with meanings on which people do not agree exactly, and they are based on extensive segments of behavior rather than short specific units. Because of the nature of these judgments, the agreement between judgments of different observers is very limited. Some data in other parts of the behavioral sciences suffer similar handicaps.

II

Words, Concepts, and Attributions

Personality today relies on words. When a word is used in a context, its meaning varies with the context. When a word is used in a verbal discussion or an essay, the verbal context helps to indicate the meaning intended. When the word occurs in a scientific statement, such as a proposition that glung is related to blap, the reader must look beyond that statement and its immediate context to try to determine what the word *glung* means. The report of the mean amount of glung, as measured by the glom test, still leaves unstated the author's denotations for glung. The author's central meaning is given to the reader only in explicit definitions and in propositions relating glung to other, equally specified concepts. Within such a scientific context, when the

22

terms are technical ones, there are no common-sense meanings to interfere with the communication between author and reader, and the extent of connotations is restricted.

Different usages of a word may have different denotations as well as different connotations. In an analysis of the multiple meanings of the term *paradigm* in the classic monograph of Kuhn (1970b), Masterman (1970) identified twenty-one different senses in which Kuhn used this central concept. Kroeber and Kluckhohn (1952) compiled and analyzed more than one hundred definitions of the term *culture*. To return to the personality domain, a close examination of writings about any single variable will typically reveal a diversity of definitions. Even for the basic term *personality*, Allport (1937) collected several dozen definitions that had been offered up to that date. When different investigators define personality differently, it is likely that they are aiming their research at different domains of phenomena as well as at different problems.

In technical writing in personality, words are usually not used as abstract symbols for some precisely identified object or property, as they are in the natural sciences. For instance, the familiar word *salt* is used by the layman to refer to a specific seasoning for food. When used by a chemist, the word *salt* has a much broader meaning, referring to a class of substances. If the chemist wants to refer to the chemical we use to season our food, she may use the words *sodium chloride* or the abstract symbols *NaCl*. Those words and symbols refer, however, to the pure compound, not the common substance with its impurities.

Words as used in writing about personality are akin to the chemical usage of *salt* as a label for a large class of substances insofar as the reader has to determine which of several referents for the word is the one the author intended. But the parallel is not close—the word *salt* has a consensually accepted meaning in chemistry, whereas no term in personality has a precise meaning on which those in the field agree. Similarly, the several substances to which the term *salt* can refer are known to chemists, and each can be identified with precision. In contrast, the various referents for a personality term cannot be identified exactly. To what does *trait* refer? And *drive*? And *attitude*? Indeed, readers of this book may at times be uncertain about the meaning I intend for one of the central concepts in the argument. Consequently, although I expect the meaning to be conveyed in the text, either explicitly or by the context, I have given definitions for these concepts in the Glossary at the end of the book.

Of the several propositions stated toward the end of Chapter One, the discussion in this chapter is directed primarily toward Proposition 2d: The meanings of words used in work on personality are to a crucial degree specific for each user. This chapter examines the fact that most of our concepts are derived from everyday and clinical experience (Proposition 1a); it also discusses the use of observers' judgments, based on impressions, as research data (Proposition 2); and the problems encountered with the use of words, problems that restrict the regularities in observations and findings and reduce the generalizability of empirical work (Proposition 4).

The Roles of Words in the Personality Field

Every discipline and every science must use words in technical discourse. In the field of personality, there is a need for greater precision in specifying the referents for the concepts used. This need is also present in many other fields, as Mandler and Kessen (1959) have shown for psychology as a whole. But words are also essential to current approaches to personality because they are intrinsic to the substance of the field, to the phenomena being studied. Although these two fundamental roles of words are interdependent, they will be examined separately.

Words enter into the investigation of personality in four ways. First, the phenomena studied include verbal acts. Since the content of speech and writing is words, the words used by people are a major part of the subject matter of personality. Second, crucial to personality is a particular kind of verbal act, involving the words that people use to describe the behavior of others and also to describe other people as entities. This descriptive material is the essence of the discipline. Although it is not generally seen as such, such material is in fact what the students of personality are trying to understand and explain, whether they realize it or not. Third, words are used in the operations of personality research. The format of many instruments for obtaining responses, such as questionnaires and rating scales, is verbal. Interviews have verbal content, and most projective techniques produce verbal protocols. Finally, investigators use words in reports of empirical studies and, as noted above, in conceptualizations. All of the last three ways in which words are used involve the construing and interpreting of behavior and the labeling of persons. Each merits closer examination.

The words that people use every day to describe another person summarize the users' perceptions and cognitions of all of the other's behaviors, both the words spoken and the actions displayed. Since so much of interpersonal communication is by means of words, people attend primarily to what others say. Even when recalling their experiences with someone, they emphasize what that person said. They are less likely to describe in words the psychomotor activity of the other person, that activity being highly familiar and ordinarily not focused on as a channel for conveying significant messages.

Strictly speaking, every act, physical or verbal, is unique. Its topography is never exactly replicated. When we think about the physical behaviors of others, we use broad terms, like *walking* or *gesturing*. But when we think about what people say, we make finer differentiations, thinking about the particular phrasing a person used or perhaps paraphrasing the verbal sequence in our own words.

The preponderant use of verbal acts to communicate, especially to communicate complex and detailed messages, is probably responsible for the emphasis in personality research on verbal content as the phenomenon to be understood. Yet the subtlety, the fine discriminations made in verbal behavior, and the uniqueness of each verbal message make it that much more difficult to understand the speaker's precise meaning, to understand the central intent and the peripheral associations involved in his utterance. The complexity and the individuality of each verbal act contribute to the lack of agreement among listeners as to the exact meaning of the speaker. The individual associations and orientations of each listener also contribute to differences in interpretation of meaning. And whatever the degree of agreement among the listeners, the extent of the congruence or discrepancy between the speaker's meaning and the interpretation of each listener is not known and ordinarily cannot be known.

A considerable part of the difficulty in achieving precise, univocal communication with words is that words are used not only as signs standing for a particular thing or even a single quality but also as indicators of a class of particulars. In everyday usage, the more abstract the word (*transportation* versus *truck*), the greater the difficulty in achieving exact consensus on its meaning. Most of the words that people use in describing the behavior of others (for example, *friendly*) are terms that summarize and abstract. The words serve to reduce an extended series of sensations, cognitions, and impressions of someone's behavior to some general tendency in the observed behaviors. Descriptions of a person's personality (such as *well adjusted*) are even more abstracted from the available phenomena provided by the person's behavior. That to which the words refer becomes increasingly more ambiguous.

I do not mean to suggest that verbal interpretations of others' behaviors and verbal attributions about persons are not of major psychological significance. In describing someone to a friend, we use words that may affect the friend's attitudes; they also seem to affect our attitudes toward the person described. Our cognitions of a person's behavior indirectly affect our behavior toward him, both when these cognitions have not been put into words and when they have. Our portrayal of another influences our expectations about that person's behavior (that is, about how we will perceive that behavior), and those expectations can affect our actions in the presence of that person.

Consider the pervasiveness of words in the many ways we collect response-data to measure personality. For convenience, the classification of modes used in *Measuring the Concepts of Personality* (Fiske, 1971, Chap. 5) will be followed. Self-descriptions, Mode 1, include the numerous kinds of questionnaires, inventories, and other paper and pencil instruments that ask the person to report about her past behavior, her view of herself, her feelings, or her usual preferences. These reports depend entirely on words. The instructions are verbal. In answering, the respondent may write a freestyle self-characterization in her own words. More usually, the investigator presents a multiple-choice instrument in which the content of the questions or items is verbal and the alternatives are in words.

Other procedures, classified as Mode 2, ask the person to report his current experiencing: his preference among stimuli provided by the investigator, his perception of a stimulus, or his judgment about it. In this mode, words are almost as universal as in Mode 1. Once again, the instructions are verbal and the response, written or spoken, is usually in words. In some instances, the subject may be asked to respond by pointing or by putting a mark under a preferred figure. Familiar exceptions not using words in the response include the Body Adjustment Test for Field Dependence and measures of category width in which the responses are numbers.

Mode 3 consists of tests of capabilities in which the person reports his solutions to problems posed by the investigator. The report states the product of a cognitive process. Here and in the next two modes, the instructions are in words. The contents of the stimulus items and of the subject's responses involve words throughout, except in measuring numerical and spatial abilities.

Measurements may be based on observations of prior behavior, as in Mode 4. The observer may refer to her recollections of prior experiences with the person to be rated, as in peer ratings, or the observer may have access to past products of that person, such as written material or formal records of achievement in school. The observer responds in words. Even when she makes ratings on a scale with several points, verbal descriptions are provided for some or all of the points. When not stated, a verbal equivalent is often implied. If the observer bases her judgments on records or products of the subject, these materials are most often in words.

Observations of current behavior, Mode 5, include interviews, projective tests, and situation tests. The person's responses in interviewing and in projective testing are primarily verbal. The drawings made in the Draw-A-Figure test are an exception; the examiner or the subject may, however, comment on these products. In other work, the behavior observed may range from primarily verbal (as in the Leaderless Group Discussion procedure) to entirely nonverbal (as in observing infant behavior).

Mode 6 provides the largest single exception to the pervasiveness of words. To obtain psychophysiological measurements, verbal interaction with the subject before or during the measurement is typically incidental to the measuring operations. The response record is usually graphic, and the derived data are usually in numerical terms.

All of these modes are used to study individual differences. Comparisons between groups can also be made with data from any of the modes. The comparisons in experimental research on personality commonly use data from Modes 5 or 6. In experimentation, the

dependent variable is usually the verbal report of the person about his
current experience after receiving a treatment—about some perception, feeling, or cognition specified by the investigator. In some
instances, the response may be a motor act that is observed and coded
by an observer.

The overwhelming dependence of personality measurement
on words has obvious implications. As Nagel (1961, p. 8) notes, the
words in ordinary speech are not sufficiently specific for scientific purposes. Although printed instructions provide a constant physical
stimulus for subjects, we have no assurance that those words have the
same meaning for each subject. Similarly, the content of items in
questionnaires is subject to varied interpretations (Benton, 1935;
Eisenberg, 1941; Kuncel, 1973). Particularly susceptible to diverse
interpretation are words for relative frequency (Simpson, 1944;
Hakel, 1968). As one might expect, even for this kind of word, the
meaning that a subject gives it varies with the verbally portrayed context in which it is placed (Pepper and Prytulak, 1974).

The field of personality, like any other discipline, uses words
for its concepts. Of particular concern for the present analysis is the
use of words to identify dimensions and other variables in the personality domain. Again, such usage is common. Concepts have to be
labeled and defined in words. In the established areas of the natural
sciences, however, each conceptual dimension has some standard
operations for measuring it; specialists have agreed on their suitabil-
ity and their coordination with the concept. These operations help to
specify the concept. For the concepts in personality theories, there are
no such procedures on which all investigators agree. The theories and
their dimensional components were created from the theorists' construing of their experience, not from the interpretation of empirical
research data. Some theorists, including Gordon Allport and Henry
Murray, developed concepts from their construing of their own experience but then went on to measure these concepts. Murray, however,
and probably also Allport, would not consider any single measurement operation as a complete reflection of a given conceptual
dimension.

Content analysis has been carried out with both a priori and a
posteriori categories. Scoring schemes aimed at concepts selected in
advance have been developed by a number of investigators, including

McClelland, Atkinson, Clark, and Lowell (1958); Dollard and Auld (1959); Gottschalk and Gleser (1969); and Loevinger and Wessler (1970). In other instances, such as the *Letters from Jenny* (Allport, 1965) as analyzed by Baldwin (1942), analysts have derived categories from the given content, typically for a particular purpose. Although investigators have worked systematically, they have constructed and interpreted the protocols in essentially the same manner that any person cognizes and labels the actions of other people.

Quite commonly in content analysis, a published guide for categorizing is modified when subsequent researchers use it, so that their several measuring procedures are not identical. In every system for content analysis, however, a considerable degree of interpretation is involved. As a consequence, the degree of intercoder agreement is restricted. Although the correlations between coders may reach .75, each coder is still contributing his individual perceptions and interpretations, and coders are not interchangeable. The proportion of variance specific to the coder is too high for precise measurement.

Concepts in personality have also been derived from empirical data. For example, Cattell (1946) began his search for a taxonomy of personality by examining the classical list of 17, 953 descriptive terms assembled by Allport and Odbert (1936). In reducing that list to manageable proportions, he made judgments about the essential equivalence of various terms, obviously on the basis of the meanings that the words had for him. His initial set of dimensions was based on a factor analysis of ratings made about males, the factors being composed of descriptive phrases that correlated with each other.

Edwards (1967) started the construction of one instrument with hundreds of statements, including attributive phrases that people used in ordinary conversation to describe people they knew. He sorted these original protocol statements into a priori categories and then factor analyzed scores for these numerous sets of items. Edwards naturally labels the factors he obtained. He seems to have limited his conceptualization of these factors essentially to the contents of the items embodied in his test, the Edwards Personality Inventory. Cattell, in contrast, uses broader labels. Arguing that he has identified universal factors, he has conducted research studies to demonstrate that his basic factors can be assessed by procedures other than his self-report inventories.

The empirical factors obtained by one investigator are not congruent with those developed by any other researcher. Although some partial correspondences and similarities can be found—for example, between the factorial scales of Cattell and Guilford (Sells, Demaree, and Will, 1970, 1971)—the average correlations between independently derived empirical dimensions are clearly below the levels necessary to conclude that the same variable has been identified in more than one study. This result is to be expected, given the findings on the covariation between independently developed instruments for assessing the same concept label (for example, Campbell and Fiske, 1959; Fiske, 1973).

No trend toward consensus on a standard set of conceptual dimensions, either from a priori theorizing or from empirical analysis, is evident. What one can see, however, are instances in which a number of investigators have seized on a particular measuring instrument when it became available. After several years, the amount of research using the instrument tapers off. Examples of instruments that have had peak periods of popularity in personality research include the Manifest Anxiety Scale (Taylor, 1953) and the R-S Scale for repression-sensitization (Byrne, 1961). A different temporal pattern may eventuate for the scale assessing internal versus external control of reinforcement, the I-E Scale of Rotter (1966), since it is linked to a developing theoretical orientation.

In more general terms, the choice of measuring procedure is typically made on dubious grounds. An investigation by Chun and others (1972) can be taken as a serious indictment of personality researchers; these authors conclude that expediency, convenience, and availability are more influential in the selection of psychological measures for use in research than are the technical qualifications of the measures. It is also true that a measuring instrument of limited psychometric adequacy can come into common use with no efforts being made to improve its quality.

The Natural History of a Personality Concept

Attributions of dispositions and other characteristics begin with social perception, that is, with the perception and interpretation of the actions of other people. Heider (1958), who has examined closely the processes involved in perceiving another person, notes the manner in which the perceiving process is affected by meanings introduced by the perceiver: "Nonspatial-temporal conditions, namely, meanings as data, are part and parcel of the perceptual process" (p. 45). A single act is often ambiguous, the surrounding stimuli helping to specify its meaning for the perceiver. For example, our perception of one person may influence our perception of another with whom he is interacting. Furthermore, the perception of a person as, for instance, courageous can be produced by many different concrete stimulus configurations.

Heider's account makes intuitive sense, at his level of analysis. It also brings out the active contribution of the perceiver to the perception of another person, and the consequent absence of a one-to-one correspondence between the physical movements of a person and the interpretations of that behavior by others. Given the picture delineated by Heider, it becomes evident how readily two perceivers may differ in their perceptions. And, insofar as attributions of characteristics to another person are based on perceptions of ongoing behaviors, the probability of disagreements in the attributions of the two perceivers is obviously high.

A person's experience with the behavior of other people is an ongoing stream punctuated by a ripple here, a swirl there, and a stretch of tortuous rapids farther along. Bruner (1958) has aptly described the perceiver's stream of experience: "In most instances, there are more things to be noticed than one can possibly register upon simultaneously . . . and even when the stimulus impact is fairly simple, there are various ways in which it can be 'looked at' or organized" (p. 86). A person has a limited span of attention and a limited span of immediate memory. "Selectivity is forced on us by the nature of these limitations" (p. 86). To economize on effort, we narrow the selectivity of attention to the essential things, "we 'recode' into simpler form the diversity of events . . . so that our limited attention and memory span can be protected" (p. 86).

When a person recalls her experience with another—either a particular interaction or a series of interactions—she may identify impressions of several segments of that experience that she has coded in much the same way. If she is talking to a third person or if she is talking to herself (thinking) about that other person, she may give a verbal label to those segments. At some other time, she is likely to use that same label for her experience with an entirely different person. For her, that label indicates a conceptual category for appropriate segments of the behavior of others as she has observed and processed such segments. In choosing her label, she draws on the vocabulary she has developed in her previous experience. Her meaning for the label is derived from hearing others use the term and noting the behaviors to which they refer, as well as from reading about people and gleaning the author's meaning for the term from the written context.

In this way, a person forms and applies her concepts for describing the behavior of other people. Her set of labels includes many labels that others have used for their concepts. She receives reinforcement for a concept when she hears another person use the same label for the behaviors that they both observe. But these two observers may be perceiving and construing those behaviors somewhat differently, even in instances where the particular behavioral events can be indicated with some precision. Opportunities for mutual confirmation of the applicability of a label are, however, usually restricted to retrievals from memory. The ephemeral nature of the referents for the label causes the concept to which it applies to be somewhat loose, both in the construing of a given observing person and in its shared meaning within the group of those employing the label.

In contrast, consider the concept labeled *broad-leaved maple*. A person acquires that concept by reading about it or by having someone describe it. Pictures or actual instances are employed. The person is given the characteristics that identify this particular tree's leaf and that distinguish it from the leaves of other trees, especially other maples—for example, size, number of main parts, and degree of seriation on the edges. Concepts of this kind can have fairly precise meanings that are consensual. The defined meaning can be quite explicit. When necessary, concrete instances of the objects falling within that class and falling outside it can be pointed out.

In personality, the shared concept lacks these aspects so necessary for exact concepts with commonly understood designations. It does not even have agreement on the wording of the defining characteristics. Still more important is the fact that the defining characteris-

tics do not refer to tangible, permanent, directly perceivable properties like size and seriation.

In spite of these limitations, the shared concept persists. We
continue to use it to label the behaviors of others. But in speaking and
thinking about these behaviors, we become elliptical. Instead of saying, "He was uncooperative today," we say, "He was uncooperative."
Later, when we think about him, we may say, "He is uncooperative."
The label for the behavior first becomes a label for the person at one
time, and later becomes the label for the person. The label is then a
trait, a disposition attributed to a person. If many people use the
label, it becomes a common trait, and some investigator may adopt it
as one dimension in his scheme for describing personality.

We have been considering traits as terms used to describe people from the viewpoint of the person doing the describing. These concepts and labels are useful to him in his cognitive functioning. But do
they have anything to do with the functioning and adapting of the
person described? Do they specify functional properties of that person? It is difficult to see how they could do so. Even when used by the
same describer, a given label refers to different physical behavior in
different behaving persons. And when the same label is used by different describers, it may not refer to the same physical action. As noted in
the preceding chapter, even investigators defining the same technical
term, such as one of Murray's needs, make references to separate
(although overlapping) sets of behaviors.

In addition, descriptions are made at diverse levels of abstraction. Beyond words for actions (like *quick*), we have words for
sequences of acts *(hurried)*, words applied to varied classes of acts *(fast
tempo)*, and words for more general categories of acts *(energetic,
driven)*. When we describe some component of a person or some
aspect of a functioning system within that organism, we may unwittingly use terms at several levels without differentiating among the
levels.

A suggestion as to how trait concepts get formed and applied
may be found in a statement by Alfred Schutz: "The individual's
common-sense knowledge of the world is a system of constructs of its
typicality" (1953, p. 4). By typicality, he seems to mean what is typical or modal. He goes on to say that this common-sense knowledge

is intersubjective and socialized, an assertion that does not necessarily mean that one person's constructs are precisely the same as everyone else's, or that everyone agrees exactly on what is typical. Some convergence, some moderate approximation is sufficient for everyday living.

One interpretation of Schutz's statement is that each person has words for what people typically do, and that insofar as people perceive similar worlds of behaving people, people will tend to use more or less the same words, these becoming the common trait descriptors. Given a sense of the mode, a person notes departures from that norm. When she describes another person, she emphasizes the ways in which the person differs from the average.

Another interpretation can also be drawn from that statement. Just as a person construes her perceptions of behaving people in terms of what is typical, so she construes her perceptions of each person in terms of what is typical for that person. Her descriptive terms for the person are intended to represent the modal features of that person's behavior, as she sees it. Concerned with the person's "typicality," she does not attend to the variation around it; she does not restrict her descriptive term to the segment of behavior that she observed under some particular set of conditions. In stating her perception of a central tendency in the person's behaviors, she does not go to the elaborate effort of specifying the range around that tendency or the sets of conditions under which she has observed the person.

The Descriptive Processes in the Individual, the Researcher, and the Observer

The infinite sequence of a person's behaviors is nonrepeating; no two acts are precisely the same in their topography. Furthermore, given this uniqueness, there can be no series of contiguous actions that recurs at a later point in time. This asserted discriminability of every action from every other action is not peculiar to psychology and personality. Natural science faces the same discriminability of each thing from every other thing. But natural science is not dismayed by this prospect; rather, it seeks regularities among objects and among events. As Wigner puts it, "physics does not endeavor to explain nature . . . it only endeavors to explain the regularities in the behavior of objects. . . . In fact, the specification of the explainable may have been the greatest discovery of physics so far" (1964, p. 995).

As living and adapting people, we try to explain everything about the behavior of other people, especially when we find some action surprising and puzzling. As scientists, perhaps we should extrapolate Wigner's view of physics to our ambitions for explaining behavior. We can search for firm regularities in behavioral events, and we can establish the limits within which each regularity can be observed. We can then seek to account for it in terms of its relationships with dependable features of the conditions, including actions and other events that precede it in some type of consistent pattern.

Each member of the laity is his own scientist, as George Kelly (1955) has suggested. Experiencing the stream of actions by others and interacting with others at a rather rapid pace, an individual develops his personal constructs for describing others. Although we know little about how children develop their personal constructs, it is likely that the process parallels other forms of cognitive development. When Waern, Hecht, and Johansson (1974) asked subjects about the behavior and feelings of children portrayed in pictures or stories, six-year-olds simply described the situation or chose interpretations tied to features of the situation. Twelve-year-olds gave more abstract answers and referred to traits.

An adult perceives regularities in the behavior of another person and, on request, will label those regularities. In construing another person, he seems to be identifying some temporal segments of the other's behavior and labeling them. His label may be applied to a single segment or may be used to describe a common feature in a series of segments that have been retrieved from memory. The lay person never demarcates any one segment from the stream. He does not indicate the boundaries, the beginning and the end of each segment. To be sure, in telling another person about the label, he may allude to a particular occasion (for example, a conversation or a social party) during which the pertinent segments of behavior occurred, but for his own purposes and for the purpose of reporting his construal to someone else, he feels no need to be more specific.

One reason why the lay person is not concerned about boundaries for segments is that he is summarizing and abstracting his experience with the other person. He may be summarizing and abstracting for ease of storage (as suggested in the earlier quotation from Bruner) or to help him understand the other person and to gain some expectation of what he is likely to perceive that person as doing when they interact in the future. Since he is concerned with labeling the person, he need not retain any impression of the detailed, specific actions on which his construal is based. Thus, in addition to the high degree of individuality in a person's cognition and interpretation of another's behavior, there is presumably much individuality in the analysis of that behavior into salient and secondary segments of unidentified lengths.

As noted earlier, the behavior that each of us observes in others is unique in that it does not exactly reproduce any other behavior. Yet there are obvious similarities between the actions of a person at different times, and there are also similarities between the actions of different persons. When we observe the behavior of a stranger or acquaintance, we may note actions that are similar to those of people we know well. To meet our need to construe observed behaviors and to label people, we may interpret those actions in terms of the attributions we have previously made to our familiar associates.

A primary argument of this volume is that, in their research, investigators utilize concepts that they have developed in their own interactions with people, either in everyday life or in the clinic. Occasionally, they may encounter a concept utilized by another researcher and adopt it if they find it useful. Practically none of the concepts studied in personality refer to features of behavior distilled from systematic observations made under standardized conditions. The primary exceptions are some labels for factors obtained by the factor analysis of test responses in the testing room. Even for these, however, the labeler frequently draws on his array of concept terms developed previously.

These terms may refer to segments of behavior of any length. An investigator concerned with individual differences may characterize a person's whole life, a period of months, or a conversation, just as the lay person does. Implicitly, she labels a person and not segments of observed behavior. She focuses on her construal of that person, taking it for granted that her descriptive terms apply for some rather extended period, several months or longer, if nothing significant occurs. Secord and Backman (1964, p. 64) refer to this assumption as "temporal extension."

In experimental research on personality, the focus of the investigator is more restricted. The investigator seeks to characterize the person's state or behavior during a relatively short period of time, usually several minutes and not more than an hour or so. Like her colleagues using other contexts for data collection, however, the experimenter does not feel it necessary to analyze this period into explicit segments. And all investigators may identify the behaviors of interest as those responses observed after the subject has been exposed to specific stimuli or questionnaire items.

An investigator obtains her data from an observer, who may be the investigator herself. When the observer is an assistant or the person being studied, the investigator can communicate her descriptive term (for a trait, motive, value, or attitude) to the observer and ask him to judge the degree of applicability of that description to the person studied. The judgment may be based on a particular period of observation, a segment of behavior he is to observe, or on his prior observations of unspecified segments of behavior.

Alternatively, the investigator can ask the observer to judge whether or not each of a series of more specific verbal statements applies to the person studied. Each of these statements may refer to a particular subconcept, one way in which the more general concept may be manifested. For example, if studying masculinity, she can ask whether the person studied likes contact sports. Or she can choose another route, providing statements from which the applicability of the target concept can be inferred. For instance, does the person tend to perceive certain kinds of images, like pipes, when confronted with ambiguous stimuli (as in the classical Terman-Miles Test of Masculinity-Femininity). These two procedures represent the sample versus sign distinction developed by Goodenough (1949), which refers to the degree of similarity between the observed behavior and the behavior to which the concept refers. That is, is the observed behavior a sample of that subsumed under the label or does it merely provide a sign, a clue from which an inference can be drawn about the applicability of the concept?

The observer may be given the freedom to analyze the behavior he observes into segments of his own choosing. Similarly, he may be permitted to use his own labels. What he does may depend on the context—for example, is the observed behavior readily labeled, or is it unusual and hard to construe (see Newtson, 1973)? More commonly, the investigator specifies the labels the observer is to use and directs him toward the segmenting of the observed behavior in terms of occurrences of designated subconcepts.

The attributing of an observer is done for purposes of research. When asked to describe another person, the observer usually comes up with six or eight phrases (Allport, 1961, pp. 366–367), but when asked specifically which of two dozen broad trait terms or which of 300 specific items characterize that person, he will make the judgments with no great difficulty. The observer's judgments in the research context are a kind of epiphenomena. They represent attributing that is done in response to the request of the investigator rather than everyday perceiving and cognizing.

There is empirical evidence (Kuncel, 1973; Minor and Fiske, 1976) indicating that observers responding to a statement about self or others draw on their memories in diverse ways and may make an interpretation of the statement that will facilitate their selection of a response. As inferred from observers' reports, the processes used in arriving at descriptions are frequently not those which the investigator intended the observers to follow. An investigator cannot assume that her observers perceive and interpret behavior as she herself does, or that their meanings for words and construct labels are the same as hers. And the greater the differences between the investigator and her observers, in prior experience and in subcultural or cultural memberships, the more probable are dissimilarities in processes of forming descriptions and in meanings for words and labels.

Raters can, of course, be given extended systematic instruction about the intended meanings for words in rating scales and about the kind of evidence they should use in making their ratings. In such work as the coding of verbal content, the judges may be trained to function in a highly routine way. In the more usual kinds of rating work, however, even trained raters are given considerable scope in the processes by which they select material as pertinent to their ratings and by which they interpret the material to arrive at their recorded judgments.

Theories as Personal Constructs

Like everyone else, those who study personality are trying to understand people as they perceive and construe them. The investigator's interpretations of people's behavior influence his research work. The theorist develops explicit statements about what he has perceived and inferred. Examination of the classical theories of personality indicates that most of their creators constructed their theories on the basis of their experience in the clinic (for example, Freud), the counseling office (Rogers), or in everyday living (Maslow). And given the different kinds of experiences on which theorists have been constructed, it is not surprising to find that they tend to refer to different phenomena. The constructs of classical theorists are personal constructs (Kelly, 1955), although they are more systematic and more explicit than those of most people. None of the grand theories have been based on research findings; none came from an effort to account for systematic, replicable observations.

Some more recent theories, of smaller scope, have been constructed in interaction with research results. Even here, however, it is doubtful that substantial modifications of conceptual propositions or of constructs have been made as a consequence of relationships demonstrated in empirical research. Perhaps exceptions might be found in the conceptual work of those relying heavily on test responses (such as Cattell and Eysenck).

One has the impression that personality theorists trust their construals of personal experience more than they trust research findings, especially those reported by other investigators. (Can they be faulted for this? Count the empirical generalizations in which you have great confidence.) Unfortunately, constructs from personal experience are rarely disconfirmed and abandoned. When an experience seems inconsistent with previous construing, it is easy to explain away the apparent discrepancy.

Classical personality theories are never stated in forms that make them falsifiable, as Popper (1959) says a good theory should be. Instead, their propositions involve words of the author's choosing, rather than standard terms with explicit definitions coordinating them with observables. Has any theorist ever said that his concept is identical with the concept given the same label, or with any concept having a different label, in someone else's theory? In much personality theorizing, even the words for the central concepts do not have the systematic quality required for scientific language. As Heider notes, "though we know the meanings of words like 'promise,' 'permit,' or 'pride' we do not know them in the same way we know the meaning of words like 'two' and 'four,' or of words like 'speed' and 'acceleration'" (1958, p. 8).

It should be evident from the preceding analysis that there is more irregularity than regularity in the descriptive processes of lay persons, investigators, and observers. Each person analyzes the behavior she observes into segments in her own way, and each applies labels as she chooses. When two observers make the same ascription to a person, the investigator cannot assume that the observers perceived that person's behavior and interpreted it in the same way. Regularity in codings of observer reports does not establish regularity and consistency in the processes yielding those reports. Similarly, the early work by Benton (1935), Eisenberg (1941), and Eisenberg and Wesman (1941) on responses to questionnaires demonstrated the various and changing ways in which subjects interpret the items.

Theories of personality are certainly interesting. We read one theory and find that it gives us a way to look at ourselves and other people. Later, when we read another theory, we may also find that intriguing and thought-provoking. And then we have a similar experience with a third theory. We have plenty of theories—in fact, too many. These theories have not provided fruitful guidance for empirical investigations leading to dependable conclusions and firm conceptual propositions. The lack of progress in the personality domain does not stem from lack of theory but from other sources, as this book seeks to demonstrate. These sources have contributed indirectly to the inadequacy of the theories. But the difficulties in personality do not originate in the theories; consequently, few references to personality theories are made in these pages.

Models for Perceptions, Predictions, and Attributions

Our understanding of the processes underlying personality data may be furthered by examining possible relevant models. If these data are seen as being perceptions, then the conceptualizations of Brunswik should be considered. One of his early models (Brunswik, 1940) identifies three components—the distal stimulus, the proximal stimulus, and the perceptual response—together with the correlations between each pair of components. This model was designed for the perception of fixed, stable stimuli. Although it could be applied to the immediate perception of a person or a momentary action, it offers little help in understanding the total process of attributing or judging.

In a subsequent discussion of social perception from photographs, Brunswik (1947) utilized a model involving "actual" scores, ecological trait-cue relationships, external cues, impression values of cues, estimated external features, and estimates made by subjects. Although this model is more comprehensive because it includes reference to stages in arriving at the final estimate, it also was intended for a situation in which the stimuli are fixed.

In the field of clinical inferences and predictions, the more lenslike model that was adapted from Brunswik's models is frequently used. In Hammond, Hursch, and Todd (1964), this model has a distal variable (criterion), input cues, and the subject's estimate (prediction), along with ecological validities (criterion-cue relationships), cue utilization (cue-prediction relationships), and the long arc relating criterion and prediction. This model has been quite useful for studies of the appropriate and inappropriate emphasis that predictors place on each of the available cues, as determined by comparing the empirical validity of the cues with the predictors' utilization of them. The research findings have thrown considerable light on the processes by which judges, in arriving at their prediction, combine the bits of information from the cues.

Yet these models and this research seem to offer little help for efforts to understand naturalistic attribution. In describing a friend or in rating a person, there is usually no objective value that the attributor is trying to approximate or predict. Since there is no criterion, such as an objective score, no functional validity can be calculated. To be sure, a very indirect estimate of the validity of a person's judgments about another might be reached from determining how successfully she was able to adapt to that person. Appraising such organismic achievement (to borrow Brunswik's phrase) would be difficult. And that estimated success would itself be a result of several other influences besides the perceiver's ability to make appropriate judgments.

Of at least equal importance is the fact that, in naturalistic attribution, the input cannot be readily analyzed into discrete cues. Naturalistic attributions are based on observing sequences of behaviors of the other person, not on looking at a photograph or studying a set of test responses or other recorded cues. In Brunswik's terms, the latter stimuli are not representative of the cues encountered in nature, although they may represent the content available to a diagnostician.

These models cannot be used for personality ratings based on observations of behavior for yet another reason. Although the cues pertinent to certain perceptions of objects can be identified, there are no standard external cues for personality attributions. Consider the rating of Murray's need for Endurance. There are no concrete acts that are clearly diagnostic. Instead, there are sequences of acts, chains of behaviors that can be labeled as exemplifying that need. But that analyzing and labeling of themes in a person's behavior is itself attributing. Free descriptions of a person, standardized ratings, and even responses to inventory items involve a complex, multistage process. Chronologically, first is the flow of speech and other actions of the person being described. From these, an observer receives a continuous flow of sensory input yielding a series of perceptions. We may presume that these perceptions are often reduced to impressions that encapsulate sequences of perceptions (or perhaps a set of similar perceptions) and that are stored in the memory. When needed, some of these impressions are retrieved.

In using the word *impression,* I am guilty of taking a term from everyday language and using it for my own purposes. Even worse, the word has already been used by many who study person perception. I mean by the term the images and other mental content about a person and the person's behavior that come to mind as we think about the person. Impressions are what we have stored in our memories about that person. They seem to be formed without effort, and they come into our awareness when we turn our thoughts to that person. I am limiting the term to this mental content before it has been reviewed and construed, before it has been cast into words, either mentally or vocally. I believe impressions exist, on the basis of my own introspections and the reports of others' introspections. My term *impression* seems very similar to *vignette* as that concept is used by Abelson (1976).

The process employed in producing a description or rating is sketched in Figure 1. This visual model has more expository than heuristic value. It is oversimplified, leaving the contribution of the observer to be inferred. To make a personality rating, the person to be rated produces a sequence of behaviors observed by the rater. In Figure 1, the sequence is undifferentiated because the only pertinent analysis is whatever differentiation is made by the observer. That behavior results in perceptions in the observer, these being grouped into impressions or somewhat inchoate characterizations. At a later time, the observer takes on the task of making a rating. The sketch does not attempt to represent that process except to indicate that the observer draws on her stored impressions (A' and D'). The lines connecting elements in the sketch indicate derivations of components from earlier components, the slope suggesting the time interval. Nothing in the sketch can be taken as a datum except the product, the rating. No utilization of cues can be determined. Without a

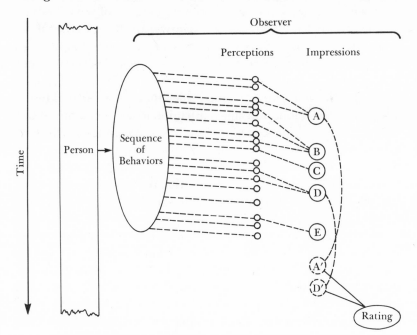

Figure 1. A Sketch of the Process Underlying a Personality Rating.

criterion in nature, no functional validity can be computed.

The reader can see for himself whether the rough schema in Figure 1 models his own experience. I will provide a personal account as an illustration. Suppose I am rating an old friend on "attention to detail." I immediately decide he is very high on that trait. Careful planning ahead is one of my vivid impressions of him. If necessary, I can retrieve from memory many instances in which I was impressed by his unusual consideration of details.

Note that, in interpreting the trait label when applying it to my friend, I have unwittingly selected one manifestation, one component for emphasis. If I had been rating another person, I might have retrieved impressions about other components of the trait, such as the care he took in preparing manuscripts—his checking of the spelling of words, his attention to punctuation, and his concern for consistency in the use of headings.

But now suppose I am rating that old friend on "manifest anxiety." I have to think about it because anxiety is not part of any impression I have formed about him. I think back to several conversations with him, searching my memories for signs of anxiety. I find very few. There have been times when he was greatly concerned about something, and the concerns were realistic, but those impressions seem irrelevant to manifest anxiety as I interpret it. So I decide to rate him as low.

It will be apparent to the reader that I have some kind of implicit notion about how much attention to detail and how much manifest anxiety is present in the people I know. At least at the final state of selecting the point on the rating scale I will mark, I compare the ratee, or my impressions of him and his behavior, to that personal norm and make each rating relative to that point. I have no clear picture, of course, whether my norm corresponds to the norm of other people.

The process involved in describing oneself on a rating scale or in response to an inventory item is rather similar to that involved in describing another. As indicated in Figure 2, a person perceives her own behavior and her internal states—feelings, thoughts, and images. She may derive general impressions from some of these perceptions. She may also have even more general impressions, which constitute an image of herself. After she has accepted the task of describing herself, she encounters a scale for rating a trait or a ques-

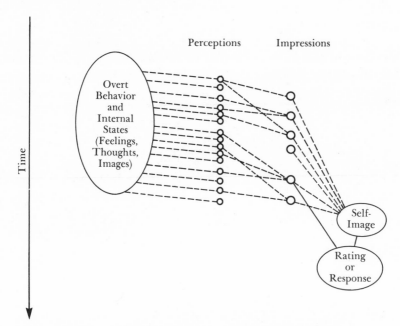

Figure 2. A Sketch of the Process Underlying Self-Descriptions.

tion about a tendency in her behavior. Either of two processes, or a combination of both, may then occur (Kuncel, 1973): She may compare the available response alternatives with her self-image, searching for the one that she feels fits best, or she may retrieve one or more impressions and select her response to fit them. These impressions may be recollections of her feelings or actions during some specific incident or during a series of occurrences of the same external situation. Note that in self-descriptions, as in descriptions of others, the generalization represented in the recorded response is formed from impressions that are themselves of an attributional, interpretive nature.

Compare these processes with the process utilized in the coding of concrete acts, as sketched in Figure 3. In an interaction involving two or more persons, there is a stream of behavior for each person. A coder watches the stream of just one person, forming a flow of perceptions. Instructed to indicate the beginning and end of each laugh, for example, the coder looks for the gestalt of perceptions that he cognizes as a laugh. These would include a sequence of vocal sounds accompanied by changes in the facial expression, pos-

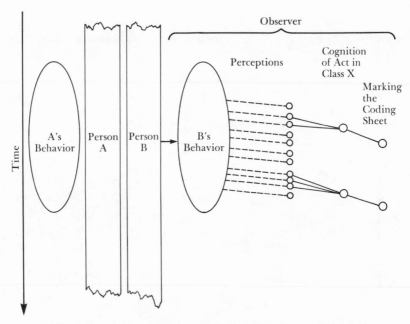

Figure 3. A Sketch of the Process in Coding Class X Acts of Person B.

sibly also accompanied by a slight backward toss of the head. Neither the vocalization nor the facial expression, occurring alone, would lead to the cognitive judgment that a laugh had occurred; only the simultaneous occurrence of both fits the observer's definition. Having made the judgment that a laugh has started, the coder marks the coding sheet to indicate that event. He then returns to scanning the stream of behavior for any subsequent cues for a laugh.

    If he is coding during observation of an ongoing interaction, the coder will be hard-pressed to note precisely the beginning and ending of each laugh of one participant, to say nothing of the laughs of several persons. While he is attending to the code sheet to record his judgment of the beginning of a laugh, he may miss the end of the laugh. The preferable procedure is to videotape the interaction so that, when a laugh has been identified, the recording can be stopped, a notation made on the code sheet, and the replay started again. In addition, the use of a recording obviously permits replay of a section when the coder is uncertain whether all the necessary cues are present. The coder can also recode the interaction at a later time to check his consistency, while other coders can independently code the recording to determine the congruence between their judgments.

As Brunswik (1956, p. 146) observes, perceptions are a subsystem of cognition. Perceptions of behaviors are rapid; cognitions and attributions are a little slower. From introspection, the task of determining an appropriate attribution seems similar to other problem solving. The observer is seeking for an attribution that satisfies ("satisfices," in Simon's terms). He considers an adjective, an alternative response printed on the page, or a step on a graphic rating scale, contemplating whether it fits his impressions. If it does not feel quite right, he rejects it and considers another alternative.

Brunswik emphasizes the lack of univocality of perceptual cues. The point is important. Certainly, there are no perceptual cues that unequivocally indicate any given personality variable. And even in the coding of simple acts like gestures and laughs, the cues are not entirely univocal. Yet it is possible to obtain fairly easily a very high level of congruence between the perceptions and cognitions of independent judges in coding such acts. This congruence is critical. Brunswik formulates "the basic requirement for scientific exactitude" as "the inter- and intra-subjective univocality of observation and communication" (1955, p. 208). A basic argument of this volume is that such univocality has not been attained and cannot be achieved for observation and communication of contemporary personality variables. In contrast, while there is some ambiguity at times in the perceptual cues for acts, very high consensus can be obtained on judgments as to the occurrence of these acts.

This examination of representations of the attributive process brings out its complexity as well as its inaccessibility. Since it cannot be directly observed, indirect methods for studying it must rely on the medium of rather equivocal words. The introspections of investigators and observers are about all the guidance available. There seem to be at least two major phases in that process of attributing: (1) the perceiving of behaviors, and (2) the formulating of a cognitive judgment based on that previous perceiving. The two phases are sequential. Although the cognizing can follow immediately on the perceiving, the cognizing usually takes place at a separate point in time. The observer may watch a segment of behavior and afterwards formulate his attributions. Much personality data involve cognizing that occurs a long time (days or months) after the perceptions on which it is based.

The first phase of attributing is particularly difficult to study because the process of perceiving and forming impressions is very rapid and almost automatic; it is so recurrent and so familiar that it is ordinarily out of the focus of attention. The second phase seems to involve little or no verbalizing to one's self as one deals with these impressions. I have asked colleagues to think out loud as they made routine evaluative ratings required for administrative purposes. Their verbalizing was associated largely with the meaning of the labels for the variables rated, with the format provided for recording the judgments, and with the meaning of one or two of the several alternative judgments permitted. There were only a few references to the impressions and recollections being reviewed to arrive at the judgments.

Progress When Not Constrained by Words

We have argued that the limited progress in the personality field can be attributed in part to its dependence on words and on psychologists' own experience and constructs and in part to the consequent lack of close consensus on attributions and constructs. In contrast, when psychologists do not study verbal phenomena and when their constructs are not derivatives of everyday experiencing and construing, some progress seems to have been made. We have learned a lot about how we do our research. We know that each procedure for collecting data has its own unique effects on our resulting measurements. More generally, different methods for assessing a trait yield somewhat different sets of data (Campbell and Fiske, 1959), and the perspective of the observer makes a difference (Cartwright, Kirtner, and Fiske, 1963). We know that psychological testing and experimenting have their own critical components of a social psychological nature. Beyond the data collection, we have psychometric theory, an impressive construction applicable to a particular kind of response data, regardless of the specific content in the test questions. And psychologists have developed elegant statistical models for analyzing the data in psychological research.

Other parts of quantitative and mathematical psychology are

also flourishing, with current work building on previous work. Brought in from outside psychology, information theory has become a powerful tool. More relevant to personality is behavior theory. The basic postulates of that theory and its established generalizations are content-free. They deal with contingencies, reinforcements, and the schedule of those reinforcements, without needing to identify the acts or the reinforcers. Quite clearly a theory about content, rather than a theory of content, is George Kelly's *Psychology of Personal Constructs* (1955). He developed nomothetic constructs that can be applied to any person's idiosyncratic constructs. For example, whatever the content of a person's personal constructs, we can measure the way in which he applies them—for instance, the number of people to which each applies. More formally, the aspects of personal constructs include permeability, dilation, tightness, and preemptiveness. This approach has been extended by Bieri (1961, 1971) and Schroder (1971). Some investigators studying perception and cognition as relevant to the personality domain have also been concerned with processes rather than the content processed. Research on cognitive controls (Gardner and others, 1959; Holzman and Klein, 1956) has studied regulatory functioning in the processing of information.

Somewhat similar is a program of investigation by Eric Klinger (Klinger, Barta, Mahoney, and others, 1976). He is studying people's current concerns, such as their exam coming next week, the date they have for tonight, or their choice of career. He is interested in the way these concerns guide the person's focus of attention and his perceptions and the way they intrude into the background of mental imagery and associations that flow through the mind when one is not preoccupied with immediate adapting to pressing stimulation. Klinger's work is not entirely content-free—for his individualized experiments, he has to create stimuli relevant to a person's current concerns. The body of his hypotheses and propositions, however, does not involve verbal representations of the content of people's current concerns or classifications of those concerns.

Another example where content is secondary can be found in actuarial or statistical prediction. A subject's response data are compared to those of groups whose performance is known, the subject is classified as more similar to one group than to the others, and that group's level of performance is the level predicted for the subject. The techniques utilized are essentially content-free. Even more dramatic are the procedures that have been developed for advising lawyers whether to accept or challenge a potential juror (Schulman and others, 1973; Saks, 1976; Zeisel and Diamond, 1976). Lawyers have, of course, made such decisions by their own rules of thumb or their intuitions throughout the history of jury selection. The new strategy consists of identifying the characteristics of those individuals who now believe the person on trial is innocent, characteristics that differentiate them from those who believe the defendant is guilty. These may include education, sex, income, beliefs, and attitudes. These discriminating attributes are then ascertained, insofar as possible, for each person called from the juror pool, and a weighted judgment is derived to predict what that person's vote would be at the end of the trial. The method assumes that potential jurors, who must not have made up their minds in advance, have implicit leanings in one direction or the other, and those leaning one way have attributes resembling those who now state their belief is in that direction. Although there has been only limited experience in applying these procedures, they appear to work. Note that the nature of the alleged offense and the content of the particular demographic or attitudinal variables found to be discriminative are irrelevant to the procedure.

In all the above instances where content is present, the investigator is not attempting to understand the meaning that someone's verbal productions have for that person and is not interpreting into substantive concepts her perceptions of that person or of his behavior. She is eliciting responses from persons, responses that can be classified mechanically or with a minimum of interpretation. Although the categories of the responses are abstract and are conceptualized, their linkage to the response data is quite explicit.

My speculation is that attempts to understand the verbal content of behavior can at best have only limited success. It will never be possible to determine exactly what each person means by each word he uses. In contrast, it is possible to have the respondent make responses about his content, his words, which can be handled objectively. Alternatively, the responses of persons to standard questions can be used to classify persons on a probabilistic basis into categories that have dependable relationships with other variables. The essential feature of the more promising approach is the avoidance of constructs generated by the respondent and of interpretive constructs stemming from the investigator's own experience.

Summary

A prime obstacle to progress stems from the fact that words pervade personality. In addition to the use of words in definitions and labels for concepts and in other aspects of theorizing, a use common to other disciplines, words are used in personality for the everyday description of people, for constructing and applying its measuring procedures, and for the responses that are converted into data. People do not agree on the meanings of descriptive terms and on the verbal definitions of concepts.

People use words in attributions that summarize their impressions of persons. Theorists go on to develop personal constructions about all their experiences with people. Labels and constructs are integrative summaries of impressions derived from assorted segments of behavior, not codes for specifiable, observable actions. Models for perception and attribution have involved fixed stimulus cues rather than the products of transitory experiences with other people. Perhaps the field can make progress when it is not constrained by words.

III

Subjectivity in
Analyzing the
Stream of Behavior

The preceding chapter examined the dependence on words in the attributing, measuring, and conceptualizing that go on in personality, pointing out the contribution of the individual person to the products of these processes. That contribution is subjective in the sense that it is specific for that individual. This chapter looks at that subjectivity. Subjectivity is implicit in Proposition 2 given in Chapter One, which points to the use of observers' interpretive judgments as research data, with the result that each datum is an observer-observed entity. It is made explicit in the statements about individuality of perceptions and processes, specific meanings for words, and specificity of observer judgments (Propositions 2c, 2d, and 2e). Of course, subjectivity is central to Proposition 1, which states that each personality investigator has been trying to understand his own perceptions, impressions, and attributions about persons and their behavior.

Analyzing the Stream of Behavior

Behavior forms a vast universe. Each person is constantly moving, constantly looking, and frequently talking. He is in an environment that is ever changing. Especially when with other people, he has a constantly varying environment flowing from their ongoing behaving. And a person's internal environment—his proprioceptive and kinesthetic sensations, his thoughts and images—is continually changing. Studying behavior in its changing milieu, Barker wrote about *The Stream of Behavior* (1963). In a later discussion of "the behavior stream," Schoenfeld and Farmer (1970) point out that the organism is always doing something.

Laboratory animals run through their mazes, choose which way to jump, and pursue their other activities without verbalizing their plans. Human beings go through many of their activities with little conscious reflection. In driving cars, they press pedals and turn steering wheels "automatically," to adapt to the traffic conditions. When conversing, they do not think out and verbalize to themselves in advance each remark they make. Thinking about behavior occurs primarily after the behavior has taken place. We reflect on our actions and on those of our associates. We try to understand behavior in the form in which we recall it. Verbalization takes place as we think back about behavior, either in private reflections or in discussion with others.

The vocabulary for describing human behavior is immense. People appear to develop words as they need them to make differentiations that are significant to them—the Eskimos have many words for snow, since distinctions among the several kinds of snow are important to them; the Arabs have many words for horse (and undoubtedly they will soon have many terms for their newly acquired automobiles, just as we do). Presumably, the range of words for describing behavior was a product of people's need to differentiate aspects of the stream of behavior they observed in others. Even for a single bipolar dimension, there are many words that have shades of meaning indicating strengths or intensities of the tendency and implying degrees of positive or negative evaluation of the behavior. For example, Goldberg (Goldberg and others, 1975) has assembled thirty-two words describing kinds of self-esteem and twenty-four for kinds of self-doubt, along with similar arrays for many other continua. The human species has amply demonstrated its great capacity for construing and interpreting behavior.

Unfortunately, human actions have a brief duration, so that the referent for a descriptive term cannot be indicated and established as readily as the referent for a particular kind of horse or a specific condition of snow. Hence, undoubtedly much redundancy occurs in the vocabulary for human behavior, along with the imprecision discussed in the previous chapter. What does last, although in a viscous and uncrystalline state, is the memory of past experiencing. It is the recollection of behavior that is construed and interpreted in verbal terms. Once given a verbal label, a piece of behavior may well be stored in a more or less stable condition identified by that label. While such recoding may be economical, as Bruner (1958, p. 86) suggests, it may distort the original experience.

The universe of the behavior of behaving persons is so extensive and diverse that it can be approached and described in an almost infinite number of ways. Within the humanities, there are the depictions of the artist and of the writer, the accounts of the historian, and the analyses of the essayist and of the philosopher. Each of these orientations implicitly or explicitly indicates a facet of human experience, the experience of the commentator or of other people. Within each orientation, the individual worker selects her own subject matter. It is not always clear whether her topic overlaps with that of her colleague, to say nothing of its overlap with the subject matter considered by a person working from a different perspective. Within the behavioral sciences, each science has its own orientation or perspective. Within psychology itself, each area takes a particular topic and typically emphasizes one kind of behavior as its object for investigation (the bar-press for learning, the mark on the answer sheet for aptitude, the verbal statement for psychotherapy). From the humanities to the psychological specialty, each approach furnishes a particular account of behavior. Each says something that cannot be translated exactly into the concepts and terminology used by any other perspective.

Although all of these disciplines can be concerned with the same phenomena, the behaviors of persons, such a statement is misleading. Each discipline deals with its own particular kind of observations. The workers within that field more or less explicitly agree on the pertinent kind of observation. Thus, the observations of one field may be distinguished by the type of person whose observations are admissible, in view of his membership in that field, and by the form in which the observation is recorded.

Underlying these distinctions is a fundamental point. Whatever the field, an observation is a product of both the observer and that which is observed. As a consequence, the observation contains a considerable amount of subjectivity. An observer may select from the stream of behavior the pieces that he observes. To a large extent, he determines the form and content of his observation on the basis of his past experience and current interests.

From the perspective of this book, the subjectivity in observations is a source of error for most research in personality and related fields. A science can advance by identifying sources of error, so that error can be measured and possibly controlled. As La Barre puts it: "All the natural sciences long since have sought to become exact sciences, first through the discernment of the *possibility* and the *nature*, and then through analysis and measurement of the *magnitude* of 'probable error' *inherent in the very process* of observation and measurement, as exemplified by chromatic and other distortion in the microscopic lens itself, and the like" (1967, p. vii). In the behavioral sciences, we have recognized that subjectivity contributes error to many kinds of observations, but we have been unable to measure the magnitude of that error with any precision. The error is not always systematic and fixed, as in the distortion introduced by a lens; it varies not only with the observer but also with the time and the conditions of the observations. For any one observer, it can vary with the person being observed and with the variable being judged.

Whether constant or variable, systematic or random, error

reduces the confidence we can place in conclusions from empirical research. The more error, the less replicable are the observations, and the less reproducible are the findings. Error reduces regularity and also constrains generalizability and external validity.

Error can of course occur in any science. For example, an observer can misread a dial or counter. Such errors are quantitative and can by themselves be measured. This chapter is concerned primarily with a different source of discrepancy between observers, disagreement on the subjective meaning assigned to observations. In making judgments about a person, the observer is attributing some degree of a quality to that person. One question is whether the assigned degree corresponds with that assigned by other observers. Another question is whether the quality itself is applicable. Even when observers are looking at the same small segment of behavior, each may assign a different quality to it. To some extent, differences in assignments reflect differences in preferred labels for construing. But there may also be differences in the type of quality assigned. These variations in qualities are the most serious product of subjectivity in observations in personality and other behavioral sciences.

It is possible to make controlled observations that minimize the subjectivity associated with the particular observer. Ongoing behavior, especially the actions of persons in the presence of other people, can be recorded in terms of simple units, and the temporal ordering of these units relative to each other can be examined. Regularities in the occurrence of a particular kind of unit or act can be discovered, especially regularities in terms of associations with other types of acts. This orderliness need not, of course, involve invariance in the sense that one kind of act always follows another. Continuing that sort of investigation, two or more kinds of acts may show the same relationship to another kind, thus permitting the formation of second-order classifications. This approach is illustrated in Duncan and Fiske (1977, Pt. III).

Subjectivity in Observations

Glass (1965, p. 1256) holds that "Science is ultimately as subjective as all other human knowledge, since it resides in the mind and the senses of the unique individual person." In his book on *The Subjective Side of Science*, Mitroff asserts that "all observations are observer dependent, dependent on the complicated and highly partial mental states of some observer. Observations are thus not neutral, because observers are not neutral with respect to what they observe. Indeed, for the act of observation to even occur, it is necessary that the observer bring with him some initial set of presuppositions about what he expects and even desires to see" (1974, p. 256). Similarly, Hanson (1958) writes that seeing (observing) is a theory-laden undertaking.

These authors write in general terms. They make statements about observation and not about concrete instances of observing. Hence, it is necessary to look more closely at these claims. In particular, among statements about subjectivity in observing, we must distinguish between statements referring to any and all observers and those that refer to the individual characteristics of a particular observer. Thus, it can be stated generally that, in order to make a specified kind of observation, all observers may need to possess certain characteristics and be in an appropriate state or have a suitable set. For example, to hear what an English-speaking person says, any observer must have good hearing and understand English. He must also be attending to the person's words and not be concentrating on his actions. The other kind of subjectivity is specific to the particular observer. For example, among a group of raters utilized in one assessment study, one rater agreed with the other raters on every variable except one, Suspicious-Trustful. Either the deviant rater was more sensitive to this trait than the other raters, or he had some kind of bias in his ratings of it.

Those who assert that the observer determines his observation more or less in line with his preconceptions fail to distinguish three types of construals, each associated with one particular role in the study of personality: that of the observer, of the person being observed, and of the investigator. (These roles are examined in more detail in Chapter Nine.) The concepts used by the observer in his construing come in part from prior experience and in part from the process of receiving instructions from the investigator. Crucial are concepts identifying the phenomenal events to be coded and concepts pertaining to the categories and scale points into which the events are to be coded. The degree to which the investigator has accurately communicated her low-order concepts to each observer can be estimated approximately by assessing the agreement between observations from independent observers. When that agreement is poor, her concepts either lack precision or precise manifestations or she has not been able to transmit them to her observers.

The construals of the persons being observed are not directly relevant here unless those persons are also in the role of observers, as in self-report procedures. Although the same basic features are found when the person observes himself and when external observers are used, there are two important differences. When using external observers, the investigator typically communicates her concept or variable to them. But when she uses self-reports, observations of self, she is less likely to do so. She does so when she asks for self-ratings on traits and enters those ratings as her data in subsequent analyses. When she is concerned with evaluative variables, as in questionnaires assessing adjustment, neuroticism, or other pathological concepts, she does not directly identify these concepts to the respondent, although the latter probably has some awareness of the type of variable being measured (Fiske, 1967).

The other difference between self-observation and external observation lies in the possibility for estimating the adequacy of the investigator's communication of her concepts. Although the judgments reported by the self-observer may provide some indirect ways to make that estimate, there is no possibility of determining agreement between independent observers since there can be only one observer in measurement procedures of this kind. As a consequence, the degree of individuality in the personal construals that the self-observer makes about the phenomena must remain essentially unknown. No one else can construe that person's behavior from the viewpoint of that person. His personal construal of the task is also rather unavailable.

Given the distinctions among these three kinds of construers, what do the assertions about the subjectivity of observation mean? We can offer at least four possible meanings, all more or less similar and some describing different perspectives on the same issue.

First, we cannot talk about concrete facts as if they were independent of conceptualizations. Citing Whitehead, Schutz notes that "the so-called concrete facts of common-sense perception are not so concrete as [they seem]. They already involve abstractions of a highly complicated nature" (1953, p. 1). We can all agree that we see, perceive, and interpret in terms of our past experiences and conceptualizations. I cannot "see" a bacterium through a microscope unless I at least know what a bacterium looks like and perhaps also know something about what a bacterium is and how to use a microscope. This interpretation refers primarily to the construals of observers, and in this sense the observational fact does depend on the observer.

Another interpretation is that the investigator's theory and more abstract concepts determine the set of categories into which observations are to be placed. This assertion is accurate; it states what the investigator should do. In the ideal situation, with the best possible set of categories, each potential phenomenological occurrence would fit into one and only one of the predetermined categories, the preconceptions and the set of categories providing the alternatives but not affecting in any way the observer's particular choice among the categories when he makes any given judgment. As argued by Scheffler in *Science and Subjectivity*, "Observation is capable of providing independent control over belief, even though it is channeled by categories, influenced by set, and describable only fallibly" (1967, p. 45). Thus, the construals of the investigator do determine the form in which the observations will be made without requiring the observations to conform to the theory.

There is, in principle, the possibility that the framework of the categories is faulty; for example, their definitions may make inevitable the finding of an empirical association between two categories. To take a trivial instance, the category "push" and the category "moves away from the other's preceding position" will have a strong association: If one person pushes the other, the other will usually be moved by that push. An investigator should critically search his categories for instances in which the definition of one category essentially requires the occurrence of an event subsumed under another category. In some cases, the relationship may be purely semantic or logical. Given human fallibility, the critical analysis of categorical frameworks may have to be done by other researchers, the initial construer being too involved in his constructs to be able to recognize defects of this kind.

A third meaning is that we see what we expect to see, we notice only the things and events which we expect to encounter. This interpretation has some validity if taken to mean that expectations guide attention and perception. We are more likely to see something we have been looking for than an equally intense sensory event that has not been anticipated. And strong expectations may even lead us to misperceive, to see something that is not there—as a fearful child on a dark road may see a goblin or ghost. Yet it is clearly not true that we see only what we expect to see and nothing else. We are frequently surprised by what we see, and very often we have no specific expectation, strong or weak.

In terms of empirical procedures, it should not be very difficult to indicate to an observer the one or more kinds of things we want him to note whenever they occur, with no hints as to when we expect them to occur or with what we expect them to be associated. In other words, the investigator should be able to communicate to the observer the observational task set for him without communicating her own expectations, stemming from her higher-level construing and conceptualizations, about associations between events.

Whether the expectations originate in the observer or have been communicated to him by the investigator, their effect can be expected to be greater when the observer is required to make interpretations and inferences than when his task is essentially recognition. The more complex and lengthy the cognitive task given to the observer, the more likely it is that his judgmental processes will be influenced by expectations.

The final and most serious interpretation of the assertions about subjectivity and preconceptualizations affecting observations is that one's observations conform to one's theory. If the investigator has a theory, and if she makes observations to give it empirical support, there is a great danger that her observations will conform to what the theory predicts. Investigators are well aware of this danger. Many of the procedural controls that have been established as norms for adequate investigation are intended to meet this potential threat. For example, it is considered most desirable to use "blind" observers, "blind" administrators of the experimental treatment, and "blind" subjects, concealing the investigator's expectations and even the nature of the treatment. The construals of the investigator regarding the relationships between constructs and the expected covariation of particular observations must be kept from the observer. And yet, as noted above, the investigator must communicate to the observer the categorical framework within which the observations are to be coded. The observer's construals of the categories must be the same as those of the investigator.

The investigator has an obligation to communicate not only with her observers but also with other investigators. While everyone would accept such a statement of principle, it is not always carried out in practice. Alleged limitations on journal space or other rationalizations are offered as reasons for not publishing a manual of one's procedures for observing and coding. Although the labels for one's categories do get published, the full definitions given to observers and the instructions for applying them should also be publicly available in full explication. Science is public knowledge, as Ziman (1968) has stressed. Any promising data-gathering techniques should be in the public domain, to be shared and to be evaluated by others, in both conceptual and empirical terms. In addition, the investigator's rationale for her categorical framework should be given, not just to try to persuade others to adopt the framework but also to permit other investigators to try developing alternatives that might be more effective.

In the history of psychology, a classic instance of observations being shaped to fit theory is found in Titchenerian introspectionism. Titchener developed a set of construals for sensory experience and internal sensations. One may speculate about the source of his constructs—presumably they came from Titchener's personal experience. He trained his students to introspect. After training, the students gave reports of their experience that agreed with Titchener's expectations. Yet investigators in other laboratories were not able to reproduce the results obtained by Titchener. The cause of the discrepancies among results from different laboratories seems obvious. Titchener communicated to his students not only what they were to observe but also (and presumably unintentionally) what they should find in their observation, what their reports should be. The psychological pressures on the student-observers must have been strong (see Schultz, 1969, pp. 215–216).

This bit of history also brings out another matter. Given the nature of the phenomena under study, there could be no independent agreement between observers on each datum. No one else can experience my introspective sensations and feelings. The apparent agreement between the reports of two observers about their introspections is a very tenuous basis for drawing conclusions.

Another part of psychological history supports the importance of having various investigators look at the same phenomena, rather than assuming that the phenomena in one laboratory must be the same as those in another because the physical appearances of the equipment and organisms are similar. Some decades ago, a vigorous theoretical argument occurred between Tolman and his followers and the group associated with the viewpoints of Hull and Spence. One focus of the disagreement was Tolman's construct of latent learning; opposing the view that learning occurs only with reinforcement, Tolman argued that rats (and presumably other organisms) learn from their experience in mazes a great deal more than just how to get to the goal box with its reinforcing reward.

An ingenious experiment designed by Jones and Fennell (1965) suggests a probable source of the disagreement between these two schools of thought. They obtained sets of rats that were pure descendants from the colonies on which each school drew for its supply. The strains seem to have been kept quite separate from each other. Rats from the colony that had supplied the Hull-Spence school behaved as their forebears had apparently behaved. After a few trials in a simple maze requiring the rat to run around a protruding partition to reach the goal box, these rats would move promptly out of the start box and proceed directly around the partition to the goal. The rats from the colony that had supplied Tolman behaved differently. When the starting box was opened, they would take their time about coming out, sniff about, amble along exploring their surroundings, and eventually move to the goal. They took much longer to get there than those in the other group. Thus, each group behaved in a way that was quite consistent with the construals of the human investigators who had studied their forebears.

Let us assume that these rats did behave in essentially the same ways as those studied by the Tolman school and by the Hull-Spence school more than a decade earlier. Let us also assume that the genetic differences between the present colonies are essentially the same as those between the colonies at the earlier time. It seems evident that the adherents in each school were studying different patterns of behavior. Within each school, there could have been agreement on the observations made on each rat. The observations of entries into blind alleys and the timing of trials could be done with close agreement by observers. Often, of course, instruments were used to record, count, and time the phenomena in this research. It seems inconceivable that no member of one school ever observed rats running in the laboratories of the other school. Perhaps when a member did, he accounted for the behavior of those foreign rats in terms of some aspect of the experimental conditions. The difference in genetic origin apparently did not suggest to anyone a genetic difference associated with temperament, with styles and rates of moving.

The moral of this episode is that investigators should not assume that their phenomena are identical with those observed by others. If investigators with differing conceptual positions cannot examine together a body of phenomena, they can certainly make recordings of behavior in their institutional setting and transmit copies of the empirical protocols to those in other locales.

After reading a draft of this book, a thoughtful person suggested that this episode in the history of psychology stemmed from the reward systems prevailing in the field. Given the fragmentation of the field into research areas that are functionally autonomous, each proceeding on its way with only occasional input from another area, the major reinforcements supplied to an investigator come from colleagues working in his field of specialization. And when a field is polarized, as the field of learning was in the early 1950s, the reinforcements come from colleagues sharing a narrow paradigm with the investigator. Under these conditions, the work stemming from a competing orientation is to be criticized, not to be assimilated. The rewards come from maintaining the thesis against the antithesis, the task of finding a synthesis requiring a detachment found only rarely among the very human members of the scientific establishment.

Returning for a moment to the third interpretation of subjectivity in observation given above—that one sees only the things that one expects to see—we find that the reverse statement applies as well: perhaps an observer's preconceptions make it unlikely that he will see anything that he does not expect. Certainly, an observer who is carefully instructed as to what he is to observe and how he is to code it may simply not perceive some aspects of the observed behavior that are very important to understanding it, since he must concentrate on his task and perform it as well as possible. When the observer has finished his work, however, it may be valuable for the investigator to question him about perceptions that were not included within the coding as he did it and events that were not covered by the assigned set of categories. More to the point, the investigator herself should be concerned with refinements in her categories and with revisions of her construing, even to the point of a complete replacement with a new conceptual framework. She should be on the lookout for anomalies in the observational data produced by her observers. Even more important, she should, from time to time, observe the phenomena herself, sometimes in terms of her standard categorical framework and sometimes with a fresh attempt simply to see what is there. (The psychology of discovery is a large and separate problem, which cannot be explored in this volume; see Hanson, 1958; Popper, 1959; Getzels and Csikszentmihalyi, 1976.)

An episode from astronomical history concerning the alleged canals on Mars is relevant here. An Italian observer perceived lines on Mars and used the word *canale* in reporting his observation. This term was translated as *canal*, although the Italian word also means channel, groove, or gully. There was much speculation about the source and interpretation of these observations. Others also "saw" the canals (Hoyt, 1976), presumably because they were convinced that the canals were there. Years later, when it was possible to obtain photographs of Mars from satellites beyond the earth's atmosphere, it became clear that there were no regular features of that sort. The episode illustrates several matters: the dangers inherent in words, the need for independent confirmation of observations (which of course occurred), and especially the need for independent evidence to support interpretations of perceptions. It also brings out the necessity of recognizing the possibility that one's perceptions are based on inadequate sensory input. Accurate observation presupposes the use of clear, strong sensory impressions.

Categorizing Behavior

Since our earlier references to categories have been in rather general terms, a closer examination is needed. Let us consider a specific action and the ways in which it might be categorized. A person raises his hand, fingers up, palm toward another person, the arm partially extended. An investigator might wish to have, as a category for coding observations, one that specified these several features. Somewhat more general would be a category for hand raised toward another. Still more general would be the category of gesture, and most general of all would be a category for movement of a hand. Each of these categories would include the categories preceding it in this list. These are, of course, only a few of the many potential categories that could be identified at points along a dimension starting with the closely specified action initially described. And, for some purposes, the dimension could extend beyond this list to even more inclusive categories of physical movement.

Beginning with the illustrative action, another list of categories could be developed along a more psychological dimension. One category might be for movements toward the other that are oppositional (rather than positive). Such a category might be included in a more general category for movements that psychologically restrain (rather than encourage) the other from moving in a particular direction. Still more inclusive would be a category for implicitly restricting the movement of the other. Beyond that, there might be categories for coercing the other, or dominating him, or acting aggressively toward him. It seems to be less obvious how to order possible categories in terms of generality for psychological dimensions than for physical ones, at least when starting with the particular hand movement indicated above.

For the physical dimension given above, it seems likely that agreement between observers would be at about the same high level for each of the categories in the series. If anything, agreement might increase as the categories became more general—the more general the category, the fewer specifications and consequently the fewer simultaneous discriminations required of the observer. In contrast, it seems safe to predict that the extent of agreement between observers would decrease with the increasing generality of the psychological categories. The more general categories are both more inclusive and more interpretive. In fact, the illustrative movement of the hand toward the other could be interpreted as indicating any of several psychological attributes.

The physical and the psychological dimensions of increasing

generality differ in another important respect. Even with the greater inclusiveness of the successive physical categories, each still applies to a movement that can occur within a fraction of a second. If the coder is recording the initiation or onset of actions, he can pinpoint the event fairly precisely in time. But it is much more difficult to locate in time the beginning of some of the psychological events as categorized above. Although some oppositional actions could be so located, the concept of restraining from movement in a particular direction and, even more clearly, the concept of restricting are very likely to require a longer period of observation (several seconds or more) to permit their application in coding. Moreover, the psychological labels can be applied to events of diverse durations, from seconds to minutes or more. (A more intensive examination of the roles of time in observing and construing behavior is made in Chapter Seven. Categorization from the viewpoint of unitizing behavior is considered in Chapter Four.)

The investigator sets up his categories for observation on the basis of his chosen level of generality, the level that he believes best corresponds to his hunches or conceptual framework. If he is working in terms of interpretive constructs, he has to reach a compromise between observational precision and coordination with his constructs. To study aggression, he can develop one category identified by a verbal definition of aggression or by a series of actions that exemplify aggression for him. Alternatively, he can develop a set of categories, one for each of the most frequent manifestations of aggression in the kinds of behavior that his observers will be watching. This multiple list should produce higher agreement between observers and certainly would permit the investigator to determine the categories for aggressive acts on which observers could most easily agree. It would also require more effort from the observers (and effort usually improves the quality of the observations). The disadvantages would include the conceptual problem involving the adequacy of the investigator's coverage of possible manifestations of aggression and the conceptual-methodological one of how he should combine the observations for the specific categories if he wishes to obtain a single index of aggression for each person observed. An advantage of establishing just a single category for aggression might be its closer congruence with the construct of aggression as the investigator was construing it.

A disadvantage would be that he could not immediately identify the sources for discrepancies between judgments by different observers.

"Aggression is characterized as injurious and destructive behavior that is socially defined as aggressive on the basis of a variety of factors, some of which reside in the evaluator rather than in the performer" (Bandura, 1973, p. 8; original italics omitted). Thus, we must consider the conduct and the social labeling of the conduct. The same action may or may not be labeled as aggressive, depending on the observer's perceptions of the circumstances and his inference about the actor's intentions. Of course every statement made about behavior, every observational report, is a labeling; whether the observer is making broad attributional ratings or is coding movements, he is utilizing concept terms involving some degree of abstraction. Some kinds of "content," however, seem more interpretive than others and seem to require larger inferential steps. Kendon (1975) argues that some classification schemes, instead of considering units of behavior, provide classes into which the observer fits behavior according to her judgment of the motive, intent, or results.

The attribution of psychological states can be a reasonably straightforward process. For example, the methods developed by Gottschalk and Gleser (1969) enable an investigator to assess anxiety and other states from a recorded verbal production—one hundred to two hundred words being sufficient. The concept of anxiety is translated into a series of characteristics, which the observer can score for the given verbal sample. Their procedure provides a systematic basis for determining the amount of anxiety to be attributed. The scoring has relatively high interobserver agreement, and the reliabilities of the total anxiety score as judged by a single scorer were found to be .80 to .86 in three samples of patients. The chief question about the method concerns the use to which the score is put. Even in measuring a state, there is a risk in generalizing the attribution beyond the five-minute period required to produce the behavior sample: To what time period does the attribution apply?

Categories for intentions or goals require a somewhat larger inferential step than do categories for states. In judging the direction of the future reference of an action, one must assess the action before deciding for what ultimate purpose or purposes it may be instrumental. Intentions or motives can be scored from productions in much the same way that a state is scored—the investigator can set up a number of features for the observer to look for. A well-known instance is the scoring of the need for achievement from stories told about pictures like those used in the Thematic Apperception Test (TAT) (McClelland, Atkinson, Clark, and Lowell, 1958). Comparatively high interobserver agreement has been obtained for achievement scores that are composites of several subscores.

The issue of external validity plagues the observation of a need or intention even more than it does the attribution of a state. Given a high achievement score derived from a sample of behavior lasting fifteen minutes or so, to what can the investigator generalize? Does the score characterize the person over a period of weeks or months? Apparently not. If the observation and coding procedure is repeated a week or so later, the new score typically has little correlation with the first one. Perhaps the assessment of needs like achievement should be interpreted as the observation of a current state of the person.

From the methodological viewpoint, one cannot object to interpretive categories for coding observations as long as the agreement between observers applying those categories is very high. Ordinarily such agreement is not high on the specific components of the scoring procedure even though the agreement between the integrative scores summing the components is good. And even for those scores, the level of agreement rarely approaches a degree of congruence justifying the treatment of the observers as interchangeable.

There remains, however, the difficulty of determining to what the attribution is assigned. In most instances, the use of interpretive categories occurs when the investigator wishes to characterize a person without reference to time or place. Since observations inevitably vary not only with the person being observed but also with the time and place in which he is observed, the scientific utility of the estimate based on a single sample of behavior is questionable. If, however, the investigator's conceptual framework brings in not only the actor but also the place and the behavioral context (derived from the time) in which each action occurs, he can avoid large inferential leaps and unknown errors of generalizing from a single observation point. In addition, he will ordinarily have a firmer data base, since his data will involve minimal differences in the judgmental processes of his observers.

The major danger in interpretive variables stems from the fact that interpretations are a kind of explanation: "She did that to hurt, and so she was aggressive"; "That behavior was intended to control the other people"; "He smiled because he was pleased." An interpretation of behavior assigns meaning to it. That meaning may be in terms of the actor's intent or goal, the behavior being seen as instrumental, or it may be in terms of the actor's direct expression of a feeling or reaction.

In our everyday discussion of people's behavior, we assign meanings of these sorts all the time, and those attributions seem useful; although they may not be optimal descriptions, they suffice. Why should we not use such meanings in our research? There are at least two reasons. First, from what perspective should these meanings be assigned? From the actor's viewpoint? If so, should we not ask her what she meant by the behavior? From the viewpoint of others interacting with her? If so, then we should ask them what the behavior meant to them. From an impartial observer's viewpoint? If so, just what is his perspective, other than that of actor or interactor? Second, these assigned meanings presume the answer to the underlying problem of understanding the behavior (Kendon, 1975); that is, they purport to explain the behavior a priori, and usually there is no opportunity to test the accuracy of that explanation.

When an observation is assigned a meaning and that meaning is used as the basis for determining the record reporting the observation, there is no way to check the interpretation. Other observers may assign similar meanings and produce corresponding data. Then the investigation is a study of these presumed meanings, not of the actual behaviors that were observed. The confirmation of hypotheses involving such meanings does not necessarily establish the accuracy of those interpretations, and the failure to confirm hypotheses does not conclusively demonstrate the inaccuracy of the interpretations occurring in the production of the data.

We say our purpose in studying behavior is to understand it. If that is so, we should not presume that we understand it and limit our study to the meanings that we or others have already given it. Following Wigner's interpretation of physics (1964), we should identify regularities in behavior and restrict ourselves to attempting to explain them. We can determine the meanings of behaviors empirically by categorizing observed behavior into discrete actions that are identified by their manifest features or patterns and then determining the complex relationships between one class of acts and each of several others. This approach is developed later, especially in Chapters Twelve and Thirteen.

One could also question the value of interpretive categories on the grounds that there is no true value that is being estimated in making attributions unqualified in terms of time and place. No one has ever attempted to specify fully what a score for a person means in terms of the complete set of hypothetical observations on which one would base the score if practical and ethical considerations did not get in the way. The difficulty can be evaded by defining the true score as the potential average judgment of all of those qualified to make attributions about the person in question (each such judge being weighted on the basis of his presumed qualifications for making a judgment, such as length of observation). But the conceptual value of such a hypothetical average seems questionable, given the low agreement ordinarily found between judges observing the same person from different vantage points.

There is no way to determine the value of the true score for one person on a single attribute. Any score is based on an observer's construal. Even when observers agree perfectly, the consensual score must be taken as the way these observers perceive and construe this person's behavior during the given period of observation. While that score is in some sense real, so is another score for that person on that conceptual dimension as obtained from other observers watching a different sample of behavior. All human construals are real and exist. A psychotic's reported construal about a person, however strange a misconstrual it may seem to be, is just as real as an observation agreed on by a number of other people. In form and in content, every observation is a function of the observer. In order to study regularities, we must minimize the contribution that the particular observer makes in her construing and interpreting. We must turn to observations that are specific to phenomena identified in time and space, observations reporting perceptions and cognitions with minimal inference.

In the natural sciences, investigators are also concerned with accurate measurements, as well as with both minimizing error and estimating the extent of error. They often make repeated measurements of the same or homogeneous objects or events under relatively fixed, specified conditions, taking the central tendency of those measurements for subsequent analyses and using the calculated variation among the measurements to estimate the degree of error. Behavioral scientists can use repeated observations by different observers to minimize the bias associated with each observer and to permit an assessment of the degree of variation among them.

The danger in considering true scores or in asking whether an observation approximates the truth lies in the attitude of the questioner. The word *truth* implies something absolute and unchanging. Scientists have to live with some degree of uncertainty and change. The history of scientific thinking is one of concepts that come and go or that change over the years. Concepts are relative to conceptualizers just as observed values for a concept are relative to observers. Scientists do not seek to approximate the truth but rather to develop concepts and theories that seem to yield increasingly more satisfactory consensual interpretations of the phenomena around them.

A major thesis of this book is that very close agreement between observers is essential to science, especially to fields studying such complex and transitory phenomena as human behaving. Given what we know about conditions associated with level of agreement (see Chapter Five), it follows that the observer should be considered an instrument. Ideally, he should be an automaton, rigorously adhering to his instructions. His role is like that of a sensor that emits a signal when it receives physical energy in a particular form (for instance, within specified wave lengths). Examples of such instruments include a burglar alarm, the heat-sensitive plug in a sprinkler system, or a metal detector.

In the observation of behavior, the sensory input to be perceived and coded is obviously not unidimensional, so these analogies are not precise. And the investigator using human detectors must recognize the limitations of such instruments. For example, a human observer must be motivated, and his motivation must be sustained. Matters of fatigue and of drift in criteria must be combated. Knowing that his observations will be checked, for example, can help an observer to sustain his efforts (Reid, 1970; Taplin and Reid, 1973).

In its ideal form, the process by which the observer arrives at his judgment can be verified independently by both the observer and the investigator. When a person is asked to add 49 and 18, he can do so and then check his work, even stating the arithmetic steps he used. The process used in making a judgment about an action can also be made explicit, although the steps are not as open to consensual validation as are steps in arithmetic. In contrast, the process used in rating a trait cannot be fully explicit, and neither the rater nor the investigator can independently check the steps in that process.

If the observer is seen as an instrument, then the concepts of communication theory can be applied. The original phenomena, the behaviors, are encoded by the observer and subsequently decoded by the investigator in data analyses. Communication theory points out that there may be "noise" associated with the coding and also with the decoding. When an observer has encoded behavior in his attributive judgment, he has added something, and he is sending a message that the investigator cannot decode precisely. But when the observer codes a gesture as occurring at an indicated moment, the investigator can decode the message without distortion from noise in the coding or decoding process.

In this discussion, as in most of this book, it has been assumed that the investigator's intention is to study behavior as it is observed by a detached observer who is not involved in that behavior itself. In this context, the goal of interchangeable observers is appropriate. But the investigator can have other legitimate objectives. She may wish to study behavior as it is interpreted in everyday interaction, or she may want to study the interpretations themselves, as a function of the particular observer. Such an investigation is concerned with the interaction between the observer and the person observed. To simplify her work, the investigator might choose to use one or more standard persons-to-be-observed. She would probably emphasize those features of the observer's interpretations that were particular to the observer. Such investigation of the attribution process, however, should be clearly separated from the study of behavior using observers as instruments (see Chapter Eleven for a detailed examination of the study of attributing).

The Interaction of Scientists and Subjects with Their Environment

In his unusual book, *The Subjective Side of Science* (1974), Mitroff reported conceptual and empirical work based on his conviction that, to understand the practice of science, one must critically appraise the actual behavior of scientists. He was concerned with the effects of new observations on scientists' beliefs and with the effects of scientists on the observations they make. He found surprisingly little change in the theoretical positions of Apollo scientists, no matter which theory they held, as the rocks were returned from the moon and were subjected to intensive analysis. Additionally, he discussed the proposition that people affect the measurements they make, a matter considered earlier in this chapter.

In personality and related fields, where the objects of study are persons, there are two ways in which the research can affect the measurable properties of those persons. First, it is quite possible that the experience of being a subject, responding to questions and reacting to experimental treatments, may have lasting effects on the person. Debriefing may not remove all effects of having been through an experiment, as Walster and others (1967) found. Although researchers certainly attempt to avoid producing any such effects, they know that it is often desirable to include a control group to be able to estimate the effects associated with having been tested before (as noted by Campbell and Stanley, 1963). Investigators assume, we must suppose, that any such effects are trivial and not harmful, although we doubt that they can offer much systematic empirical evidence that no harmful effects ever occur.

Second, psychologists have established that research procedures have effects on the measurements obtained. The problem of the social psychology of the psychological experiment has received much attention in recent years (see the papers in Miller, 1972, and the overview in Fiske, 1971, Chap. 10). The experimenter can affect his obtained data in many ways, as Rosenthal (1966) has shown. A person being observed reacts to being observed; a subject in a laboratory reacts to the laboratory; a person being tested reacts to the examiner, the room, and the instructions and content of the test. In each instance, the reaction may affect the measurements that are made. Although the ideal solution to this problem is unobtrusive measurement (Webb, Campbell, Schwartz, and Sechrest, 1966), it has proved very difficult to make systematic observations for comparisons between individuals without either violating ethical principles or letting the individuals know they are being observed. A partial resolution is to make recordings of behavior under natural or naturalistic conditions (openly and with permission). If the recording is continued long enough, and if the people observed are engaged in some activity, they seem to become relatively comfortable, and their behavior appears to be reasonably spontaneous and natural, in spite of the recording. It is particularly important that they not have any specific information about the purposes of the research or the investigator's constructs and expectations. They can, of course, be told that they can learn the results of the research at a later time.

Mitroff's emphasis on the behavior of scientists is important. Many aspects of scientific activity are subjective, irrational, or relative. Scientists are human creatures, with motives and feelings like those of their fellows. Scientists and students of scientific activity must recognize these facts. Yet objectivity must not be confined to testing the end products of scientific work; it "is a property of the whole process of doing science" (Mitroff, 1974, p. 240). We must try to understand how to extract the objective from the subjective, how to elicit consensual observations from inherently personal observers.

This chapter has examined subjectivity in observation. I do not argue, however, for elimination of all subjectivity in studying behavior. Once the investigator has collected and analyzed his data and determined his findings, he must try to understand and interpret them. This step can be highly personal and subjective, for this work follows no formal, impersonal rules. When a possible interpretation occurs to him, however, he must evaluate it systematically, weighing the evidence for and against it and making his assessment explicit for others. More generally, in Reichenbach's context of discovery (1938), the most creative aspect of science, the investigator is pursuing new ideas and new ways of seeing phenomena, and here he is highly subjective. It is here that a major principle of Feyerabend, "anything goes" (1975, p. 10), really holds.

Summary

The stream of behavior has been observed and construed from many orientations. Construals are subjective, and any observation is subjective also because it is dependent on the observer and his mental processes. Although there is agreement on the presence of subjectivity in observations, that assertion has several interpretations. Two important ones are that we observe what we expect to observe and that our observations conform to our theory. To what extent are these true for observations in personality research?

Categorizations of behavior are also subjective. When observers interpret behavior, they assign meanings. Although science requires the use of human observations, the observer can be used as an instrument that is interchangeable with other human instruments. Replicable observations are necessary for reproducible findings and generalizability of conclusions.

IV

Units for Observations, Measurements, and Analyses

"Relative to the importance of the issue, there has been very little research on the way we 'chunk' behaviors into meaningful units. In fact, psychologists often make a priori assumptions about behavioral units when investigating how we perceive others" (Hayden, 1975, p. 400). Although Hayden was writing about the perceptions of persons, the problem of behavioral units is not restricted to that topic. Central to personality and much of psychology is the cognitive analysis carried out by perceivers.

One consequence of the subjectivity in observations that was examined in the last chapter is that a judgment by an observer is attributed to a person typically without restriction as to time or situa-

76

tion (see Proposition 2b, Chapter One), that is, without reference to the segment of behavior on which the judgment was based. Such judgments may be based on segments of almost any duration. The investigator ordinarily does not specify the segment, although she may limit the duration of the period during which the person is observed. The investigator is rather casual about this matter because she and other investigators of personality have failed to locate conceptually useful units in the stream of behavioral phenomena (see Proposition 5). The preceding chapters have dealt with both natural processes and processes in measuring personality. Placing its primary emphasis on measurement, this chapter will consider several ways in which the problem of units enters the study of behavior and people.

First, there is the question of units in the objects being studied, the identification of each "thing" that is to be measured. In the personality domain, the answer is obvious: The unit is the person whose behavior we are describing. Each measurement is assigned to a person. But we are not measuring persons as objects; we are measuring the behavior of behaving persons.

Second, the behavior of a person must be analyzed into units associated with the measurements of that stream of behavior. The *unit of observation* is the segment of that stream utilized for any given observation. In experimental work, the unit is explicitly the subject's behavior after some experimental stimulus or manipulation. For a rating of a friend, the implicit unit may be the total time the rater has been with the friend. Thus, a single observation may be made for a unit of observation that has a very brief duration, for a unit that extends over years, or for a unit with some intermediate duration.

Each observer has a total *period of observation* for each subject observed. That period may be composed of just one unit of observation or many units, according to the task set for the observer. In experimental research, that period includes all the time the subject is being observed. The investigator may ask the observer to use as his unit of observation that whole period or may designate one or more specific units, such as after Stimulus A and again after Stimulus B. For ratings of a friend, the period of observation is the entire set of occasions when the observer has been with the friend. The observer may be instructed to use the whole period as his unit of observation, making one rating for the total period. Alternatively, he may be instructed to rate his friend as the friend behaves in a particular situation, the unit of observation then being instances of that situation, such as social occasions when others were present.

A third kind of unit or differentiation involves the aspect of the behavior segment selected for study. This aspect is the variable or dimension in some conceptual framework that is filtered out of the behavioral flow during the segment. Note that the variable may refer to a quality of only one component in the behaving. For example, within a single segment, it may be the loudness of the person's speech or the rapidity of his movements that is observed. Alternatively, the variable may be more comprehensive, such as the perceived tenseness in the whole segment of behavior.

Fourth, there is the unit in the measuring process—the particular cognitive action of some observer that results in the reported value used by the investigator in his analysis. Each such unit in the measuring process produces a *unit of measurement*, for which the very general term *response* is often used. The unit may be a mark on a scale, a word, a number, or some other response that the investigator can code as a number.

Finally, there is the *unit of analysis*. In simple correlation and contingency analyses, this unit consists of the pairing of a unit of measurement from one array of observations with a unit of measurement for the same object or event in a second array. In other forms of analysis, the value of the observed variable for an object or event is associated with a category or level, on another variable, to which the object or event has been previously assigned.

Various usages of the term *unit* will be examined in the following pages. The differentiation among five types of units given above is intended to alert the reader to the danger of confusing one problem of unitizing with some other one. Note also that *unit* refers to an element in a set. The set can be one that is readily differentiated into elements, as in the identification of the several persons in a group, or it can refer to a compound that can be analyzed in more than one way, as in the identification of elements in behavior.

Units in Personality Research Today

In conventional work on personality, the thing being studied —and therefore the unit to be measured—is the person. Attributes are assigned to the individual, typically without restriction as to time or place. I have argued earlier that the objective in personality research has been to understand the person as we see him, that is, to understand the particular cognitions that we have about that person. In everyday life, these cognitions are the end products of processes involving perceiving and construing the behavior of the other and interpreting that behavior in terms of its implications for us. For example, given our perceptions of a person's intentions, what should be our expectations about that person's future behavior? The complexity and individuality of these processes contribute heavily to the idiosyncratic aspects of a personality description in everyday life and to the specificity components in personality measurements.

Although the unit of observation is frequently the observer's entire experience with the person observed, it can be a much shorter period. The investigator may instruct the observer to make a sequence of judgments during a period of observation. Although the investigator can indicate how the entire period is to be unitized for this purpose, she can also leave that to the observer. It is instructive to consider the activity of the observer while carrying out such a differentiation.

In one of the few systematic studies of the observing process, Dickman asked subjects to break up a behavioral sequence into units. He concluded that " 'the stream of behavior' attains orderliness in the eyes of other humans to the extent that goals and motives are imputed to the behavior" (1963, pp. 40–41). Newtson (1973, 1976) has also studied how an observer breaks up a sequence of behavior into what he judges to be natural and meaningful units. Newtson has found that, for a given sequence, the number of units and the location of the divisions between them are relatively stable for a given observer, both within one observing session and between two sessions five weeks apart. Observers, however, are flexible. When instructed to identify the largest or the smallest units meaningful to them, they can do so readily, the latter instruction leading also to more units, more attributions, and more differentiated impressions of the person observed. Newtson quite appropriately suggests that "the perceiver actively participates in the organization of observed behavior into meaningful units and thus actively controls his information from that behavior" (1973, p. 28).

The intervals marked by observers as changes in actions appear to be places in the sequence that convey more information than other intervals. These "break points," as Newtson calls them, are places where there is a perceived change in a phenomenal feature being monitored by the observer, a change conveying information (Newtson and Engquist, 1976). Although the average time between break points varies considerably with the instructional set given to the observers, it seems to be roughly 15 seconds for neutral instructions.

Newtson has been exploring fairly naturalistic processes of observation. Understandably, he has asked his subjects to watch prepared tapes with just one actor, rather than using more complex materials. Yet his work does bring out the observer's contribution to the cognizing and construing process in observations, when the observer is relatively unrestricted by the investigator. In systematic observation, the challenge is to guide the observer's energies and activities toward the data-gathering objectives sought by the investigator.

The length of the unit identified by a subject has been shown by Ebbeson, Cohen, and Lane (1975) to vary with the investigator's instruction. When instructed to form an impression of what the actor was like, subjects formed units that were about twice as long as those marked by subjects instructed to remember what the actor did. Even with the latter instruction, however, the units were roughly seven seconds long. Although these findings are from a laboratory investigation, they do suggest that persons usually construe and interpret behavior in chunks lasting at least several seconds.

In most research on personality, the investigator determines the chunking of behavior. He establishes the unit of measurement as the response made by the observer to the stimulus designated by the investigator. For many procedures, that unit is simply the response to an item on a questionnaire. In research using paper and pencil instruments, the behaviors recorded and analyzed are the observer's responses in the testing room, each behavior being determined by the task set for her, by the particular item (which can be seen as the stimulus), and by the content retrieved from memory in reaction to that stimulus. That behavior is functional with respect to that situation. In most research on personality, the chunking is distinct from the original behavior of the person being measured, even if that person is the observer (as in self-report procedures).

For many paper and pencil instruments, the observer makes a response to a stimulus or an item referring to a class of behaviors that is only a small part of the broad aspect of the person's behavior being studied. For example, within the area of the person's social behavior, the aspect may be the trait of friendliness, and one item may refer to friendliness with children, another to friendliness with strangers, and so on. The responses to these numerous items are pooled to obtain a composite score or datum, which is entered into the investigator's analysis. In other instances, as in a single rating for a given trait, the unit of measurement refers directly to the entire aspect being measured, so that the rating becomes the datum without any further processing of that unit of measurement. Thus, a datum may be simply a single unit of measurement, or it may be derived by the pooling of several units.

Let us consider more closely the characteristics of each datum used in standard research on personality. Each datum is taken as referring to (a) a person (b) at some point in time or during some temporal interval, and involving (c) some quality or aspect of (d) some portion of his activity. The person and the time reference are easy to identify, and hence we can fairly readily obtain good agreement on these characteristics. There are, of course, difficulties with respect to time (examined in Chapter Seven). Yet the point in time or the period of time can be designated adequately when the investigator chooses to do so.

The portion of activity to be observed is the source of many of the difficulties in personality measurement. That portion is rarely stated explicitly. This neglect or oversight stems from several sources. We typically have spent so much time interacting with the person being rated that we do not stop to think about what aspects of his behavior we focus on. Even more important, we form our impressions of the other in a global manner, without trying to justify them by reference to particular acts at certain moments.

Let us be more specific. Even when a segment of behavior has been indicated for us as observers, we are usually not told what components of the person's behavior during that period we should watch —his words, his manner of talking, his facial expressions, his movements, or whatever. We may be asked to decide how friendly, how assertive, or how tense he is during that period. At the most, we may be given some synonyms for each of these attributes and perhaps a few of the behavioral cues to look for. But the unit to which each rating will be assigned is the entire stream of behavior during the designated period of time, not some restricted component, such as the verbal behavior or the psychomotor actions. Given this freedom, you may emphasize tone of voice when you are making ratings of friendliness or assertiveness, while I may emphasize posture and gesture. As a consequence, the discrepancy between our ratings may stem from the difference in the components of behavior noted as well as from the difference in the interpretations of that behavior. One step toward increasing the degree of interchangeability between observers is the specification of the components and aspects to be observed within the multifaceted stream of the ongoing behavior. Such specification is necessary if the study of behavior pertinent to the personality domain is to become more rigorous and if the data are to be generalizable over observers.

The thoughtful reader will have noted that the two characteristics of a datum, the *quality* noted in the *portion* of behavioral activity, have been handled rather loosely in this book. This treatment was due in part to the desire to avoid complexities in exposition and in part to the desire to start from the viewpoint of the reader whose field is personality. These two characteristics of a datum are not emphasized in most of personality or in many other parts of psychology. The typical variable is usually taken as a quality of behavior as an entity, it being deemed unnecessary to specify the component of behavior to which the variable applies.

In the personality sphere, the usual attributive judgment does not specify any aspects or components of behavior. In attributing, observers frequently attend to particular, salient behaviors of the person observed. Such behaviors include actions that depart from our expectations for that person or for people in general or that we see as having important meaning. End products, such as solutions to problems, decisions reached, or evaluations made, are noted more carefully than the series of acts or mental steps taken to reach those products. Usually, the entire sequence resulting in the product is perceived and interpreted as a whole.

A crucial point here is the fact that the length of the behavioral units, the size of the chunks, is usually ignored both in everyday attribution and in personality measurement. The naturalistic chunking of behavior probably varies with the kind of concerns we have about the other person in an interaction. But in scientific research, the units must be explicit and appropriate to the problem at hand. Behavior as we experience it is not obviously segmented—it is more or less continuous and flowing. Hence, it can be arbitrarily chunked into coarse or fine units.

As an illustration, consider one game in a set of tennis. There are several explicit elements or points, each being the series of strokes terminating when the ball is not returned by one player into the other's half of the court. In discussing tennis, people may refer to one point, and perhaps even to one stroke of one player during that point. But consider the complexity of the behavior between two of a player's strokes. After hitting the ball, the player moves to prepare for the opponent's return of the ball. As soon as the opponent hits it (or as the opponent swings his racquet toward the ball), the player moves her body toward the appropriate spot to hit the ball. Once there, she positions herself for the stroke and swings her racquet back. She then swings it forward to hit the ball, and watches its course away from her.

These phases form a sequence of behaviors within just one stroke or one turn in the longer interchange that results in a point in tennis. Although each phase could be a unit for the analysis of the tennis game, each phase can be further subdivided with respect to the movements or position of feet, torso, head, arm with racquet, or other arm. This example may seem contrived, and in one sense it is. An investigator might well choose to work at one of these several levels, but he would be extracting that aspect of the behavior from the total match. What the observer and each of the players ordinarily attend to is the outcome of each point, since that outcome contributes to the total enterprise, the whole game. They also attend to the skill manifested in each stroke. Both the outcome of the point and the competence displayed by the successful stroke provide these persons with information that has meaning for them.

Just as a tennis match can be viewed as a hierarchy of levels of analysis, so can a personality trait. Consider attributing the trait of dominance to someone. That attribution may be broadly interpreted as the person's having acted to affect the actions or beliefs of others. But how did he produce that effect? His action may be analyzed as taking the initiative, as persuading, as directing, or as leading. Moreover, the act of directing can be characterized by level of subtlety, and that level can be divided into verbal or physical actions. Finally, each action can be further broken down.

What level does the investigator select? The usual one is the global trait attribution, because that is the level at which we ordinarily think about people and construe their behavior. But that level has little relationship to the stream of behavior. An attribution may or may not affect the observer's subsequent behavior and will only indirectly affect the behavior of the person observed. More useful is the classification by form of dominating. Still more fruitful is classification by the actual action that impinges on the other person. What is of most significance is whatever can be determined to be related most closely to the behavior of the other. The selection of level of unit should be guided by its fruitfulness, that is, by the degree to which it enables meaningful empirical relationships to be obtained.

In considering possible levels for analysis in personality attributions, two hierarchies seem to be discernible. One is the breadth of the labels for units at each level. Dominating is broader than directing, which is more inclusive than commanding, and so on. The other is the implicit generalization from the attributing. We are referring here to the extent to which the observer intends to describe the person as he usually is, as opposed to simply labeling the particular chunk of behavior he has observed; for example, there is a range between "he orders people around" and "at that moment, he ordered the other person to do something."

These potential levels for behavioral analysis can be presented as meaningful alternatives because people do describe behaviors at each of these levels. When we approach personality from the standard perspective, which is dependent on the cognitive-interpretive process of an observer, the extensive literature demonstrates that there is almost no limit to the variety of conceptualizations that can be studied.

By analogy from other disciplines, we should be looking for the most basic functional units of behavior—units that cannot be further analyzed within the particular problem being attacked. In the analysis of spoken or written language protocols, the word may be the ultimate unit. In behavioral analysis, the unit should be the smallest act that makes a difference for the problem being investigated. If the researcher is studying the taking of speaking turns in a conversation, certain acts of the speaker seem to play central functional roles: for example, the initiation, continuation, or termination of a gesture; turning the head toward or away from the auditor (Duncan and Fiske, 1977). Each of these acts has been found to be associated with the course of the turn-taking, within Duncan's turn-taking system. While it is obvious that an act like gesturing can be analyzed by pattern of movement, speed of movement, and other characteristics, the effective unit of behavior within this sytem is the occurrence or termination of certain acts, these being conceptualized as cues by which a signal is given. The analysis of the behaviors in conversation at the level of these acts has been found to be productive; the acts of one person are empirically related to the acts of the other person.

The characteristics of a datum listed above also apply for an act as a datum. The act is identified as made by a person. Its moment of occurence relative to other acts is noted. The act is found within some component of the person's behavior. For example, a gesture is defined as one kind of movement of the hand. Its quality is made explicit in the definition differentiating it from other movements of the hand, such as touching one's body or clothing. For each recorded datum in the study of such acts, each of these characteristics is fully explicit and available for checking against independent observation and data production by a separate observer.

Underlying this discussion are some issues basic to the argument of this book: regularity, reproducibility, and generalizability. At such levels of analysis as the act, the data from one observer replicate very highly the data from another, and we can generalize over observers. With that base, regularities can be identified more confidently, and the replicability of findings can be assessed with less ambiguity.

The Unit of Analysis

The matter of the unit for scientific analysis is quite straightforward. As construed here, the unit of analysis is the combination of two units of measurement, one from the array obtained by one measuring operation and the other from an array obtained from a separate operation. The specification of the units of measurement has the value of indicating the nature of the analysis being made. When the two arrays of measurements are composed of attributions, the research question is the extent to which attributions of one variable covary with those of another. When the two kinds of attribution are made by the same observer, the contribution of components common to the cognizing processes for the two variables must be considered, as D'Andrade (1974) and Shweder (1975) have pointed out. Even when each array is produced by a different observer, it is difficult to account for any obtained relationship. Perhaps overlapping meanings for the trait terms are involved. If not, what is the substantive implication of determining that two sets of cognitions about a person are related?

When the unit of analysis is a pair of acts, the interpretation is often direct. Suppose that one act comes from one person in a conversation and the other from the other person. Suppose also that the temporal interval between the two acts is brief—a second or two. If act B occurs when the other person has just made act A, and tends not to occur when act A has not appeared, it seems safe to conclude that a relationship exists. The occurrence of A changes the situation for the other person, and act B can also be seen as one response to that change. Of course, act B may also be found to be associated with a later act, act C, so the occurrence of B is itself a change of situation contributing to the occurrence of C. Within a sequence of behaviors, each act can be construed both as a response and as a stimulus or initiation.

The role of time should be apparent here. As Kurt Lewin has pointed out, the factors affecting behavior must be present in some form at the time the behavior occurs. Even though an act of the other person receives only peripheral notice as one attends to what one or the other is saying, it can be assumed to have registered and to be held within memory for at least a few seconds. In fact, what is retained could well be the message conveyed by the signal that the act manifested. In contrast, any assumptions about the temporal relationships between two dispositions indexed by trait attributions must be highly tenuous.

This examination of units makes some distinctions that are useful for understanding research in personality, especially research focusing on the behaviors of individuals. The matter of units becomes more complex in experimental work, where the investigator seeks to give the same treatment to groups of individuals. In that situation, the basic unit of measurement may be the response of one individual to the treatment. But different experimenters may administer the treatment in somewhat different ways, so that the important unit of analysis involves the mean measurement of the individuals treated by one particular person. Here and in other contexts, the measurements for individuals have to be aggregated because some kind of dependency is present. Problems of aggregating will be considered briefly in Chapter Six. The complex and critical issues in person-treatment interactions and in aggregation cannot, however, be examined intensively within the scope of this book.

A Systematic Analysis of the Measurement Unit in Personality Research

Central to the critique of personality research being presented in Part One is the examination of the unit of measurement. A compilation of the basic aspects of that unit will help explicate that analysis. These aspects will be contrasted to those for an alternative measurement unit basic to a major proposal given in Part Two. The alternative unit of measurement is presented as it is found in the study of interpersonal behavior, a topic of major concern to those working in the personality area. This application of the general approach has been selected because I am very familiar with it (see Duncan and Fiske, 1977).

The alternative measurement unit is based on an approach in which the act is the unit of observation producing a unit of measurement, rather than the unit of observation typical of the standard approach to personality measurement, that unit being a segment of behavior with varying and usually unspecified duration. This approach has been used earlier in the discussion because the contrast between it and the standard approach serves to highlight the nature of the standard orientation to behaving persons. Understanding and conceptualization are promoted not only by descriptions in familiar terms but also by delineation of contrasts and antitheses. Since this alternative, the act approach, is still something of an ideal, it can be presented as a pure case that is easy to characterize. Yet that feature makes it harder to illustrate in concrete terms because there are few

pertinent examples. The prime example used throughout this book
is the investigation of face-to-face interaction by Duncan and Fiske
(1977, especially Pt. III). Among the many acts in that research are
smiles, laughs, nods, gazes, and gestures. Other examples include the
research on greeting behavior by Kendon and Ferber (1973), on the
initiation of conversations by Cary (1974), and the work of Hess (1973,
Chap. 8) on the imprinting of animals in the natural setting.

The essence of the act approach is the nature of the data used.
Each datum is the observation of the occurrence of an act. Although
each kind of act is given a verbal label for convenient reference, the
category is defined primarily by pointing to examples included
within it and examples that are excluded. In this type of classifying,
such pointing often communicates better than verbal definitions,
enabling observers to identify more clearly the boundaries of each
category. A fundamental requirement for the methodological
acceptability of an act category is consensus between observers in
their judgments that an act has occurred or not occurred. A very high
standard approximating perfect agreement between observers is set.

Strictly speaking, the identification of an observed act requires
two discrete judgments: first, that the act has started, and second, that
the act has terminated. Hence, each act can produce two data, one
from the judgment of the initiation of the act (the onset) and one from
the termination (the offset). Although each of these is usually
recorded, the investigator may be interested only in the initiation of
some classes of acts that are very brief, such as a nod or a "yeah." Each
onset or offset is a behavioral event, a change in behavior. As Harré
says, "Only changes, whether of things or of processes, need to be
explained" (1970, p. 7). General psychology has long known that
both the onset and the offset of physical stimulation can be stimuli. In
studying actions as they impinge on both the actor and other people,
the investigator should consider both the beginning and the end of an
act as potentially effective units of measurement. The act approach
analyzes behavior into units that are often much shorter than those
formed by Newtson's subjects in the work on unitizing discussed earlier in this chapter. In both instances, however, the general principle
holds: A change in behavior conveys information.

In the act approach, the observational record identifies not
only the actor but also his immediate status or role in the interaction,

coded in terms of other acts, such as his status as the speaker in a conversation. The judgment is recorded on a temporal continuum, which can be chronological time or interaction time. Thus, the judgment that an act has been initiated requires an additional judgment as to the ordinal position of that onset relative to other acts of the actor and of others participating in the interaction. The locations of this and other acts may all be placed on a scale of chronological time, independently and objectively marked (for example, see Kaye, 1977a), or they may be identified relative to each other. Although the choice will be determined by the investigator's interests, there are sound practical and theoretical reasons for preferring to locate each act relative to other acts.

Table 1 lists the characteristics of interpretive, attributive judgments as used in personality research and those of observed acts. Since most of these characteristics have been discussed earlier, a detailed consideration will not be necessary here. Some comments and explication may, however, be helpful.

The orientation in studying attributive judgments has typically been that of individual differences, or what Cronbach (1957) has identified as correlational psychology, studying covariation over persons with an effort to minimize the differences between treatments of those persons. The technical term *treatment* can be generalized here to include the procedure for measuring and the particular observer used for each person measured. In this volume, it has been argued that differences between treatments have been substantial and that the attempt to minimize them has had only limited success. Experimental psychology, the other discipline identified by Cronbach, compares treatments while seeking to minimize variance associated with persons. Personality research falling within this rubric has not been notably successful in minimizing either effects associated with persons or effects involving person-treatment interaction. (Although the term *interaction* is being used in its technical, statistical sense, it also can be given a psychological interpretation here.) The pervasiveness of person-treatment interaction and the relative strength of its effects are so marked that Cronbach has recently written a sequel to his 1957 paper in which he expresses "pessimism about our predominant norms and strategies" (1975, p. 116). It is certainly true that reactions of persons to tests and to experimental treatments have had serious

Table 1. Characteristics of Two Kinds of Measurement Units.

Category	Attributive Judgments (Personality Today)	Observed Acts (An Alternative Approach)
1. The phenomena	Perceptions and interpretations of the behavior of a specified person	The actions of a person
2. The unit of observation	A segment of behavior, which may be limited by the research conditions or only by the observer's experience	Each action, in the segment of behavior designated by the investigator, of the class to be recorded
3. The phenomena utilized for each unit of measurement	All those in the segment of behavior (as in category 2) that the observer deems relevant	The initiation or the termination of each act of the designated class
4. The variable to be coded	A concept subsuming qualitative variations (any of several qualitatively different acts are indicators)	A low-level concept subsuming only quantitative variations
5. Potential consensus on the verbal definition of the variable	Varying, but usually limited	High
6. The observer	A particular person, usually with a relationship to the observed person in their everyday lives	Any person who has been given minimal instruction; observers are interchangeable
7. The cognitive process of the observer	Given the task assigned, what impressions are retrieved or formed? Which of the permissible alternative judgments (explicit or implicit) fits these impressions?	Is that change in behavior an instance of category? (Yes or No)
8. The degree of inference or interpretation required	Varies from moderate to very high, depending on the variable	Minimal or none at all
9. The unit of measurement	The observer's judgment	The observer's judgment
10. Identification given to the unit of measurement	The person being observed	(1) The status of the actor (for example, as speaker or auditor) and (2) the

11. Datum entered into the analysis (the value given to that unit of measurement)	(1) The rating (if task is to rate a concept) or (2) the score for a subconcept (as expressed in an item)	sequential position of the act relative to other acts or to time
12. Form of observer's response	Words or mark that stands for words	The occurrence or nonoccurrence of the act in proximity to the occurrence or nonoccurrence of another act by the same or a different actor
13. Agreement between data from two observers	Partial to close (depending on the specificity and concreteness of the concept)	Mark indicating initiation or termination of an act of the designated class
14. Permissibility of self-observation	Yes, for most concepts	Close to very close
15. Pertinence of estimate of homogeneity (or internal consistency, in classical psychometric terms) of resulting data	High	No
16. Internal validity of measures	Must be demonstrated in each instance	None
17. External validity	Must be demonstrated	Presumed to be high
18. Congruence between construct and measuring operation (one aspect of construct validity)	Must be established	Must be demonstrated
		Manifest, based on content validity
19. Relationships	(1) Does the attributed judgment co-vary over people with another variable? or (2) is the mean attributed judgment related to a treatment or a condition?	Does one act precede a given act? If so, are there other acts that also precede it? Is the occurrence of a pair of acts associated with occurrence of some third act?
20. That which the investigator seeks to understand	The person as his behavior is perceived and construed	The inter-act sequences of behavior within a general context
21. Prognosis based on current evidence	Permanently handicapped	Appears promising

consequences for research on personality. Here again, the difficulties being noted in this book apply to both of Cronbach's disciplines— the experimental study of personality and the study of individual differences.

The act approach as exemplified here appears to fall within the experimental discipline, with the important qualification that the treatment is not manipulated by the investigator. Instead, he observes what precedes and what succeeds a naturally occurring act. That categorization of the act approach does not, however, exclude the possibility of looking for individual styles or strategies in interactions, as in the correlational discipline. Especially when the observed regularities among kinds of acts indicate options for a participant, individuals may be consistent within one interaction, and perhaps over a set of similar interactions, in their exercising or not exercising a given option and in their preferences among alternative cues for a recurring signal (see Chapter Twelve; Duncan and Fiske, 1977, Pt. IV). Hence, the act approach does permit the study of individual differences.

Additional comments are needed for specific parts of Table 1. The segment of behavior referred to in the unit of observation for attributive judgments seems unrestricted when the observer is free to draw on any recollections he may retrieve of his past observations in interaction with the person studied. Yet it is restricted, of course, to just those occasions of prior interaction. It is more clearly restricted when the observer watches a situation test. A more complex example is the person's behavior during an interview, including the content of what she says. While the behavior base is what the interviewer sees and hears, that base includes the interviewee's reports of perceptions and construals of her own behavior occurring before the interview.

Speculation about the mental activity of the observers working within the two orientations brings out an instructive contrast. In making an attributive rating, the observer scans his memories, seeking to retrieve impressions pertinent to the concept he is to rate. For the most part, these are positive instances recalling behaviors that are subsumed under the concept, although he may also recall situations where manifestations of such behaviors would ordinarily occur but did not. In coding an act, however, the observer searches for occurrences. He focuses on the part of the body where the pertinent movement would appear. In effect, he notes every instance of movement in that part of the body and makes a judgment as to whether it is an instance of the act to be recorded or of some other act. For example, to record gesturing, the observer watches the hands. If a hand moves, does it touch some part of the actor's clothing or body? If so, it is a nonmeasurement. Thus, in the coding of acts, there are many judgments of nonoccurrence, which are evident on the coding sheet from the absence of any mark. A vacant unit of measurement, a nonmeasurement, contains information and can, of course, be used as a datum entered into the analysis.

The postulation that, in the act approach, the concepts subsume only quantitative variation (category 4 in Table 1) is somewhat overstated. It is intended to indicate that the essential features necessary to identify an act are taken to be qualities, the quantitative degree being ignored. The extent to which the forehead dips in a nod is not judged in identifying a nod. The spatial extent of gesture movements is irrelevant in coding the presence of gestures. And it is obvious that gestures show wide qualitative variations in such features as amount of the arm that moves, direction of movement, and speed of movement. The distinction between quality and quantity as applied to actions is not clear-cut. A more accurate assertion would be that the range of variation in the acts judged to fall into a specified class is smaller than the range of variation among the behaviors subsumed under a typical personality concept. The methodological point is that, even when the investigator is not restricting herself to ostensive definitions, the recognition rules for inclusion and exclusion can be explicit for the coding of acts.

With respect to the identification given to the datum from an attributive judgment (category 10), it may be added that the role of the observer making the judgment is identified for each set of judgments (the roles here being those implied under category 6, such as self, peer, or interviewer). And of course the context may be specified, especially in experimental research; the judgment may refer to the behavior observed after a treatment or after a designated stimulus.

An attributive judgment, then, is associated with an observer, a person observed, and a more or less extended but undifferentiated segment of that person's behavior. The coding of an act is identified by the specified status of the actor at that moment and by the location of the physical action not only in space but also in time, either chronological or psychological as relative to other acts. Since the referent for the attributive judgment cannot be closely specified, it cannot be reexamined. Not only can an act as coded from a videotape be checked for accuracy of coding, but the act can be recoded readily if the investigator refines his coding scheme.

A Comparison Between an Attributive Judgment and the Coding of an Act

Since Table 1 contains many abstract terms, let us consider two concrete examples in order to make sure that the references of the various terms are reasonably clear. The first example is the rating of a person's friendliness on the basis of a half-hour observation period—perhaps a situation test such as a leaderless group discussion. The second is the recording of a person's smiles from a videotape of that same discussion. The examples were chosen because smiling is, of course, considered as a sign of friendliness. For the judgment attributing some degree of friendliness, the observer utilizes her perceptions of the person. In this instance, the unit of observation is the entire duration of the situation test. While watching the discussion, the observer may make mental or written notes of any behavior possibly related to friendliness. Alternatively, she may simply watch and later recall her perceptions and impressions of the person's behavior for evidence pertinent to that trait.

The concept of friendliness has no standard definition in the personality literature. Each person who has written about it (or its synonym, sociability) has his own definitions. A conference aimed at defining the term, however, could probably arrive at a definition that was fairly acceptable to all the participants. Even so, some differences of opinion would be expressed about which behaviors could always be used as indicators of friendliness whenever they were observed, which usually indicated the trait, and which would do so only once in a while.

The cognitive process of the observer in making the rating involves reviewing her memory traces of the person's behavior and recalling the impressions she formed during the discussion, with the goal of determining which of the degrees of friendliness stated on the rating form is most applicable. In doing so, she may recall her impression that the other people in the group seemed to like the ratee—they gazed at him and smiled at him. She could well interpret these responses as indicating friendliness in the person being rated.

The unit of measurement here is the value on the rating scale marked by the observer to code her interpretive judgment. It is identified with the person being rated and with the situation test. Although the investigator might utilize that single rating in his analyses, he is more likely to average it with ratings from one or more additional observers. Each pair of observers might agree fairly well (.50?) on their ratings.

The investigator would have to take steps to ascertain that his observers were really rating friendliness and not unwittingly indicating how much they personally liked the person. He would also have to establish that ratings of friendliness made in one situation test with a particular set of persons in the group could be generalized to tests with others in the group, to other situational tests—and, in fact, to friendliness in general.

Now consider the coding of smiling. Although the coding might go on while the coder was watching the discussion, it would be better practice to make a videotape so that replays were possible. The observer watches the face of the person, scanning the changing picture for signs of a smile. Her unit of observation is the appearance of the constellation of characteristics that she deems to indicate a smile; a bit later, her next unit of observation is the disappearance of that constellation.

The observer's process in coding is simply deciding whether each change in the person's behavior, but specifically in the facial expression, constitutes a smile or not. Little interpretation and no inference are involved. The measurement unit is the observer's mark on the coding sheet to indicate the initiation or termination of a smile. That mark is located on a continuum designated by other actions, such as the syllable being spoken at that moment, the locus of the mark permitting the investigator to know who was smiling and what else was going on at that moment (for example, whether or not the person was talking). Observers can agree closely on the coding of smiles. No psychometric estimate of internal consistency is appropriate here. There are no problems about the validity of the measurements. There could, however, be some question raised about the external validity of the obtained relationships, depending on the investigator's stated generalization of his findings to other kinds of situations.

At this point, many readers will be feeling skeptical about the value of studying such acts as smiles, nods, and gestures. The potential value of the act approach will be examined closely in Chapters Twelve and Thirteen, but it seems appropriate to mention here some of the reasons for believing that an emphasis on acts will be fruitful and may in fact prove necessary for the future progress of the field. One reason is our evident inability, in the past, to make clear, substantive progress by studying the summarizing judgments that have constituted most of our data. If there is no way to remedy the problems associated with those judgments, we should consider new approaches to the understanding of interactions and other behavior pertinent to the field of personality.

Another reason is the possibility that sequences of acts are the basic phenomena in the personality domain. One or more acts of one person are followed by acts from another person, and these acts are in turn followed by acts of the first. Each act may be a response and also a stimulus. Interaction occurs at this level of analysis and on a moment-to-moment basis. The interaction between two persons does not consist of a time period of several minutes during which one person manifests affiliation and aggression while the other displays dominance and aggression. Instead, there is a sequence of acts carried out by the two participants. During the course of the actual behavior, each person may begin to form impressions of the other. After the interaction is terminated, each may make attributions about the other, spontaneously or on request of an investigator. While these attributions are important phenomena in their own right, they are the products of the interaction and not the interaction itself. Hence, the study of these acts is crucial to the understanding of interactions.

A third reason for being interested in acts is the possibility that they may throw light on the things we have been studying, attributive judgments. We may be able to learn how acts contribute to attributions. We may also find that several acts are empirically associated with each of certain common attributive concepts. For example, empirical support for the impression of an association between the act of smiling and the judgment of friendliness is provided by Shrout (1976) in a study with larger objectives.

A moment's reflection on the connotations of the terms *judgment* and *act* may be instructive. Judgment implies a judge, who is the observer. This association reminds us that, in attributions, we are dealing with a judge-judged entity or what we called earlier an observer-observed entity. The particular judge is part of the identification of the datum. In comparison, act implies an actor. The emphasis is on a person who is acting, that is, behaving. The contrast, then, is between the question "Who is making a decision?" and the question "What is going on?"

Summary

Pervasive in the study of behavior is the problem of units and unitizing. Particularly important for personality research is the identification of the unit of observation, the segment of behavior utilized for a given judgment. There is also the unit of measurement, the recorded product of the observational process. That value may be combined with others to obtain the datum entered into statistical analyses. The unit of analysis is construed as two units of measurement or two data taken together. The measurement unit in personality research, an attributive judgment, can be contrasted to a measurement unit that is the coding of an act, the two units differing in many characteristics.

V

Agreement and Disagreement Among Observations

As earlier chapters have pointed out, the stream of behavior can be unitized at many different levels, and people vary in their unitizing of a behavior protocol. Moreover, different people give different meanings to the words that pervade personality and its measurement. As a consequence of the several contributions of the specific observer to his observations, the judgments of independent observers do not agree well and are not interchangeable (see Proposition 2e, Chapter One). A necessary condition for a science, however, is agreement between observations. A science builds cumulatively, one scientist basing his work on that of predecessors. He must be able to depend on that prior work. Published findings can be used by him only if he can accept the

98

quality of the observations from which they were derived. A central aspect of that quality is the agreement between observers, which must be so close that the observations made by separate observers are essentially interchangeable. These assertions apply to both of the scientific disciplines identified by Cronbach (1957), the correlational study of individuals and the experimental investigation of general effects. But what do we mean by the term *agreement?* And how does the concept of the interchangeability of observers apply to studying the phenomena in personality and similar domains?

Agreement among observers is one kind of agreement among scientists. The many published statements about agreement refer to a variety of meanings for the term *agreement.* Ziman writes that science is public knowledge; its "goal is a *consensus* of rational opinion over the widest possible field" (1968, p. 9). Each scientist tries to maximize his area of agreement with others. In his classic monograph, Kuhn proposes that agreement on a paradigm is the criterion for a realized science, as opposed to the "incommensurable ways of seeing the world and of practicing science in it" (1970b, p. 4) that are found in the developmental, prescientific stages of most sciences. Among his apparent meanings for the term *paradigm* (see Masterman, 1970, and Kuhn, 1974) are those involving the sharing of values, exemplars, beliefs in particular models, and symbolic generalizations (as in equations for general laws). In concordance with statements of this sort, it seems reasonable to postulate that a science is characterized by consensus among its practitioners on some theoretical propositions, some concepts, and some empirical generalizations. The qualifier "some" is important because the active scientist is often more aware of his disagreements with his colleagues working at the frontiers than of his points of agreement on basic matters as stated in textbooks.

Glass gives another view: "In the last analysis, science is the common fund of agreement between individual interpretations of nature" (1965, p. 1256). He goes on to state that "science is ultimately as subjective as all other human knowledge, since it resides in the mind and the senses of the unique individual person. . . . All that can be claimed for science is that it focuses upon those primary observations about which human observers (most of them) can agree" (p. 1256). In a statement that comes close to the major thesis of this volume, Glass says that "the objectivity of science depends wholly upon the ability of different observers to agree about their data and their processes of thought" (p. 1256). Stevens (1935, p. 327) expresses a similar viewpoint: "'Objectivity' in science is attained only when facts can be regarded as independent of the observer; for science deals only with those aspects of nature which all normal men can observe alike." Earlier, N. R. Campbell ([1921] 1952, p. 27) stated that "Science is the study of those judgments concerning which universal agreement can be obtained."

Most of the authors of these statements about agreement on observations and on the data derived from them did not develop the point in much detail, perhaps because it seemed so obvious. Karl Popper (1959) did discuss the importance of intersubjective consensus. Churchman (1959) briefly considered accuracy in terms of deviation from the truth. And, at a highly abstract level, the notion of approximation to an explicated "universe value" is central to the work of Cronbach, Gleser, Nanda, and Rajaratnam on *The Dependability of Behavioral Measurements* (1972). Their focus is on estimating the generalizability of a set of data. Our concern here is the endemic problem underlying the need for such estimation, the unsatisfactory levels of agreements between observations and between observers.

The concept of agreement enters into science at many levels. These can be placed in a rough hierarchy. There is, at the most general level, agreement on beliefs about science and how to do it. For each established science, those working within it have agreement on the paradigm and on the basic theory, including agreement on propositions that relate one concept to another and hence on the concepts and their basic definitions. Within a firmly based science, such as one that fits Kuhn's conception (1970b) of normal science, the practitioners agree not only on the definitions and referents of a concept but presumably also on its relative significance and centrality within the conceptual matrix of that science. Turning to the empirical side, scientists in an established field have agreement on the replicability of some empirical findings and on the adequacy of certain procedures for measuring each of the basic concepts.

For a given piece of empirical research, there are several matters on which scientists who examine it may or may not agree. One is the internal validity of the design, the extent to which the plan of

investigation permits the investigator to interpret her obtained relationships as she does (Campbell and Stanley, 1963). More differences
of opinion occur regarding the external validity of the study, the
extent to which the findings have generalizability beyond the particular components of the specific study to populations of people, to
classes of contexts, and to sets of stimuli.

For a single investigation, scientists assume that the operations for obtaining descriptive statistics and for testing hypotheses
were correctly carried out, and that they or other persons could replicate the calculations and the obtained values. They also assume that
if, following the same observational and coding procedures as the
original investigator, they themselves had made the observations or
processed the recorded protocols, they would have produced essentially the same set of data as that utilized by the original investigator.
Although their data might not be fully identical with the original, the
differences would have been so few and so small that they would have
been able to obtain almost identical descriptive statistics and make
identical statistical decisions.

The preceding applications of the term *agreement* do not
exhaust all of the meanings that the term may have, yet their variety
reminds us to be cautious about interpreting statements referring to
agreement among the scientists working within a particular discipline. As we pointed out in Chapter One, personality lacks consensus
at the levels of concepts and theory. This diversity stems in large part
from the limited agreement between observers. We cannot build a science in domains like personality until our investigations focus on
observations on which observers agree to the extent that the observations of one observer are essentially interchangeable with those of
other observers, that is, so closely congruent that data derived from
any one observer will yield the same findings as those obtained from
another observer. Where sets of observations are interchangeable,
their analysis will have the same implications for our concepts and
conceptual relationships. Within a science, agreement at the higher,
more abstract levels can be obtained only when there is congruence
among observations from separate observers. (That assertion neglects
the obvious possibility of consensus on a proposed theory that has not
been tested empirically. It is also true that converts to a faith may
agree on the doctrines of that faith, no matter what correspondence

exists between the personal perceptions of the several converts.)

The matter of agreement between observations is part of the basic and inclusive topic of generalizability. Under this heading fall the standard concepts of reliability and validity. We must be very clear about what all these terms and their subconcepts mean. *Reliability* ordinarily refers to the dependability of measurements, to the extent to which separate measurements of an attribute for a given object are reproducible. One form of reliability is the agreement between observations made more or less simultaneously about an attribute of a given object under given conditions. Another form of reliability, the one emphasized in test theory, is internal consistency, the degree of agreement among a set of observations that are compiled into a single composite score. An index of internal consistency assesses the extent to which that score can be expected to agree with another score, actual or hypothetical, from a separate set of very similar observations. Note that, although the index does not refer directly to agreement between single observations, it has a mathematical relationship to such agreement (as given in the classical Spearman-Brown formula). The third type of reliability is stability, the agreement between measurements of objects made at one time with measurements of the same objects made at another time with no changes in the measuring procedure.

These three kinds of indices are ordinarily used for scores entered into statistical analyses. As such, they indicate the degree of confidence with which the investigator can consider his measurements to apply to his objects—his subjects in personality research—regardless of observer, stimuli used in measuring, or time when measured, respectively. Obviously, the dependability or reproducibility of his findings and the subsequent generalizability of his conceptual conclusions are based in part on this dependability of basic measurements.

In this book, I am arguing that the investigator's confidence in his measurements must be limited. Measurements in the personality domain are affected by time, that is, by recent experiences of the persons measured. They also vary with the particular stimuli or items used to elicit responses (for example, see Fiske, 1973). But even more critical is their variation over observers. This chapter is concerned with the necessity of minimizing that variation between observers, reducing it as close as possible to zero. If we can eliminate the undependability associated with observers, we can have sufficient confidence in measurements of behavioral events under known conditions and in empirical findings to be able to make generalizable statements about relationships among behaviors and between behavioral acts and other variables.

Observers as Measuring Instruments

A classical definition of measurement states that measurement is the assigning of numerals to properties of objects on the basis of rules. In research on behavior, we rarely have a complete set of explicit rules for assigning ratings to observed behavior. For the present context, however, the most relevant part of the definition is the term *assigning*. It implies activity on the part of the measurer, the observer. If data are to have scientific utility, the assigning must be done according to rule. Implicit in the classical discussion of measurement is the notion that measurers follow the same rules. As a consequence, it is assumed that two measurers will assign the same numeral to the same property of a given object.

In the natural sciences, two observers can usually read scales and dials with minimal discrepancies between their readings, that is, between the numerals they assign. When the science requires a very high degree of precision, so that the observer's "personal equation" is of concern, a permanent record of the dial is made so that the location of the pointer at any given moment can be determined with almost perfect agreement, with one reader essentially replicating the readings of any other reader. (We are describing here the situation in advanced areas of research in the natural sciences, after answers have been found for the vital questions of what should be measured and how to measure it.)

Personality research also uses permanent records, but its recordings are of people's behavior, not of the readings on measuring instruments. Obviously, videotape, motion picture, or audio recordings are highly desirable since they permit an observer to make judgments without being concerned about missing some of the action—he can always replay the recording. In addition, when there is a discrepancy between the judgments of two observers, they can always reexamine the section of the protocol on which their judgments differ to try to identify the source of the discrepancy. At least as important is the possibility of utilizing the recordings to make observations on new variables that the investigator had not included in his original plans. The chief disadvantages of recording include the fact that the recording instrument may have to be more evident and obtrusive than an observer (for example, an observer behind a one-way glass) and that the range of the recorder may be less than that of a human observer on the spot; the lens angle may be less than that of the eye and audio-recordings may not have the same spectrum as the human ear.

Personality research is not ready for the use of mechanical instruments to measure its variables. It has not even reached agreement on what variables it should study. In addition, the variables that are studied cannot be operationalized in a way that would permit the use of instruments providing dial readings as the data. The variables are construed as categories of heterogeneous behaviors; no instrument could possibly be constructed to record and process such a diverse set of actions. Furthermore, there is good reason to question whether investigators will ever agree on particular overt movements as indicators for the concepts that are currently being studied. Human observers will, therefore, continue to be a central part of the procedures by which the field of personality obtains its data. In the few instances where instruments can be used (as in measuring pertinent psychophysiological variables), observers may still have to be employed not only to do clerical counting but also to make judgments about patterns, such as wave forms.

The task given to the observer should, however, be as simple and direct as possible. The goal should be to utilize the observer as a rather complex coding instrument. To maximize the potential agreement between observers and to avoid the development of cliquish or provincial observational and coding procedures that cannot be readily transferred to other persons in other locales, it seems best at present to use lay observers. That is, the task given to the observer should not require expert knowledge. Our observers should not have to be trained intensively, as are pathologists who must make decisions from X rays or from an anatomical slide. Our knowledge is not as advanced as theirs.

The problem is, of course, not specific to personality.

Throughout the social sciences, "people have been used as measuring instruments," as D'Andrade (1974, p. 159) has aptly put it. People are quite exceptional measuring instruments that can be used in a diversity of ways. The fundamental issue is how to use them. In Part Two, we propose that the investigator first examine the basic nature of the problem he is studying and then determine the best way to employ human measuring instruments for his particular purpose. Here, however, we are concerned with the adequacy of human observers as they have been used in personality research, with the extent to which they agree with each other, and with the effect of the limited empirical agreement on the current status of the field and on the likelihood of any major breakthroughs in the foreseeable future.

There are numerous kinds of personality observations. Does the requirement of high interobserver agreement apply equally to all of them? The most prevalent kind of procedure in personality is the paper and pencil instrument: the inventory, the questionnaire, the attitude scale. The observable behavior for this procedure consists of the subject's responses. There is no problem of agreement in scoring these responses; the clerical activity can be performed with essentially perfect consensus between scorers. In fact, however, that scoring is for judgments made by the subject in accordance with the task instructions. The subject is the observer, the only observer. There can be no comparison between observers for self-report data.

Psychophysiological measurements, such as heart rate, muscular tension, and pupil size, are typically made with instruments that record the variable in the form of a tracing. The coding of tracings is not as easy as the scoring of multiple-choice tests. For example, the scanning of an electroencephalogram for the occurrences of a particular wave form is a demanding task, and the assessment of intercoder agreement is essential. Since the matter of agreement between such coders is different from the question of agreement between observers in other kinds of personality research, that kind of intercoder agreement will not be examined in this volume.

Within the other procedures for gathering personality observations, two major categories are apparent. In the first, the investigator delineates and circumscribes the period of observation, the segment of behavior that the observer is to observe and judge. For instance, the observer may be asked to watch a person in a situation test or a child during recess in the school yard. The investigator may provide a product of the person's activity as the object to be examined and judged. The material may be free-response protocols from projective techniques or products of activities outside the testing room, such as letters or school essays. In this category, the judgments are ordinarily made immediately after the observer has perceived the specified segment of behavior; in some instances, the observer makes and records judgments while the person observed is still under observation (for example, when recording all instances of one child hitting another).

The other major category involves judgments based on more remote memories of the person's behavior. Instead of making the judgments seconds or minutes after perceiving the behavior, the observer may draw on recollections of what she perceived days, months, or years earlier. Here, the period of observation was originally a series of segments of behavior. (For the biases introduced by reliance on recollections, see Shweder, 1972, 1975, and D'Andrade, 1965, 1974.) The judgments in this category are typically ratings, and usually they are ratings of fairly broad variables, such as traits or dispositions. The judgments in the first category may be either ratings or codings, the latter referring to the observer tallying instances of behavior falling into a specified class.

Agreement Between Observers in Personality Research

Anyone who has some familiarity with published research in personality is aware that the typical degree of agreement is limited. But what do we mean by good agreement? When I asked some colleagues what they considered to be good agreement, the median of their estimated coefficients was .7; it was .9 for excellent agreement and .4 for poor. Of course, the expected level of agreement depends in part on the particular conditions and on the variables being observed or rated. Actual agreement on the units of measurement is generally poor by these standards. Investigators tend to think of interobserver agreement in terms of the estimated reliability of the datum they use in their analyses. Thus, if an investigator has four raters and averages their ratings, he reports the reliability coefficient for those mean ratings (a value estimating how well those means would correlate with an independent team of four raters rating the same behavior). Hence, the rough norms given above are considerably higher than the values that one tends to find for correlations between two observers. For example, Norman and Goldberg (1966) report estimated reliabilities for single raters, that is, estimated correlations between one rater and another, averaging .15 for raters who knew the persons fairly well and .20 for raters who knew each other very well (for example, Peace Corps trainees after three months of intensive interpersonal contact). In an assessment project (Kelly and Fiske, 1951), peers who had lived and been tested together for a week had an average agreement between pairs of .26. Pairs of students rating other members of residential groups after living together for several months agreed at about the same level (.24) in a study by Jackson, Neill, and Bevan (1973).

Those values are for the second category of procedures mentioned earlier, where the ratings are made from memories extending back over time. What do we find for the first category, for conditions where the raters have observed a limited sample of behavior and make their ratings immediately afterward? In our assessment project, observers watched people in several situation tests lasting two or three hours all together. The average agreement between pairs of observers was .21. Another study using situation tests (Magnusson and Heffler, 1969) found considerably higher agreement between pairs of observers, averaging about .50 for a single situation and a bit higher for two or three situations. They used trained raters to assess leadership, cooperative ability, and self-confidence. Their unusually high level of agreement may have been helped by the particular research conditions. The raters made ratings for only one person in a group of three, using a finely scored graphic scale. A study using situation tests but untrained raters (Fiske and Cox, 1960) obtained an average agreement between pairs of raters of only .16. In this particular instance, the data are for correlations between a peer who was a participant observer and a peer who just watched and rated.

Investigators usually do not publish these values for the single rater but rather the higher values for the mean rating of a team of several raters. And all of these figures are for single variables (for example, a single rating of cooperation or of leadership). The reliability of scores that combine a series of subscales is much higher, just as the reliability of the total score for a test is well above that of the response to a single item, there being a well-known Spearman-Brown relation-

ship between the reliability for one observation and that for a combination of observations. Thus, the average interrater agreement of .90
reported by Stanton and Litwak (1955) is for scores based on summing
ratings for twenty separate items. Application of the Spearman-
Brown formula yields an estimate of .31 for agreement on just one of
their items. Similarly, the interjudge agreement values between .90
and .96 that McFall and Lillesand (1971) report for judgments of
acceptance or refusal of unreasonable requests are based on composites from eight role-playing situations. The estimate for a single situation is about .62.

These two studies have been cited by Goldfried and Sprafkin
(1974) as evidence of the high agreement that can be obtained between
observers. Of course, by adding more items to the composite, the reliability of the composite can be raised even further, just as an average
intercorrelation of only .05 between pairs of items can be utilized to
obtain a test score with reliability over .90 simply by summing over
two hundred items. Especially in examining findings on agreements
between observers, the distinction between the single response made
by the observer (the unit of measurement) and the datum entered into
the investigator's analyses is crucial.

The several values cited above are from studies that were readily available to me or that were part of my own work. These findings
are reasonably representative in showing that the typical agreement
between two observers is quite limited. In contrast, Beekman (1973)
obtained interobserver agreements averaging .95 for coding each of
several dozen acts, including nods, smiles, laughs, gestures, and inter-
ruptions. Some of these reliabilities were based on just two-and-a-
half minutes of the interaction. These indices for the score summing
each observer's codings for the given time period are representative of
agreements obtained for such coding. For example, Rosenfeld (1966)
reports reliabilities ranging from .85 to 1.00, with a median of .96. For
particular acts found to be pertinent to the taking of speaking turns in
a conversation, Duncan has recorded comparable values (Duncan and
Fiske, 1977, p. 342). These findings suggest that very good agreement
can be obtained between pairs of observers when they code actions as
they occur (naturally or on the video screen) rather than depending on
memory, even short-term memory, as in ratings made immediately
after a thirty-minute period of observation. The specificity and explic-

itness of the actions to be coded also contribute to the level of agreement.

The levels of agreement between two observers that are attained in personality research are an insufficient base for sound empirical work. Even when reliability coefficients for such agreement are on the order of .6 or .7, substantial contributions to the variance of the ratings are coming from sources associated with the individual rater. In principle, one might argue that the variance that is specific to an individual rater is random error and can be accepted as undesirable but unavoidable; although such error hampers the investigator, it can be handled by utilizing enough raters to obtain a reliability estimate close to the ideal, 1.00. But such an estimate would simply indicate that, in principle, if another large group of very similar raters were available to make additional ratings, their average ratings would correlate almost perfectly with the averages of the first group. These averages would still have little conceptual value and would not refer to anything in the observable world. They are hardly more meaningful than the statement that the average woman in this country is .17 pregnant or that the average adult male is .73 married.

The individual ratings combined into the averages are not accurate ratings that have been contaminated by random errors. It has long been known that the individual rater contributes biases to his ratings, systematic components that may be associated with all of his ratings, including ratings for a given concept or for one person or kind of person (Guilford, 1936). The classical example is the *halo effect,* the label given to a general pattern of unduly favorable ratings. That term is, however, an interpretation made by the investigator. Very little is known about how such a pattern is actually produced by a rater. But we do know that how the rater makes her ratings, how she construes the concept being rated, and how she reacts to the ratee as a whole person can affect her ratings. The rater's perception and cognition of the ratee's behavior are always somewhat individualistic.

The situation is even worse when each rater has had her own period of observation involving a specific set of experiences in interacting with the ratee. In many instances, the rater has been part of what the ratee has reacted to, and hence different raters may have observed different physical behaviors in the ratee. Even when the rater has not actually interacted with the person but has observed him unobtrusively, she will be basing her ratings on observations made over a period of time—perhaps five minutes, perhaps an hour, perhaps many hours. At the time of making the rating, she must retrieve and synthesize her memories of these observations and then make her rating on the variable specified. The many opportunities for the rater's own personality to have effects on her judgments are obvious.

Possible Remedies for Observer Disagreement

There are several reasons why observers do not agree with each other any better than these figures indicate. As noted in Chapter Two, observers interpret somewhat differently the words in the instructions given to them, the words in the descriptions of the variables they are to judge, and the words in the alternatives provided for them. In addition, the physical events—the movements and sounds of the person being observed—are perceived and cognized differently, leading to differences in interpretations and attributions and hence to observations containing considerable subjectivity—as pointed out in Chapter Three.

Do these general sources of disagreements between observers present an insoluble problem? Is it not possible to measure each of these effects in each observer and, by appropriate adjustments of their recorded observations, arrive at higher levels of agreement? Can we calibrate observers, as Luce (1972) has suggested is necessary in psychophysics and as Weick (1968) has considered for observational methods? This solution does not appear to be feasible. One major obstacle is the lack of an adequate standard against which to calibrate. Another is that observers are not sufficiently consistent in their processing of perceptual material. If we know that a clock consistently gains five minutes a day, and if we also know when it was last set correctly, we can calculate the correct time from the present position of its hands. Unfortunately, observers do not have such dependable biases. We cannot ascertain, once and for all, how an observer always interprets a particular word. We cannot be sure that his interpretation of a particular physical movement will always be the same.

Considerable work has been done on sources of potential distortion in self-reports, the easiest data for personality researchers to obtain. For example, the potential contributions of response biases or styles are well known. But suppose we learn, from a measuring procedure designed for the specific purpose, that a person has a tendency to mark more "yes" than "no" responses, a disposition that has been labeled *acquiescence*. Can we then use this information to adjust his score on a scale designed to measure achievement? Regrettably, we cannot do so with much confidence. Different measures of acquiescence do not, themselves, agree very highly with each other. Hence, a person may tend to mark the "yes" responses on our corrective procedure aimed at acquiescence but not do so on the achievement scale.

Personality researchers are aware of the typical levels of rater agreement and of ways to maximize that agreement (Guilford, 1936). They realize, for example, that the training of raters ordinarily leads to better agreement. The investigator can profitably discuss with the raters the meaning of each concept being rated and can identify the cues to be taken as evidence of the strength of the disposition being judged. Raters can be reminded of common rater biases and habits. More important is quality control. The investigator can determine the extent to which each rater agrees with other raters and work to raise levels that are unsatisfactory. She can eliminate raters who are found to be doing poorly when compared to some immediate criterion, such as the modal rating. (In principle, of course, by making these evaluations she may be eliminating the more perceptive raters, who may prove to be more accurate in terms of subsequent criteria.) Other ways of maintaining quality include periodic checking of raters against other raters or against some standard during the days or weeks over which the ratings are being made. To counteract the decline in observer-criterion agreement after the training period, the investigator can let the rater know that his performance is constantly under scrutiny (Reid, 1970; Taplin and Reid, 1973). Further suggestions for maximizing the quality of observations are given in O'Leary and Kent (1973).

The problem of maintaining quality stems in part from the fact that a rater is not dependable over time. Moreover, raters generally vary in their judgments from one day to another. When two raters do not agree on a particular day, it may be due in part to such temporal fluctuations in their ratings. The investigator can, if she wishes, estimate the agreement of each rater with himself and then see whether, when the two sets of ratings are corrected for their unreliability, the estimated agreement between them is near 1.00. If so, the problem lies in intraindividual disagreement rather than in interindividual disagreement.

The training of raters is probably more effective for specific variables than for global ones, even though the level of agreement for specific variables is typically higher than that for general variables when there has been little or no training. In this context, *specific* refers both to the degree of concreteness of the behavioral categories and to the restriction of the temporal segment of behavior being rated. Mash and McElwee (1974), for example, found that category complexity was associated with poorer observer performance. If raters are asked to note whether, during a clearly indicated interval of time, a person talked, they will agree quite closely. For ratings of how loudly he spoke, the agreement will be lower. For ratings of how friendly he was during the time period, the agreement will be still lower. And estimates of his ego strength will probably show the least agreement of all. Judges will agree poorly when the rated variable is abstract, requiring the rater to extract, consider, and infer from a variety of evidence.

Some years ago, Donald Campbell formulated a conjecture summarizing the matter: "The greater the direct accessibility of the stimuli to sense receptors, the greater the intersubjective verifiability of the observation. The weaker or the more intangible, indirect, or abstract the stimulus attribute, the more the observations are subject to distortion" (1961, p. 340). Reviewing "systematic observational methods," Weick (1968) found that subsequent work had supported this general proposition.

In most instances, it is wise to select observers who have some familiarity with the substantive topic. The observers can then be trained for the specific work required by the research plan. But the investigator must realize that demonstrated agreement between his observers is a necessary but not sufficient condition for dependable observations that will contribute to sound scientific findings. As noted in Chapter Three, agreement can result from training observers to interpret what they see in a manner that conforms to the particular expectations of the investigator.

Although the several factors affecting interrater agreement have been known for some time, the typical level of agreement reported in the literature of recent decades seems to be rising little, if at all. Personality investigators have accepted the general levels that they and their colleagues obtain, and they evince little concern with the matter. For one thing, most researchers pick for study a set of phenomena and construe them in terms of selected variables, measuring the variables as well as the nature of their concepts and the available measuring techniques will permit. Among factors affecting their choice of a research problem, they do not ordinarily include the extent to which observers producing the research data can agree with each other.

Absolute and Relative Agreement

Let us spell out the basic paradigm for examining agreement between observations.

1. A pool of qualified observers is specified. These will be either lay persons given some minimal instruction or professionals with certain experiential qualifications.
2. Two or more observers are drawn randomly from that pool.
3. Each observer is instructed as to the discriminations he is to make: to what aspect of some ongoing sequences of behaviors, some recording of behaviors, or some product of past behaviors he is to attend, and what decisions he is to make about what he perceives.
4. He is informed about the scale he is to use in reporting his judgment: the basic facet or dimension represented by the scale, and the definitions of the several categories for a nominal scale or of the several steps for an ordered scale.
5. He is then directed to his period of observation, to the particular series of phenomena he is to observe.
6. He may be instructed about his unit of observation—the moment at which he is to observe, make his judgment, and record it (producing a unit of measurement).

There is little ambiguity about what phenomena are to be observed (number 5) and when to observe them (6), so these need cause no particular difficulty. In contrast, the instructions to each observer (3) are very likely to affect the obtained level of agreement.

The more complex and detailed the instructions, the greater the likelihood that an observer will forget one part of the instructions, that he will emphasize certain parts in an individualistic way, and that he will have the opportunity of interpreting the total set of instructions in his own way. Each of these possibilities can contribute to lowering the agreement between his observations and those of others. Much the same kinds of considerations apply to the scale for reporting (number 4 in the paradigm). In particular, the more abstract the basic dimension, and the more psychologically complex the concept involved, the greater the likelihood of disagreements in its applications.

Suppose we have two observers, and each goes through the identical observational procedure, independently making his own set of observations. How do we assess the degree of correspondence between those sets of observations? Much of psychology, especially psychometrics, has emphasized agreement on the relative position of each observation within the array identified with a particular rater. Thus, one choice is the conventional procedure of assessing agreement by the Pearson correlation coefficient. An alternative is the measurement of absolute agreement. For example, we can use the intraclass correlation (Haggard, 1958), which assesses the interchangeability of two or more observations for the same event or object being rated, regardless of the source of those observations. When this coefficient is used for this purpose, the variance of the two or more observations for one object is compared with the variance of the mean observations for the several objects, and the degree of correspondence among the observations of each object is evaluated in terms of the degree to which the several objects are differentiated.

These choices illustrate two classes of available statistical measures of relationship (as considered in Bishop, Fienberg, and Holland, 1975, Chap. 11). One class includes various measures of association, such as the Pearson r and the several coefficients based on it. These indices ignore all characteristics of the data except the relative position of each datum within its own array. They say nothing about congruence; in computing the Pearson r, for example, the two arrays of observations can be on different scales. When applied to agreement between observers, they assess the degree to which one observer's placement of an object, relative to his placements of other observed objects, corresponds to the relative placement made by another observer. In effect, they ask whether the two observers discriminate each object from the others in the same way. The interobserver coefficients cited earlier in this chapter are of this form. Such coefficients assess relative agreement, not the degree to which the judgments of observers are identical and interchangeable.

The other class involves measures of congruence. In this context, perfect congruence refers to two observations being identical. The extent of congruence is the extent of absolute agreement. Statisticians often restrict the term *agreement* to just this type of correspondence. For scaled data, the intraclass correlation, mentioned earlier, is usually used. For categorical data, Cohen's kappa (1960) is most appropriate, especially for determining degree of congruence. The more familiar chi-square assesses all kinds of association, including systematic disagreements, and hence is less useful in this context. Other useful statistics for agreement include the indices described by Goodman and Kruskal (1954), Scott (1955), and Holly and Linert (1974). These assess congruence between matched pairs of observations. As Krippendorff (1970) has pointed out, many of these coefficients are the complements of the ratio of the observed disagreement to the disagreement expected on the basis of chance. The form of these coefficients, 1 - X/Y, may have the psychological advantage of reminding the investigator that his norm should be 1, perfect agreement, rather than better-than-chance agreement.

Many of these statistics are scaled in terms of the maximum amount of agreement possible for the set of data, given the sets of marginal values (the numbers of observations that each observer places in the several categories). Such indices have certain advantages. They permit ready comparisons between levels of agreement obtained with different measuring operations. They also permit tests of the statistical significance of agreement, although such tests are hardly necessary when the investigator is striving to achieve perfect congruence. Viewed in terms of the standard of exact correspondence, these indices have the weakness of not revealing the extent to which the two sets of observations disagree on the total frequencies for each category (that is, on the marginals). In addition to the standard indices, an investigator may wish to determine the degree of correspondence on these marginal frequencies for each classification, assessed perhaps as a percentage of the mean frequency placed in that class. Such an analysis would enable him to identify those classes (categories or scale steps) on which the observations disagreed most.

Let us look more closely at assessing agreement in observations of behavior. When the investigator delineates the behavior to be observed and judged, she may ask the observer to make one judgment of the total segment of behavior or one judgment for each demarcated portion of that segment—for example, each five minutes as marked by a signal. The determination of interobserver agreement is easy for the data derived from such tasks. But suppose the investigator asks the observer to note every time that a child hits another child; how can the investigator calculate the agreement between that observer and another? If she assumes that there are no false positives—that every judged hit was a correct judgment—then she can take the total number of instances so judged by either observer as her base. But if some physical contacts are ambiguous and may not be hits, she has no satisfactory base. The best procedure appears to involve arbitrarily breaking the temporal period into units of observation. For each unit, the investigator can then record each observer as noting a hit or not and can calculate the extent of congruence between their sequences of judgments. But when the act being judged is a rare one, the investigator must realize that her observers could agree by chance on a very large proportion of the units, where both made judgments that the act did not occur. Of course, the investigator may be interested only in the total frequency of a given act within the designated segment; if so, she need only compare the totals produced by each observer. Such a comparison, a rather common procedure, ignores the question of congruence between judgments of each occurrence of the act.

The coding of an act as present or absent is an instance of categorical measurement—measuring with categories that have no inherent order. Such measurement appears to be more primitive than measurement based on ordered scales (for instance, a rating scale with six ordered scale points). It has the merit, however, of being absolute— the observation either does or does not fall into that class. The gain from this quality depends, of course, on the clarity with which the classes can be specified and the consequent ease with which each observation can be judged to fall into a class or to fall outside that class.

In contrast, most ordered scales utilized in personality measurement do not have precise definitions for each point specified on that scale. The words or phrases used to label each point have imprecise and varying meanings (especially when they refer to relative frequency, as discussed in Chapter Two). On a scale for strength of an attitude or disposition, the delineation for any one point must usually be interpreted by the observer within the context of the specifications for adjacent points. There is some arbitrariness in the set of steps indicated for any given scale, in the sense that a smaller or larger number of steps could have been specified, and each step could have been described in different words.

Congruence can also be assessed for ordered psychological scales, the criterion being the percentage of correspondence of scale points assigned. Note that, when the scale lacks a true zero point, the standard cannot be the percentage of discrepancy of each observation relative to the magnitude of the mean observation. Zero on a scale for friendliness or for intelligence is an arbitrary function of the scale, unlike zero on a dimension like length or weight.

It is well known that agreement defined as congruence will vary inversely with the number of categories made available to the observers or the number of steps on an ordered scale, assuming that the total range is kept constant. The finer the discriminations required of the observers, the lower their exact congruence can be expected to be. Where the scale for recording judgments has numerous equal intervals, observers may not agree on the precise step in every instance. The investigator might then decide to combine adjacent steps, thereby reducing the total number of intervals being analyzed. Alternatively, she may determine the number of steps between each pair of judgments and compute the average difference (squaring these differences if she wishes to give greater weight to the larger discrepancies).

In assessing agreement, the adequacy of the sample is a critical matter. The sample is composed of units of observation. Each unit can be identified with one observed person and with one segment of behavior. In considering the degree of agreement between observers, we are interested in two universes, that for segments of the behavior of one person and that for several persons. When we speak of a sample of persons, we are actually referring to a set of segments of behavior, one for each person. If the behavior sample has a restricted range on the variable being studied, the discrepancies between judgments for each unit of observation will appear relatively large. But if the sampling of units of observation from the universe of interest has been adequate and unbiased, the relative agreement can be estimated more accurately. All too often, the investigator is concerned with a hypothetical universe that cannot be described with sufficient specification to permit the application of sound sampling procedures. Recall that, within the paradigm sketched earlier, any obtained estimate of the agreement between two observers pertains to the total setting, including as components the task assigned to observers, the scale for reporting, the body of phenomena observed, and the times at which observations were made. The observed level of agreement is a function of all these components.

Less familiar is the sampling of observers. In some psychological research, the identification of the population from which observers are drawn presents no difficulties. For example, in laboratory research, anyone who knows the procedures and the phenomena can be utilized. The situation here is similar to that in the natural sciences: any person can be considered a member of the pool of interchangeable observers after he has been given sufficient instructions and training. Note, however, that the notion of interchangeability does not mean indifference as to the person who observes; it does not mean that any person will do. Interchangeability always has limits that should be specified. Although the requirements for acceptable observers are fairly obvious in laboratory sciences, they are not so obvious in personality and related fields. In laboratory observations, the usual task for the observer is relatively straightforward and manifest; in judgments about behavior, the cognitive processing required of the observer is rarely examined because it is so natural, so often practiced in everyday living, that it is erroneously assumed to be understood.

For personality investigations, the appropriate pool of observers is not easily ascertained and may not be readily accessible. Rarely can the pool of acceptable and interchangeable observers be specified. If the role of the observer is that of a professional trained in interviewing or in some other diagnostic procedure, then some specification is possible. But if each potential observer has a unique status relative to the person observed, then there can be no pool, or at most a small one.

At any one time, a person ordinarily has only one therapist, one supervisor, and one spouse. Some classes of relatives, such as children or parents, may not be seen as interchangeable because they differ in sex. Even within the categories of peers (coworkers or friends), similar distinctions may be necessary.

The single observer in the personality area can, however, be specified on at least two facets. One facet pertains to the segments of the observed person's behavior that the observer has perceived. Has he seen the person at work or at play; with superiors, peers, or inferiors; with men or with women? The other and more significant facet is the particular relationship of the observer to the observed. Insofar as that relationship has unique qualities, and insofar as the observer's task requires interpretive judgments, no pool of interchangeable observers exists, only a limited number of human individuals.

Much of personality data derive directly or indirectly from self-observation, and for these data there is only one observer, the person himself. Our heavy reliance on judgments made by the subject under study stems from several sources. First, it is often much more convenient to ask the person about himself, rather than to ask several others about him. Even more important is the fact that such reports are typically more direct than reports by others. If an investigator is interested in the person's preferences, self-report seems more suitable than making indirect inferences from lengthy observation of what the person does or says. When the substantive topic involves feelings or other internal states, inferences of external observers become even more tenuous. Finally, the measurement of aptitude or achievement requires the use of response data produced by the person, and much of the methodology utilized in the assessment of personality variables has been adapted from that developed for measuring aptitude and achievement. Since mental test theory has been constructed primarily for such self-report data, it has little to say about the issues of the interchangeability of observers. The exception is the concern for the estimated reliability of pooled ratings, which borrows the reasoning used for the reliability of items or tests.

When the method of measurement involves the use of a specified single observer, especially when that observer is the person himself, it is not possible to assess the adequacy of that observer in any fully satisfactory way. The investigator can, of course, readily identify gross failures to follow the instructions stemming from failure to understand the task posed or from simple lack of cooperation. All other evidence on the quality of self-report judgments—for example, the presence of regularities in the response patterns that would occur by chance very rarely—must be indirect. Very long sequences of responses in the same class ("yes" responses, for instance) and long sequences of alternating responses (yes, no, yes, no) cast doubt on the cooperativeness of the person. The other kinds of regularities that have been identified and analyzed have typically been construed as indicating the strength of some intruding extraneous variable other than the one the investigator sought to assess. Examples are the several response sets or styles; acquiescence, favorable self-presentation, and defensiveness have been investigated extensively (Fiske, 1971, pp. 213–220). Although the potential confounding effects from these unwanted sources of variance are particularly serious in assessing personality variables, they cannot be ignored in other areas utilizing self-reports, such as in some measuring of attitudes. Even in measuring capacities, response sets like cautiousness about committing oneself may be found.

Assessing the adequacy of self-report judgments is difficult because the self-observer is not a mechanical instrument that has fixed biasing features—he does not consistently rate himself two scale points or 25 percent higher than he should. Similarly, the observer who is rating other people does not consistently depart from some independent criterion in a given direction to a fixed degree. His idiosyncratic contributions to his ratings appear to vary with the person rated and with the variable he is rating. In technical terms, there is considerable observer-target interaction, observer-variable interaction, and even observer-target-variable interaction, with none of these being sufficiently regular and dependable to permit adequate assessment of their contributions.

Agreement Between Observations of Different Events

Up to this point, we have focused primarily on agreement between observers looking at the same object or phenomenon, that is, having the same period or even unit of observation. The matter of agreement between observations, however, is not limited to that case.

It also involves agreement between observations of two or more different units of one person's behavior and extends to agreement between observations of units from different persons.

For comparison, consider disciplines where another kind of agreement is fundamental—agreement between readings from instruments. An instrument must yield essentially the same reading whenever it is applied to the same object. That is, when the object can be assumed to be unchanged in the interval between two applications of the measuring instrument, the investigator expects the two readings to be interchangeable. In parallel fashion, the investigator in these disciplines expects that two instruments designed to measure the same property of objects will give interchangeable readings. She expects congruence both when the conditions permit the two instruments to be applied simultaneously and also when the object is assumed to be constant over some period of time during which the two instruments can be applied successively. Each instrument may, of course, have some individuality so that it has to be calibrated in order to make its readings congruent with those of some standard instrument. The transformation in a calibration is assumed to be point for point: C, D, and E on the scale for one instrument are to be read as identical to k, l, and m, respectively, on the scale for the other. Such calibration is tested to ensure its dependability over any given series of applications.

In personality and related disciplines, instruments yielding readings are not available, and so those kinds of agreement are not pertinent. What is pertinent is the matter of agreement between observations made at different moments in time. Just as the investigator fortunate enough to have instruments assumes that, under appropriate circumstances, readings on different occasions will be interchangeable, so the personality investigator assumes that observations at different times, and hence based on different units of observation, will agree with each other. Both are making the same assumption—that the property of interest in the observed object is essentially constant over the period of time sampled by the two points when observations are made. This steady-state assumption is made by generalizability theory, as Jones (1977) has pointed out.

The assumption that the attribute being measured is stable over some period of time is a reasonable one when that attribute is a property like length and weight in simple physical measurements. In fields like personality, however, many attributes of interest cannot be assessed as directly as length can be. To measure length, it is only necessary that the object stay still for the period required to make the observation. In contrast, personality measurement is concerned with the occurrence or nonoccurrence of an event. More generally, the behavioral sciences study the behaving of organisms. Behaving is essentially the changing of the position of the body or a part of it in space. The behavioral scientist classifies these changes as events of one kind or another. She may either scan the stream of behaving for the occurrence of a specific event or produce a change in the environment (a physical stimulus or an item to be read and answered) and then classify the subsequent change in the organism's activity, the behavioral act or response. Taking the extreme instances, determining whether or not a particular act occurs within some circumscribed period of time is substantively distinct from determining the value for some presumably stable attribute of a presumably inert, passive object. The primary difference is associated with the vitality of the organism as it constantly changes its behaving, concurrent with the constant changing of the total external environment around it. Hence, a crucial matter in the measurement of behavior is determining whether two of its phenomena, two behavioral events, are equivalent.

As earlier chapters have pointed out, science looks for regularities. Recall the quotation from Wigner that physics "only endeavors to explain the regularities in the behavior of objects" (1964, p. 995). For behavioral science, the objects are persons. The problem is to analyze behavior into units and to find classes of these units of observation. Empirical research then seeks relationships among these classes or between a class and some other variable. But the first step is the forming of classes, a matter that comes down to the question of whether two units of observation, two events, are interchangeable with respect to their membership in some class. Although the nature of the class need not concern us at the moment, it should be noted that the class is determined by the purposes of the particular investigation. Thus, the same event may be placed in one class for one research purpose and in another class for a different investigation.

We can begin by asking whether two given events observed for the same organism are interchangeable. On psychological grounds, we would not expect equivalence unless the state of the organism and the total circumstances surrounding the event are the same at the two moments of observation. Although the correspondence of these two states cannot readily be determined, it is possible to note whether the preceding events, which are likely to leave residual effects on those states, have been the same. This level of equivalence or interchangeability is unduly strict and would lead to many classes of events, each with few instances in it. More reasonable are classes for recurring events that take similar form although the behavioral events preceding them are slightly different and the environment is slightly different. In these instances of recurrence, the organism's response may be repeated when it will serve the same function or have the same instrumental role as it did before. Thus, two units of observation may produce the same unit of measurement for the organism even though the two corresponding environments are different.

Equally fundamental, and more relevant to standard behavioral research, is the question of the equivalence of two events involving different organisms. Do they fall into the same category for classifying behavioral acts? Can the observations of those events be taken as yielding two data with the same value? These are the kinds of questions that each investigator has to answer, explicitly or implicitly, for the specific events involved in the observations of his observers. All too often, the answers are taken for granted, and yet the assumptions made by the investigator about the equivalence of behavioral events involving different organisms are basic to all of his compiling of data and reporting of findings.

This discussion of events has assumed that three steps have been taken: The phenomena being studied have been analyzed into explicit events, units have been demarcated by some rules, and agreement has been reached on the application of these rules to determine the boundaries of each event. The problem of unitizing a behavioral protocol is a very difficult one, as we saw in the preceding chapter (for a specific instance, see Duncan and Fiske, 1977, pp. 164–175). The problem has been resolved readily and simply in standard psychometric procedures that indicate the alternative responses permitted for each stimulus item; each recorded response is considered an event.

We have examined correspondence between events in very general terms. When an investigator is studying broad concepts, such as the common traits of personality, he must consider the various problems and questions raised above. For such an investigator, the events of interest are usually complex, since they involve several distinct sequential components extended over time. In contrast, there need be little difficulty in obtaining agreement between observations of events when the event selected for study is a manifest act, such as a smile or a gesture. The act can be defined in words and illustrated with examples from videotapes so that the observers can agree readily on occurrences of the act in the recordings they observe. Each occurrence yields a unit of measurement, and each unit of behavior without an occurrence yields an implicit unit of measurement with a null value. Even when these occurrences involve the same actor at different times or different actors who execute the act with varying topographies or physical patterns (for example, gestures can take different paths), the coding of these events into the designated categories presents few complications.

Thus, the matter of agreement between observations begins with the problem of agreement on the identification of the units to be observed. Once the units have been marked off, we can ask whether observers agree on their observations of the same unit of one person's behavior. But we must also ask whether observers agree on observations of two or more units of that person's behavior that fall into the same class (again, as determined by the purposes of the investigation). Finally, we have to assess agreement between observations of behavioral units from different persons.

Reliability and Validity as Provincial Psychological Constructs

Each concept that psychologists use in their work on the individual differences between persons is heterogeneous. It refers to a set of several broadly defined aspects of behavioral events that are usually extended in time. Although psychologists are not interested in the lengths of checkmarks on answer sheets, they may be interested in expansiveness, defined as the disposition to make long, comprehensive movements in writing, in hand movements, in tosses of the head, and in the sweep of the arms in gesturing. It is obvious that a meticulous assessment of expansiveness would require the measurement of at least one aspect of units of writing and of at least one aspect of units of gestures. Interpersonally oriented dispositions, such as friendliness, are also heterogeneous. In order to measure them carefully, the several relevant sequences of behavior have to be unitized in some way, and the aspect of each kind of sequence pertinent to the concept must be identified.

In assessing a psychological concept, psychologists implicitly grant that it refers to several qualitatively different aspects of units in several distinct kinds of behavior. Friendliness may be indexed by smiles and gazes at another person who is talking to the observed person, by offering the hand at greeting or departing, by tone of voice and choice of words when speaking, or by other cues. In the usual approach to this personality variable, each of these qualitatively different events has aspects that are used as cues in judging friendliness. In making global judgments, the relative weights to be given to positive cues and to counterindicating cues are left to the intuition of the observer. In systematic measuring procedures, a number of separate questions may be posed for the observer (the subject himself or someone else), and the response to each question is classified as positive (indicating friendliness) or not. Each positive response is then treated as interchangeable with any other positive response, and the total number of such responses is determined for the person being observed and measured. Each of these responses is taken as the occurrence of the same event or, more precisely, as the occurrence of an event that has a particular aspect, the marking of a keyed response. The several events are the same in the sense that they are treated as members of the same class.

Psychologists do not attribute a disposition to a person on the basis of observing one unit of behavior that can be characterized as having an aspect indicating that disposition. The nature of the concepts used in studying individual differences, especially within the area of personality, is such that investigators will not attribute a concept label to a person without multiple instances of observations identified with that concept; typically, the investigator also requires that the several instances fall into more than one of the distinctive classes of actions subsumed by the concept as described.

Which aspects of behavior to include within a concept is determined before the investigation begins. As a consequence, investigators usually differ in their specifications of these aspects, each investigator having his own conceptualization for the disposition. But once the list of relevant behaviors has been compiled, the investigator is faced with the problem of how the observations of diverse behaviors should be combined. The usual procedure in psychometric work is to give each equal weight. The problem of combining separate molecular observations into a composite score closely parallels the problem of combining molar, composite scores from discrete operations into a single index. Both problems will be examined more closely in the next chapter.

For comparison with the measurement of friendliness, consider the observation of nods during a conversation. If a psychologist is interested in the occurrence of nods in temporal conjunction with an act of the other person in the interaction, she need be concerned only with the degree of agreement between observers watching the live or videotaped interaction (see, for example, Duncan and Fiske, 1977, pp. 340–342). For each unit of the interaction, she will want the observers to agree that the auditor did or did not nod. She may also want the observers to agree on the location of each nod relative to the sequence of other acts by the speaker or the auditor. No other kind of reliability is pertinent. Unless she is also concerned with individual differences in the frequency of nodding after some other act, the stability of nodding in the auditor is not relevant. Notions of internal consistency do not apply. Questions of validity need not trouble her if she and her observers can independently identify any events containing the aspect of a nod and any events not containing that aspect.

Perhaps the investigator wishes to determine whether the frequency of nods is correlated with ratings of general friendliness. Once again, for her measurement of nods, the only crucial concern is agreement between observers. In this case, the investigator need not examine the agreement on each specific occurrence; she will be content if the number of nods observed by one observer corresponds closely with that of another observer for each protocol being scored. She may be interested in the stability of nod scores: for repeated interactions between the person being scored and the same other, do the several nod scores agree relatively closely? She cannot usefully apply the idea of internal consistency. She could segment the conversation and see whether the nodding while listening occurred irregularly or evenly, but the interpretation of that determination would be difficult unless she had further information about the other actions occurring in temporal contiguity with nods.

This investigator would also have to determine the empirical generality of nod scores over conditions. In particular, she would want to know whether it varied with the person's partner in the conversation. She would also need to find out whether nodding in informal social interactions was closely related to nodding in instrumental interactions, such as employment interviews. Once again, the usual validity concerns seem irrelevant here. The nod score is a direct indicant of the concept of nodding, a highly homogeneous concept, rather than an indirect measure for a construal of the phenomena.

When the investigator turns to her other concept, friendliness, she must consider all the usual matters of reliability and validity for any measure she uses. If she selects peer ratings, she must determine the degree of agreement between peers in their rating of the trait of friendliness. This agreement, however, is between observers who have observed different although overlapping periods of the person's behavior. Hence, it is not exactly the same as the agreement between observers discussed earlier. It includes to some degree agreement between observations of sets of behaviors that can be distinguished in terms of the conditions surrounding each set. Each peer may have seen the person in circumstances that are not exactly the same as those in which other peers saw him; each peer has his own period of observation. Even if the set of behaviors constituting each peer's period of observation is not explicitly identified, the investigator can treat it like a separate item in a test. The rating of each peer is a unit of measurement based on a single unit of observation similar to that in the response to a specific stimulus item.

The stability of ratings by peers is not ordinarily examined. Note that two questions may be involved. First, do these peers give the same ratings at a separate, later time when they have had no additional experience with the person during the interval? Second, does the modal peer rating of friendliness change over time as the peers have additional interactions with the person?

Peer ratings would seem to have face validity, especially if the investigator has restricted her concept of friendliness to friendliness as perceived by peers. She would, however, want to consider whether the conditions under which the ratings were made might have affected the ratings. Criterion-related validity is not an issue here since the investigator does not view these peer ratings as a substitute for some superior index of friendliness or as a possible predictor for some criterion to be obtained at a later time. The construct validity of her measuring operation also seems sufficient here, without being examined empirically. The validity of her construct in its nomological net is a separate issue, which involves the findings from her analysis of the covariation with nod scores.

Now suppose that another investigator, instead of asking peers for ratings of friendliness, asks them a series of questions presumably pertinent to friendliness. Rather than defining friendliness as what peers perceive to be friendliness, he is defining it implicitly as the series of behaviors embedded in his several questions. If he accepts that definition, he is in the same position as the other investigator, who uses global ratings. More typically, the investigator views his several questions as pertinent but indirect means for estimating friendliness as he defines it. In this case, he must be concerned with several kinds of reliability and validity. Comparing the several responses to each question would indicate whether these observers agreed with each other (ignoring their different experiences with the person). The stability of these responses or of sums over questions would be an appropriate concern for the investigator. And internal consistency, the extent to which the several questions covaried over persons observed, would be highly pertinent.

This investigator would also consider the validity of his set of questions as a measuring instrument. He could have judges assess his questions, separately and as a set, for their relevance to friendliness. He could correlate the scores from these questions with some superior measure of friendliness, if he could identify such a measure. And, at least in principle, he would utilize the relationships between these scores and other scores, including those for nods, in assessing the construct validity of his measure.

This lengthy consideration of hypothetical investigators has indicated the many questions that careful investigators should answer when studying global and heterogeneous concepts rather than more simple ones. Given their heterogeneous concepts, most investigators in personality have not been concerned with obtaining close agreement among observers for each observation. Although these investigators consider agreement between observations of a single organism at two different times, they have not given it the emphasis it merits. The major focus has been on ensuring some covariation between events involving the same organism reacting to separate environmental events, such as various item stimuli (the fact that these events occur at slightly different moments is considered secondary—with some justification).

Many of the concerns pertaining to the generalizability of a measuring operation—that is, to its reliability and validity—do not apply to operations for certain kinds of concepts. For example, when the concept is at a low denotative level of abstraction, being essentially a label for perceptions-cognitions where the perceiver and the conditions for making observations are specified and where high observer agreement can be demonstrated, the only relevant generalizability issues are simple empirical ones concerning external validity: Do the relationships found for the obtained indices under one set of conditions also hold for other sets of conditions, and if so, what kinds of conditions?

Generalizability in its several aspects is involved, however, when empirical research is undertaken on certain concepts common in personality and other parts of psychology. This kind of concept has an independent existence, being part of the culture before any efforts were made to measure it in research. If an investigator develops a procedure to measure one of these concepts and finds that his procedure has poor reliability and questionable validity, many of his colleagues will ignore his findings, convinced that he has failed to capture the full flavor and range of the concept as they construe it.

Such a concept will usually have a rich connotative aura for each scholar using it. Each worker will have a large number of prior perceptions and experiences to which he has applied the term. Finally, a concept of this sort will usually have an implicit attributional function. Devised originally to describe observed behavior, it has come to be employed as an attribute of persons—a shorthand way of saying that some persons manifest a considerable amount of the behavior described by the concept.

Recognizing the vagueness in these old concepts from their culture, psychologists have sought more precise concepts. Years ago, psychologists measured intelligence. Now, *intelligence* is a term for an area of functioning that has been analyzed into many narrowly defined abilities. During World War I, psychologists measured neuroticism. Now they measure anxiety, repression, sensitivity, and other more specific conditions. But anxiety itself has many forms. These more specific concepts are still highly heterogeneous, and hence the various issues involving generalizability must be raised about each operation for measuring them.

When a concept is derived from interactions with people in everyday living or in the clinic, it takes on an existence of its own and is almost impregnable. It may be assailed by systematic empirical research, but it will rarely be destroyed. In the more advanced sciences, laymen's concepts have either disappeared or have been limited to more precise meanings associated with objective ways of observing their occurrences. The central concepts in those fields typically stem from theorizing tied to research work, and such concepts are linked to generally accepted ways of measuring them. If psychology is not advancing by studying its a priori concepts, it may be time to develop concepts a posteriori from fresh empirical observations.

In the early parts of this chapter, an argument was made for interchangeability among observers. Observers can be interchangeable when they are asked to attend to aspects of behavior that can be indicated with high precision. *Precision* here refers to the clarity of the definition of the concept, including clear indications of which occurrences fall within the concept and which do not. When a personality concept is defined verbally, one cannot tell whether the concept has the same meaning for different investigators, even if they should happen to accept the particular set of words formulated for the definition. The extent to which the concept has common meaning can be ascertained only by determining agreement on concrete instances of its manifestation or by seeing whether researchers use the same operations for measuring it. But popularity of a particular measuring procedure is not pertinent if researchers discuss their findings in general terms invoking connotations not linked to the procedure. The use of several measuring procedures that yield measurements that covary to some limited extent (the usual finding) is not sufficient unless there is a rationale specifying how each procedure is related to the others in a pattern pertinent to the overall concept.

As an illustration, consider the term *friendliness* (or the more systematic term, *affiliation*). How should friendliness as perceived by acquaintances relate to friendliness as judged by close friends and as judged by spouse? Should self-report on friendliness covary with these other measures? Where do ratings of friendliness from stories the person produces in reaction to TAT pictures and from sentence completions fit into the picture? No one appears to have specified the patterns of scores from independent procedures that indicate each of the degrees of a personality concept like friendliness. The usual approach is to give each procedure equal weight. If, however, one procedure is found empirically to produce scores that are uncorrelated with those from other procedures, it is often treated as measuring a separate form of the concept, such as its latent form.

From the preceding discussion, it becomes apparent that the limited agreement between definitions of concepts, the limited covariation between separate observations and between independent scores, and the limited progress in personality and similar domains are closely interrelated. It is certainly time for a reexamination of our basic (but often unstated) assumptions, of our objectives, and of our procedural tactics.

Reliability and validity are provincial psychological constructs. They are crucial within that province where the focus is on broad and loose constructs with heterogeneous manifestations, especially when the objective is to estimate some general, unqualified score for a person, without restriction as to the circumstances under which manifestations of that construct may occur. The concepts prevalent in personality and common in other parts of behavioral science are indeed fuzzy and have indeterminate connotations, as Nagel (1961) has characterized them. In contrast, constructs embedded in theories built on empirical research are less troubled by those problems. Similarly, matters of reliability are particularly irksome when one attempts to measure vague concepts. Sciences with more precise constructs developed from systematic observations place their primary emphasis on achieving an essential interchangeability of instruments and of observations. That same interchangeability is also essential to the behavioral sciences because it is the foundation for obtaining reproducible findings and for any subsequent generalizing of conclusions.

Summary

A science can be seen as consisting of matters on which its practitioners have consensus. Especially pertinent are agreements on basic theory, fundamental concepts, standard methods, and replicable empirical findings. All of these are built on close agreement, virtual congruence, on empirical observations. The human observers must be interchangeable.

The obtained levels of agreement between observers in personality and related fields are low in absolute terms and poor in comparison with those in the natural sciences, not only in correlational, individual-differences research but also in experimental studies using personality variables. We can expect little improvement in agreement on judgments for global variables. For observations of specific, concrete variables, however, very good agreement can be obtained. Although the ideal is congruent observations and interchangeable observers, agreement is commonly measured in terms of relative position in each observer's array of measurements. In addition to agreement between observations of the same behavior, personality has been concerned with agreement between observations of separate events, as in determining the stability and internal consistency of test scores.

Reliability and validity are provincial psychological constructs that are needed for evaluating measures of global concepts. Of the various aspects of generalizability, interobserver agreement is the only one essential for observations of low-order concepts, such as simple, overt acts.

VI

Generalizing from Observation, Attribution, and Covariation

After a person has seen a friend a number of times, he may have occasion to describe that friend. Choosing his words with some care, he attributes several qualities to him. He generalizes from his observations of the friend's behavior to make his attributions. Suppose he says his friend is both friendly and relaxed. He may then think about another person whom he sees as unfriendly and tense. It may occur to him that friendly people are usually more relaxed than unfriendly people. If so, he is generalizing from his attributions to a relationship or covariation between attributions.

Personality research involves similar generalizations and includes another—the generalization from attributive judgments made by one person or in one situation to general characterizations of the person. Since an observer's integrating or synthesizing of impressions to arrive at an attributive judgment has been examined in earlier chapters, that kind of generalizing will not be considered here. Instead, this chapter will look at the generalizing employed in aggregating or pooling judgments to get a datum for statistical analysis. It will also deal with generalizing from that datum to a characterization of the person and generalizing from obtained associations between such data or characterizations to broad statements of relationships. As pointed out in Propositions 3 and 4 (Chapter One), many of these generalizations seem unwarranted. Finally, although we will be considering the behaviors of observers, we will emphasize the behaviors of investigators.

Pooling Observations

To obtain a representative index for a person, the investigator is not content with a single observation or a single unit of measurement, such as the person's response to one question about himself. Unless the response is a global rating on the concept, it is taken as referring to only one of the various manifestations of the concept. Furthermore, the investigator does not trust a single observation—she recognizes from her training and experience that it is undependable, since the probability of replicating that observation is clearly less than 1.00. If the same observer responds again in a week, the likelihood that he will give the same response is high but not certain. Conceptually, the investigator will say that she realizes that the observer's response is probably affected by a number of influences other than the actual phenomena—the person's behavior. Although she knows that these effects exist, she cannot entirely eliminate their contributions to the observation. (For convenience in this discussion, we are using the term *observation* to refer to the most elemental unit of measurement or response employed by the investigator; each of these units is viewed as based on a unit of observation.)

The typical way of handling this problem is to pool the unit of measurement from a single observation with measurements from other observations. If the other observations come from other observers, the investigator hopes that the extraneous effects influencing one observation are counterbalanced by independent effects on other observations, so that the average is less biased than any one of the values contributing to it. She seeks, in this way, to minimize the contribution of the individual observers. Another common form of pooling involves combining the several measurements or responses to discrete questions pertaining to portions of the concept's domain, such as responses to a self-report questionnaire. The prevalent method of pooling consists of counting the number of those responses that have been labeled a priori as indicating applicability of the concept. The investigator ordinarily has no explicit rationale for this last scoring procedure. If asked, she will probably say that, as far as she knows, a positive response to any one of the questions means as much as any other positive response, so she is weighting them equally. It is likely that she has not thought out whether a positive response to one question makes less probable a positive response to some other; for example, a person may have adopted one way to satisfy a need in preference to any other way. If anything, the investigator is likely to assume some positive covariation between responses. Empirical evidence, of course, shows that the average correlation among such responses is extremely low—often about .02, sometimes around .07, and only occasionally over .12 (Fiske, 1966).

The investigator who scores responses by counting is employing the compensatory model from the set of composition models delineated by Coombs (1964). In this model, a postive response to one item can compensate for a negative response to another item. Other composition models utilize separate responses or indices for the several major components of the disposition being assessed. For example, a person may be labeled careless if he frequently loses things because he leaves his belongings scattered about, even though he is moderately careful about the condition of his car and about balancing his checkbook; another person may be labeled careless because he neglects the condition of his car. Analysis of patterns of acts suggests that broad labels like *careless* may not adequately fit the particular patterns of actions observed in many individuals.

Sophisticated methods of psychological measurement are being developed, including functional measurement (Anderson,

1970, 1976, 1977) and conjoint measurement (Coombs, Dawes, and Tversky, 1970). At present, however, such elegant methods can be of little help. The difficulties in personality measurement are primitive, extending back to the origins of the data, so that it has not been possible to establish agreed-on components that might be integrated by these developing methods.

From the Datum to the Inferred Attribute

Our discussion thus far has dealt with what Campbell and Stanley (1963) have identified as the external validity of a score obtained by pooling the observations from several observers or the several responses by one observer. Although each observer has, in fact, already integrated a set of impressions in order to arrive at his response, the investigator goes one step further and integrates several such responses. She is seeking a measure that has validity beyond the circumstances in which the data were collected. She wants an index that represents the degree of applicability of her concept to that person over all places and all times. She generalizes from observations collected within a narrow span of time to a characterization of the person over some unspecified but much more extended period; she assumes that the degree of applicability of a concept to a person is rather stable.

The external validity of measurements is interpreted in this context as the extent to which they correlate with some hypothetical perfect scores that are not confounded with variance from the specific conditions or the specific measuring procedure. If an investigator is willing to make some assumptions, she can roughly estimate this external validity. It is rare, however, for an investigator to give up the use of a measuring procedure because of its apparently limited external validity. She typically continues to use her measuring operations if she can find any empirical evidence in their favor, even when it is clear that the procedures get at only part of her concept, get at it from only one point of view, or show limited covariation with procedures designed by others to measure the same general concept (Fiske, 1971, 1973; Mischel, 1968). Her difficulties in procuring adequate procedures for assessing her concept do not shake her faith in the existence of her concept or in its appropriateness for use in research in personality.

One important facet of observations over which the investigator generalizes is place. The extent to which an investigator can generalize from observations collected in just one measuring place, even if they involve memories, is limited. Although other places put the person in a setting where evaluation does occur, measurement (or evaluation) is only rarely the principal reason for the person's presence there. And even for unobtrusive measurement (Webb, Campbell, Schwartz, and Sechrest, 1966), each place or setting has its own characteristics that affect the behavior observed in it. Hence, it is not surprising that the external validity of a measuring procedure is greatly restricted by the unusualness of the situation in which it is applied. Insofar as behavior is a function of the situation, the more similar two situations are, or are perceived to be, the more similar a person's behaviors in the two situations will be. In contrast, the more unusual a situation, the less likely it is that behaviors observed within it will be observed in other situations. A testing situation is distinctly unusual. Entirely aside from the novel stimuli that compose the testing materials, the general conditions are atypical to the point of being unique. Since the person usually knows that he is being tested, he is likely to suffer evaluation apprehension (Rosenberg, 1969), just as he does in academic examinations. But unlike a person facing academic examinations, the subject in personality research has only a general idea about what characteristics are being assessed (Fiske, 1967). Other components of the situation, such as the personality of the examiner, may also have effects. It is a reactive human being who takes our tests and plays the role of subject in our laboratory experiments (Fiske, 1971, Chap. 10; Silverman, 1977).

The original rationale for conditions in a testing room was probably the analogy of the laboratory in the natural sciences. In a laboratory, the experimenter can control the conditions, such as temperature and humidity, that might affect the observations. Irrelevant influences can be eliminated so that the specimens are not contaminated. But the analogy breaks down when one considers the extraneous, obtrusive factors present in measuring personality. Although the testing room may eliminate distractions, it introduces effective, impertinent background stimuli that are likely to affect the responses to those other stimuli that the examiner carefully presents for the subjects' reactions.

Thus, the testing room and the testing stimuli together constitute a unique situation, which cannot be considered as representative of any class of situations ordinarily encountered by the persons being tested (Fiske and Butler, 1963). Consequently, the extent to which the empirical findings can be generalized is clearly restricted, and the external validity of measurements made in that situation is distinctly limited. All of these problems are well known to the careful, experienced investigator, and yet the custom is to pay minimal attention to them because there is little that can be done to alleviate them. In fact, the extent to which these extraneous factors affect our measurements is very difficult to estimate since we cannot compare them with measurements made with the same testing stimuli in other situations. We must be on our guard, however, against developing merely a psychology of personality-in-the-testing-room.

In principle, it should be possible to measure the attributes of each situation in which we obtain measurements. If we could also measure the attributes of situations in everyday life, we might then be able to make estimates of the comparability of the two types of situations and even devise methods for making dependable extrapolations from our measurement situations. But that ideal is quite unobtainable now because we simply cannot measure all the significant features of situations. Even if we could, we would be dealing only with averages for people in general. We would still face the more difficult question of measuring the attributes of each situation as it impinged on each individual being studied, the attributes as perceived by that individual.

The true nature of the testing situation can be realized if we stop to consider that the data collected there have no function in human behavior, other than in the behavior of personality researchers. The attributions used as data are ordinarily produced for research purposes, as stated in Proposition 2a, Chapter One. Only the investigator interacts with them. Ratings do not affect either the person assessed (who is usually not aware of their content) or the observers. Although making self-ratings may affect a person, the investigator hopes that such an effect will be negligible, and he certainly does not collect self-report data in order to produce an effect. It can be granted that, in describing a friend to an investigator, the observer may become aware of impressions and cognitions not previously verbalized to himself, and this awareness could affect somewhat his later interaction with the friend. And it must also be granted that an assessment, such as a psychodiagnostic report, that has been read by a diagnostician or therapist can affect his behavior in later interactions with the patient. But, for the most part, personality data are appendages to the main stream of human behavior. They are produced under the special circumstances of assessment rather than in the course of natural interactions between people. Since they are not identical with the impressions and interpretations of others that occur outside the testing room, they may not have the same functional relationships.

Furthermore, attributions are cognitions about what has been observed. Weick has suggested that it "may be that cognition has little effect on behavior, because it follows rather than precedes behavior. Cognitions may be retrospective; they may make sense of what has happened rather than what will happen" (1969, p. 30). He goes on to say that "too little attention has been paid to actions and too much to cognitions, plans, and beliefs" (1969, p. 30). We must also recall that naturally occurring cognitions can be at varying levels of abstraction, from "That was a friendly thing to do" to "She is a friendly person." The levels of abstraction dictated by investigators in their questionnaires and rating scales may, at best, correspond to only some of the levels in natural cognitions.

Some psychometricians may argue that the average rating obtained from several raters gives a dependable datum because it reflects the common component in the several ratings and hence gives a good estimate of the underlying disposition as it exists in the person rated. But how does such a disposition function in the person's behavior? It is not the impression the person has of himself; rather, it is estimated from the judgments of others. The degree of the disposition estimated by the psychometrician from the ratings is unknown to the other persons, the raters. Instead, each of them has his own impression, which determined the rating he assigned to the person. Although we must grant that one's impressions of a person may contribute to one's expectations about his behavior and consequently have some functional role in interactions with that person, the more important factor is one's impression during the actual interaction. Of most importance in affecting one's behavior with another person are one's perception and interpretation of the other's actions as they occur over time.

Ralph Gerard used to relate the story of the squirrel-hunter and his double-barreled gun. Seeing a squirrel in a tree, he fires one barrel, the shot passing one foot to the left of the squirrel. The hunter fires the second barrel, only to have the shot go one foot to the right of the squirrel. But the squirrel falls down dead, killed by the law of central tendency. When two raters have different impressions about a person, the raters and the person may be affected by each impression but not by the mean rating.

The difficulties encountered with averaging judgments stem from the use of abstract, a priori concepts. An investigator does not have to start off with such concepts, which cannot be adequately measured and which, as a consequence, are quite unlikely to be modified or discarded in the light of empirical findings. He has the alternative of beginning by identifying actions that he believes may be important in the structure of behavior and then developing ways of obtaining sound measurements of their occurrence, along with the occurrence of other actions. One form of that strategy is illustrated in the act approach (sketched in Chapter Four and developed in Chapter Twelve). The objective can be to find actions that are followed by the same or highly similar changes in the environment, animate or inanimate.

The notion of functional equivalence was discussed forty years ago by Heinrich Klüver (1936) in a neglected article published in *Character and Personality*. He points out that stimuli are equivalent if they evoke the same reaction. Although his emphasis is on stimuli, responses can also be functionally equivalent, since a response can become a stimulus. The importance of an action stems largely from its effects in terms of the reactions of the actor and of other persons to it. One illustration is found in animal behavior, where investigators have noted diverse ways that animals evoke the same reaction in others. For example, the ways that males may mark their territory to deter other males from entering it vary with the species, but all have the same effect.

Another example of seeking interchangeability in empirical data can be found in Duncan's research on the turn system in conversational interactions (Duncan and Fiske, 1977, Chap. 11). In these investigations, a number of acts were identified in recorded protocols, their moments of onset and of offset being carefully located relative to other acts. Examination of the transcriptions suggested that certain acts occurred frequently before a particular point, such as the end of a speaking turn. It was later determined that these acts were functionally equivalent: The number of such acts observed, regardless of which particular kinds of acts they were, was associated with the likelihood of a smooth transition from one person speaking to the other speaking, as opposed to simultaneous talking. The unit of study was often an act by one participant and a subsequent act by the other, the frequency of such action sequences being checked against the frequency of just one of the acts or of neither act. Further research may show the first half of the sequence to be equivalent to other acts that show the same association with the subsequent act. Replication studies can establish whether these relationships and equivalences can be generalized to other conversations.

As in all sciences, the determination of class membership for actions must be empirical. Although prior conceptualizations may provide guidance, investigators must demonstrate in their data that certain behaviors are functionally equivalent in the particular context being studied. Some classes of equivalent actions may be found to characterize all human behavior. More typically, classes will turn out to be pertinent only for a culture or a subculture. A few classes may be found to apply just to one small group.

Questions of pooling and of functional equivalence involve matters of regularities and interchangeable events. Beginning with concepts that show limited regularity across their heterogeneous components and trying to build on limited levels of covariation among measurements of those concepts have not paid off well in terms of positive discoveries. An alternative strategy (discussed in detail in Chapter Twelve) is to start with categories of highly uniform actions and seek regularities in their co-occurrences. Regularities among observations must be demonstrated, not just predicted or assumed. The basic question for personality and also for other behavioral sciences is, quite simply: What stimuli are functionally equivalent and what actions are functionally equivalent?

Specificity in Measuring Operations

Several kinds of incongruences plague research in personality. In addition to differences between observers, there are effects associated with instructions and with other conditions of testing and discrepancies between measurements taken at different times. All of these intrusive effects on measurements weaken their generalizability. Just as an estimate based on measurements with large variation is less trustworthy than one based on a set of very similar scores, so the extrapolation from a group of heterogeneous observations is less dependable than one derived from more homogeneous judgments.

At least as important as any of these differences are the differences between measurements obtained by independent procedures for assessing the same concept. The poor agreement between such procedures has been noted by many writers (for example, Vernon, 1953; Campbell and Fiske, 1959; Mischel, 1968). Whenever two procedures differ in the task given to the observer, the procedures can be expected to yield scores with limited intercorrelation. The two tasks may differ in only one aspect, and still the correlation between them will be low. The primary exception is the special instance in which an investigator sets out to construct alternative forms for a test, the two forms setting the same task for the observer and differing only in content. The reasonably high intercorrelations between the forms occur because the content is based on just one person's construal of the concept being measured, and hence the items in one form may correlate with items in the other form to the same (low) degree that they do with each other. When two instruments for assessing the same concept label are constructed by separate investigators, however, they have distinctly lower intercorrelations (see, for example, Butt and Fiske, 1969; Fiske, 1973). The literature is replete with findings of low intercorrelations among procedures purporting to measure the same concept. Anyone using several independent procedures in a study of a single concept will obtain that result. And, although the procedures may involve different observers, the same finding occurs when the same observer, such as the self, is used. In spite of this picture, many investigators use only one procedure for each of their concepts and generalize from its specific measurements to the concept as a whole.

The methodological consequences of this specificity are profound. If measurements of a concept are dependent on the procedure used, how can relationships to those measurements be interpreted? Strictly speaking, any obtained associations must be taken as holding only for that particular form of the concept, for that concept-method entity. Even if similar associations (perhaps correlations around .3) are found for other procedures aimed at the same concept, the investigator must be cautious about assuming that the consistency of his findings indicates that he has contributed to establishing a set of relationships—all too many of the positive associations found in personality research are around that level of correlation. He can safely assume that two procedures are measuring essentially the same construct only if they show the same pattern of relationships, large and small, over a number of correlates. I have described this process elsewhere as one of extrinsic convergent validity (Fiske, 1971, p. 245).

One strategy for dealing with this specificity of measuring operations is to identify subconstructs that are particular forms of the general construct (Fiske, 1971, pp. 255-256). Jackson, Ahmed, and Heapy (1976) provide an example in their analysis of achievement. A related approach is to study semantically related constructs that can be subsumed under a broad term, as Stricker, Messick, and Jackson (1970) did for reactions to group pressure. Even for narrowed concepts, however, no more than moderate agreement between independent measuring procedures can be expected in the light of published findings.

Another, more extreme strategy is that of strict operationalism. Each procedure can be taken as measuring a separate concept. Most investigators are unwilling to adopt this viewpoint because they are trying to measure the general concept, not some special form of the concept as it is found in a single procedure, and they are not interested in theorizing about a concept-as-embedded-in-a-procedure. They do not want to make the effort to determine how the characteristics of the particular operation generate the specificity in its measurements. Their reluctance is understandable. For them, the measuring procedure is only instrumental; it is not a phenomenon to be understood in its own right.

Another proposed strategy is the explicit use of multiple operations. Some optimists argue that the solution to the problem posed by low covariation among sources of measurements is a reliance on a combination of procedures rather than on any single one. That proposal does have pragmatic value—a composite score will be more dependable and will be less likely to omit important aspects of the concept at which the measuring is aimed. Yet, in view of the general finding that different sets of operations yield different scores, how should one proceed in selecting the procedures to include among the multiple operations? We know that they should be as varied as possible, for example, with respect to the roles and the perspectives of the observers to be used. Yet we cannot make informed decisions when we know so little about our concepts and about the coordination between a concept and each specific procedure for measuring it. An additional problem is the weight to be given each operation when one seeks a combined score. A promising solution is indicated by the evidence that unit weights yield very dependable findings in predictive studies (Dawes and Corrigan, 1974; Einhorn and Hogarth, 1975).

An example may illustrate. How should an investigator measure the need for achievement? There are many measuring procedures aimed at that concept, including several self-report questionnaires, a procedure for scoring stories told in response to TAT-like cards selected for this purpose (McClelland, Atkinson, Clark, and Lowell, 1958), and a procedure for scoring a person's doodles (Aronson, 1958). Previous research indicates that a composite score based on three questionnaires would agree only moderately well with a score composed of one questionnaire, one TAT-type measure, and the doodles test. And for the latter composite score, should the questionnaire component receive double weight, to balance the two projective tests? If the investigator wishes to use more sophisticated weighting based on a multiple regression analysis, what would be his dependent variable? The need for achievement has no standard, observable criterion measure.

The investigator's decisions would depend on the particular way in which he construes the need for achievement. For example, McClelland (1958) argues that it and other motives can be adequately assessed only by a TAT-type procedure. Given the present state of affairs in personality research, it is certainly desirable to make a separate analysis for each of several procedures for measuring a concept, in addition to any examination of a composite score. Even better are parallel studies varying at least the sample of persons and preferably the context as well. These would be frustrating for the investigator since relationships among scores from separate procedures are likely to change with alterations in these conditions.

The orientation in this discussion of multiple operations has been primarily empirical, but the basic problem is conceptual and methodological. A truly adequate definition and delineation of a concept would make explicit the appropriate procedure for measuring it. When the concept is explicitly broad, the conceptualizer may decide that it cannot be measured by any one technique, that it can best be approximated by some specified composite obtained from designated component scores obtained by particular methods. This possibility seems reasonable in the abstract, but its implementation would encounter too many serious difficulties to make it practicable.

Amorphous Relationships Between Polymorphous Concepts

We turn now to generalizing from empirical findings. Just as no one is content with a single observation, so no one should be content with a single occurrence of an obtained relationship. Observations can be multiplied fairly easily, but the repetition of an empirical study takes much more time and energy. Hence, an investigator is predisposed to generalize from his obtained finding. Before considering that matter, let us look at the generalizing that is done about each of the sets of scores or other measurements. What conceptual interpretation does the investigator give to each score?

Suppose that several observations have been pooled to arrive at a datum or score for a person. What does such an attributed score mean? What can be done with it? For example, take the statement, "Joe Smythe was rated high on affiliation." What does that statement mean? The only definite, fully specified part is the designation of the person referred to—there should be no problem about identifying who Joe Smythe is. The elliptical phrase "was rated" can be taken to indicate certain observers who made ratings under certain conditions. The investigator can report who the observers were and what the conditions were.

Finally, what does "high on affiliation" mean? It implies, first, that the rating or mean rating given to Joe was higher than some norm, such as the ratings given to a majority of those rated in more or less the same way. If, instead of high, the statement had used a specific number, that number would have to be referred to some set of norms or some distribution in print or in some people's heads. The term *affiliation* can be viewed as referring to a particular procedure: some instrument with demonstrable format and content. But only a skeptical methodologist would want to know what the instrument was. Most readers accept the large inferential leap from the rating procedure to the unqualified attribution of affiliation. "High on affiliation" implies that Joe tends to seek out people and likes to be with people. Perhaps more than most people, he initiates, maintains, and deepens relationships with others—all of which is a lot to infer from the single statement. And, of course, one does not know in what ways Joe shows his affiliative tendency. The heterogeneity of such manifestations for a common large concept has been discussed earlier and needs no further comment here.

A more complete interpretation of the statement about Joe could be given as a generalization predicting that, if a full description of all of Joe's behavior were obtained, it would show that he engaged in several behaviors subsumed under the category of affiliation more frequently or more intensely than the average person. The prediction would be qualified by some phrase like "under circumstances when affiliative behaviors could occur." But over what period of time would this protocol of Joe's behaviors have to extend? An hour would not be enough. A day might catch him in an atypical state. A week? (But a week of vacation or of hard work?) A couple of months? That should be enough time. The predicted attribution should not be required to hold for several years or a whole lifetime.

Now suppose an investigator wished to determine the relationship between affiliation and social values (defined as valuing the social aspect of things, as opposed to such other aspects as the economic or the aesthetic). He asks Joe to take the Allport-Vernon-Lindzey Study of Values and finds that Joe's score on social values is high. Repeating his observations on a number of other people, the investigator obtains two arrays of scores or attributions and correlates them, finding the correlation to be, say, .50. So measurements of affiliation and social values covary over persons.

What does that empirical finding mean? Strictly speaking, the investigator found that persons rated as affiliative report a relatively high interest in social concerns. At that level of generalization, the investigator may have uncovered a purely semantic relationship. The terms *affiliative* and *values social concerns* in these scales may have overlapping or very similar meanings. The investigator might reason that people rated by others as affiliative are likely to rate themselves as affiliative, and people who rate themselves as affiliative are likely to rate themselves as high on social values because the two terms have similar meanings and references. Alternatively, if Joe attributes social values to himself, it is likely that others will rate him as having social values and, in addition, will rate him as affiliative because they perceive the two terms as having similar meanings. The significance of semantic overlap has been pointed out by D'Andrade (1965, 1974) and Shweder (1972, 1975).

What else might the obtained relationship mean? It could mean that complete behavioral descriptions of the people assessed would show that those with many affiliative behaviors also did many things indicating social concerns, while people showing little of one set of behaviors also showed little of the other. But what would that mean? The two sets of behaviors might occur in complementary fashion—at times when a person showed social concerns, he was not affiliative, and when he was affiliative, he did not show social concerns. But that kind of relationship would seem less likely than a supplementary patterning over time, the two sets of behaviors tending to occur at the same times in the behavioral records. Yet what would the supplementary pattern mean? That the expression of social concerns tended to follow affiliative behaviors, or the reverse?

The ambiguity of interpreting an empirical finding that two attributions are correlated is particularly evident when the two attributions are made by the person about himself. It is evident that such an empirical finding means simply that persons reporting that they perceive themselves as having a high degree of one variable also report self-perceptions of having a high degree of the other, with similar correspondence between low reports. Such covariation could, of course, stem from response sets. If the "yes" responses on each scale are the keyed ones, yes-saying or acquiescence may be operating; if both variables are positively valued, some persons may be seeking to present themselves favorably on both scales, while others are trying to be more candid about admitting their deficiencies.

But does the relationship between two variables as determined from response behaviors in the testing room correspond in size to the relationship between the variables as determined from the everyday behavior of the same subjects? The investigator studying the paper and pencil responses is using as his unit of analysis each person's pair of scores from his tests. Another investigator looking at actual behavior has in his unit of analysis a pair of measurements derived from observing physical behaviors. Need the findings from their analyses correspond? The self-attributions are actions in response to test stimuli. The actions in the everyday behavior are in response to quite different stimuli. Since the linkages between self-report and observed behavior are at best modest, the likelihood that the relationship obtained for self-descriptions reflects the relationship for relevant behaviors outside the testing room is small.

A number of interpretations, then, are possible for an obtained relationship between two sets of attributions. Such a relationship may mean only that attributors perceive the attributes as related. It may mean that attributors have impressions or construals of people's behavior relevant to the two attributes and that these construals overlap. It can also be taken as indicating that the two sets of referent behaviors covary over people. And, instead of that macroscopic view, it could mean that an expression of a general social concern tends to follow or tends to precede an affiliative action. Each of these is a broad generalization suggested by the specific, restricted study but not firmly supported by it.

The hypothetical investigator might not assign any further meaning to the hypothetical obtained relationship between affiliation and social concerns because he could recognize that it was dependent on the observers who produced his data. The given relationship might not be found for data from other kinds of observers. It might even not appear for the same observers if they were responding to a rather different procedure for rating affiliation or for reporting social concerns. The interpretation of such a finding may also depend on the particular wording that an investigator employs. In survey research, for example, a slight, apparently innocuous change of wording may affect the results of an opinion poll. In an experiment on attributions, Gurwitz and Panciera (1975) found that the effects of their independent variables on attributions of freedom depended on the wording of the measure of freedom. They concluded that an experimenter's choice of wording can affect the conclusions he draws.

There is yet another complication. An observed relationship between two variables may hold for one specified group of persons but not for another. In the intriguing study by Bem and Allen (1974), ratings of observers on the trait of friendliness showed more agreement for persons who rated themselves as consistent in their friendliness across situations than for persons who described themselves as less consistent. In addition, a measure of extraversion correlated more highly with observer ratings for the consistent group than for the less consistent group. These provocative results must be interpreted cautiously for two reasons: similar strong findings were not obtained for the trait of conscientiousness, and prior research on separate variables that moderate or suppress empirical relationships has typically had difficulty in confirming original results in subsequent replication studies. It does, however, seem probable that some people's behavior varies more with the situation than that of others, as the work of Snyder (1976) also suggests.

Covariation of Composites and of Instances

Does the same ambiguity of interpretation appear for relationships between attributes that were judged from the same sample of behavior? For example, if observers rate friendliness and talkativeness from watching a situation test, is the obtained correlation between these attributes equally difficult to interpret? The answer is yes. The correlation may stem from the semantic associations of the observers, especially if the ratings are made from memory. But most important is the fact that a sizable correlation tells us nothing about the functional relationship between friendly and talking behaviors. Were the spontaneous, extended segments of speech generally friendly in tone? Were the participants apparently friendly only when they were talking? The obtained correlation does not tell us anything about the behavior of the participants, not even about the temporal associations of actions that were clearly talking or friendly.

An extended example of the limitations of summarizing scores can be found in a report by Duncan and Fiske (1977, Pt. II). We coded a large number of rather molecular acts for a series of interactions. We obtained relatively few dependable relationships. On the other hand, using some of these interactions, a separate set of analyses looked for temporal contiguities between one act and another act of the same person or the partner. Patterns of relationships were discovered and confirmed. We found, for example, that the initiation of a gesture is often associated with beginning a speaking turn, that the termination of gesturing is one cue for readiness to yield the speaking turn, but that continuing to gesture negates other cues ordinarily signaling such readiness. If the other person starts to talk while the speaker is still gesturing, an interruption or simultaneous talking occurs. This set of relationships between one kind of act, gesturing, and other acts was much more informative than our findings that total time speaking was correlated with total time gesturing but not correlated with average duration of gestures while speaking.

Another case in point involves a research program on a group of art students. In their study of creativity, Getzels and Csikszentmihalyi (1976) began by administering several conventional paper and pencil personality inventories. A number of interesting, although not very surprising, correlations were obtained. For example, the grades received by male students for work in studio correlated -.40 with the Economic value score from the Allport-Vernon-Lindzey Study of Values, even though the mean Economic score for the whole group was below the norm given in the test manual. Yet the findings threw no light on the creative process as it occurred in more and in less successful students. So these investigators then asked each student, whom they knew well by this time, to produce a still life under somewhat standardized conditions. Observations of that work sample as it progressed revealed that the way the more creative students went about the task was not the same as that used by less creative students. The more creative spent more time handling the objects available to them, turning them and examining them from different angles. Their tactics were different—involving different actions. Hence, their approach could be described in terms of fairly discrete, brief acts as well as in terms of more general, abstracted characteristics, all of which could be subsumed under the attributed label *discovery-orientation*.

For these latter analyses, the criterion of creativity was not derived from coding of actions. It was the average judgment of art critics evaluating the work sample produced for this investigation. That judgment was also correlated with ratings made several years later on the students' subsequent success as creative artists. Since creativity is defined by society (by art critics, in this instance), it was necessary to utilize attributions of creativity in this investigation. But these rat-

ings and the students' self-attributions conveyed limited information. They were generalized ascriptions not referring to particular
occasions. Even the evaluations of the work samples were judgments
of the final product as it stood, and did not give any information
revealing how the students' actions contributed to that final product.
Observations that generalize over time, especially when the time
period is not specified, can yield relationships with other variables, of
course, but the meaning of those relationships is difficult to establish.
Creativity is manifested in creating, in a sequence of varied actions
that change the material with which the artist is interacting. To
understand creative activity, the investigator must look at the actions
involved, not at attributions that someone makes about the artist.

Generalizing from Experimental Research

Most of this chapter has dealt with correlational research in
which attributions are made about persons and in which covariation
of attributions over persons is the investigator's focus. In Cronbach's
(1957) other scientific discipline, experimental research, there are
also problems in generalizing. Since the laboratory is at least as atypical of everyday environments as the testing room, the experimenter
faces the question of generalizing her findings from that unusual context. Moreover, laboratory subjects are as reactive as people being
tested. They may try to play the role of subject as they understand it,
or they may play games with the experimenter, trying to guess what
her purposes are. Differences in these reactions serve to increase the
interindividual variation that the experimenter is trying to minimize.
Silverman (1977) has summarized much of the research on the subject
as subject.

The experimenter must also determine whether her experimental stimuli can be considered to be representative of the naturally
occurring stimuli to which she wishes to generalize. In the present
state of psychological knowledge, it is difficult to extract the pure
essence of the physical or behavioral stimuli encountered in the everyday world. The identification of basic dimensions for stimuli has not
been firmly established. As a consequence, the experimenter often
finds that her empirical variables are incomplete representations of
her general concepts and that findings obtained from analyzing one

variable are not replicated in analyses of another variable. In sum, the external validity of experimental research, especially in the personality domain, remains in much doubt.

Experimental research does, of course, pool and aggregate multiple trials for one person or trials for different persons. In studying evoked potentials in the brain, the same stimulus is repeated many times, and the many responses are averaged, with the expectation that the small common effect will emerge through all the random effects ("noise") associated with the separate trials. In this and other work using repeated trials, the investigator knows of no explicit difference between trials except their temporal order. Hence, the pooling of trials is reasonable. Note the contrast between the pooling of observed responses and the pooling of manifestly different questions in a test or ratings by clearly distinct raters. In spite of differences between contents of items, responses are pooled when they have one property in common. For ability or achievement tests, responses considered correct are aggregated; in personality testing, the aggregated responses are those previously keyed as indicating the disposition being measured.

For both experimental and correlational research, a larger aggregation problem concerns the entities being studied—are they individuals or groups? And what is the connection between relationships from individual data and those from group data? These questions are more critical for other social sciences than they are for personality. Thus, educational research often involves measurements that are means for whole classrooms and has to consider what the relationships among such means tell about individual children. (For technical work on aggregation, especially in sociology, see Hannan, 1971a, 1971b.)

Summary

Naturally but injudiciously, without a sound rationale, we generalize from an observation, an attribution, a single measuring procedure, or an empirical relationship. Neither the lay person nor the investigator is concerned with any particular observation; each combines a set of impressions or observations into a generalized attribution that ordinarily is not qualified in any way. More specifically, the investigator uses several kinds of generalizing. His observers generalize from impressions to attributive judgments. He pools these judgments to obtain a score for the person being studied. He generalizes from that specific score, inferring from it an attribute characterizing the person. Finding an empirical association between a set of such scores and another set for a different attribute, he generalizes to a relationship between the concepts involved in the attributions. The external validity of attributions—their generalizability beyond the circumstances in which they are made—must be critically examined and questioned, especially when the attributive judgments are made in a testing room. Experimental research has comparable difficulties in demonstrating the external validity of its measurements and findings.

Like researchers in other areas, the personality investigator seeks sets of observations that can be classed together as functionally equivalent in terms of their relationships to units in other classes. Yet the scores he obtains from each independent measuring operation contain much specificity. No fully adequate conceptual rationale has been developed for combining the data from multiple operations. Not only is the meaning of a summarizing attribution unclear but the interpretation of a relationship between sets of attributions is also uncertain. Any generalization of an obtained relationship between specific procedures is risky. In contrast, the empirical investigation of covariation between sequential actions provides a firmer basis for controlled, explicit conceptual work.

VII

Crucial Roles of Time
in Behavior and
in Personality

Time has been brought into the discussion of most topics in the preceding chapters. It is central to the study of behavior, and it is a factor in many difficulties facing research and measurement in the personality domain. Yet, as noted in Proposition 6 (Chapter One), time has been relatively neglected. The importance of time provides the rationale for this chapter, which brings together and examines the significant ways in which time pervades the themes we have been considering.

154

Time is a peculiar dimension. In the study of behavior, time itself is irrelevant. What is important is the frame of reference it provides for the investigator. We can identify eight different roles played by time in personality research.

First, time is used to determine the length of the period of observation, be it seconds or years, on which a unit of observation (such as a rating) is based. Yet it is not the duration of observation that actually interests us. We use duration as a rough indicant of the amount of behavior observed.

Second, in a related but not identical role, time is used to indicate the period to which an attribution applies. That period may be only a portion of our total period of observing a person. We may say, for instance, that a person was depressed yesterday. But to what period are we referring when we just say that he is depressed?

Third, time is used to designate the duration of a psychological process in either the observer or the person observed. In instances in which we cannot readily study a central process, such as cognizing or choosing an alternative response to a test item, we get indirect information from knowing the duration of the process. We know empirically that practiced activities require shorter periods of time, and we assume that processes taking longer periods are more complex or at least have more phases.

Fourth, and probably more important than the first three roles, is the use of time to identify when an event occurred or, more exactly, when a measurement was made. This datum enables us, in turn, to gather two other pieces of information, each of which involves a different role of time. Fifth, then, we use time to state which of two events or actions occurred earlier, and sixth, to measure the interval between them. That interval is related to the expected strength of the impact of the first action on the second. The longer the interval, the greater the amount of intervening behavior or other events and consequently the weaker the impact is likely to be. Furthermore, when two actions are judged to fall into the same class, the interval between them can be one datum used to determine the average interval or rate of occurrence for that class of actions.

Seventh, knowing when an observed action occurred permits us to determine the exact state of the person's whole external environment immediately preceding the action. Similarly, knowing when an interpretive judgment was made enables us to determine the conditions preceding it. In a sense, time can identify for us the specific place or setting for the behavior as measured.

Finally, time has a related role in any consideration of the person's internal environment—his state or mood. Although these environments will be almost identical for two measurements made a few minutes apart, they will vary over different hours of the day and different days. Thus, identifying when a measurement was made enables us to locate it relative to other measurements and also to relate the measurement to the existing external and internal conditions.

All of these roles of time will enter into the several topics of this chapter. Note that some, such as the last two, refer primarily to the behavior of the observed persons, while others are largely concerned with the responding behavior of the observer.

Time in Attribution

A plausible account of the manner in which impressions are formed by making inferences from brief actions is provided by Secord and Backman: "One of the most widespread perceptual-cognitive processes operating in impression formation is *temporal extension*. This takes place when a perceiver regards a momentary characteristic of the person as if it were an enduring attribute. For example, a smile usually means that the stimulus person is momentarily responding in a friendly fashion, but the perceiver may infer from this expression the enduring attributes *good-tempered* or *easygoing*. Or a single action by another person may lead to judgments of lasting characteristics" (1964, p. 64). Although the major basis for their statement and for my agreement with it is probably introspective, the processes they describe undoubtedly occur. A single action may yield an impression that is converted into a tentative attribution. Subsequent actions and their consequent impressions may reinforce the attribution, so that it is no longer tentative.

The attribution of a personality characteristic is usually assigned to the person without reference to time; in academic terms, attributions have tenure, being made "without limit of time." The human being has been called a time-binding organism, and when one describes another person, one is integrating observations over several periods of time and inferring a property that is believed to endure for some unspecified duration.

Thus, an attribute is construed as pertaining to the person and not to her behavior. We do not expect every act and every sequence of the person's behavior to manifest the attribute in some discernible form. It is as though we talked about the weather in a city in terms of the average annual temperature, rainfall, humidity, wind velocity, and hours of sunshine, and then tried to use this information to predict the weather on a given day or to understand a particular meteorological event that occurred there. But the weather on one day is more closely related to the weather on the day before than to the average weather. At any one hour, the prediction of a storm depends on many specific observations of the conditions in the area around that city. Analogously, we cannot understand a person's behavior at one point in time in terms of averaged or abstracted features of her past behavior, especially when we have no knowledge about such contextual matters as the preceding actions of other persons interacting with the person.

Attributing in the natural world outside the testing room is the product of mental activity. As indicated earlier, it takes some small effort to find an appropriate label for a person or for a segment of her behavior. Attributing takes longer than perceiving. It is more than recognizing; it is cognizing that is interpretive, in which one finds the most appropriate categorical label from a long list of stored descriptors—and the longer the list, the longer the time, in seconds or fractions of a second, that the search and selection process takes.

In obtaining attributive judgments from observers, the investigator should consider effects associated with the length of the period of observation, especially when the entire period is the unit of observation from which a unit of measurement is obtained. One might assume that the longer the observation period, the longer the cognitive processing required to arrive at a judgment. In fact, however, longer periods of cognitive activity are likely to be associated with less dependable judgments in terms of consistency over occasions for judging, a point we will return to later. Experience with observers yields the impression that the extent of their cognitive activity in forming a judgment is not related to length of observation period but instead is approximately constant for short periods (such as the duration of a situation test) and for longer periods. In both cases, the judgments probably involve a few visual images rather than many and are derived from summarizing impressions that may or may not have been verbalized previously.

Mental products are not restricted by time. The solution of a problem exists as long as it is remembered or the record of it remains. Bits of knowledge are similarly time-free. Once we have learned a telephone number, it exists in our memory store for a long time, especially if it is recalled and rehearsed from time to time. An attribution is a bit of knowing. Its longevity is unrelated to the duration of the brief cognitive process by which it came to exist.

Research on perception has identified a number of constancies in human information processing, including object constancy, size constancy, and color constancy. It would appear that people also assume person constancy. Over a long period of time, a person has much the same physical appearance and manifests the same psychomotor patterns of speaking and moving. Largely from these constancies, we come to expect a high degree of constancy in behavior. Our construing of a person seems to provide some functional utility and psychological economy, since it guides future perceptions and interpretations of her observed behavior.

Perhaps Piaget's concept of conservation (1965) is pertinent here. That concept refers to the judgment that an object or some material has retained a fundamental property even though the object has gone through a transformation. It involves the denying of an apparent perception, calling it illusory on the basis of a preemptive axiom regarding the constancy of some material property. Elkind (1967) argues that fundamental to conservation is the recognition of identity. Conservation of identity is seen in the decision that a transformation of the material in one respect, such as general shape, does not alter other properties, such as weight.

Just as the child learns about the conservation of weight and volume, so perhaps he also learns about the conservation of a person's identity in spite of changes of apparel—swimming trunks, an overcoat, or a masked costume. And if a given volume of water retains both its volume and its wetness when poured into a different container, so should the perceived properties or attributes of a person be conserved when in different clothes or in a different context. The person remains the person, therefore his attributes remain his attributes. And they are *his* attributes: We give them to him and not to his behavior. Consequently, he and the attributes we have assigned to him persist in time, whether or not his behaviors persist in our memory store.

Attributions differ in their remoteness from observed actions and in their removal from the scale of time. Global, comprehensive attributions are generalizations many steps away from observations and actions. Terms like *distinguished* and *able* are not linked to specific acts. Labels like *creative* and *pleasant,* though not quite as abstract, are still several steps removed from momentary perceptions of others. Words like *orderly* and *assertive* begin to suggest particular behaviors. Descriptors like *graceful* and *jittery* can be applied to particular actions lasting only a second or two. All of these labels are used to characterize people, but they vary greatly in their usefulness for describing behavior as it is immediately observed.

Although attributions are often made without temporal restrictions, personality is also analyzed at a number of levels that can be identified with segments of behavior having different durations. These levels are degrees on a continuum from temporal specificity to temporal generality. Some earlier psychologists studied life histories. In capsule form, a description of a life might state: He wanted to become a great violinist, and he gradually became one. The first half of the description characterizes the person over a period of many decades; the second covers a period overlapping most of that period as the person progressed toward his goal. Today, such comprehensive studies of lives are more prevalent in biography or history than in psychology, although some psychobiographies do appear, even for living people. More within the realm of personality research would be analyses involving shorter time periods: He practiced faithfully, and he acquired exceptional skill. Less abstract would be this description: One day he watched a virtuoso, closely observing his bowing, and learned a new way of phrasing. Still considering the same person, a description might note: He watched to see what the virtuoso did at a particular point in the score; and perceiving something he had not noticed before, he had an insight into a more effective style in bowing.

Investigators study personality at a range of levels. The resulting measurements are thus derived from longer or shorter segments of behavior. Psychopathological status before psychotherapy may be represented by a single number—in this instance, one end of the time period, the start of treatment, is clearly indicated. Behavior over a week in a ward may be rated. A score may also be derived from responses during a fifteen-minute test. We can and do construe at any and all of these levels. Moreover, we can and do use the same label or variable for our measurements pertaining to these assorted segments of time. Once a time-free attribution is made, the scope of behavior from which it was derived is immaterial. Thus, a measurement stops the flow of time and compresses the sequence of actions into a single observed value. The investigator then determines whether an array of such values for several persons covaries with some other array or has a central tendency that is higher when some identified event precedes the period of time to which the values apply.

Perhaps all measurements indicate status for some interval of time, however brief. Measurements not only in psychology but also in other sciences can be viewed in this light. The moment in time at which the measurement is made must be explicit and must enter into our interpretation of that measurement and of its relationships with other data. (This statement applies to the second, fifth, seventh, and eighth roles of time listed earlier.) Furthermore, there is reason to believe that, with notable exceptions in geology and astronomy, much scientific progress has been associated with the degree to which the concepts studied and measured are of low orders of abstraction and pertain to brief time periods. Actions and reactions in mechanics and chemistry are rapid. Actions and reactions in psychology are also rapid, although not quite at the same order of magnitude.

What goes on in a person can, of course, be studied on a very fine time scale. The neuropsychological and psychophysiological processes underlying overt activity occur at very fast rates, requiring temporal measurements in terms of milliseconds. Physical actions, including speaking, can be studied on almost as fine a temporal scale. Very brief stimuli apparently can be perceived and reacted to; tachistoscopic exposures as short as four milliseconds have been used in research reported by Silverman (1976). But most of psychology in general and personality in particular is not concerned with that level of analysis. For example, the physics of music deals with hundreds of cycles per second, the effective events being vibrations that are rapid changes in time. Yet the study of sound as perceived and music as experienced is concerned, not with that level, but with a somewhat more gross scale of time.

What level or order of temporal magnitude should investigators select for studying phenomena in the personality domain? Although many levels have been tried, none have become standard. The most common is the trait or dispositional level, with unspecified temporal boundaries. Others should be intensively investigated. In this volume, I have emphasized a comparatively fine level of analysis, identifying acts that may be of quite brief duration and yet can readily be perceived by other people. What is important is behaving, and behaving consists of changes in activity—that is, the initiations or terminations of acts. For purposes of analysis, these events are taken as instantaneous even though a finer-grained examination might reveal a period of many milliseconds as the time required for an act to be initiated.

What order of temporal duration is involved in molecular acts that can be discerned by other people? We know that people can see and hear events lasting just a small fraction of a second. In laboratory research, reaction times approach 200 milliseconds. Micromomentary facial expressions of similar duration have been identified (Haggard and Isaacs, 1966). The eyebrow flash in greetings, noted by Eibl-Eibesfeldt (1972), is quick. Very rapid movements of the eyes are detectable. A change of visual focus is quite evident to an observer able to see the person's eyes. A rapid glance away and back can be noted, even though the duration is some small part of a second. In fact, a series of alternating shifts in the directions of gazes of two persons can occur in less than a second, as observed in one protocol obtained by Cary (1974) in preliminary work on the initiation of conversations. In this instance, the coding of the glancing required minute analysis of the videotape—the sequence was not obvious in the first or second playing of the tape. Since we cannot determine whether each of the participants actually perceived all of the ocular movements of the other, the psychological interpretation of the protocol must be taken as no more than suggestive. Another relevant piece of evidence is the time interval between one person terminating and the other initiating a speaking turn. In data published by Jaffe and Feldstein (1970), some means for that interval are less than a second. Attributive acts take longer times, on the order of several seconds. Subjects can read a questionnaire item aloud and respond to it with an interval of only a second or two between the question and the answer. In group administration of inventories, most subjects will average ten seconds or less for reading and marking each item.

The rapid pace of interaction with the environment has been noted by various writers, although absolute temporal values are not given. For example, Piaget points out that "behavior is at the mercy of every possible disequilibrating factor, since it is always dependent on an environment which has no fixed limits and is constantly fluctuating" (1971, p. 37). A person's actions keep pace with these rapid changes in the external environment as well as with changes in his internal environment. Students of personality and other disciplines in behavioral science have generally neglected the very rapid pace of action in a person's interaction with both the physical and the human environment.

Time in the Study of Relationships

Our consideration of the significance of time for the study of behavior requires us to extend the discussion of relationships given in the last chapter. Time plays crucial roles in our efforts to establish and interpret relationships. Much of personality has looked for covariations of attributes over people. The implicit paradigm has been that labeled R-R (for example, by Bergman and Spence, 1944). Although that symbolization indicates the correlation of responses, it can be used to stand for the correlation between response tendencies or dispositions. Within this loose paradigm, broad and global concepts are often studied. Furthermore, this approach ignores time. The two response tendencies are treated as coexisting during some unspecified period of time. This laxity permits the use of generalized attributions made on the basis of unidentified segments of behavior.

Not all personality research looking for relationships between broad concepts has ignored time. Developmental research looks for relationships between a descriptive concept assessed at one age and a similar concept or an environmental variable assessed at an earlier age. And experimental work is explicitly time-related. One component, the condition manipulated, precedes the period during which the behavioral variable is observed. To test whether frustration leads to aggression, for example, the experimenter seeks to produce a state of frustration, which he expects to be followed by a state with a low threshold for aggressive responses.

In much classical psychology, the paradigm is labeled *S-R*, stimulus followed by response. In using this paradigm, the psychologist concentrates her attention on the behavior observed after the stimulus is presented, looking for forms of behavior found after the stimulus but not found in the absence of the stimulus. In contrast to those doing R-R research, the S-R psychologist has the advantage of being able to limit her observation to some designated brief period after the onset of the stimulus. She also can restrict her codes for behaviors to concepts presumed pertinent to the fact that the stimulus has occurred.

A major contribution of Skinner has been his emphasis on what happens after the behavior of interest. Instrumental conditioning involves a univocal act studied chronologically, in terms of the reinforcing events that have followed the prior occurrences of that act. Just as a response in the S-R approach may be looked at as that which follows a stimulus, so a reinforcement in Skinner's paradigm is that which follows the act. Since the reinforcement can be taken as stimulating the organism, the paradigm involves interaction between the organism and the environment—the organism starting the process by its act, the environment responding, and the organism subsequently repeating (or not repeating) the same act. This paradigm can therefore be viewed as asking not only how the environment affects the organism's behavior but also how the organism's behavior affects the environment. Note that both the act and the subsequent change in the environment can, in the experimental setting, be identified unequivocally, with perfect observer agreement.

Similar analyses can be made of behavior in naturalistic settings. In the study of acts, the protocol of the streams of behavior of people is coded into sequences of acts by one or another person, each act being located in time relative to the other acts. Given such coded data, it is possible to identify a particular class of acts and to determine what other categories of acts tend to be found just before and just after the instances in the class of interest. This approach can be seen as the study of acts in their action contexts.

An act can thus be analyzed as related both to actions that follow it and to actions that precede it. In classical terms, an investigator might want to conceptualize that act as both a stimulus for later acts and as a response to prior ones. The subsequent actions might also be construed as reinforcements. But the terminology of behavior theory is not essential to the analysis of acts in their action contexts, and that terminology has the unfortunate feature of narrowing the way in which an act is studied. Whereas in classical S-R psychology, the variance of the response act is considered to be largely accounted for by the designated stimulus, an act analysis takes a broader view. It treats relationships between successive acts as probabilistic, and it includes the concept of alternative classes of acts that are interchangeable in terms of their relationships with subsequent acts. More complete statements about classes of acts being subsumed under a broad category and about options and strategies in interactive behavior can be found in Duncan and Fiske (1977, Pt. IV).

As in work stemming from behavior theory, the act approach utilizes data based on relatively brief temporal segments. Each observation refers to an act taking perhaps a fraction of a second, perhaps a few seconds, with the onset of the act being viewed as psychologically instantaneous. Each conceptual pairing of an act with a subsequent act involves a relatively short period of time, again with a lower limit of less than a second but extending to somewhat longer durations. The behaving, the psychological process, is thus studied as it occurs. That statement should be obvious. It is made because the same statement cannot be made about research utilizing data pertaining to the usual attributions employed in research on personality.

Consider the proposition that anxiety is related to affiliative behavior more closely in first-born children than in others, as Schachter (1959) has studied it. Anxiety was assumed to be present in his subjects as a consequence of experimental procedures. Each subject was then told she would have to wait for ten minutes for the next part of the experiment and was given a choice between waiting alone or with others. A higher proportion of first-born subjects indicated a preference for waiting with others.

Schachter appropriately assumed that the anxiety generated by his instructions would persist over a period of several minutes. While in that state, the subject was given an opportunity to perform an affiliative act. Whether or not she indicated that she wished to perform that act was the critical datum. The merit of this research lies in the generation of the psychological processes that the investigator wished to study. While anxious, did the subject manifest affiliation? The affiliative act, or more accurately the indicated affiliative preference, occurred during the anxiety state. The two psychological events overlapped temporally.

Contrast that research with a hypothetical study of the relationship between anxiety and affiliation. In this study, the investigator might measure anxiety and affiliation by any of several attributive procedures: self-ratings, questionnaires, ratings by peers, judgments from projective protocols. The processes of measuring each of these variables would be closely continuous in time. The behaviors utilized as the basis for these attributions could, however, have occurred any time in the fairly recent past. Suppose a moderate correlation was obtained between the array of scores for anxiety and a parallel array of affiliation scores for the same subjects. How might that relationship be interpreted? There are many possibilities. (1) When a person experiences anxiety, he is more likely to manifest affiliation. Thus, anxiety-prone persons are more affiliative. (2) When a person acts affiliatively, he may experience rejection, which makes him feel anxious. Thus, people who are highly affiliative experience more anxiety. (3) People are more likely to feel anxious when they are alone; hence, people who are high on anxiety learn to seek out others as a way of minimizing the likelihood of their feeling anxious. (4) People who attend more to their feelings than to the outside world will be more aware of their anxieties and will report more anxiety. They will also be more interested in being with others in order to learn whether others have feelings like theirs.

The first two interpretations postulate that the occurrence of feelings or behavior categorized under one of the variables is followed closely in time by the occurrence of the other. The hypothetical data, however, provide no way to check this postulation. The other interpretations do not require the temporal juxtaposition of the two occurrences. Instead, they have to postulate intermediate processes. And the last three interpretations are minitheories introducing additional variables. Whichever interpretation the investigator selects, he must check it by additional research involving the examination of actual occurrences of feelings and actions. Eventually, he must study behaving people rather than attributions made by observers who themselves are behaving in a measurement situation.

Findings on relationships between attributions have made very limited contributions to our understanding of behavior. Since attributions ordinarily are based on unspecified but presumably lengthy segments of behavior, they do not tell us about the continuing occurrences of actions, reactions, and sequences of actions. In addition, the length of the interval between perceiving behavior and coding or judging it is important. When observers make attributions after observing a segment of behavior, the intercorrelations among the attributed variables may be much larger than the correlations among the same variables when observers mark each relevant action as it occurs during that segment. The immediate recording of behaviors subsumed under each variable yields a score that has less covariation with other, similarly coded variables than does the post hoc summarizing judgment for each variable—a judgment relying on assorted memory traces and impressions formed earlier, during the observing of the segment. Hence, the obtained correlations between attributed traits can be determined more by cognitive processes in the rater than by co-occurrences of identifiable physical acts. As indicated earlier, this point has been made clearly by Shweder (1972, 1975) and D'Andrade (1965, 1974). Trait scores from attributions and from coded actions are not comparable because they are obtained by processes in the observers that involve time in different ways.

Time in Science

I have argued here that measurements must have specific temporal referents and that personality research has been held back by its emphasis on attributional data lacking temporal referents. The asserted importance of specifying time and of examining observations in a temporal framework stems from a belief that the understanding of the behavior relevant to personality requires much the same tactics and strategies employed in other scientific work. We should assume that the same approach will be effective in this domain unless and until it has been demonstrated to be inappropriate or insufficient. Granted that the phenomena of personality look different from those of the natural sciences, are they fundamentally different? Personality involves processes, behaving, acting. Physics and chemistry also study processes. Even if the latter processes are judged to be different in kind, are the processes in biology different? Perhaps we can learn from that field.

Time plays an essential role in modern physics, especially in relativity theory. In biology, large orders of time are involved in evolutionary studies, and extended periods must be included in developmental investigations. Physiology examines rather rapid processes, and neurology studies even more rapid ones. Economics involves temporal ordering, especially in econometrics. Time plays a central role in areas of psychology that seem to have made some progress, such as conditioning, learning, and perception.

Some natural sciences, as they have progressed, have brought smaller and smaller units into their investigations. For example, biology has proceeded from studying organisms to studying organs, from organs to cells, and from cells to their components and to molecular processes. Shorter and shorter time periods also appear to be involved. Physics is now concerned with particles that exist for only infinitesimal parts of a second; biology has moved from examining physiological processes of comparatively long duration to chemical processes that are almost instantaneous. Although the scientist can construe processes with either long or short intervals between their stages, improvements in observing and measuring have enabled him to study processes with shorter and shorter durations.

Psychological processes can occur within a fraction of a second. A classical example is simple reaction time, which can average a fifth of a second. Although reactions to more complex stimuli may take somewhat longer fractions of a second, interactions between person and environment in that order of magnitude are part of the phenomena of interest to students of personality. They are amenable to systematic investigation using interchangeable observers. Personality investigators need not confine their work to construing and studying gross processes involving components that can be located only approximately on the scale of time.

Psychologists have found two strategies to be fruitful. In addition to the study of relatively homogeneous events—stimuli or acts that can be placed into classes with minimal variance among the instances grouped together—there is the strategy of emphasizing brief time periods. Their joint application has been particularly evident in laboratory research in which the phenomena studied are processes as they occur. Sensory psychology now includes the recording of the evoked neural potentials that follow the stimulus. In perceptual psychology, the course of change in pupil size is being traced. A technique that psycholinguistics has found valuable is shadowing, speaking aloud what is being heard from earphones. An intriguing finding here is the very small interval between the moment of hearing and the moment of repeating: It can average less than half a second in some persons.

The laboratory has also been used for research on personality and related areas, including social psychology. For the most part, the temporal relationships involved here have been of much larger orders of magnitude. Often the experimental manipulation itself requires one to many minutes. The response occurs from a few seconds to a number of minutes later. In contrast to these orders of temporal relationships, large and vaguely indicated intervals occur between the manifested variables in research utilizing attributions. For that work, no specification is made of either the intervals or the temporal order of the events of interest.

The temporal interval between the measurements of two variables deserves closer scrutiny. We recognize today that the organism should be seen as active. Many complex processes are continually occurring within it. When an organism receives sensory input from a stimulus, more occurs than just the flicking of a neural switch or relay. The organism actively processes the input. From this orientation, it seems highly probable that the strength of an empirical relationship in psychology should be a function of the temporal interval between the input event and the output event. The longer the interval, the longer the period of cognitive processing of that input will be and the greater the opportunity for new inputs to interact with it and to have other effects. Hence, the longer that interval, the weaker and less regular the input's effect on the output will be. A basic axiom underlying this speculation is the Lewinian assertion that action is a function of factors and conditions existing at the moment, the past influencing the present action only insofar as it is somehow currently represented in the organism.

But what does this hypothesis about strength of relationship decreasing with length of the interval between input and output have to do with personality? Consider first the situation in which the input is an act of another person. It seems likely that, in general, a given output act will have stronger relationships to acts occurring immediately before it than to acts more remote in time. Now consider the case where the input is a question or item in a measuring procedure and the output is a response or an attributive judgment. For the usual items in self-report questionnaires, there is some evidence that the strength of the relationship between a response and an item is higher with shorter temporal intervals and that longer latencies of response occur with factors linked to less stable responses (Kuncel, 1973; Kuncel and Fiske, 1974). Perhaps the test responses with longer latencies are influenced by a number of separate inputs, including memories and impressions retrieved in processing the item.

Finally, consider the case of attributions made about another person. Although the immediate input, the item or scale, constrains the response, the observer's selection among the alternatives available to her is the product of her cognitive processing of memories about the person being judged. Extrapolating from studies of memory in general, we can hypothesize that the longer the interval between the original behavior and the time of making the attribution, the fewer the details of that behavior that can be recalled and, in all probability, the greater the alteration of the original perceptions during that interval. Hence, the longer the interval, the weaker the association will be between original perceptions and the current attribution. In addition, it seems likely that the strength of the relationship between two attributions should be a function of the proximity of the times when the attributions are made. This generalization seems plausible for the situation in which the two attributions are made by the same observer, longer intervals between judgments permitting more modification of impressions and also the acquisition of new impressions. In addition, it should hold for separate observers, since longer intervals would allow the judge making the later judgment to see behaviors that occurred after the first observer's judgments were made. Thus, just as the strength of the relationship between two actions will tend to weaken, so will the relationship between attributive judgments tend to weaken as the interval between them increases.

Time and Place

The behavior of a person is, to a considerable degree, a function of his environment. A person reacts to his environment, and as that environment or setting changes over time, his behavior is likely to change. A comprehensive analysis of a person's behavior would probably emphasize place more than time, since a change in place always involves a change in time, whereas a change in time need not involve a change in place. Yet even when a person remains in the same external setting during just a short time, there is often, we infer, a change in the person's internal environment—his mood or his state of activation may be altered. As noted earlier, we can use time as a way to identify the state of external and internal factors affecting behavior.

Place and *environment* are very broad terms that are often used when it is difficult to be more specific. They refer to two types of possible influences on behavior—the external stimuli that change over time and the standing conditions or continuing characteristics of the physical and psychological setting. As can be seen in the thoughtful review by Pervin (in press), investigators in the personality domain have had difficulty in conceptualizing both the setting and its components because they have sought to interpret and make attributions about them, just as they make attributions about persons. Perhaps this difficulty can be avoided by limiting our identification of conditions to simple features that can be labeled with low-order concepts on which observers can agree readily and well. If observers produce interchangeable descriptions of these features, it seems reasonable to assume that the persons being studied in that setting would also agree with these descriptions. Since the more general, interpretive level of portraying settings has not proved fruitful, it is time to try working at a lower observational level requiring less inference.

Despite my earlier statement that place may be a more comprehensive variable than time, I have not stressed place in this volume. Although several of the basic arguments in this book could have been recast with an emphasis on place, the decision to put the stress on time was determined by a concern with processes, with behavioral sequences, and with internal processes in observers. In that context, time is a more important frame of reference than place.

Summary

Although any attribution is based on observing only a temporal segment of a person's behavior, the attribution is usually assigned to the person without specifying the period of time to which it is deemed applicable. The time of attribution and the interval between it and the observed behavior being interpreted are important but neglected specifications of such personality data. Specifying the time an action was initiated enables the investigator to determine the preceding actions or other environmental events and the existing situational conditions. Increasing the precision with which the measurement of an event is located in time increases the possibility of identifying the factors determining it.

Relationships between attributions convey limited meaning when there are no temporal reference points. In contrast, less tenuous inferences can be made about empirical relationships between acts located closely together in time or between such an act and an immediately preceding environmental event. Perhaps the strength of a relationship between two acts or events is a function of the temporal interval between them. The comparative neglect of time may have seriously handicapped research in personality and related areas.

Research Decisions, Strategies, and Generalizability

VIII

Generalizability
of Alternative
Research Choices

In Part One I developed a critical analysis of current practice in personality research. In Part Two I will offer several proposals that may enable the field to make progress. In particular, the identification and application of certain strategies may help move the field toward becoming a science. The proposed strategies are not new ways of conducting empirical studies. They are differentiations among approaches that have been used, their explicit identification enabling us to perceive their potential strengths and weaknesses and thus to

175

determine when to use them and what they may yield. Each strategy has its uses, each can be applied to a class of problems, and each can contribute to our understanding of human behavior. An investigator can profit from examining the strategy that he is following. From time to time, he must stand back and gain some perspective on his own work, in order to judge whether his research operations are actually directed toward his ultimate objectives.

One way in which strategies must be examined is in terms of the generalizations appropriate for them. The kinds and extents of such generalizations are determined in large part by the decisions made by the investigator at various points in his planning. This chapter examines the fundamental issue of generalizability and presents the basic decisions made implicitly or explicitly as an investigator formulates his research plan.

Before looking at these matters, we need to consider briefly a larger question. What is common to the approach of the natural sciences and that of the behavioral sciences? More specifically, to what extent can the approach that has proved so successful in the natural sciences be used in the behavioral sciences? What norms and ideals from the natural sciences are applicable in the behavioral sciences? As I have suggested in Part One, I am convinced that the best hope for understanding personality phenomena and related phenomena within the behavioral sciences is to identify the critical features of the approach in the natural sciences and to apply those features as fully as possible in the behavioral sciences. Although we have adapted some of those features in our scientific work, we have failed to recognize the essential significance of others.

Scientific Method and Scientific Disciplines

Does a unique field require its own scientific approach? Some writers argue that, since the human species is unique, it must be studied by approaches that are developed just for the study of people, regardless of the approaches that have been applied successfully to other fields. More particularly, they say that personality is a topic with its own highly individualistic characteristics. If the method of natural science is not effective in studying personality, then new methods must be devised. There can be no question about the uniqueness of the human species, in terms of its having characteristics that make it appear separate from other species. And no other topic seems to resemble personality closely. Even accepting these propositions, however, we need not accept the conclusions that have been drawn from them.

The phenomena of human behavior, and especially of personality, stem in large part from one unique characteristic of human beings, language. Without attempting to pin down the exact definition of that term, most of us can probably agree that no other species displays this capacity in the developed form possessed by human beings. This feature does not, however, make it necessary to develop a new method for studying man. Just as the physiology of human beings can be studied by many of the techniques used to study the physiology of animals, so the behavior of humans and of animals can be studied by similar methods. Language can be taken as verbal behavior and studied by methods adapted to that particular substantive field.

Language does seem to present a unique difficulty when one is concerned with its content, that is, its meaning. Although observers can reach consensus on what words are spoken by a person, close agreement on the exact meanings of those words is difficult to obtain. Reference to authoritative dictionaries is no solution, since many words have several definitions. Investigators cannot expect to obtain congruent data from observers on the meaning of most sentences. At the very least, there is the question of whose meaning is sought. A priori, it seems reasonable to suggest that a sentence has some meaning for the speaker, some meaning for the person to whom it was addressed, and some meaning for disinterested observers. Although it is difficult to determine the extent of overlap among these meanings, they are not likely to be identical or interchangeable. In contrast, the structure of a sentence appears to present fewer difficulties. It is possible to analyze the components of a sentence in such ways that there can be very high agreement among observers. Hence, some aspects of language can be approached by investigators who have set for themselves the standard of high consensus.

The uniqueness of the species does not necessarily require that the scientific study of human beings follow methods and standards specific to that enterprise. We should do what we can within the code of science in general. If we ultimately find that the approach of natural science does not enable us to make progress, then we shall have to examine the possibility of modifying that code. Perhaps we have misunderstood or misinterpreted its norms as they apply to the study of persons. More likely is the possibility that we have not framed our questions and stated our problems in fruitful forms.

Before we can determine whether or not the scientific method can be applied to the study of people, we must examine what is meant by the term *scientific method*. It clearly does not point to a homogeneous entity. It has been used to refer to the basic axioms or assumptions of scientists, to ways of reasoning, to rules for evidence, to methods for observing and for collecting data, and other things. What appears to be common to the several natural sciences are the first three items in that list. Most practitioners in those fields appear to agree on certain basic axioms, such as the postulate of determinism (at least for most of the range of phenomena they investigate). They also agree that reasoning must be logical and internally consistent. They accept the norm that empirical evidence must be public, that observational data must be on the record, and that the methods for obtaining them must be stated in a fashion that permits other investigators, at least in principle, to replicate the empirical operations.

In contrast, each natural science makes observations by methods that are appropriate to the phenomena it studies. Most of these methods involve ways of recording physical properties of the objects under study. The particular instruments, of course, take quite different forms, from the radar telescope to the electron microscope, and from the spectroscope to the acoustical analyzer. But whatever the instrumentation for collecting data, it must be such that others can use the same devices or close copies of them and obtain highly congruent, if not essentially identical, observations. The instrumentation also must be selected for the problem at hand.

There is one critical difference between the behavioral sciences and the natural sciences. The natural sciences are concerned with two kinds of phenomena: properties and processes. On the one hand, these sciences observe and classify properties of objects. The specification of the objects studied includes identifying their locus in space. The assignment of an attribute to an object is made at an identified point in time. In many instances, the attribute is taken as a lasting property of the object. Implicitly or explicitly, however, the period of time during which that attribute characterizes the object is indicated. On the other hand, these sciences study processes. The investigator makes observations of changes occurring over time in a particular object or, more usually, in a particular system of objects. The critical feature is that his observations pertain to an ostensive system, one that can be pointed at. He identifies the spatial locus of the processes he is studying. He also specifies the times or at least the temporal sequence of his observations.

Most of the behavioral sciences are not concerned with the relatively enduring properties of objects. They do not study people's heights or the color of their eyes. For the most part, the behavioral sciences are concerned with behavioral processes. When the behavior is overt moving and speaking and is analyzed and classified in terms of its overt characteristics, the behavioral scientist proceeds in much the same manner as his colleague in the natural sciences. His observations pertain to objects—persons or parts of persons—that can be located in space and time: this person raised his hand; that person spoke the word *no*.

More typically in personality and related fields, however, the locus of the process is uncertain. When an observer makes an attribution about an observed segment of an actor's behavior, where is the attribute located? Many would argue that it is located in the physical movements of the actor. Insofar as the observation is a summarizing attribution, however, it cannot be precisely located. It is not tied to any particular movement or pattern of movement at a given moment, but rather to a pattern of actions extending over the duration of the behavior segment. Others would argue that the attribute is located in the perceptual-cognitive processes of the observer. But where are those located? The locus includes not only the observer's sensory receptors and pathways but also his central nervous system, particularly his brain. The process occurs somewhere within the black box.

A critical difference, then, between the study of physical objects and the study of human beings is the extent to which the phenomena being observed can be explicitly located in time and space (see Lachenmeyer, 1972, 1973). In the natural sciences, an observation can be specified in terms of the physical object or system about which it is made. The series of observations for a process are identified sequentially in time. Although it is true that parts of natural science have successfully studied the functioning of black boxes without being able to state exactly what was going on within the boxes, the boundaries of those boxes have been explicit.

In contrast, an observational datum in the behavioral sciences is typically taken as referring to a person over some segment of time. It is usually assigned to a total process occurring in time without specifying the system in any but the most general terms. Since it is difficult to locate the phenomena precisely, especially when the observational period is lengthy, we identify the phenomena with the person observed, and our interpretation of what we see becomes an attribution to the person, without restriction as to time or place.

Let us look at the question of method in terms of the investigator studying people, our pervasive concern in Part Two. Each investigator initiating a program of research in personality or a related field needs to identify her objective. She must spell out the world of phenomena she is trying to understand. (The term *world* is used here to indicate a domain of interest that is large but that is more readily conceived and comprehended than a universe.) Everything depends on that choice. The presumed nature of that world directs the investigator in her decisions about the methods she will use to investigate it and about the phenomena she will select for empirical examination. Her axioms and principles of scientific effort will, of course, be much the same as those of any other investigator; yet the manner in which she implements those guidelines may be specific to the world she seeks to understand.

She must identify that world of phenomena explicitly because of the peculiar nature of the phenomena in the disciplines concerned with human nature. The investigator in these disciplines brings to her scientific work a wealth of rough generalizations, efficient rules of thumb for interacting with other people, and various ideas about human nature. Ordinarily, the investigator's initial view of her target phenomena is derived primarily from her everyday experience. At the beginning, she is not trying to understand a body of observations systematically made by herself or by others in the role of researcher; instead, she is intrigued by her informal experience. But her initial view of the target phenomena is not just an amorphous mass of prior experiences. Since she is interested in those phenomena, she has already reflected about them. She has verbalized to herself or discussed with others her impressions about the world. She has applied lay concepts to the phenomena, so that she cannot claim to be starting with a completely open mind. She has tentative preconceptions. When she stops to delineate her target phenomena, she will be manifesting some of her preconceptions by her very choice of words for formulating her description.

In investigating personality, have we been looking at the right phenomena and asking the right questions? Gertrude Stein, on her deathbed, was asked: "What is the answer?" In reply, she asked: "What is the question?" A primary objective in science is formulating productive questions. Indeed, a major part of scientific progress has depended on asking the right question. If this proposition has been true for the natural sciences, it should hold for the behavioral sciences. "Why did I dream about sailing?" is not a scientific question. Science is concerned with the general, not the idiosyncratic. "Are dreams influenced by spirits?" is not amenable to scientific study until an adequate definition is given for the term *spirits* and an acceptable method for observing them is developed. "Are dreams influenced by experiences preceding sleep?" can be studied scientifically. But for an empirical investigation, the question must be qualified and restricted further. For example, the question might be stated in a more testable form as "Is the content of reported dreams related to the content of experiences in the two hours preceding falling asleep?" The scientific study of that question would of course require the investigator to develop methods of classifying the contents of dreams and of waking experience so that high levels of interobserver agreement could be obtained in coding them.

The game of science, however, is much more exciting than just trying to frame researchable questions. The challenge is to find the problem and to formulate the basic question that will open up new ways of construing and approaching the phenomena of interest. In a sense, the challenge is to decide which phenomena are those that must be understood if the science is to progress. It is not possible to state rules for finding problems that will revolutionize a field. In any area there are few scientists who make such contributions, and each of them has his own style. Perhaps the most that any scientist can do is to maintain a set toward problem finding (Getzels, 1964) and to persist in being discovery-oriented (Getzels, 1964; Getzels and Csikszentmi-halyi, 1976). Although the work of a scientist in the context of justifi-cation (Reichenbach, 1938) must be public and consensual, the activ-ity of a scientist in the context of discovery is personal, even idiosyncratic, and perhaps unfathomable. Only the products of that activity must be shared and understood by others.

Generalizing Beyond Empirical Observations

In personality and related fields, both investigators and theor-ists generalize very casually from the findings based on a set of obser-vations to some unspecified world of behavioral phenomena. Such inductive leaps are made in spite of the prevalence, if not universality, of our experience showing that these generalizations hold only to some much attenuated degree, if at all. Sometimes a finding is not reproduced when another study draws a second sample of persons from what is apparently the same population. More typically, another investigator doing his own research modifies one or more aspects of the original study and then cannot be certain whether his failure to obtain the same results stemmed from his different sample of persons, his particular execution of the experimental plan, or his modifications of that plan. As a consequence, we have achieved no established generalizations. Any general statements on which most workers would agree would have to be worded in very loose terms and could have no boundary conditions specified for them.

Within the broad concept of generalizability, then, one par-ticular type is the reproducibility of empirical findings—the extent to which the results from one study reproduce those from another, inde-pendent investigation. At a lower level of abstraction is replication of particular observations. Attributional judgments can be seen as restricting generalizability because findings derived from that kind of datum are not exactly reproducible. Attributional judgments are individualistic and particularistic. They have limited replicability over observers and even limited replicability from time to time in suc-cessive judgments of each particular observer. Hence, an investigator using them cannot generalize his findings with much confidence. As the research literature shows, the likelihood of his obtaining highly congruent findings in a subsequent repetition of his research study is low. The findings may be somewhat similar, but similarity of findings is not sufficient to establish any general conclusion except in very loose form, such as "under certain conditions, X tends to be related to Y."

We are also unable to generalize across methods for obtaining observations (Fiske, 1971, 1973). When two instruments for assessing the same concept are used, the findings from one do not agree closely with those from the other. Hence, even our loose general statements must ordinarily be qualified by specification of the measuring procedure, such as "X as measured by procedure x' tends to be related to Y as measured by y'."

Generalizability involves more than replicability of observations made about the same set of phenomena and reproducibility of findings on parallel sets of phenomena. In most scientific work, the investigator wants to generalize from the results of his study to some much larger set of objects or events. Since his study examines only a sample from the population, the confidence with which he can generalize to the population depends on the representativeness of his sample. The most common concern is about the adequacy of sampling persons. Given a population of people in which the investigator is interested, how representative is his sample of persons? Technical developments in sampling theory and practice have produced ways of obtaining highly representative samples of people. The excellence of sampling in survey research is well established.

The notion of representativeness of sampling is very difficult to apply in the behavioral sciences. Precise sampling requires an explicit statement of the characteristics delineating the population to be sampled. In our present state of knowledge, we are ordinarily unable to state the characteristics pertinent to our research problem. This handicap applies not only to most sampling of persons but also to other aspects of investigations. Even if we are able to sample *actors* (borrowing that useful term from Runkel and McGrath, 1972), we cannot specify the population of their behaviors that we would like to sample. To spell out the population of behaviors, we would have to specify the conditions within which those behaviors might occur: the physical setting, the other persons present, and perhaps the basis for their being there.

There is an additional consideration. Suppose we could state in words the particular features of some population of behaviors. We still could not possibly sample it in a representative fashion. Such sampling requires a listing of the population, a clearly impossible task. Just as the sampling of the national population of persons is based on the census, so a sampling of behaviors would have to be derived from a listing of all relevant behaviors, together with specifications of the conditions surrounding them. At the present time, we are quite unable to do so. We should, however, proceed as far as we can toward the delineation of any population in which we are interested. Such specification would give investigators a more exact description of what they are studying and would give readers of research reports a more specific definition of the domain to which findings apply.

For our purposes, the population of central interest is the population of observations. This population is delineated by a set of features pertaining to the actors, to the behaviors to be observed, to the conditions under which the observations are made, to the observers, and to the observers' processes in making the observations. Although the adequacy of a sample from some population of observations cannot be defended by spelling out the procedures for identifying the sample, as it can in survey research, an estimate of the representativeness of our sample can be made. The empirical test of representativeness is the degree to which the statistics from our study can be reproduced in subsequent studies of samples obtained from presumably the same population. Unfortunately, that criterion is rather vague: to decide whether the samples in several studies were drawn from the same population of observations, what norm should the investigator use in evaluating the congruence among their statistical findings?

Finally, the degree of representativeness of the sample and the consequent confidence in generalization depend on another factor, the heterogeneity of the population. Strictly speaking, the heterogeneity of population should not be a matter of concern. Formal sampling theory takes it into account with little difficulty. For any one characteristic, the variation in the sample can be used to estimate the variation in the population from which it was drawn. The more heterogeneous that population, however, the larger the expected departure of the sample mean from the population mean.

The behavioral sciences face three serious problems: the qualitative heterogeneity of the population of actors, stimuli, and conditions; the difficulty encountered in identifying the pertinent characteristics of each population; and the consequent difficulties encountered in sampling representatively and in determining the degree and types of bias. The pessimistic view of social science presented by Cronbach (1975) appears to be derived in large part from the difficulties observed in obtaining reproducible findings, presumably because he considers a highly complex population of observations. All of its pertinent characteristics cannot be identified or at least cannot be handled within any feasible research plan.

In our contemporary state of limited scientific knowledge about behavior, it would appear that the more components of the population of observations we can identify (at least analytically), the less congruence we should expect between findings from separate investigations. We must take into account not only observable components but also assumed components. For example, although we cannot directly observe the cognitive processes of our observers, we have reason to believe that such processes are themselves highly complex and heterogeneous.

Generalizability is not viewed here as a dichotomous variable. Just as there are degrees to which one set of observations replicates another set, and just as there is variation in the extent to which one set of findings reproduces those from another sample of the same population, so generalizability is a matter of degree. The underlying variable is really the confidence with which the investigator states a conclusion applied to the population of interest, or his level of subjective probability that the conclusion is correct.

Our discussion thus far has emphasized a restricted kind of generalizability, the probability that the empirical finding obtained in a research study applies to the population of observations that is of interest to the investigator. Given R—the observed magnitude of the relationship between measure x' and measure y'—how confidently can the investigator generalize that finding and assert that the relationship between x' and y' in the population is essentially of that magnitude? But generalizability also refers to the confidence to be placed in an inference from sample findings to a loosely conceived universe. For example, the investigator obviously wants to generalize her empirical finding about her measures of x' and y' to the conclusion that X and Y, the concepts represented by those measures, are related to the degree R. Such an inference must assume that the concepts are fully indexed by those measures (a clearly untenable assumption, since it is contrary to fact in most instances) and that the array of scores for each measuring procedure reflects the postulated true scores on that concept so closely that the particular measure of relationship would yield the value R if applied to those true scores.

Returning again to the personality investigator, we find that generalizability is pertinent to a fundamental dilemma confronting her. She must decide either to select her problem first and then seek the best information obtainable to throw light on that problem or to set her norms for the kind of work she will do and then determine her problem within the possibilities permitted by those standards. The first alternative will be chosen by the investigator who believes that her problem area is of such basic significance that she must attack it by whatever methods are available or can be devised. Even though ideal data and elegant research designs cannot be used, she will do the best she can with fallible data and imperfect designs. And she will accept the fact that all of her generalizations must be tenuous and uncertain. The second alternative will be chosen by the investigator who is convinced that she must meet some basic standards if her research is to contribute to progress toward a scientific understanding of human behavior. By meeting those standards, she can ordinarily have some confidence in her generalizations.

The presentation of this dilemma should not be taken too literally. Few scientists actually formulate explicit norms for their research activity and then look for a problem that does not violate them. An investigator may, however, become interested in a problem and try to devise ways of studying it empirically. After some thought, she may conclude that, for that problem, there is no research design with a good likelihood of yielding dependable findings. She may then seek to reformulate the problem or turn to a problem more amenable to sound research planning.

A statement of preference may be in order here. Of the two approaches, I prefer the second alternative. I have worked, at times, on what I felt were highly significant problems that could not be studied by elegant methods, and I certainly intend to do so again when the occasion arises. But when I follow my personal inclinations, I shall choose the second alternative because I am convinced that an essential quality for a science is consensus on the fundamental observations from which it is constructed and on the explicit definitions for the major, established constructs. When constructs and observations are firmly linked, there can also be consensus on some established relationships between the constructs. I do not see this norm as requiring that investigators commit themselves to working in just one direction, either from the level of observations toward the development of constructs or from the level of constructs and their postulated interrelationships toward their empirical testing. Each investigator can and will proceed according to his own style. The starting point is not crucial scientifically, although it may affect the investigator's cognitive processes. Essential for effective work, however, is a continuing interplay between constructs and observations. Observations must be guided by constructs, and constructs must be refined, modified, or discarded in the light of observational data.

Within the norm of consensus, we can seek to identify regularities and to determine the range of phenomena to which they apply. It is obvious that any regularity—any relationship between two constructs or between two sets of measurements—should be expected to hold only under certain conditions. A major part of the scientific enterprise is the determination of those conditions for each identified regularity.

The requirement of a high level of consensus is restrictive. In the past, much work in personality has not been able to meet this standard. I grant that this requirement may make it impossible to investigate scientifically many problems that are of great inherent interest to people. But the richness of human life may never be understood by scientific investigation. In a thoughtful discussion of this matter, Kelman writes about "the inevitable tension between the scientific study of man and humanistic values" (1968, p. 109). Much of my private experience, much that goes on within my mind without any direct manifestation in my verbal or physical behavior, cannot be observed by any other person, let alone by two or more other persons whose observations can be compared. Topics that cannot be studied within the scope provided by the norm of close consensus must be left for other disciplines that are interested in the way that particular individuals have construed their experience, individuals who have offered conceptualizations that others can share to a limited extent. For centuries, brillant minds have worked within these disciplines. The products of their thinking are a kind of knowledge that, although it has enriched our lives, is not the corpus of a science.

The Basic Decisions

In the orientation developed in this section for investigators in personality and related fields, each investigator makes several decisions concerning the kind of problem he will attack, the kind of phenomena he will study, the kind of data he will utilize, and the kind of setting in which he will collect his data. As in the points of decision analyzed by Runkel and McGrath (1972) in their examination of the research process in studies of human behavior, there are no correct choices. Each of the alternatives has its advantages and its disadvantages.

The several decisions are presented separately, for clarity of exposition. They are, however, interrelated in some instances, one choice typically being associated with a particular alternative for another decision. Moreover, one choice may restrict the possible choices for some other decisions, as discussed in the next chapter. The proposed orientation is essentially methodological. By his several decisions, the investigator determines the way in which he will do his scientific work. Taken together, his choices constitute his strategy, and that strategy limits the range of problems on which he can work. This restriction, however, applies more to the formulation of the problem than to the problem itself. A problem can be viewed in different ways and can be attacked by different strategies. The investigator's strategy will require him to construe his problem in a manner that conforms to his several decisions.

The investigator who first identifies his problem area and then delineates a particular question as the focus for his work will usually find that he too has implicitly limited the possible ways in which he can seek an empirical answer to his question. For example, the investigator may want to determine the value of a certain psychotherapeutic treatment and may decide to ask whether it relieves personal distress. If he means this question to refer to the inner experience of clients, he has restricted himself to assessing the clients' expressions of distress. But what is an expression of distress? Some observer must make the interpretation that certain utterances indicate distress and others do not. At the least, some one must decide that certain client responses to multiple-choice alternatives provide a basis for inferring distress.

Ordinarily, the several fundamental choices are not deliberated, and each decision is not made explicitly. The implicit decisions are often determined by the investigator's interests and values, with minimal reflection on the rejected alternatives. An investigator who is entering one of these fields of study, however, may find it valuable to think about the choices available to him. All too often, an investigator becomes committed to one particular strategy for fortuitous or pragmatic reasons. Often, he pursues the strategy in which he happened to receive his training in graduate school.

Dissatisfied with the research approach they have been following, some experienced investigators may be ready to consider a different strategy. Most established investigators, however, will persist in working on their old problem by their chosen methods. For them, the following discussion may be useful in helping them to gain some perspective on their own styles, preferences, and methods. They can see which of the conceptualized strategies they have been following and may recognize the preconceptions that they have brought to their observing and construing.

The delineation of decisions made by investigators may also be of value for readers of research reports. By identifying the choices made implicitly or explicitly by the author of the report, a reader can make guesses about the author's orientation and about the preconceptions and values that may have influenced the way in which she went about the investigation. The reader may then be led to opinions about the soundness of the author's interpretations and conclusions.

The decisions are grouped here by topic. For each decision, two or more questions are posed and contrasted. The investigator makes a choice by assenting to one question or another.

The Kind of Problem

Decision 1: "What kind of problem am I trying to solve?"

1a: "Shall I try to solve a problem presented to me by the society in which I live?" The investigator in personality or a related field can decide to tackle a problem directly pertinent to her society, such as a problem concerning human welfare confronting her and her fellow-citizens. It may deal with the adjustment or psychopathology of people; the fit between an individual and an institution (a school or a business); or the fit between the individual and the social system, as in delinquency and criminology. A prime example is the problem of optimal psychological treatment for those with personal difficulties. Another example is the evaluation of a social program.

The problem need not be explicitly presented by society; the phrasing is figurative, not literal. Such a problem might be handed to the investigator by society, but more generally it is simply a problem with which society is concerned. The identifying feature of this kind of problem is a focus on the whole person as he is seen and described by others. As noted earlier, these attributional evaluations are ordinarily made about people without restriction to a given time or place. Most of personality theory, normal and abnormal, has this focus.

1b: "Shall I work on a problem that I identify, seeing it as critical to gaining an understanding of human behavior and functioning?" The investigator can select or invent her own topic and problem within the study of human behavior. She may select the problem because she sees it as relevant to her theory or to someone else's. She may simply dig into an area that intrigues her, applying some procedure for observing and collecting data.

A reader may feel that he could answer yes to both of these questions. He can be interested ultimately in contributing to the solution of a societal problem even though the phenomena he is studying do not pertain to the person as a whole or to judgments about persons or categories of persons. If so, he has selected his own problem. In Decision 1, the distinction involves the directness of the attack on the societal problem.

A societal problem, since it is stated in society's terms, must be investigated by means of societal concepts. Because these lay concepts are broad and can be applied only by making attributional judgments, the basic observational data will show limited agreement between observers and limited replication of observations over observers. Hence, the obtained sample of observations will have restricted representativeness. It cannot be taken as a dependable sample drawn from a well-defined population. As a consequence, any empirical finding will not be reproduced exactly, and it can only be generalized with very limited confidence.

The investigator choosing her own problem does not face these inherent restrictions. The extent to which her observations are replicable, her samples are representative, and her findings are reproducible will depend on the particular problem she selects and on the methods by which she attacks it. In principle, the range on each of these properties is great, extending from the limited scope that hampers her colleague working on a societal problem to however broad a scope is possible within the study of human behavior (a factor we do not yet know).

Most investigators will be able to determine fairly easily which kind of problem they are investigating. They can usually trace the way they came to their problem. Someone else looking at the research operations of an investigator, however, may not be able to make that identification. In some instances, for example, the kind of procedure and the type of data would seem to indicate the choice of a societal problem (such as research involving opinions about mental illness), even though the investigator had formulated her research questions and had drawn her conclusions in terms of some problem of her own devising. In such a case, the use of opinions and even attributional judgments may simply have been the best available means she could find to throw light on that problem.

The Kind of Phenomena

The term *phenomena* refers to the raw material to be studied, that about which the investigator is thinking as he selects his problem and begins to plan his attack on it. At first, he may well perceive this material in a naive, intuitive way; later, he will usually move toward a more explicit verbal formulation of the matter on which he focuses. *Phenomena* refers to the material studied before any systematic analysis, labeling, or construing takes place. Such phenomena can be taken as occurring in the world at large.

Decision 2: "In what population of actors am I interested?" Some actors must generate the phenomena of concern to the investigator. The investigator must consider the specifications of his population of actors. Are they all human beings, just those from a particular culture, or those from a restricted subculture within that culture (such as Americans who are living outside of institutions)? What age groups are in his population? Is he interested only in mature adults, or does he wish to include youths and adolescents? Is he concerned with both women and men? Once the investigator has decided on his population of actors and has specified the characteristics of that population, the familiar considerations about sampling of persons can be applied. The generalizability of his findings will be in part a function of whatever representativeness is obtained by his procedures for sampling that population.

Decision 3: "What behavior of these actors shall I study?" Any one investigator is interested only in part of what people do. More generally but somewhat more accurately, he decides what part of their functioning is of concern to him. The essence of behavioral science is the study of behaving, of adapting and maladapting, of moving and speaking. Behaving can be analyzed and construed in many ways. For the purposes of this discussion, there are two main classes.

3a: "Shall I study expressions about people?" These are, implicitly or explicitly, attributions that result from the observer's internal perceptual-cognitive processes.

3b: "Shall I study moving and speaking, as in motor acts and vocal acts?" Vocal acts are of course motor acts, but their importance in behavior requires designating them as a separate class because they are perceived as differing from other psychomotor activity. Vocal acts are treated here as acts, usually without considering the words uttered or their meanings.

This distinction is made from an external viewpoint, involving the orientation of the person who is making the classification. It is essentially the contrast between interpretive judgments and simple observations examined earlier. Although that choice determines the task of the observer and the processes he uses in making an observation (Decision 6, to follow), we are concerned here with the orientation of the investigator as he considers the phenomena he will study.

The phenomena in the first alternative are verbalizations that people make about people. They include direct attributions and statements that suggest or imply the speaker's construal of a person. Often we sense or interpret an evaluative aspect in that construal.

Expressions about people are drawn from a very heterogeneous world. As a consequence, any sampling from it is bound to have much variation between samples, and the degree of representativeness will be hard to estimate adequately. Hence, any generalization of findings must be tenuous.

The clearest examples of acts can be found in the work of some ethologists studying birds, animals, and persons. These acts are the immediately perceptible actions of an organism. Essentially of the same kind are the acts that constitute the phenomena for most research related to behavior theory or to nonverbal communication. The observations of acts have proved to be highly replicable over observers. Although there are sampling matters to be considered, the pertinent population of acts can ordinarily be specified so that the degree of representativeness can be determined. Given these conditions, generalizability should be rather high. In fact, some investigators, such as Eibl-Eibesfeldt (1972), seem to be finding generalizability even across cultures.

Although these two classes are of central importance in the study of personality, they do not by any means cover the whole range of relevant phenomena. Additional classes include verbalizations about things and verbalizations expressing the speaker's feelings and other inner experience. The emphasis on verbal productions indicates the central position, in personality research, of communication. Interpersonal behavior is a prime focus of personality.

But what about the inner psychological processes in people? Why are no classes of phenomena identified for intentions, emotions, hopes, and fantasies or for needs, attitudes, values, traits, defenses, and controls? There are no categories for these technical or common-language terms because they are construals about observations. They are expressions about people. Each attribution of a property to a person is a bit of observer behavior, a product of the complex interaction in which an observer perceives some actions of an actor and proceeds to cognize and interpret it in a particular way. All of the internal processes discussed in personality theorizing are conceptualizations constructed by the observer's processes. Although we do not usually consider a theorist to be an observer, his conceptual statements can be included in the category of expressions about people.

The Kind of Observational Data

Once the investigator has decided on the kind of problem and the kind of phenomena, she must decide the kind of observational data she will obtain. The phenomena she studies must be experienced by someone. Who will observe them and how will he observe?

Decision 4: "What type of person will my observer be?"

4a: "Shall I use a professional observer?" Some kinds of observations require an observer with extensive experience and training.

4b: "Shall I use a person observing himself as actor?" This is probably the most common choice in personality research today. In self-report procedures, the roles of observer and actor are played by the same individual, who observes by looking within and attending to his feelings or his impressions of his prior experiences.

4c: "Shall I use a lay person?" For many problems, the observer can be almost anyone who has been motivated to carry out the observational task. We can consider a lay observer to be a person who has had no extensive prior training or experience in the role of observer. The category includes observers who are instructed on the spot, in a minute or two, as well as persons who are trained for perhaps an hour or more for the particular observational task.

When using professional observers, the investigator needs to consider the population from which they are drawn. What qualifications of training and experience characterize that population? Furthermore, are there particular specifications regarding theoretical orientation that must be stated? A psychoanalytically oriented investigator would rarely want to use observers who adhered to behavior theory.

In self-report procedures, where each person is observing himself, the population of pertinent observers consists of just one person, the subject describing himself. No other observer can make that kind of report about the subject. The only kind of replication of observations that is pertinent in this instance is the repetition of the same self-report procedure at another time.

When the investigator uses lay observers, she is sampling from a very large population of observers. Her sample is usually a sample of convenience, a group of students who are available for part-time work. The implicit population consists of adults who are at least reasonably well motivated to execute their observational task carefully, who are of average intelligence or better, and who have no serious sensory handicaps. Investigators rarely use observers who are not part of the academic community, so that there is little or no evidence on the generalizability of observations from their sample. The investigator should, nevertheless, be able to generalize to the total population of possible observers.

Decision 5: "Which set of persons am I studying?"

5a: "Am I interested primarily in the behavior of my observers?" The answer is affirmative when studying the process of observing and the differences between observers, with little or no concern about the particular actors they happen to observe. For example, the investigator may be studying the process of attributing. Paradigms for the steps involved in studying attributive processes are discussed in Chapter Eleven. At this point, it is only necessary to indicate that in some strategies, the investigator has observers judging actors in order to study judging, so that in fact the investigator is observing those who are designated as observers. Since the investigator who is studying judging and attributing is studying his observers, he must determine the population from which they are drawn and the representativeness of his sample. His observers are really his subjects, so that the usual considerations of subject sampling apply.

5b: "Am I interested primarily in the behavior of the actors who are being observed by my observers?" This is the usual case. When the investigator is interested in the behaviors of the actors who are being observed, no problems of representativeness and generalizability are added to those noted in connection with decisions discussed above.

Decision 6: "What processes does my observational task require?"

6a: "Am I seeking judgmental data that require interpretation and inference on the part of my observers?"

6b: "Am I seeking simple, observational data that my observers can produce by perceptual-cognitive processes involving recognition and identification, with little if any inference?"

The distinction is in terms of the kinds of cognitive processes that, the investigator presumes, occur in his observers as they go about their task. He cannot, of course, examine those processes directly. In determining which type of process predominates, he can make his own observations and introspect to try to identify his cognitive process, or he can ask observers to report their recollections about their processes. He can also ignore the whole question and simply concern himself with determining the degree of agreement among his observers. Is it sufficiently high that his observers are essentially interchangeable, or is it only moderate because each observer is, in some fashion, contributing variance to his set of observations? In the subsequent discussion, we shall assume that the investigator making Choice 6b does have interchangeable observers.

It seems obvious that the simpler the psychological processes involved in the observational task, the higher the degree of obtained replication of observations over observers. In addition, when these processes involve recognition and identification, each observer can readily check each of his own observations, going through the same process again before reporting his cognitive product; he has a fairly clear criterion against which to compare his observation. When the observer is interpreting or inferring, however, he is less likely to review his processing, in part at least because it is more complex and takes longer to do so.

If observers undertake the same observational task with the same phenomena at a different time, an observer whose task is recognition or identification will be much more likely to replicate his own observations than will one making interpretations or inferences. This within-observer dependability is a major factor in the higher degree of replicability over observers who are carrying out the simpler observational task.

Common to simple observing and interpretive judging is the fact that neither can be taken as a sample of any population other than one of similar processes in research observers. Although each kind of process resembles cognitive functions used commonly in everyday life, its application in the research setting is best viewed as a special case. Its representativeness with respect to any population of processes cannot readily be determined empirically. In addition, these two processes do have common aspects. Each involves observing in the broad sense of attending to what is going on; each also involves cognizing the observed behavior and giving a label to it.

Decision 7: "What further choices shall I make about the kind of observational data?"

Several other decisions are made implicitly or explicitly. These need not be discussed since they have been examined in different contexts earlier in this volume. Drawing on Table 1 (Chapter Four), we can see choices concerning the unit of observation, the variable to be coded, the unit of measurement, and the identification given to the unit of measurement. Of central significance is the length of the behavioral segment used for each unit of observation. Is it very brief (on the order of a second), or is it extended (anywhere from several seconds through minutes to hours or more)?

The Conditions Under Which the Phenomena Will Be Experienced by Observers

This topic includes many features of the investigator's research plan, only three of these being stated here as explicit decisions.

Decision 8: "Will my observers be aware of their research participation?"

8a: "Shall I use observers who did not know that their reports would be used later for research purposes?" Such observers have made their reports for other reasons. They may have graded students; they may have rated job performance for administrative purposes. These reports affect, or could affect, the lives of the actors observed. Knowing about any potential consequences will usually have more influence on the observers than knowing that their observations will be used in research.

8b: "Shall I use observers who know that they are making reports for research purposes?" Such observers include the usual observers in a laboratory, observers of actors in ordinary situations (children in a playground, for instance), and all persons responding to self-report instruments.

At first thought, it may seem preferable to use observers who are not aware that their observations will be used for research purposes. Just as actors react to being observed, so observers react to knowing that their reports will be studied and used. Hence, just as unobtrusive measurement (Webb, Campbell, Schwartz, and Sechrest, 1966) avoids actors' reactions, so unobtrusive use of observations avoids observers' reactions. And certainly it seems true that the use of observers who are not aware of their research participation yields broader representativeness of their observations, since the observations can be taken as drawn from some large natural population.

But just what is that population of observations? Can reports made for one real-life purpose be grouped with those made for a different purpose? In fact, the population can be described only in very general terms. The conditions for these natural observations are very heterogeneous. Even for student grades, we can have little assurance that different teachers are making their judgments under the same conditions or with the same criteria. In fact, it is likely that the basis for one teacher's judgments differs from student to student. Thus, in the everyday world, there are many unknown and unknowable influences affecting any set of archival reports. Moreover, the use of past records may involve problems regarding confidentiality and the right to privacy.

When the observers know that their reports will be used for research purposes, and especially when they make their reports in accord with the investigator's instructions, we can reasonably expect greater replication across observers and higher reproducibility of findings. The observer population being sampled seems more homogeneous. Hence, it is likely that greater generalizability can be associated with the use of aware observers, especially when the observational task requires little training.

Decision 9: "Will the actors be aware of their involvement in my research?"

9a: "Shall I allow the persons observed, the actors, to know that they are being observed for the purposes of my research?" The answer has to be in the affirmative in most cases in which the investigator selects the exact setting and the specific stimuli preceding the behavior to be observed, as in observations in a laboratory or testing room, where the investigator can prevent the occurrence of the most unwanted stimuli. Under these conditions, he will ordinarily produce the behavior he wishes to observe by instructing the person to attend to his stimuli and to respond as he specifies or by presenting strong stimuli to which the person is bound to react.

9b: "Shall I not allow the observed persons to know that they are being observed for the purposes of my research?'' The exceptional cases in which the investigator can manipulate stimuli without the subjects' awareness that research is under way include such deceptions as observing people in a waiting room before they are called to serve as research subjects or observing in a field experiment, as in studies of bystanders' reactions. The actors are also ignorant when observers are asked to rate people whom they know but who are not present.

Keeping the actors unaware that they are being observed is certainly the ideal condition from the investigator's perspective. That condition, however, raises serious ethical questions, along with questions about informed consent and invasion of privacy. Although they cannot be examined here, there are socially acceptable possibilities for observing people in public places where the individuals are not identified in the records and where there is no possible risk of their being embarrassed or even that anyone who knows them will see the observations.

When actors are aware that they are being observed, that awareness can be a major influence on their behavior. Consequently, data collected under this condition are restricted and cannot be assumed to be representative of any population of observations where this qualification is absent. The investigator using aware subjects must consider whether this potential influence does affect his results. Since awareness does not have uniform effects on all subjects, the population of observations about aware subjects is likely to be heterogeneous. It is clear that, in the absence of empirical evidence on the matter, confident generalizations cannot be made from aware subjects to unaware people.

Decision 10: ''What will be the source of the stimuli experienced by my actors?''

10a: ''Shall I manipulate the stimuli preceding the behavior being observed?'' Such control and manipulation are central features of the classical psychological experiment. If the investigator provides standard stimuli, she can compare the responses made to each of them.

10b: ''Shall I study naturally occurring stimuli?'' Pursuing this tactic, the investigator records certain behaviors and then determines what the immediately preceding conditions were—what environmental events and what other actions occurred shortly before the acts selected for study? This is the tactic used by Duncan and Fiske (1977) in their study of *Face-to-Face Interaction.*

In principle, the degree to which observers agree should not be a function of the choice between manipulated and naturally occurring stimuli, especially when the behaviors have been recorded and the observers are simply observing the replay of the recording. With manipulated stimuli, to be sure, the temporal locus of the behavioral response to be observed is more apparent, and the observers' typical task is to decide which of several alternative response categories is manifested. In some cases, this task may be easier than scanning an ongoing recording for every instance of a particular action category.

The manipulation of stimuli permits the investigator to provide precisely the same physical stimuli to one actor on several occasions and to any actor on any occasion. Hence, we expect greater reproducibility of behaviors than when the stimuli are natural ones and the identical physical stimulus is less likely to recur. With the greater control of stimuli, the investigator does anticipate greater reproducibility of findings. The investigator can ensure that the stimuli she uses are a highly representative sample of some well-specified population of stimuli. For example, she can carefully stratify her experimental stimuli along one or more continua. What she loses, however, is representativeness of stimuli as they occur in the natural universe (Brunswik, 1956). This is the classical trade-off between the experiment and the field study. The representativeness of the stimuli is important insofar as it affects the representativeness of the behavior being studied and the observations of that behavior. Generalization from reactions to a restricted sample of stimuli to reactions occurring in the natural world is highly problematic and must be defended in each instance.

There are cases where stimuli are manipulated within a natural setting, as in recent social psychological experiments on the bystander. More commonly, stimuli are manipulated in a research setting that is not representative of the population of settings within which behavior occurs in nature. Hence, the use of manipulated stimuli tends to be associated with conditions from which generalization to everyday behavior is difficult to justify. This whole set of issues has been extensively considered by Aronson and Carlsmith (1968). More recently, Tunnell (1977) has identified three dimensions in the

naturalness characterizing field research: behavior, setting, and treatment. Decision 10 pertains to treatment—would the environmental
event have occurred without the investigator's presence? The awareness of research participation (Decision 9) is a consequence of being
in a setting to which the actor is not naturally exposed. As pointed out
earlier, in Proposition 2a (Chapter One) and elsewhere, the behavior
elicited in research on personality and some other topics is generally
not part of the actors' natural responses.

This discussion about the source of the stimuli should make
evident the fact that these decisions are made by all investigators
working within the personality domain or a related area. The investigator performing experiments in his laboratory makes these decisions
just like his colleague studying individual differences, although some
of the alternatives chosen by the experimenter are different from
those selected by his colleague.

The preceding list of decisions and choices has presented the
choices as starkly contrasted with each other. Are the choices mutually exclusive? Are they exhaustive categories or is there a middle
ground between them? Some choices actually made by investigators
can be construed as involving each of the contrasted choices to at
least a minimal degree. For example, in considering the kind of problem, there are instances that do not fall neatly within just one category. Although the study of pathological processes generated for
research purposes and other work in experimental psychopathology
can be recognized as derived from society's concern for personal
adjustment (Choice 1a), research of this kind deals with problems
identified by investigators from their conceptualizations of the topic.
Research on attributional processes may be seeking to determine how
descriptive judgments are influenced by the evaluative appraisals so
prevalent in societal problems.

It is also evident that no sharp line can be drawn between recognition and identification processes and interpretive processes in the
observer (Decision 6). The observer is typically given a concept, in
technical terms or in everyday language, that he is to apply to the
observed behavior. That concept can vary in concreteness and abstraction from "moves hand" to "threatens" to "acts aggressively." Similarly, the manipulation of stimuli (Decision 10) can vary from none at
all to the introduction of strongly stressful stimuli. More generally,

control of the observational conditions is absent in studying archival data, limited in selecting natural situations in which to observe actors, strong in most laboratory work, and especially strong in studies of sensory restriction.

Any choice falling between the two specified extremes involves a decision concerning the extent to which the investigator is willing to accept some pertinent restriction. In each instance, of course, he gains something in return for what he gives up. Some would say that the decisions involve choices of values. Runkel and McGrath (1972, p. 115) suggest that realism, precision, and generality cannot be maximized simultaneously.

Although the relative rather than categorical nature of these choices must be granted, we will, for ease of discussion, consider each decision as dichotomous. It is more convenient to talk about a particular strategy as defined by the set of choices from opposing categories, one choice for each decision. In spite of this oversimplification, the points made about a given strategy should hold for another approach characterized by a set of choices falling toward the same end of the decision continuum.

The strategy formed by the investigator's several choices is not a research design but rather a delineation of the kind of research he will do and a circumscription of the content of the phenomena that interest him and of the kind of observations and data that he will use. A full research plan requires many more decisions, some identifying more specifically the content of the choices indicated above, and some dealing with matters not considered here, such as the compiling and statistical analysis of the data. In the present context, the term *strategy* refers to general orientation and manner of proceeding, not to the complete set of particular tactics followed in a single research study.

All the decisions and their associated choices are brought together in Table 2 for easy reference. The reader will recognize that I have ordered the alternative choices for each decision in terms of my interpretation of their desirability: I see the ideal strategy for psychological research as including Choices 1b, 3b, 4c, 5b, 6b, 8b, 9b, and 10b. The rationale for this preference is simply the greater expected degree of generalizability associated with these choices. I readily grant the tremendous practical difficulties, if not the impossibility, of fully implementing this ideal.

Illustrations of the Decisions in Three Studies

To make these construed decisions more concrete, we can examine the choices made in three investigations. In the Psychotherapy Change Project, Cartwright, Kirtner, and Fiske (1963) set out to study the structure of psychotherapeutic change. Our basic plan consisted of administering a set of procedures to clients before and after a course of counseling, deriving a score on each measure for the change between the two testings, and factor-analyzing these scores. The problem was societal (Choice 1a). We wanted to know just what were the basic changes associated with psychotherapy, as part of a concern for understanding the therapeutic process. In the original conception, the population of actors (Decision 2) was clients coming for treatment. Later, as we learned about method factors and as we studied the data, the actors became the people making the judgments about the clients—the therapists, the diagnosticians, and the clients themselves.

The behaviors selected for study were expressions about people (Choice 3a), that is, about the clients. We analyzed both the expressions that clients made about themselves and expressions that others made about them. The observers (Decision 4) included both professionals and self-observers. We started to study clients as actors (Choice 5b). As the study developed, the observers themselves became our actors, since we turned to studying their judgmental behaviors. All data required interpretation and inference (6a) except the clerical determination of length of therapy. Both observers and actors were aware of their research participation (8b and 9a). In the original conception, the stimuli encountered by the actors (the clients) were naturally occurring ones (10b). As the study was ultimately construed, however, the data were viewed as the observers' behaviors in response to the items in the several instruments (10a).

When we originally decided to study psychotherapeutic change, we felt we had no alternative to most of the choices we made. We took it for granted that attributional judgments were required. Both ethics and the nature of our problem made it necessary for observers and actors to know that they were participating in the research. We did not give any serious consideration to identifying potential measures of change that could be obtained without inter-

Table 2. The Basic Decisions.

Topic	Decision	Choices
A. The kind of problem	1: What kind of problem am I trying to solve?	1a: Shall I try to solve a problem presented to me by the society in which I live? 1b: Shall I work on a problem that I identify, seeing it as critical to gaining an understanding of human behavior and functioning?
B. The kind of phenomena	2: In what population of actors am I interested?	
	3: What behavior of these actors shall I study?	3a: Shall I study expressions about people? 3b: Shall I study moving and speaking, as in motor acts and vocal acts?
C. The kind of observational data	4: What type of person will my observer be?	4a: Shall I use a professional observer? 4b: Shall I use a person observing himself as actor? 4c: Shall I use a lay observer?
	5: What set of persons am I studying?	5a: Am I interested primarily in the behavior of my observers? 5b: Am I interested primarily in the behavior of the actors who are being observed by my observers?
	6: What processes does my observational task require?	6a: Am I seeking judgmental data that require interpretation and inference on the part of my observers?

6b: Am I seeking simple observational data that my observers can produce by perceptual-cognitive processes involving recognition and identification, with little if any inference?

7: What further choices shall I make about the kind of observational data?

8: Will my observers be aware of their research participation?

8a: Shall I use observers who did not know that their reports would be used later for research purposes?

8b: Shall I use observers who know they are making reports for research purposes?

9: Will the actors be aware of their involvement in my research?

9a: Shall I allow the persons observed, the actors, to know that they are being observed for the purposes of my research?

9b: Shall I not allow the observed persons to know that they are being observed for the purposes of my research?

10: What will be the source of the stimuli experienced by my actors?

10a: Shall I manipulate the stimuli preceding the behavior being observed?

10b: Shall I study naturally occurring stimuli?

D. The conditions under which the phenomena will be experienced by observers pretive and inferential judgments. Since our resources were limited, we decided to omit the use of lay observers, of such significant others as spouses or peers.

In another research program, a pilot study explored the relationship between scores for acts in a brief interaction with a stranger, before a video camera, and attributions made by an observer watching the videotape. More favorable attributions seemed to be made about actors with higher scores on a variety of acts, including nods, smiles, laughs, gazes, leg movements, and gestures. The investigator (Shrout, 1976) then planned and executed a systematic study, varying the sex of the observer and the sex of the actor.

The problem was identified by the investigator (1b) as relevant to understanding factors associated with attributions. The population (Decision 2) was in part selected for convenience. The actors were graduate students in professional schools who had been videotaped for another study (Beekman, 1973; Duncan and Fiske, 1977). The observers were people of about the same age, some enrolled in the university and some living near it.

The behaviors of concern were expressions about people (3a) and the plan required lay observers (4c). The people who filled the role of actors were those doing the observing and attributing (5a) since it was their behavior that was of interest. Their data clearly required interpretation and inference (6a). Both the data producers and the original participants in the taped interaction knew they were participating in research (8b and 9a). Those reporting their attributions experienced fairly naturally occurring stimuli (10b), the taped behavior not involving any stimuli manipulated by the investigator. The original choice of problem determined several subsequent decisions, such as the choice of lay observers and the attention to attributions. Note that the study made use of the previous scoring of the original actors' actions from the taped interactions. Since this scoring required only recognition and identification, it was done with very high interobserver agreement.

Another facet of the study also brings out the fact that several chains of decisions may be required, one for each measuring procedure used and one or more for each substudy or each question asked. Each attribution was scored by the investigator for favorableness. That scoring involved cognitive functioning of a simple clerical type

—the investigator recorded the favorableness value for each attributed adjective. But to obtain that value, he utilized a different set of observers, whose task was just to judge the favorableness of each adjective on the checklist. (Those judgments had moderately good interobserver agreement.)

The third research example used some of those same videotapes, along with others. Duncan (1972; Duncan and Fiske, 1977, Pt. III) analyzed the cues by which a speaker signals that he is ready to relinquish the speaking turn to the auditor. Duncan discovered several acts that occur in the second or two before one person stops speaking and the other begins, as well as at various other points in a conversation. These acts include not only the presence of certain linguistic and paralinguistic features but also the termination of one act, gesturing.

The problem was clearly the investigator's invention (1b). The population studied included both graduate students and others. The behavior was moving and speaking (3b). The observers were essentially lay persons (4c) in that they used only their everyday experience plus a little training in which the several acts were pointed out on practice tapes. The actors were the people conversing with each other (5b). The observations required only recognition and identification (6b). Both observers and actors knew they were participating in research (8b and 9a) and the stimuli were relatively natural (10b).

This study differs from the two preceding ones in many ways, but primarily in the focus on moving and speaking and on an observing task requiring only recognition and identification. Although Duncan, in the replication study examined here, had definite expectations derived from his preceding empirical analyses, he began this research program with no preconceptions about the particular cues or even about the signaling of readiness to relinquish the speaking turn. Similarly, Shrout started without any expectations about favorableness. In contrast, the project on psychotherapeutic change began with prior conceptualizations of dimensions along which change was expected to occur. These included the scales of the MMPI and the Scales of Behavioral Adequacy created for that project. The research question was: Which scales would change together? Since the Behavioral Adequacy Scales were used, in one form or another, by the client, the therapist, and two diagnosticians, one strong possibility seemed to be that the same scale or set of scales would covary over the parallel sets of data from the several observers. From prior experience, lay and clinical, it seemed almost certain that change would be associated with factors related to some classification of the multiple measures and not with a single global factor of change. The factors that actually emerged were related to the viewpoints of the observers and were interpreted as method factors.

Summary

The task for personality and related fields is the same as that for science generally, to find clear regularities and consistencies in the phenomena being studied. These phenomena are processes that cannot be located precisely in directly observable organic systems. This fact increases the difficulties in replicating observations and in reproducing findings. An associated problem is that of determining the populations that the observed sample can be considered to represent. Representativeness, replicability, and reproducibility are components of the key concept, generalizability. The populations especially pertinent to this book are those of phenomena and of observations. We are concerned with an entity, the observed behavior of a person in a context. We wish to generalize to some world composed of these entities. But to what world can we generalize and with what degree of confidence?

In developing his plan for a research program and in undertaking each empirical study, the investigator makes a series of decisions either implicitly or explicitly. He decides whether his problem will be one presented by society or one of his own invention. He must choose the actors and the kind of behavior he will study. He must decide who his observers will be and what processes his observational task will require. These processes may involve making interpretations or just identifying simple events as they occur. He must determine whether his observers and his actors will be aware of their participation in his research and whether he will use natural or manipulated stimuli. For each decision, the alternative chosen by the investigator determines one feature of the world to which he can generalize. Taken together, his several choices constitute a strategy that delineates the world of observations to which he may be able to generalize his empirical findings.

IX

Decisions, Strategies,
and Research Behaviors

This chapter considers some effects of the research decisions delineated in the last chapter, taken singly or as a set. Each choice not only
points the investigator in one direction but also rules out another
choice, thus restricting the phenomena he can study and the conclusions he can draw. His choices determine the kind and the extent of
the generalizations that he can make from his empirical findings.
Similarly, each set of decisions, each strategy adopted by the investigator, constrains generalizability. The chapter also looks at the
research topics falling within each of four major strategies. Then,
turning to the research activity itself, we find that the investigator's
choice of strategy determines for his research study the appropriate
behavior processes in his actors, his observers, and himself.

The sequences of these processes are analyzed in the last part of the chapter.

The Generality of the Decisions

These investigator decisions were formulated for research in personality and related fields. Are they specific to such research, or are they made in all scientific research? The investigator in the natural sciences makes several of these decisions. The physicist can choose between a societal problem and one he identifies in basic physics. He can seek to invent a process for producing nuclear energy that has few potentially harmful side effects, or he can study an atomic particle. The physicist works in a laboratory; his colleague in astronomy or geology, however, may study naturally occurring events, especially infrequent ones like eclipses and earthquakes. The investigator in astronomy or geology then has the problem of establishing that his observations were determined by the physical events to which he attributes them and not by other variables that he has not identified or controlled. Thus, in selecting the problem (Decision 1, Table 2), in choosing the objects or events to be observed (Decision 2), and in deciding whether or not to use naturally occurring phenomena (Decision 10), investigators in the natural sciences are making decisions of the same kind as those of the behavioral scientist.

Unlike the behavioral scientist, however, the investigator in the natural sciences does not feel that he has any choice about the kind of observational task he will use—he must utilize observations from interchangeable observers (Choice 6b). Typically, he obtains a permanent recording of the events he is studying, so that he and others can check and recheck the readings derived from the experiment. The observer is used as a reader or sensor, not as an interpreter. In some instances, especially in the early stages of a research program, it may be necessary to identify complex patterns that cannot immediately be specified in concrete terms, such as the paths of a particle and of its products when it disintegrates or the form of an electroencephalographic wave. Although these patterns are difficult to identify, they can be examined closely in recordings. They are hardly comparable to the complex mental processes involved in summarizing and interpreting impressions of an extended period of observation of human behavior.

The parallel between investigators in behavioral sciences and those in the natural sciences does not hold for other decisions and choices. There is nothing in the natural sciences closely comparable to Decision 3, what type of actors' behavior to study, since they do not study the behavior of actors—with the possible exceptions of some borderline fields, like psychopharmacology, that do use reports of actors about their feelings and experiences. Again, the natural scientist ordinarily uses only professional observers, although lay observers could make many of the observations he needs. And there is no observer observing himself (Choice 4b). Similarly, the natural scientist does not treat the observing process in his observers as a primary object for study (as in Choice 5a).

We can see, then, that there are some fundamental matters of concern to all scientists, whatever their field of study. All of the decisions that must be made by the natural scientist must also be made by the behavioral scientist. The investigator in the behavioral sciences must, however, make additional decisions stemming from the particular nature of the phenomena in which he is interested.

The Consequences of a Single Decision

The several decisions are not completely independent, at least in practice. One choice constrains the alternatives that would otherwise be available in other decisions. If the investigator chooses to work on a societal problem (Choice 1a), he will find that he can study societal concepts most directly only by using naturally occurring attributional judgments, judgments centering on an evaluation of some kind. These judgments must be made by natural observers, who will turn out not to be interchangeable. In the most direct attack on a societal problem, the observer has already made her judgments as part of her normal activities, not knowing that they would be used for research. Her judgments are on record, in some file. Under these circumstances, of course, the person is not observed for research purposes and his behavior occurs with natural stimuli. In terms of the decisions outlined in Table 2, then, the investigator choosing to work most directly on a societal problem has implicitly chosen alternatives 3a, 5a, 6a, 8a, 9b, and 10b. If that investigator chooses to obtain some judgments specifically for the purposes of his research, he substitutes 8b for 8a in that list of specifications.

A less direct attack on a societal problem might use fairly objective social indicators from archival sources. For example, the investigator might wish to represent the welfare of a group by average income; amount of living space; ownership of refrigerators, cars, or washing machines; and similar indices that might be available from some kind of prior census. He would probably assume, with limited justification, that he could treat the respondents to the census as interchangeable observers—the census-takers being recorders here. His choices would then involve 4b, 5a, and 6b. The investigator could also decide to use, as social indicators, self-reported feelings of wellbeing (Bradburn and Caplovitz, 1965; Bradburn, 1969), perhaps through a social survey. If the investigator construes the behavior he is observing as that summarized and interpreted by his respondents, his choices are 3a, 4c, 5b, 6a, 8b, 9a, and 10b. If he views his respondents' replies in the survey as the behavior being observed, he has implicitly chosen 3a, 4b, 5a, 6a, 8b, 9a, and 10a, these choices referring to the behavior elicited by the interviewer's questions.

Also indirect is the experimental study of dynamics and pathology in the personality sphere, as in generating anxiety in the laboratory. In this kind of work, the investigator chooses to manipulate the stimuli. He also uses observers who know that, for research purposes, they are making observations; the people they observe usually know that their behavior is being observed. Ordinarily, the observers must make inferential judgments. Hence, the specifications are 3a, 5b, 6a, 8b, 9a, and 10a.

Looking at just one decision, we may ask what constraints result from the choice of interchangeable observers (6b). If the investigator gives high priority to obtaining observational data from interchangeable observers, they will almost inevitably be aware that they are making reports to someone. In principle, their awareness should not provide any serious inherent restriction on other choices. If the investigator also selects a societal problem (1a), archival records are probably the main feasible source of data. Although these may already be coded in usable form, they are more likely to be discursive accounts that must be categorized or scaled by the observers. Another possibility occurs in research on behavior modification, such as desensitization, where the behavior being modified is construed in terms of reasonably objective, manifest acts.

The investigator using interchangeable observers on a problem of his own invention (1b) should, in general, have no restrictions on his other decisions. It is true, however, that he will have great difficulty arranging any conditions in which the observers are unaware that they are making observations for his research and in which the person is unaware that he is being observed. There is the additional consideration that such conditions probably violate the ethical principles of informed consent and the right to privacy. With respect to the persons observed, it can be argued that their privacy is not invaded and they are not put at any risk, psychological or otherwise, when observations are made in a public place without identifying the persons or permitting such identification from recordings in which the persons can be recognized. Such an investigator should probably consult disinterested colleagues to obtain impartial opinions about these matters.

Ethical matters are also involved in decisions about conditions for obtaining observations (Decisions 8, 9, and 10). In addition, these choices impose restrictions on the particular problem the investigator can select for his research. If he does not want his actors to be aware of their research participation, he cannot effectively study the content of dreams and other fantasy. If he chooses to study naturally occurring stimuli, he will have great difficulty in systematically investigating attributional judgments. The extent of these restrictions may depend on the ingenuity of the investigator and on his willingness to utilize indirect procedures for attacking his problem. Furthermore, if his observers do not know that their reports are being used for research, it is not likely that the investigator will find that the observers are interchangeable, that he can manipulate stimuli, and that the persons observed know that they are being observed for the research. The decision to use aware observers is usually made together with the decision to manipulate stimuli.

Constraints on Generalizability

For each decision, the choice made by the investigator restricts what he can do. Taking the investigator's several choices together as a strategy, we find that the strategy as a whole constrains the external validity, the generalizability of the investigator's research findings.

Those findings can be generalized with some confidence to an appropriate composite population defined by the sampling of several univariate populations—actors, behaviors, observers, and settings. If enough investigators work within a single strategy over enough time, some body of knowledge will be produced. But that body of knowledge must be viewed as a separate discipline or field of study.

When an investigator reads about the findings of investigators pursuing strategies other than his, he must be cautious about generalizing his own work beyond the domain identified with his strategy. Yet he should and normally he will compare his findings with those of such investigators.If his strategy and that of another investigator differ only in one choice (for example, he uses professional observers, while his colleague uses lay observers), and if both of them obtain essentially the same findings and draw almost identical conclusions, then these two investigators may decide that their strategies can be merged, because the choice on which they differ is not critical for the substantive topic they are studying. But caution is essential here. The judgment that the differentiating choice is insignificant should be reserved until congruence between the yields of the two adjacent strategies has been demonstrated for a number of topics and no major exceptions have been found.

It is possible that the number of strategies that are significantly different in terms of their yields will be far less than the very large number of theoretically separate strategies that could be formed from all possible combinations of choices. For the present, however, the narrower perspective is best. To avoid self-deception and overgeneralization, the investigator should restrict his conclusions and his published speculations to the domain circumscribed by his set of choices. Progress in the early stages of a science is slow, and firmly establishing some findings within a restricted area is the only safe basis for dependable generalizations linking that area to others.

A major, perhaps mortal, flaw in much personality research has been the implicit or explicit generalizing beyond the domain appropriate to the populations of persons, settings, stimuli, observers, and behaviors that can be said to have been represented adequately by the research. The results obtained from a particular strategy are all too freely generalized to the natural world. The great majority of published reports come to conclusions that are not explicitly restricted to the domain actually investigated.

The situation is usually much more complex than I have indicated thus far. Even within a set of particular choices constituting a strategy, a single study or research program may have specific characteristics unlike those for other research in the same strategy. The obvious example is the stimuli chosen for manipulation within any one strategy that includes Choice 10a. The stimuli may be verbal questions, pictorial material, or the actions of fellow-subjects or of confederates. Another example is the kind of interpretation and inference required of observers within Choice 6a. Different statements of instructions to observers may invoke separate modal processes and hence may be associated with different qualitative findings. Thus, within a strategy, generalizability must first be demonstrated for a specified set of conditions. Then generalizability to other sets of conditions can be determined empirically. Only when generalizations have been described and established within the limits of one strategy can we begin to think about possible generalizability beyond the limits associated with that strategy.

My own preference for the strategy formed from the last choices listed for the several decisions is based on the belief that it provides a shorter route to the goal of understanding the behaving we see in the natural world. Of course, the problem of confident, justifiable generalization is not avoided in this strategy. In fact, these choices typically involve more diverse and uncontrolled universes than the alternative choices. For example, all lay observers, taken together, are a more heterogeneous group than professional observers, in spite of the latter's diverse theoretical orientations. Similarly, the range of naturally occurring stimuli seems much vaster than the range that can feasibly be manipulated. Hence, insofar as the investigator cannot sample natural stimuli systematically, she must intentionally draw samples that are widely diverse. This more extensive sampling of the more heterogeneous populations may well lead to more differentiated research investigations and consequently to the necessity of a larger number of investigations before a conclusion can be firmly established.

Much of this general analysis must be qualified when we consider some single, substantive problem. For example, we do not ordinarily want to generalize to all lay observers. We would be happy to believe that we could generalize to almost anyone who had at least average intelligence, who was motivated to serve in that role, and who was found empirically to make observations that agreed closely with those from an assortment of other observers. In similar fashion, for any topic where the use of naturally occurring stimuli is appropriate, the content of the topic will greatly reduce the universe to be sampled. Work on conversational interactions can begin with relatively free conversations between strangers brought together for research purposes, allowing them to produce the stimuli. Then important findings can be tested in interactions between different types of persons, not just those most convenient for the investigator. Once a set of conclusions has been established for interactions between strangers, the investigator can begin to examine conversations between people who know each other. She may find that some general statements hold only for strangers and that some apply only to people who know each other well and are at ease in their conversations. She might also discover a relationship applicable to any conversation in her culture. It is, of course, essential to determine the universe for which a generalization holds.

Broad Strategies in Current Research Topics

The examination of research practices in personality and related fields developed in Part One indicates that some investigator decisions have been of major importance to the current state of these areas. The implicit choice of behavior to be studied has been predominantly that of expressions about people (3a). Closely associated with that decision is the selection of processes required by the observational task (Decision 6), the most common implicit choice being to use data requiring interpretation and inference on the part of the observer producing them (6a). For simplicity of exposition, Decisions 3 and 6 are merged in the discussion that follows, since Choice 3a is usually associated with Choice 6a, and 3b with 6b. It is rather uncommon to give observers the task of identifying words in expressions about people (6b with 3a). Asking observers to make judgments solely on the basis of actions with no verbal content (6a with 3b) is an unusual experimental manipulation in which the stimuli are silent films or stick figures.

The other central decision has been the selection of the kind of problem to be studied (Decision 1). If we take it as one major classification and the choice of behavior to be studied (Decision 3) as another, we can identify four broad strategies from the cross-classification of these two dichotomous variables (Table 3). The

Table 3. Four Broad Strategies.

Choice of Phenomena	*Choice of Problem*	
	1a: Societal problem	1b: Investigator-identified problem
3a: Expressions about people	Strategy 1: Societal problem studied with data drawn from expressions about people. (Example: Psychotherapy Change Project.)	Strategy 3: Investigator-identified problem studied with data drawn from expressions about people. (Example: Contribution of acts to favorable attribution.)
3b: Motor and vocal acts	Strategy 2: Societal problem studied with data drawn from motor and vocal acts. (No example.)	Strategy 4: Investigator-identified problem studied with data drawn from motor and vocal acts. (Example: Cues signaling readiness to relinquish the speaking turn.)

resulting schema is, of course, a coarse oversimplification that blurs a number of valuable distinctions and ignores the fact that the variables are actually continual rather than categorical. Three of the four cells have an example drawn from those used in Chapter Eight to illustrate the basic decisions. The strategy associated with each of these cells will be critically examined in a later chapter.

Some current research topics that seem to fall into the strategies given in Table 3 are listed below.

- Strategy 1: Evaluative judgments of persons, using natural raters, such as (a) adjustment to job (adequacy of performance, conformity to expectations of others, leadership), (b) adjustment to significant others, (c) adjustment to society (such as delinquency), (d) adjust-

ment to self; psychotherapeutic treatments; evaluations of treatment programs and other social programs; experimental
psychopathology.
- Strategy 1 or 2: Social indicators; behavior modification.
- Strategy 3: Attributions, such as (a) the content of attributions, (b)
covariation among attributions, (c) common-sense psychology, (d)
processes in attributing.
- Strategy 3 or 4: Social learning theory.
- Strategy 4: Behavior theory, pupillometrics, ethology, nonverbal
communication, acts in interactions.

Most of applied personality research falls within Strategy 1,
which involves a societal problem studied with data determined in
part by the particular observer. Interpretations or inferences are inevitable antecedents of evaluations of persons. Work on social indicators
may use either attributive judgments or data on which qualified
observers can agree readily (A. Campbell, 1976; Fox, 1974). Both
kinds of observational data, 3a and 3b, are also used in work on behavior modification. For example, although much of the data in that
area involves observations of manifest acts on which high interobserver agreement can be obtained, interview judgments and various
kinds of self-reports are also used (Ciminero, Calhoun, and Adams,
1977).

The striking feature of the list above is the lack of current
research topics using Strategy 2 only. Aside from research on social
indicators and on behavior modification, are there any topics falling
within the category of societal problems that have been or can be
investigated by studying motor or verbal acts and using observers who
are essentially interchangeable? The only topic appropriately categorized as using Strategy 2 is applied social indicators. In addition to
the indicators of general social well-being, there are indicators for
particular social problems, and some of these measures are sufficiently
objective to yield very high interobserver agreement. To assess intoxi-
cation in drivers, for example, relatively objective devices are available. Instances of littering and of violating traffic rules can be
observed with excellent congruence of observations. Basic political
participation can be assessed by determining whether a citizen has
voted in an election. Note that, in each of these examples, the state-

ment of the social problem specifies a behavioral act or a physiological condition.

These cases involve objective measurements for the criterion variable. An occasional investigation of other social problems does use essentially interchangeable observers for measuring one set of variables. For instance, Hargreaves (1972) studied a series of interviews with each of three patients showing motor retardation and found that the interviews in which the patients were judged as depressed differed from those in which they were judged as recovered, using the variables of loudness, time to respond, utterance length, and word rate. Although the criterion here was based on judgments and although the findings may be viewed as operational specifications of elements in those global judgments, the study does provide one further bit of evidence that the investigation of societal problems need not be restricted to data based on attributive, interpretive judgments.

The preceding list gives illustrations of current research using Strategy 3 or 4, in which the research problems are identified by the investigator herself. There is little uncertainty in classifying topics as falling within this category as opposed to that for societal problems. There is also little difficulty in identifying topics that involve data about motor and vocal acts obtained from recognition and identification processes within essentially interchangeable observers. What does raise problems is the broad area of attributions. These expressions about people have been taken as involving data determined in part by the particular observers. If an investigator asks people about the meanings of attributional terms or about associations and overlap among such terms, those people's responses form her data. Of course, the responses from each respondent depend to a considerable degree on that individual respondent. But suppose the investigator wishes to study the extent of overlap between individual descriptions of some target person. Perhaps she has had several friends describe that person. She may ask whether their descriptions are sufficiently similar to permit a judge to distinguish them from descriptions pertaining to other people. Since her judges must make interpretations of those descriptions, she will find that her several judges show only limited agreement for their identifications of several descriptions as pertaining to the same target person (see Bourne, 1977). Her strategy, therefore, falls within Strategy 3.

If this investigator has obtained descriptions on a standard instrument, such as an adjective checklist, she can objectively count the number of adjectives that both respondents use in describing a given target. In this instance, her strategy involves interchangeable clerks and falls within Strategy 4. (In fact, Bourne used both objective counts of overlap on adjective checklists and judges' matchings of the total protocols from these lists, along with similar scorings of agreements on other descriptive procedures.)

We can see, then, that the broad strategy of studying attributions can involve one or two sets of observer processes. In the simpler instance, the investigator just gives her observers the task of making attributions about some actors; these observers generate her data, and only their cognitive processes are involved. In the more complex instance, the investigator gets people to produce protocols describing actors and then gives these protocols to observers, who will make the judgments that form her observational data. For our purposes, the primary concern is the observational process leading to the data that the investigator enters into her analyses. If these data are cognitions about observations reported by an earlier set of observers, the investigator's task in interpreting her findings is considerably more complex than when the data are obtained from observers observing the actors directly. Whenever two sets of observer processes are used, the investigator must distinguish between the settings for each. The behavior of actors is affected by their setting; similarly, the behavior of the person doing the initial observing and the behavior of the observer making judgments about those earlier judgments are influenced by the particular setting.

At first glance, the topics associated with Strategy 4 in the earlier list, involving recognition and identification processes in observers, may seem far removed from personality. It is true that they do not concern what we usually mean by *personality* in the everyday usage of that term. Yet behavior theory has led to behavior modification, a major treatment technique today. Ethology, nonverbal communication, and acts in interactions deal with general dispositions and actions that are pertinent to interpersonal relationships. Pupillometrics studies both general and individual reactions to arousing stimuli. Other research on individual differences can be done in this area, as proposed by Duncan and Fiske (1977, pp. 329–337).

The Central Roles in Personality Research

We have been examining the decisions implicitly or explicitly made by the investigator before carrying out his research operations. Let us turn now to the research itself and see what actually goes on in investigations conducted according to each of the major strategies. Although this examination will deal with some matters considered earlier, it will take a different perspective, which may help us to understand more completely the current state of personality research. This perspective will also help to clarify the distinctiveness of the several strategies that are the central focus of Part Two.

We must recognize the critical fact that most behaviors used in current personality research are produced in reaction to the task set by the investigator and are not part of the everyday lives of people, as noted in Proposition 2a (Chapter One). The major function of such behaviors is in the professional activity of the investigator. The apparent exceptions to this rule, as in naturalistic observation, are more apparent than real. Tunnell (1977) found very few studies that were natural along all three of his dimensions: behavior, setting, and treatment. And even in seemingly very natural research, the data are likely to be derived from interpretive judgments that observers make in accordance with the investigator's instructions.

The behaviors used in personality research are associated with three roles: investigator, observer, and actor. The investigator initially sets the observational task for his observers; later he processes and analyzes the records they produce. The actor produces the behavioral phenomena. These are what the observer perceives, cognizes, and processes in generating his observational records, his units of measurement. The actor may himself be cognizing and interpreting some behavior of still other actors, so that he too is observing. What the actor does, however, is viewed as secondary in the present analysis.

The three roles are not identified as persons because the same person may play two roles. In some clinical research, the investigator is also the observer. Unless he also utilizes other observers, however, we view his products as the case studies of a diagnostician or a therapist. Quite prevalent is the use of the same person as observer and actor. In all multiple-choice procedures involving self-reports, one person, who has been the actor producing the behavior now being cognized, takes on the role of observer and produces his interpretive judgments as data for the investigator. When an investigator uses his own self-reports as data, thus playing all three roles, we take his product as a study of just one person and wait for additional studies before spending much effort on thinking about implications of the findings.

Among the many activities that can be identified within the investigator's role in research, there is the apparently mundane task of taking the records made by observers and transforming them for entry into statistical analyses. In some instances, the transformation may be a direct copying of the observers' numerical responses onto a code sheet for keypunching, each unit of measurement from the observer becoming a single datum. More often, each response is routinely transformed into a value on a numerical scale or is combined with several responses into a single datum. The combining typically consists of scoring the units of measurement and summing or averaging the units from one observer or from several raters.

Although this behavior of the investigator or of her assistant is routine, this step in research should not be passed over without examination. It implements a judgment about translating the observer behaviors into some variable that is relevant to one of the investigator's concepts. The investigator must decide what translation best represents her concept. The important point about this investigator behavior is that it is specifiable, objective, public, readily replicable, and hence subject to intersubjective testability.

The behaviors of the person in the role of observer have been examined closely in earlier portions of this book. These behaviors are obviously crucial because they lead to the data generated in the research. In the present discussion, the critical aspect of these behaviors is, once again, whether the observers' records agree so closely that they are essentially interchangeable. The argument has been that such congruence is possible where the observers' task involves the processes of recognizing and identifying, processes usually associated with construing the observed behaviors in terms of acts. The alternative case, in which observers agree no better than moderately, is typically found when the processing requires interpretation and inference.

Finally, there is the behavior observed, the behavior of actors. These, the phenomena being studied, may take any of several forms.

They may be currently perceived behavior, as in observations in the laboratory or in the field. More commonly, they are the behaviors observed in the past, either in oneself for self-reports or in others for peer ratings. They can also be records of past behavior, archival material, or protocols for projective techniques.

To summarize, the general paradigm for the research behaviors in personality and related fields looks like this:

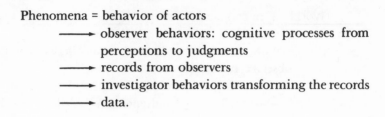

Phenomena = behavior of actors
⟶ observer behaviors: cognitive processes from perceptions to judgments
⟶ records from observers
⟶ investigator behaviors transforming the records
⟶ data.

In this schema, that which follows an arrow is derived in some way from that which precedes it.

This paradigm is oversimplified in one respect: The phenomena must be analyzed more fully. It is essential to differentiate among the world of phenomena in which the investigator is interested, the population of phenomena accessible to the investigator, and the sample actually observed. Hence the paradigm should begin as follows:

(World of phenomena chosen for study by the investigator ⟶)
Accessible population of phenomena of actor behavior ⟶
Sample of phenomena used by investigator = behavior of his actors
⟶ observer behaviors
and other steps as above.

The parentheses are used to emphasize the fact that the designated world is not wholly accessible to the investigator.

In much research on human behavior, the research phases of the paradigm are more complicated. A substantial portion of personality research has, as its phenomena to be observed, expressions about people, these expressions being the products of cognitive processes in the actors. For example, the products produced by the actors may be letters of recommendation that are read and judged by observers to rate applicants for a job or training program. Although the observers often make judgments about the authors of such letters, their primary concern is with the applicants that the referees have observed. The actors are the referees and the actors' behaviors are the letters. The paradigm here is as follows:

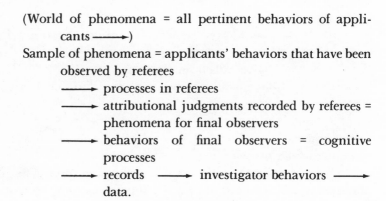

(World of phenomena = all pertinent behaviors of applicants ⎯⎯→)

Sample of phenomena = applicants' behaviors that have been observed by referees

⎯⎯→ processes in referees

⎯⎯→ attributional judgments recorded by referees = phenomena for final observers

⎯⎯→ behaviors of final observers = cognitive processes

⎯⎯→ records ⎯⎯→ investigator behaviors ⎯⎯→ data.

Note that there are two sets of attributional judgments in this paradigm, the usual and inevitable ones made by the final observers and the ones made earlier by those whose role is actor but who also are observing and attributing. Note also the several kinds of generalization involved in this paradigm. First, the consumer of these letters of recommendation hopes that the sample of the applicant's behavior that has been observed by the referee adequately represents the world of relevant applicant behavior. Second, she hopes that the attributional judgments made by a referee represent the population of such judgments that might be made. She knows, of course, that this sample is actually biased since the applicant naturally selects those referees whose judgments will, he believes, be most favorable. Third, the consumer assumes that the sample of observed past behavior can be generalized to future behavior or, more precisely, that judgments about the prior behavior can be generalized to predict judgments about future behavior. Lastly, there is the generalizing from the final observer in this process—the consumer of the letters—to those who will be making evaluative judgments about the applicant if he is accepted. It is little wonder that letters of recommendation are often such poor predictors.

Research on attribution utilizes this more complex paradigm when it is concerned with how a given class of people are described and labeled by other people. More frequently, research on attribution is directly concerned with the actors who are doing the attributing, regardless of the persons about which those attributions are made. The attributions are taken as behavioral products that the final observers perceive and cognize, either recognizing and counting words and other simple features of the descriptions or interpreting the contents of the attributions.

It is difficult to make the necessary differentiations for such an analysis of research roles and associated behaviors. Because the natural tendency is to focus on the phenomena being observed, whatever they are, it is easy to overlook the significance of the crucial aspect, the role and the behavior of the final observers. Adding to the difficulty in conceptualizing these paradigms is the diversity of procedures used to produce data for research on personality. In terms of the complexity of the cognizing, the procedures vary from copying academic grades recorded by registrars to making interpretive judgments about others' attributions based on some unknown and unspecifiable behavioral protocol. The investigator is usually interested in the phenomena that are the input for the observer' processes, the goings-on in the behavioral world that led to those processes. Yet he has no direct knowledge about the behavior of his actors; he knows only what is filtered out by his observers in their perceptual-cognitive processes leading to the overt records that are mechanically transformed to data.

Another confusing matter is the distinction between what the investigator thinks about and what he actually studies, between the world of phenomena and the sample of phenomena in the preceding paradigms. The investigator has a conceptual label for his research topic identifying the world of phenomena relevant to him. When he thinks about his topic, he thinks about the label and about instances drawn from that world of phenomena. In contrast, when he conducts his research, he attends to the small set of phenomena he has produced. In spite of his involvement, he must decide objectively whether his sample of observed phenomena represents a population corresponding to some portion of the vaguely defined world of phenomena he has been thinking about. For example, the investigator may be interested in the favorableness of attributions made about others in everyday living; he asks observers to describe actors whom they have seen for ten minutes and then assesses the favorableness of those descriptions. Although observers will readily carry out this experimental task, the investigator must carefully determine how adequately his set of research phenomena typifies the world of everyday attributing. How common is it for a person to make a multiattribute description of another after a short period of detached observation?

Research Roles and Behaviors in the Current Strategies

Let us consider how the analyses of the preceding pages apply to three of the four broad strategies identified in Table 3 (the three for which there are examples of current research): Strategies 1, 3, and 4. Strategy 1, societal problems using evaluations of people, involves attributive judgments made for practical purposes in the everyday world. These are the phenomena of interest to investigators following the societal strategy. In research on a societal problem, the role of the investigator is the universal one outlined above—he transforms records into data. The observers' records that are processed by the investigator may come from archives, the judgments having been made and recorded for purposes not connected with the investigator's research. Alternatively, the records may have been made for research purposes, at the request of the investigator.

Ordinarily, the observers are *natural raters*—to adopt the term used by Kellam, Branch, Agrawal, and Ensminger (1975)—people who make evaluative judgments about the actors in everyday life. These judgments typically have consequences for the lives of those judged. For example, both a teacher's grading and a teacher's appraisal of a student as a person have some effect on the student's later life. If natural raters are not used, the observers are essentially surrogates for them. When the investigator employs observers to make evaluative judgments, the persons filling that role are usually professionals who are asked to make the judgments as if they were natural raters.

The actors are ordinarily clients, the people about whom decisions must be made in order to help them or to help society. The ultimate concern is with the behavior of these clients in the real world of the human society. This behavior may be reported by the client to his therapist. Frequently, however, the observers see only the behavior of the client in the treatment situation, the psychotherapeutic interaction, or the hospital ward, the judgments about that behavior being presumed to generalize to the rest of the client's behavior.

For those who investigate societal problems, the phenomena of interest are evaluative judgments made for practical purposes in the everyday world. Note that these phenomena may or may not be those observed for producing the data used by the investigators. When the investigator takes archival records and transcribes them into data, with no interpretive process intervening, she is studying a sample from the world of phenomena with which she is concerned. The judgments made by natural raters as a part of the ongoing procedures of the institution are formulated with that context in mind, are reported on the standard instrument used in that institution, and are intended for people who may be making decisions about the clients at a later time. In contrast, as soon as the investigator asks observers, natural raters or others, to make judgments for the purposes of her research, she is introducing possible effects associated with the research task. She is sampling a different population of phenomena. The judgments that she studies and analyzes are made with the research instructions in mind, and the judgments conform to the format of the instrument provided.

To illustrate the paradigm for societal problems, we can use the evaluation of client status after treatment. We will assume that the therapist has written a report on his judgment of the client at that time and that other observers then make judgments quantifying such reports.

(World of phenomena = evaluative judgments made for decisions in everyday living ———)
———→ records of judgments = phenomena for final observers
———→ processes in final observers
———→ records ———→ investigator behaviors ———→ data.

This example of assessing status in societal terms is fairly typical of societal problems involving the personality of clients. It may also apply to assessment of applicants for training or employment, as in the example given earlier. Societal problems, however, take many forms, and no single paradigmatic scheme can represent all of them. Their standard feature is the central emphasis on evaluative judgments.

In research using Strategy 3, research on attribution, the phenomenal world of interest is composed of the cognitive processes of people in some subcultures as they observe and describe other people. The investigator rarely studies a sample of these phenomena (for an exception, see Baldwin, 1942, and Allport, 1965). Ordinarily, the investigator elicits attributions for research purposes, asking people to describe themselves or others. Here the paradigm looks like this:

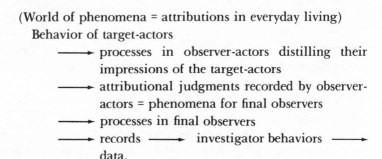

(World of phenomena = attributions in everyday living)
Behavior of target-actors
⟶ processes in observer-actors distilling their impressions of the target-actors
⟶ attributional judgments recorded by observer-actors = phenomena for final observers
⟶ processes in final observers
⟶ records ⟶ investigator behaviors ⟶ data.

Although the processes in the final observers can be recognizing and identifying, they typically involve interpretation and inference. Note the disjunction at the beginning of this paradigm. The investigator's research topic is natural attributing done after observing natural behavior. In his empirical study, the research process starts with some behavior of target-actors. That behavior may be naturally occurring behavior as recalled by observer-actors, or it may be behavior of the target-actors in a setting arranged by the investigator. In either case, the observer-actors do not make their attributions when and where they feel like it. Instead, they produce their judgments in response to the instructions of the investigator and record them in the form he specifies. In most cases, these particular judgments would not have been expressed if the investigator had not intervened. Although at some time these observer-actors might have verbalized to themselves or to someone else some judgments about the target-actors, they would have used words of their own choice and would not have made as many specific judgments. It is clear that the population of attributions from which the investigator is sampling is distinctive, being characterized by the requirements of the research task. That population cannot be taken as representing the world of naturally occurring attributions. The investigator assumes that, regardless of the different reasons for making attributions in his testing room as opposed to the outside world, the processes will be essentially the same. This assumption is rarely, if ever, tested.

In research using Strategy 4, research on acts, the phenomena of interest are acts in the everyday world. The investigator ordinarily has an expectation that these acts contain potential information for some other person or possibly for the actor himself. We need not debate the question of intention in the actor—the acts may be purely expressive, from the viewpoint of the actor, and yet convey information to other actors.

Since the investigator is interested in naturally occurring behavior, he tries to observe in nature. Outstanding examples in animal ethology are the extensive work of Lorenz (1970-71) and the recent work of Hess (1973, Chap. 8). In human ethology, there is the work of Eibl-Eibesfeld (1972).

When the investigator is unable to observe in a truly natural situation, he observes in as naturalistic a setting as possible, taking into account ethical considerations, the right to privacy, and the appropriateness of informed consent. Much of the work in this area utilizes observations made by the investigator himself. Given his expectations, however, it is necessary to establish his agreement with other observers. The paradigm in research on actional problems is simple:

(World of phenomena = behavior construed as natural
   acts ⟶)
Sample of phenomena = behavior that can be observed
   conveniently
      ⟶ observer processing by recognition and iden-
      tification
      ⟶ observer records
      ⟶ investigator transformations
      ⟶ data.

In the ethological work with animals, the investigators have often been able to observe directly the phenomena of interest to them. They have found means of making their observations unobtrusively, so that the organisms do not react to the procedures for observing. In some work with human beings, the observer has used a camera that is pointed in one direction, the observer also facing that direction, while the images seen by the observer and recorded on his film are those at ninety degrees from the apparent line of sight (Hass, as reported by Eibl-Eibesfeld, 1970, p. 413). In other instances, the presence of the observer or the recording equipment is obvious. The actors, however, may not know when observations or recordings are being made. Even when they do know, the process may be continued so long that the attention of the actors is directed primarily elsewhere, and the reactive effects of the observing, although difficult to estimate, appear to be small. In all these instances where the observer or the recording equipment is visible, they become part of the background stimulation. Once the recording has started, the observer introduces no new stimuli.

The Distinctiveness of the Three Strategies

The emphasis in the preceding discussion has been on the differences among the strategies resulting from the major decisions made by the investigator. Left for the active reader who wishes to do so is the task of looking for similarities among the three strategies and the research associated with each. For example, the strategy for societal problems involving evaluative judgments and the strategy directed at attributions do have components in common. Regardless of the presence of similarities, however, the quality and extent of the differences are sufficient to identify them as distinctive realms of investigation.

It must be recognized, of course, that the classification developed here is a coarse one. It is possible to identify research topics that do not fit neatly into the three major categories. Of particular importance is research directed toward problems that involve two or more areas, research that may link them together. One instance is the study by Shrout (1976) considered in Chapter Eight. This research involved both acts and attributions. In addition, it was concerned with favorableness of attributions, a topic relevant to the societal area even though the study itself is far removed from the real-world problems toward which the societal strategy is directed. When a problem involves more than one area, it can be classified in terms of the phenomena for which an explanation is sought—attributional behavior in this instance. And, of course, a single investigation may include several research questions, one falling in one category and others falling in other categories.

In spite of the differences, we can hope that connections will eventually be made between strategies and between the topics subsumed under them, just as fields have developed between older disciplines in the natural sciences, such as biochemistry, biophysics, and astrophysics. The generation of those joint fields has, however, been made possible by introducing constructs from one field into research in the other field and by bringing over agreed-on measuring procedures for these constructs. In contrast, each major strategy in personality research has its own set of provincial concepts and its own units of observation and measurement. As long as the data and the conceptual networks are so separate, there can be few sound connections between them. But most central is the distinctiveness of the three sets of phenomena, the happenings being studied. The investigation of societal problems centers on evaluations of persons made instrumentally, for practical purposes. The study of attributing as it occurs naturally, almost as an end in itself, is concerned with a wider, more heterogeneous class of processes. Research on behaving as behaving focuses on manifest behavioral events, on actions and sequences of actions. These three sets of phenomena are fairly readily discriminated. Granted that each set is not the only group of phenomena that can be studied under the given strategy, the strategies do point toward different phenomenal events.

Insofar as each strategy leads to productive research, a set of empirical findings and general propositions will be developed for the particular world of phenomena toward which that strategy is aimed. Well-designed research studies will permit generalization to that world. No matter how excellent the research plan, however, the results from a study conducted within one strategy cannot be generalized to the different worlds of phenomena being examined by other strategies.

Although the different strategies investigate distinct sets of phenomena, it is disturbing to realize that there should be psychological connections among the three realms. Behavioral acts, together with the content of the person's speech, must be the raw material from which impressions are derived and attributions eventually constructed. Similarly, it seems reasonable to assume that impressions and attributions form the basis for the evaluative judgments studied in societal problems. Yet we cannot anticipate seeing soon the reduction of attributions to acts and the reduction of evaluative judgments to attributions. For what is physically identical behavior, each individual constructs her attributions in her own way. The products of two people making attributions are as discriminable as the paintings of two artists portraying the same person or as the accounts of two reporters writing about the same presidential press conference. In reconstructing an evaluative judgment, we have only these individualistic attributions on which to build. And we do not know what other personal and contextual factors have entered into the formation of that judgment.

William James (1890) argued that each of us recognizes that there are many worlds, such as the world of sensation and the world of science. Each, he says, is real while we are attending to it. Perhaps, when we are attending to societal problems, we are attending to a world of evaluative judgments about persons and society, a world involving parts of James' "various worlds of individual opinion" (p. 293), part of his "world of 'idols of the tribe,' illusions or prejudices common to the race" (p. 292), and parts of other worlds. When we study attributional problems, each person's attributions (individual opinions) constitute for us a real world unto itself. In the study of actions, the discriminated behaviors also constitute a real world for us. In Part One, I have argued that personality research has taken the world of people's construals and interpretations of other people's behaviors as a real world. In James' frame of reference, it is a real world for those attending to it. The question I am asking here is the extent to which each of the strategies outlined above can become a world of science.

Summary

The framework of decisions, developed in Chapter Eight, reveals the methodological diversity in research on personality and related topics. Although some of the decisions are also made by natural scientists, some are pertinent only to behavioral science. For any decision, each available choice has its advantages and its disadvantages. Some decisions necessarily constrain other choices. Using the choice between a problem presented by society and one identified by the investigator as one classification, together with the combined choices of type of observational data and kind of observer processes as another, we can identify a set of four potential strategies, three of which have been extensively pursued in work on societal problems, in studies of attribution, and in studies of actions. These three will be analyzed in Chapters Ten through Thirteen. Each strategy is distinctive. Empirical findings generated by one strategy cannot be generalized beyond it.

The conduct of research in personality and related fields utilizes persons in three roles: investigator, observer, and actor. A set of behaviors is associated with each role. From these behaviors, paradigms for research processes can be indicated. Each of the major strategies formed from patterns of investigator decisions has its own paradigm or paradigms. This analysis brings out once again the distinctiveness of the several strategies and the limits to generalizing from the findings from each. Since each investigates its own separate set of phenomena, it seems unlikely that the strategies will ever converge.

X

The Strategy for Studying Societal Problems

The investigator's decisions to study a problem presented by society and to use expressions about people as his phenomena (Choices 1a and 3a, respectively) identify Strategy 1, the strategy for societal problems. The investigator using expressions about people ordinarily sets for his observers a task involving interpretation and inference (Choice 6a). This chapter will examine the strategy for studying societal problems. The next chapters will look at the strategies for studying attributions and for studying actions.

Societal problems are found in many domains and disciplines. In addition to mental health and illness, sources of societal problems include delinquency and other antisocial behavior; drug use and abuse; education; personnel selection and classification; and other topics dealing with personal, social, and institutional welfare. The new field of environmental psychology (Altman, 1976; Ittelson and others, 1974) is replete with societal problems. The phenomena of personality are pertinent to a majority of these diverse topics.

Yet the investigation of societal problems must be seen as distinct from research aimed at building a basic science by discovering fundamental constructs and determining their interrelationships within a nomological net. Unlike the orientation of a person who has identified his own research problem, the orientation of an investigator studying a social problem must include the recognition that his data come from judgments that are relative to the observer and cannot be taken as impartial records of behavior. He must accept the fact that the problem often involves utilitarian concepts derived from people's common sense, instead of constructs from a basic science. The investigator will be examining associations among variables selected as pertinent to the particular question being explored, the measuring procedures for those variables often being developed or adapted for the task at hand. Thus, findings from investigating a psychotherapeutic treatment or an assessment technique for personnel selection do not add to our basic scientific knowledge. From analyzing and thinking about such findings, however, the investigator or his colleague may get the idea for a new basic construct or possible relationship that becomes the focus of subsequent research in a different context.

Society needs whatever help it can get from the behavioral sciences. MacRae (1976) argues that social science has an important social function but is not carrying it out well. He proposes that universities be reorganized to perform this function better. People who face these problems often come to individual behavioral scientists for advice and assistance. At times, these scientists can offer their considered opinions, developed not only from their personal experience but also from what they perceive as relevant empirical findings; at other times, the scientists can offer more direct assistance, especially regarding methods for obtaining and analyzing the data for developing solutions to the problems. But behavioral scientists do not have an extensive body of fundamental scientific knowledge that can be brought to bear on societal problems. Especially in the field of personality, there is little if anything that has been firmly established and consensually agreed on.

Hence, societal problems are not applied science in the sense of applying basic science to a practical, mundane question. The investigation of such problems is not engineering, in which the knowledge in a basic field is brought to bear on a tangible matter in the everyday world. Nevertheless, the study of societal problems can utilize the general scientific approach and the established methodology for behavioral research. Although it can share these with research following other strategies, the special nature of the substantive material makes it necessary to differentiate research on societal problems from other fields of investigation.

The extent of psychologists' awareness of social problems and concern about them is suggested by a study directed by Lipsey. Most graduate students (92 percent) in a representative sample of departments said that "academic psychology *should* be concerned with contemporary social problems" (1974, p. 542). Almost as large a group (90 percent) "said they did *not* think that academic psychology was making a significant contribution to the needed solutions" (p. 542). The comparable figures for a random sample of faculty members in graduate departments were a little lower.

The investigation of applied problems was one characteristic of the early stages in several behavioral sciences. Decades ago, sociologists studied delinquency. Some of the first psychologists worked on maladjustment and mental illness along with psychiatrists, who have always been predominantly concerned with those problems. From his broad perspective on psychology, Sigmund Koch writes: "At the time of its conception, psychology was unique in the extent to which its institutionalization preceded its content and its methods preceded its problems. If there are keys to history, this statement is surely a key to the history of modern psychology. Never had a group of thinkers been given so sharply specific an invitation to create. Never had inquiring men been so harried by social wish, cultural optimism, extrinsic prescription, the advance scheduling of ways and means" (1974, p. 15).

In addition to having societal problems presented to them, behavioral scientists have been aware of these needs from their own everyday experience. In a natural science, a scientist may not become acquainted with a research topic and may not be able to identify a critical research question until he has studied the science in academic courses. In contrast, many behavioral scientists enter their chosen discipline because they are already interested in the content and issues.

They come to the field with knowledge of these matters preformulated in everyday language, and they readily pick up the technical jargon because it refers to everyday experience rather than to precise technical terms linked to laboratory operations with which only the initiated are familiar.

Behavioral scientists are aware of the magnitude and importance of social problems. George Miller (1969), an experimental psychologist, devoted his APA presidential address to "Psychology as a Means of Promoting Human Welfare." Yet many scientists do not want to get involved. Some prefer to identify their own research topics, often selecting ones on which they can work readily because the methods have already been developed. Others feel that they can offer little help—although they know a number of pertinent theories, they are dubious whether extant conceptualizations have much applicability and usefulness for specific problems. Perhaps a majority of investigators see themselves as pure scientists, not as engineers. And it is true that most behavioral scientists have had little or no experience in working on applied problems.

Behavioral scientists, even those who would like to work on these problems, are often deterred by the immensity and difficulty of the issues. Consider a problem very close to the vocational home of these scientists—the evaluation of faculty performance. As Dael Wolfle puts it: "The proper basis for judgment should, of course, be the faculty's educational objectives and the extent to which those objectives are achieved. The trouble with this proposition, however, is that no one knows how to measure with any satisfactory degree of completeness or accuracy what really happens to different kinds of students as a direct consequence of their experience at different kinds of institutions of higher learning" (1973, p. 131).

The Characteristics of Societal Problems

Society is concerned with several kinds of problems. One is helping persons or groups who are perceived as needing assistance. The obvious example is those who have psychological problems and who are seen in clinics, hospitals, and private practice. Other examples are those judged to be handicapped or socially disadvantaged.

Another kind of problem pertains to institutions. For instance,

what can be done to make a particular firm more efficient? Improve
the quality of internal communication structures? Raise the morale
of workers? Increase job satisfaction? Select new personnel in a better
way? Other topics of this kind include leadership effectiveness and the
success of teaching and training activities. Some problems concern
both the individual and the institution. In the selection of graduate
students, one objective is identifying those applicants who will be
capable of using the opportunity that the university can offer them
for developing their competence in a discipline. Another objective is
to find those applicants who will best fit the personal objectives of the
faculty and the aspiration of the university for students whose later
careers will add to its reputation.

A third kind of problem has a wider scope. People in government and people in a position to facilitate social research and social
programs are concerned with formulating policy about activities undertaken to help people. Is this treatment or training program effective? Is it worth the expense? The growing field of evaluation research,
considered later in this chapter, is concerned with these practical
questions. Still more generally, there are questions about the quality
of life. Although there have been indicators of the economic health of
a country for years, only recently has there been a comparable concern
for the social and psychological well-being of people in general. This
concern has sought social indicators that would provide policymak-
ers with information about these matters (for example, Campbell,
Converse, and Rodgers, 1976; Fox, 1974). With regard to policy
research, Coleman says that "the research problem originates outside
the discipline, in the world of action" (1972, p. 3). This characterization applies generally to the study of societal problems.

In each type of societal problem, there is a general process that
can be sketched, using the format given in Chapter Nine, as follows:

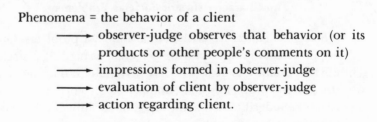

This paradigm need not occur in full form. The observer-judge may go from her impressions to her action regarding the client without formulating an explicit judgment or at least without making that judgment a matter of public record. Moreover, the action may be taken either by the observer-judge or by someone else. In certain cases, the decision may be that no action should be taken at this time. For example, a foreman may review the work of an employee, judge that it has been only marginally adequate, and decide that no action is needed. Thus, evaluative judgments pervade societal problems and their investigation. The investigator may, however, focus on the evaluation (for example, a rating on a health-sickness scale), on the decision (this client should have psychotherapy), or on the action (the client was given the opportunity to begin psychotherapeutic treatment).

These judgments involve the evaluation of human performance, on or off the job. The clinician encounters people judged to be adapting to and coping with their environment and themselves in an unsatisfactory or unsatisfying way. Institutional executives assess the total performance of the institution, based on the performance of each member. Those with a broad concern for society attend to the performance of general programs institutionalized by government actions. Social indicators reflect the performance of society for its members.

In most instances, the evaluation of performance leads to a practical, concrete decision: to treat or not to treat; to administer one treatment or another; to hire or not to hire; to continue a program or to terminate it. Once the decision has been made, it is ordinarily implemented—by the decision maker or by someone else. Thus, societal problems are action-oriented. When the problem concerns individuals, the decision is acted on rather directly, so that the welfare of those persons will be improved. But when the problem involves an institution, the decision is more instrumental; and any resulting action pertains to the ultimate objectives of that institution, usually in an indirect fashion. In principle, the evaluative judgments made for work on an institutional problem are in terms of criteria formulated to be congruent with those objectives (see Fiske, 1951).

As this discussion indicates, several sets of persons are involved in societal problems—the client, the person administering the treatment, the evaluator, and the decision maker. There may be others with some stake in the problem, such as persons close to the client. The researcher undertaking work on a societal problem must recognize these diverse roles, each with its own perspective, values, and objectives. In analyses of research on program evaluation, Coleman (1972, pp. 15–17) has indicated these roles in policy research, and Riecken and Boruch (1974, Chap. 7) have pointed them out in social experimentation. Frequently, the investigator must work out her research plan cooperatively with people in several of these roles. And she must appreciate the fact that, in addition to general evaluation apprehension (Rosenberg, 1969), clients, therapists and others giving treatments, and administrators do not like to have their performances evaluated (see Boen, 1975).

Although another important characteristic of societal problems is fairly obvious, it must be mentioned here because it has major implications for research investigations in this area. Each such problem is posed within a set of specific conditions. Some of these conditions are taken for granted and hence are not specified. For example, in deciding what treatment to give, the practitioner assumes he will treat within the setting of his agency. And he does not explicitly examine his own characteristics—his own training and experiences—as restricting the alternatives available to him or as affecting his perception of their comparative desirability. In similar fashion, he may overlook the fact that his institution both limits his choices and influences the potential effectiveness of possible treatments.

Particular conditions are also involved in personnel selection. What leads these applicants to apply to this organization? What demands do the working or training conditions make on accepted applicants? How are the criterion judgments about performance made by the pertinent supervisors or trainers? Stern, Stein, and Bloom (1956) have illustrated the importance of analyzing a selection problem in terms of the values of those making the final evaluative judgments.

The investigator who has committed herself to research on a societal problem must take these limiting conditions into account. She cannot base her research plan on any generalization from prior empirical work, especially laboratory studies, without deciding that the generalization should hold under the given conditions for her problem. Even if there exists an empirical generalization from a number of other studies in different settings, she must judge whether it is likely to hold in her specific instance.

In conducting her study, the investigator must identify and assess the conditions under which she collects her observations so that she can report them as qualifiers of her findings. Even if she is working to optimize the decisions among courses of action within a single organization, she must be able to point out what she sees as potentially limiting conditions so that her findings will be applied cautiously when changes in those conditions are evident. Her findings may be affected by a wide variety of factors, and appropriately so —she is seeking to help a decision maker whose choice of a course of action must take into account many and diverse matters. In contrast, the investigator selecting his own research problem can choose his conditions so as to minimize the influence of most factors that he construes as outside his problem as he has formulated it.

One more important characteristic of societal problems must be pointed out. The concepts used in stating and investigating societal problems originate in society. The concepts held by the investigator and the decision maker come from their socialization—their internalization and interpretation of what society wants—and from their personal experience. As such, their conceptualizations have all the limitations of personality concepts as discussed in earlier chapters. The investigator and the decision maker may, of course, modify society's concepts rather than adopting them outright. And they will formulate them in their own conceptual language, weighting each component as they deem best. In many situations, the investigator and the decision maker may help to determine the form of criterion concepts, working with the administrator to analyze the basis for evaluations and the factors to be considered. All of these people are, however, working with the performance of the person as they construe it. Moreover, they take that performance as a set of phenomena outside themselves. The characteristics attributed to the clinic client are seen as located within the client. The qualifications of the job applicant are attributed to him. In point of fact, these judgments are attributions resulting from the construing and evaluating processes in the judge. A major feature of work on societal problems is the joint nature of the observational datum—each involves not only the behavior of the client but also the interpretive activity of the attributer-evaluator.

Consider, for example, the investigation and treatment of maladjustment. Peers, family, and other members of society point out the persons whom they perceive as maladjusted and those who indicate distress or a desire for help in coping. These identifications are made, for the most part, by natural raters—the potential clients themselves, those who are personally concerned about them, or those who encounter the client in such roles as teacher or supervisor. These lay evaluations are followed by more systematic professional evalua- tions, the decision maker utilizing his own set of concepts for diag- nosing and predicting.

The investigator conducting research in this area finds that the natural raters agree among themselves only moderately, each rater making his judgments on the basis of his own personal experience with the client as he has interacted with him. The investigator also finds that different professional evaluators reach different conclu- sions about the client, depending not only on the type of diagnostic procedures used but also on their own ways of construing maladjust- ment. And if the investigator studies the treatments administered by several therapists, he finds variation among the therapists' objectives. The contribution of the evaluator, lay or professional, to the stated evaluation must not be ignored. In the formulation of a societal prob- lem, the considerable contribution of the persons presenting it must be recognized by the investigator. What implicit assumptions have been introduced into that formulation? A thoughtful article by Caplan and Nelson (1973) has considered the way that societal prob- lems are defined. They argue that problem definition is often person- centered and that the causes of social problems tend to be seen as resid- ing in individuals, not in their environments.

The investigator who chooses to work on a societal problem should do so with full awareness of the orientation that she is adopt- ing. What are the unstated presuppositions underlying society's view of the problem? What is the theoretical perspective taken by the investigator herself? She should also consider whether the problem as presented to her is formulated from an unproductive or even errone- ous point of view. Industrial psychologists have known for years that part of their work is to help their sponsor in analyzing and formulat- ing the problem. In other contexts, similar reeducation of the sponsor will often be necessary.

Research on Societal Problems

Our examination of research on societal problems will emphasize two general problems: decisions for treatments of classes of individuals, and selections among applicants for training or for jobs. While these do not cover the full range of problems, they are fairly typical. They have also been chosen because I have had some experience in working on each of them. The discussion will distinguish between in-house studies, conducted primarily for the benefit of a single institution, and in-society investigations, seeking findings that can be generalized with some degree of confidence to part of the society—to a class of agencies, organizations, or institutions. The in-society study is formulated to yield findings with wide applicability. The in-house study is ordinarily designed to contribute to administrative decisions seeking to maximize the effectiveness of the particular organization, and hence uses clients and observers from that one institution. The initial focus will be primarily on the in-house study.

For the investigator working on a societal problem, some things are in his favor. One is the obvious fact that the pertinent phenomena occur naturally, so that he does not have to contrive conditions and stimuli. Even the central material, the evaluative judgments, are ordinarily made in a routine way. Another advantage lies in the motivations of both clients and observer-judges. Although the investigator may need to introduce additional evaluation procedures, his observers will take their judgment task seriously, recognizing the importance of the evaluative process.

When an investigator elects to work on a societal problem that some sponsors have posed for him, he has the advantage of having a fairly clear orientation and direction. If he takes his problem just as presented to him by those sponsors, however, he is highly constrained. He must develop a research plan that appears pertinent to his societal sponsors. If not, he must persuade them that his plan will contribute to the solution of the problem as they see it. Although by drawing on his everyday experience he can usually understand their view of the problem, he may find it hard to educate his sponsors to the point where they can understand his arguments for formulating the research plan in a technically preferable way. And although his everyday experience may at first seem an advantage in preparing to work on the problem, his feeling of familiarity may deceive him into believing that he understands it well at the outset.

Replicability of Societal Phenomena. The phenomena of concern for a treatment problem are manifestations of behaviors that someone considers undesirable. Although they are often called *symptoms,* that label is unsuitable here because it implies that the concern is with the inferred disease or disability and not with the behaviors themselves. Yet the symptom label has the value of calling attention to the fact that society is concerned with the implications of the behavior, with the inference or prediction from the observed symptomatic behavior to the later behavior of the client. We must also note that these behaviors are identified and named by some observer.

In a curious way, these behaviors do not have to be taken as a sample of other behaviors. They are sufficient in themselves to identify the person as a client. If one behavior has been observed enough times, or if enough different behaviors have been observed, the client is identified as needing treatment. The only necessary generalization about the behaviors is the assumption that, since behavior tends to be consistent over time, the occurrence of these behaviors is a sufficient basis for predicting their future occurrence, and that is what treatment may be aimed at preventing.

In a selection problem, the phenomena are the behaviors used as a basis for the initial decision and those used at a later time as a basis for the criterion decision. Methodologically, these two sets of behaviors have much in common. Both are taken as performance and both involve observations that are interpreted and transformed into ratings or scores of some kind. At the time of selection, judgments about the applicant's behaviors have only modest agreement and replicability. Two evaluations in letters of recommendation for different applicants often seem to agree about as well as two letters about the same applicant—there is limited differentiation between applicants. Judgments based on interviews also show restricted replicability. Subsequently, the separate criterion measures of performance will also have so little covariation that they cannot be considered to replicate each other. If these are ratings, it is frequently not even possible to obtain judgments from a second observer with a given perspective. Just as a client ordinarily has only one therapist, an employee usually has only one immediate supervisor, so there may be no population of potential criterion judges but only a single judge. In contrast, the scoring of responses on a selection test is obviously replicated easily. Yet the responses themselves are specific to the test, and replication can be attempted only by readministering the same test. The score from one test cannot be closely replicated by another test unless the two tests are essentially parallel forms differing only in the particular content of the items.

The selection decision, to admit for training or to employ, is a judgment based on a set of heterogeneous information, much of which is attributional and interpretive. The final decision may be made by one person or by combining the judgments of several persons. The combining can be done clerically or by discussion and voting. Thus, the phenomena in societal problems are processed by observers who produce evaluative judgments. These are essentially the same as the interpretive, attributional judgments examined extensively in earlier chapters. They differ from the more general type of attributions in their focus on one variable, relative adequacy of performance or of expected performance. They may also differ in being more removed from direct observation of behavior. The final evaluative judgments are often based on intermediate judgments made by other observers.

Replicability can be increased by the common scientific practice of averaging a number of observations. Although a single observation may have a sizable error component, the averaging of several observations tends to let many errors cancel each other. This practice is effective insofar as the errors are random and are not correlated across observations, but it does not help cope with systematic errors consistent across observations. Although the classical theory of test scores builds on the assumption of uncorrelated errors, it does make the verifiable prediction that scores based on more items will be ordinarily more dependable, that is, more replicable.

Similarly, the mean of several ratings is more dependable than a single rating. Why then can we not use this established principle to increase the replicability of evaluative judgments to whatever level is required? Such averaging is often impractical if not impossible. There may simply be no pool of potential raters on which to draw. And even when other raters are available, it may be too expensive to use enough of them to obtain mean ratings with very high replicability (that is, mean ratings that would correlate highly with those from an independent set of raters).

For homogeneous quantitative dimensions, such as length, the averaging of several measurements works well, especially if a separate instrument is used for each of the observations. But evaluations of performance are complex, qualitative judgments, which are forced onto a single dimension only with difficulty. The evaluation made by each observer has its own qualitative aspects and its own structure, as can be seen in letters of recommendation. If one judge evaluates favorably because she sees the candidate as responsible, a second judge evaluates favorably on the basis of the candidate's sociability, and a third evaluates favorably on the basis of initiative, the favorable mean evaluation lacks consensual content.

Average evaluative judgments are undoubtedly more replicable than the judgment of an individual and should certainly be used wherever possible. But such averaging combines judgments that have different compositions, and hence the interpretation of an average rating is uncertain. Even more important, a mean rating is one step removed from the individual ratings it summarizes, and hence is one more step away from the original phenomena of interest, the behaviors.

Reproducibility and Generalizability. Once a research study on a societal problem has been completed, what can the investigator do to determine the extent to which its findings are reproducible? Where does she turn for another sample? Ordinarily, the population of persons has not been specified, and no explicit sampling has been carried out. Instead, the investigator is likely to have used a captive group of persons, a "sample of opportunity."

Similarly, she is likely to be at a loss when it comes to considering other components of the research plan. Were her observers drawn from some population that can be sampled anew? Or do her circumstances limit her to using the same observers again, thereby restricting the generality of any replicated findings? The investigator not only must specify all the pertinent conditions in her research but also must establish replicability of judgments as to those specifications. Her personal appraisal describing the selection interview or the tape of verbal therapy is not sufficient. Almost inevitably, instead of objective measurements of the conditions, judgments about them must be used, and these complex judgments can be replicated only to a limited degree.

It is true, of course, that an investigator can conduct a number of studies on the same problem, varying the persons studied, the observers used, and other features of the research plan. If she obtains findings that are closely reproduced in the series of studies, she can sketch out roughly for each component of her plan the range of conditions under which her established findings seem to hold. Would that any of us could be so fortunate! In research on societal problems, it is rare for any two studies to have highly congruent findings, to say nothing of more than two. Even if the findings of one study are rather well reproduced in a second study, the investigator must be cautious about her interpretations. In both studies, some unrecognized variable may be operating such that her observed effects cannot be confidently attributed to the presumed determining factors. Technically speaking, even when the findings of a study have been reproduced subsequently, the study may lack internal validity (Campbell and Stanley, 1963).

With limited replication of observations and with limited reproducibility of findings, there can be only very restricted generalizability. Even the generalizability of an in-house study to its own particular population is limited. For example, suppose that a study comparing two treatments administered to clients of a designated category is done in 1978. Surely it can be generalized to 1979, and probably even to 1982. We tend to believe that generalizing to future times is quite justified. But, as we saw earlier, it is not the chronological time but the set of conditions that matters. When given the next year, will the two treatments remain the same? Will they be more beneficial because they have been practiced more often, or will they be less beneficial because the interest in a new technique has waned? It is notorious that each new therapy has a higher success rate when first reported than at later times. Will the therapists perform the same way next year, or will they go about their treatment work more mechanically? Will the clients placed in the designated category next year be comparable to those so classified this year, especially if there is a new diagnostician next year?

The same kind of limitation is inevitably present in selection research. In a standard plan, a new potential predictor is added to the established selection procedures, but its scores are not used in selection decisions. When criterion measurements have been made, the investigator then determines whether the new predictor would have improved the efficiency of selection. If so, the new procedure is added to the predictor battery and is used to select and reject future applicants. But once the procedure is used in actual selection, there is no way of precisely checking its predictive value again. In spite of indirect analyses, such as correlating its scores for accepted applicants with the criterion measure, there is no certainty that the predictor continues to be related to performance among borderline or rejected applicants. The continued use of a selection procedure validated at a previous time is an act of faith based on the belief that the characteristics of the applicant population and the requirements of the job or training program have continued to remain constant in the intervening years.

In-Society Research. We have thus far emphasized in-house research within a single agency or organization. What additional considerations apply to in-society research involving several institutions—research that seeks conclusions applicable throughout a society or a subsociety? A central issue is representativeness. How can the investigator draw a sample of persons, behaviors, events, or conditions from a group of relevant institutions? In principle, he would simply list the population of interest and apply a standard sampling procedure, seeking a fully random sample or a stratified sample, as appropriate. But rarely will he be in a position to develop any actual listing of his population. What agencies should be included in a study of treatments for persons in distress? Which universities should be included in a study of selection for training in social psychology? The boundaries of such classifications are fuzzy at best.

There is also a pragmatic question—is such in-society research feasible in a democratic society? Can an investigator obtain the necessary cooperation from the array of institutions that he selects for his sample? Will those institutions be willing either to make available their present files or to spend the time and energy carrying out the data-gathering procedures specified in the investigator's research plan? It seems highly unlikely that the investigator can count on obtaining the considerable degree of cooperation required for implementing any planned in-society research. And refusals of cooperation would almost certainly bias his obtained sample in unknown or unknowable ways. Finally, as in all behavioral research, the investigator must consider the people studied. Can the cooperation of all designated individuals be obtained in an ethical way? Do individual refusals bias the findings? And what effects on the observations are contributed by the subjects' knowledge that they are subjects?

More fundamental is the problem of interaction between the client and the treatment, a problem thoroughly examined by Cronbach and Snow (1977) in the educational domain. They conclude that, although well-substantiated findings about interactions between student characteristics and educational treatments are scarce, such interactions clearly exist (see also Cronbach, 1975). Much educational research involves standardized tests. Granted that subject-test interactions are always likely, tests of aptitude and achievement avoid the difficulties associated with interpretive and evaluative judgments about others. Societal problems involve many kinds of interactions, some of them pertaining to judgments that are themselves judge-judged interactions. All of these interactions reduce the generalizability of findings from research on these problems.

What Can Be Done

The tremendous difficulties encountered in trying to carry out elegantly rigorous research on societal problems does not mean that behavioral scientists can do no useful research in this area. Investigators must simply be realistic in viewing both societal problems and their own work on those problems. They must see their research studies in perspective, recognizing what their findings can contribute and what conclusions can be drawn from their data and being careful not to imply that they have found general propositions with wide applicability. In addition to direct attacks on societal problems, behavioral scientists can make descriptive and analytic studies and can conduct pertinent methodological research.

Descriptive and Analytic Studies. The investigator can make substantial contributions to solving societal problems by precise descriptive studies in a single organization. Most agencies and institutions do not conduct periodic surveys of their effectiveness. Treatment agencies rarely produce annual reports summarizing, not just the number of persons treated or the number of treatment hours, but the effectiveness of their treatments. Training institutions may report the number of persons completing training but omit any appraisal of the proficiencies of their graduates.

The paucity of actuarial data on effectiveness is a consequence of the perennial criterion problem. An adequate assessment of persons who have completed treatment or training is expensive; most institutions opt for allocating their scarce resources to more treatment or training rather than to intensive measurement of outcome. An additional consideration is the nature of institutional objectives. Both in treating and in training, definitive evidence of effectiveness is not available immediately. Adequate assessments by criterion measures must evaluate performance over a period of years. At the end of that period, the institution is often doing its work in a different way, and the treaters and trainers have changed. Hence, any conclusions about effectiveness some years ago may be viewed as not applicable to present practices.

Some accounting is nevertheless desirable. It is easy for practitioners to develop beliefs about their work that are not entirely accurate, and these beliefs persist in the absence of any evidence to the contrary. An illustrative incident concerns two clinical diagnosticians who were convinced that their assessments from projective tests agreed well. After reading empirical reports of low agreement between other diagnosticians, they decided to gather systematic evidence on their own degree of consensus. They made independent assessments of a series of consecutive cases referred to them and carefully tallied the degree of agreement. Much to their chagrin, they discovered that it was very poor. Their prior belief was apparently a function of selective recall, of remembering those instances where they did agree or where they were able to persuade themselves that the two assessments could be reconciled as consistent and forgetting or explaining away the numerous other cases.

A more serious example is the occurrence of harmful consequences from psychotherapeutic treatment (Strupp and Hadley, 1977; Lambert, Bergin, and Collins, 1978). For many years, in reports of therapeutic outcome, the poorest outcome was identified by such categories as "no improvement" or "essentially no change."

Only in recent years have investigators included a category for "worse off at the end of treatment." Fortunately, the proportion of cases falling in such categories is rather small. Relative frequency, however, is not the central concern. Today, psychotherapists must confront the fact that some persons are actually hurt by psychotherapy. The crucial problem is how to prevent such harm. Should such persons be given a quite different kind of treatment? Should they receive no psychotherapy at all? Or should more care be exercised in matching the client with the therapist?

To solve that problem and to answer those questions, one must decide what is a negative effect of psychotherapy. Strupp, Hadley, and Gomes-Schwartz (1977) note that the criteria for identifying such effects are uncertain. This state of affairs is not surprising in view of the fact that assessing any outcome from psychotherapy requires a value judgment. Judgments about positive and negative effects depend to some degree on the viewpoint and vested interests of the judge.

The example of negative effects brings out a very important function of descriptive studies—they point out that something exists, at least in the judgment of the investigator; they indicate that certain things can happen. A descriptive study may have no systematic generalizability in the strict sense that has been examined in preceding chapters. Yet it can have important implications. The observation of one white crow permits the general statement that white crows exist, that not all crows are black. By noting the unusual or unexpected occurrence, a descriptive study can help to delineate the boundaries of a classification and the range within which a general proposition holds.

Descriptive studies can also have practical consequences. As an example, early research at the Counseling Center of the University of Chicago (Cartwright, 1955) produced a graph indicating the mean success rating by counselors for cases with varying numbers of therapeutic interviews. There was a generally positive relationship. The graph showed, however, a smooth dip in the region between thirteen and twenty-one interviews, and that region was labeled the *failure zone*. When similar data were examined several years later, there was no dip in that region; instead, there was a dip for cases where the number of interviews was in the twenties. Although intensive investigation of these phenomena was not carried out, it seems likely that counselors learned about the earlier findings and modified their behavior in their counseling interviews, or possibly in their ratings at the end of treatment, in a way that yielded the shift in that zone.

Descriptive research must not be seen as trivial and minor. As indicated earlier, societal problems stem from actual activities in the real world when one person is making a decision that affects another person in an important way. The decision may be made by persons administering treatments, making personnel selections, or setting policy. In reaching their decisions, they utilize whatever information they have, no matter how fallible and undependable it may be. They draw on their own subjective impressions and their own intuitive generalizations. The investigator who gathers pertinent data in a systematic fashion can contribute to the quality of those decisions by providing the decision maker with better information on which to base his decision.

The findings of descriptive studies are often counterintuitive, failing to support the general impressions that people have built up from their experience—impressions that all too often are selective and biased. Although descriptive studies may occasionally report relationships that are opposite in direction from expectations, more typically they will simply indicate that an expected relationship is not present in the data. Such studies contribute to the negative knowledge discussed in Chapter One. Such knowledge is important because it jolts us out of our unfounded belief that we do understand and thus makes it possible for us to examine alternative conceptualizations in our search for empirically supported understanding.

Finally, descriptive studies can be useful at the societal level. Even when systematic, comprehensive investigations involving several institutions or contexts are not feasible, reported in-house studies can be compiled and carefully analyzed. The reviewer must take into account the complex determination of the empirical phenomena in any one study. For instance, a report entitled "Planning of Research on Effectiveness of Psychotherapy" (Fiske and others, 1970) outlines the numerous components in such research and points out the obligations of the investigator to provide information on each. Although published papers do not usually give all the relevant information, some useful compilations of findings can be made. For example,

Luborsky and others (1971) have pulled together the findings from 166 studies of psychotherapy. For any one issue, their set of results often shows a trend rather than a strong relationship. Yet their summarizations do indicate problems deserving investigation and findings meriting additional study. In a later paper, Luborsky, Singer, and Luborsky (1975) examined the smaller body of research comparing psychotherapies with each other and with other treatments. Granting the unknown biases in the set of published papers they could examine, their report on insignificant differences among outcomes of different psychotherapies is an important conclusion. An example in another area was mentioned earlier—Cronbach and Snow (1977) made a painstaking, critical review of studies of interactions between pupil characteristics and educational treatments, concluding that few findings in this area have been well established. The nearest thing to confirmed generalizations about societal problems are the final judgments in such reviews, especially when based on a finding occurring in all or almost all of the pertinent studies reviewed. Regrettably, such congruence among results is more common for null relationships than for strong associations.

In addition to descriptive studies, analytic research can be profitable in this area. The several components in each class of societal problem should be identified and investigated. For example, within the psychotherapy area, the contributions of therapist and client expectancies to outcome need further documentation. A related topic is the utility of the orientation interview described by Orne and Wender (1968), an interview designed to let the therapy client know what is likely to happen and hence what the therapist expects to occur. In personnel work, the components of job satisfaction and the factors contributing to evaluations of job performance have been determined.

Clearly desirable is an intensive examination of the terms in which societal problems are posed. The problems that stem from the use of such vague verbal labels have been examined in Chapter Two and the difficulties with the meanings of attributive statements were noted in Chapter Three. The topic is also related to the subject of the next chapter. A brief consideration is, nevertheless, appropriate here. Relatively little space in this book has been devoted to the meanings of concepts and attributions, but we must make an explicit distinction here between two broad types of meaning. One is the meaning intended by observers making interpretive attributions to others, judgments of the kind examined repeatedly in this book. These meanings have considerable specificity associated with the individual attributer. The other is the meaning of a concept within a scientific context. Following Feigl, that meaning is taken as specified only by the place of the concept "in the entire theoretical system involving the postulates, definitions, correspondence rules, and finally the operational definitions" (1970, p. 7). Rather than being to some significant degree idiosyncratic, that kind of meaning is shared among those scientists working within the particular domain.

The meanings of such societal concepts as *adjustment* and *mental health* have been extensively studied (for instance, see Jahoda, 1958). There is an enormous conceptual literature on these topics. Yet little research seems to have been done on the heterogeneous meanings that these terms appear to have for practitioners and on the complex nature of the meaning that such terms have for the individual professional worker. Perhaps the range of attitudes toward mental illness (Rabkin, 1972) stems in part from the variation in meanings for that term. In the domain of training and other personnel activity, similar research and analysis are needed on concepts of adequate performance.

The investigation of society's concepts may need to be carried out in naturalistic settings, rather than by gathering responses to multiple-choice scales. Investigators could look for answers to questions like the following: When a professional indicates that a client is in need of treatment, what specific behaviors does he cite? When a client says that he has benefited from a treatment, what evidence does he offer? When an evaluator judges a person to be performing his work well, what does he say about the person's products?

Protocols of the kind just mentioned can also be used for work on the evaluative process. Since evaluations are central to societal problems, it is necessary to learn how these evaluations are made. To study this topic, observations in natural settings are preferable. If, however, the investigator queries a supervisor repeatedly about her evaluation of an employee, he will be likely to affect the evaluation. The supervisor may feel she has to make an evaluative judgment before she is ready to do so. And once she has stated her judgment publicly, she is less likely to modify it in the face of evidence indicating that it is not correct.

Many questions can be asked about the evaluative judgments routinely made by supervisors or other natural raters. Does the rater base his evaluation on behaviors relevant to performance or on trivial characteristics of the person's appearance or interacting? Does the rater implicitly use a disjunctive model, basing his final overall rating on the weakest component of the person's performance? Conversely, if the person is very good in some one area, does the rater ignore weaknesses in other areas? Ideally, these questions should be pursued by statistical analyses that do not intrude on the natural process.

The extensive literature on judgment and on decision making suggests that progress is being made toward some understanding of these processes. Although most of the research has been done under experimental conditions, some investigations have utilized judgments made in the real world, such as those determining acceptance or rejection for training. Further research is needed on the applicability of these experimental findings to natural judgments and decisions. The designing of such research will challenge the ingenuity and creativity of investigators.

Methodology. A major type of fruitful research on societal problems is methodological. Investigators can examine methods for obtaining evaluative judgments that measure diagnostic, predictive, or criterion variables. They can also develop appropriate quantitative methods and designs for the kinds of research required in this domain. The contributions of these investigators should be shown to hold empirically over a variety of substantive content.

For example, it is generally accepted that the quality of evaluative judgments is improved if the evaluators make a series of judgments about components before making their overall evaluation. An instrument that requires the evaluator to consider each of the several aspects of job performance will yield summary ratings that are not as impressionistic and as susceptible to the overweighting of one aspect as those obtained by a scale that simply asks for a single overall judgment. Again, evaluations that require comparing persons by ordering them provide more discriminations than just rating each person on a standard scale. The classical "man-to-man" rating procedure, conceived many decades ago, can be applied on a person-to-person basis today. It is often true that the more effort required of a respondent, the better the quality of his responses will be—provided that the respondent is sufficiently motivated to carry out the judging task conscientiously.

A major methodological finding of central importance to research on societal problems is the low correlation between independent methods of measuring adaptation and performance. Evidence supporting the general concept of method variance (Campbell and Fiske, 1959) is well established. Each type of method contributes specific variance to its measurements. In particular, evaluative judgments made by persons with different perspectives and sources of information tend to have limited agreement with each other. Related to that generalization is the lack of consensus between independent measures of effects of treatments. These general propositions are well documented in diverse empirical investigations, and they have significant implications for a variety of societal problems. The investigator should obtain evaluations from all perspectives and persons relevant to the given problem. She should analyze the effect of a treatment as assessed by each distinguishable type of evaluation.

Method factors must be taken into account when planning research in this area. Furthermore, investigations should be directed at the identification of the several possible kinds of method effects that can impair such research. For example, to what extent does the segment of observed behavior on which the judge bases his evaluation contribute to the judgment? Is such contribution minimal when the judge has observed the person in a reasonable variety of contexts? Again, how and when does the format of the evaluation instrument make a difference? Are effects associated with format small in comparison to those associated with the evaluator's knowledge of the use to which his evaluations will be put?

Multiple operations are essential for assessing outcome or any other central variable of interest in a societal problem. At a somewhat more general level, a promising type of program design involves convergent approaches in which the target is studied in several distinctive ways, each having its own empirical procedures and its own ways of measuring the central variables. As an example, the nature of the interaction in the therapeutic process can be approached by identifying certain apparently critical moments in the course of the therapy hour. Videotape recordings of these segments can be studied by independent observers. The passages can be played back to the therapist, and she can be asked what she felt was going on in each. Under some circumstances, similar stimulated recall might be used with the client. And perhaps the psychophysiological concomitants can also be examined.

The above example seems practicable, at least in principle, because the events to be studied can be identified in space and time. But what about the effects of therapeutic treatment that occur between formal sessions? Once again, we can ask the client what happened, and we can ask the therapist her opinion about what happened and about what the client reports as having happened. Our data would be relatively unsatisfactory, however. At the most, we would have only verbal reports from deeply involved persons, reports that have been filtered through memory.

We can agree on the desirability of approaching any behavioral research topic by more than one strategy and from more than one perspective. It does seem, however, that the program design labeled *converging operations* by Garner (1974) is appropriate only for fields more advanced than personality and others involved in societal problems. For the application of that design, the phenomena at issue must be identified and delineated much more explicitly and definitively than can be done for the phenomena being considered here.

Another general proposition is that the strongest consistencies over time are found when measurements of the same kind are made in similar settings. The best prediction of how a person will perform on a given task or in a given role is that he will do as he did the last time. The best predictor of job performance or of gain from a training experience is a work sample of the person's performance under working or training conditions. (For example, the best single predictor of grade-point average is previous grade-point average.) McClelland (1972) extends this proposition, arguing that, to predict actions, one should use actions, and to predict opinions, one should use opinion measures. Consistency of behavior is not only higher when the setting and task are the same but also when the kind of phenomenon is the same.

The design of experiments forms another large class of methodological contributions to the investigation of societal problems.

The difficulties encountered in determining how to measure gain from treatment for individuals have been exposed and examined. One important product of these methodological papers has been the argument by Cronbach and Furby (1970) that it is rarely, if ever, necessary to design a study involving the gain or change scores for individuals. Research on treatments can be conducted more effectively by designs involving group differences in scores at a point in time. Other major developments in designs for societal problems will be considered later.

History shows that progress can be made in developing the methodology for research on societal problems. We should be able to improve the quality of the evaluative judgments that are the central data for research on these problems. No matter how strong our desires to find immediate solutions to matters that concern all of us, we may have to take a coldly pragmatic attitude and work first on the means for moving toward those idealistic ends. We must have optimal measuring procedures. We must find feasible and effective research designs.

But why should the methodological investigator believe that she can make any general contribution when her substantively oriented colleague faces such overwhelming obstacles to generalizability? In addition to arguing from history, she can have other reasons. What the methodologist studies are matters common to a variety of substantive areas. If those who evaluate performance are helped by explication of the several components of performance, it is reasonable to expect that the same kind of explication will aid those who evaluate adaptation. The process of evaluation has much in common in the two settings. The methodologist also faces a somewhat easier task. A study of outcome for treatments may take years to complete, and hence any repetitions of that study will take another block of years. In contrast, methodological studies can often be completed within a much shorter period, so that both the investigator and her colleagues can attempt to replicate her findings much more readily. Although it is just as necessary to replicate substantive findings, it is more likely that the necessary set of investigations will be carried out, and soon.

Methodological studies are concerned with the relatively objective and public components in the research process, such as the printed instruments and the procedures for processing responses into data and data into findings. The investigator wishing to compare two formats for a rating scale can readily communicate to others what those scales looked like. The investigator comparing two treatments has a much more difficult descriptive task, and his colleague trying to repeat his study cannot be sure that his attempts to replicate those treatments with other therapists were successful reproductions.

Research on methodological issues in the investigation of societal problems is a kind of engineering. Methodology has developed some generalizations that appear to hold fairly widely. The question is to determine when and how they apply to these problems. In contrast, substantive research on societal problems can hardly be viewed as engineering, since such research has few if any general laws from which to derive expected applications to the particular circumstances of the societal problem.

This discussion has omitted any reference to substantive theory. Cannot the investigator studying a societal problem bring to bear her knowledge of personality theory and other kinds of theories? I grant that the theoretical viewpoint of an investigator may affect the way she approaches a societal problem and may influence her choices of particular variables to introduce into her research plan. It is also possible that she may be able to derive from personality theory some conceptual proposition that will guide her in formulating her experimental hypothesis. I have, however, omitted any discussion of personality theory because I do not see such theory as having any clear, direct, logically compelling relevance for most societal problems. These problems concern such specifics as this treatment, that person's maladjustment, someone else's performance on his job. What is pertinent is how these are perceived, interpreted, and judged by people in various roles. Furthermore, as argued earlier in this book, I see personality theories as attributional abstractions stemming from the theorists' interpretations of their own personal experience. As such, the linkages between theoretical constructs and empirical measuring procedures are tenuous, if indeed they exist at all.

The Evaluation of Social Programs. A new field, evaluation research, has been identified in recent years. It is concerned with the methodology of evaluating the effectiveness of social programs that treat people to improve their welfare. Included within this rubric are programs concerned not only with mental health but also with delin-

quency, criminology, law, education, and socioeconomics. Headstart
and the Income Maintenance study are two of the best-known programs that have been evaluated. These empirical evaluations constitute a major variety of research on societal problems and deserve
examination here because they help us see what can be done.

This research has yielded a number of important findings. The
Manhattan Bail Project (Botein, 1964–65; Sturz, 1962, 1967) is an
excellent illustration. For a group of prisoners accused of felonies and
misdemeanors but not very serious crimes, studies of their prior histories and their roots in the community were made to determine
whether to recommend pretrial release without bail. Those for whom
that recommendation was judged appropriate were divided randomly
into two groups. Nothing was done for the control group, but favorable recommendations were made to the judge for the experimental
group. The judge granted parole to many more in the experimental
group than in the control group. Almost every one of the experimental group showed up in court for trial. In addition, a much
larger proportion of people in that group were either acquitted or
had their cases dismissed. Similar projects have since been started
in other cities.

Evaluation research has shown the value of searching for
objective indices of outcome wherever possible. In the Bail Project, all
the criteria were objective. Note, however, that evaluative judgments
were required to determine who should be recommended for parole.
In mental health and rehabilitation, objective indices are also available for many of the objectives.

The field of evaluation research has made many methodological contributions. Although some writers have argued that true
experiments with randomization are not possible or even desirable in
this area, others have disagreed (see, for example, Riecken and
Boruch, 1974; Bennett and Lumsdaine, 1975). But where experiments
cannot be done, various quasi-experimental designs may be valuable.
Since the classic monograph of Campbell and Stanley (1963), many
possible designs have been identified and appraised. Perhaps the most
important product has been the formulation of numerous threats to
validity. These include both threats to the internal validity of interpretations and conclusions drawn from the particular data of an

investigation, and threats to external validity, generalizations beyond those data (Cook and Campbell, 1976).

By using these methodological developments along with prior methodology, behavioral scientists can do effective work on societal problems. Each such investigation, however, must be planned and executed with great care. Insofar as possible, the criterion measures should be objective indices rather than evaluative judgments. The external validity of such research—the extent to which the findings of a single study can be generalized with confidence—will depend largely on the avoidance of interpretive judgments in the treatment itself and in the assessment of outcome. Unusual care is necessary in designing and carrying out a study evaluating a treatment program because the costs of such an investigation are great, and, consequently, few will be done. Replication within a single investigation or one experimental program, as in the Headstart and Income Maintenance research, becomes almost essential—when will funds be available for repeating those studies?

One ultimate criterion in science is reproducibility of findings. Perhaps what is needed today is methodological work on the problem of designing modest studies in such a way that the findings of several can be integrated confidently so that firm conclusions can be established. Given a number of separate investigations designed and carried out so that their results can be compared and amalgamated, we may learn more than we do from a single investigation costing the same total amount.

The many behavioral scientists who want to make contributions that are steps toward the resolution of societal problems can do effective work. They must recognize, of course, that their work is largely specific to current problems, since societal problems are formulated in contemporary terms. Treatments aimed at ameliorating these problems are such complex entities that it is very difficult to determine whether a treatment administered by certain people in one context can be considered essentially the same as a purportedly similar treatment given elsewhere. And even when the full specifications of a successful treatment can be determined, only the first step has been taken toward any contribution to basic science. Much additional research is necessary to identify the active elements or compounds in that treatment. We should not forget, however, that important advances in science have resulted from research on applied problems by investigators who had the genius to conceive and demonstrate the underlying fundamental laws.

Temporal Relativity

Earlier in this chapter, the question of generalizing from one setting to another, from one institution to another, was discussed. It was pointed out that the same agency or the same organization may be different at a later time, when the pertinent personnel have changed. Societal problems are presented in terms of particular persons in a particular setting at a particular time.

Gergen (1973) has argued the provocative thesis that social psychology is primarily a historical inquiry. Theories of social behavior reflect contemporary history, and psychological knowledge can affect the behavior on which that knowledge is based. His thesis undoubtedly has some validity, especially over long periods of time. Does it apply to societal problems? It is true that the conception of mental illness has changed greatly over the centuries and varies somewhat from place to place in the contemporary world. From the viewpoint of this book, however, the crucial consideration is that societal concepts change over time—what was once considered appropriate behavior may no longer be seen as necessary or even desirable. The conception of adequate adapting and coping has also changed over time. In some instances, the public view of adequate performance on the job has also been altered.

Insofar as the variables being judged are societal concepts, the judgments of observers will be time-bound to some degree. Even when the label remains essentially the same, the way in which observers interpret that label and perhaps even the processes they use in formulating judgments may change over the years. Assessing the degree of that change would, of course, be extremely difficult. Some idea of the magnitude of potential effects can be obtained by comparing observers who are members of diverse contemporary cultural groups. Any investigation of that topic, however, faces tremendous difficulties of translating the concepts. It is significant that a language may not have words for concepts frequently used in other languages. Even the familiar phrase *thank you* has no direct equivalent in some dialects.

Cronbach (1975) has made a related point pertaining to smaller entities than cultures or cultural epochs. He notes that empirical generalizations decay over time. A generalization is a working hypothesis that must be demonstrated to hold for the given set of local conditions to which one wishes to apply it. In his view, "though enduring systematic theories about man in society are not likely to be achieved, systematic inquiry can realistically hope to make two contributions. One reasonable aspiration is to assess local events accurately, to improve short-run control (Glass, 1972). The other reasonable aspiration is to develop explanatory concepts, concepts that will help people use their heads" (1975, p. 126).

The pointing up of historical, cultural, and subcultural differences in observed effects does not mean that behavioral science is impossible. It does mean that care must be taken in claiming generalizability of findings. Scientists must not be so provincial as to assume implicitly that their given behavioral findings hold universally and for all time. Part of their task is to establish the cultural limits within which their tentative generalizations hold. Behavioral scientists should make more explicit the social conditions under which they collected their data.

Most likely to change over cultures and times are content and meaning, especially where words are involved. Other approaches to human behavior are likely to be more general. Just as physiology obeys much the same laws regardless of the particular foods and beverages consumed, so some psychological processes seem fairly general. Instrumental conditioning would seem to be one example, and operant conditioning another. Laws about sensory, perceptual, and cognitive processes may be established as general across culture and over time. It may well be that generalizations about cognizing behavior and making attributions to people will have considerable replicability, if not universality. And, although there may be changes in the particular actions in the action sequences from which the rules observed in face-to-face interactions are derived, the structuring of interactions may be as dependable as the pupillometric response or the duck's response to her duckling.

What then is the strategy for studying societal problems? It consists of recognizing what can and what cannot be done in investigating these problems. The investigator must recognize the fundamental and pervasive role of attributive judgments evaluating the performance of those on whom the problem focuses. In planning her research, she must realize that her complex variables cannot be completely analyzed into components observable by simple processes involving just recognition and identification. She has to accept the fact that these factors and the various interactions between judges and judged, between treaters and treated, make it very difficult to interpret her empirical findings. In addition to internal validity, there is the more serious question of external validity. Although she may feel considerable confidence in her interpretations of her results, the extent to which they apply beyond her particular data is always questionable. Nevertheless, actions have to be taken and decisions have to be made in the real world. A well-designed and carefully executed investigation of a societal problem does make available better information than can be obtained by other means. Behavioral scientists can make contributions toward resolving specific societal problems even though those contributions do not add to our basic scientific knowledge about behavior.

When we read a report of societal research, we should not expect the findings to have the universality of an established chemical or physical equation. Investigations can make different kinds of contributions. As consumers of research reports, we should consider not only what the investigator found in her data but also whether she is justified in interpreting those findings as she does. If so, to what circumscribed domain might those findings prove to be generalizable? Even more important, what new ideas does the study suggest? Does it indicate that some unexpected kind of relationship may exist? Does it call for some change? Does it reveal some unrecognized assumption or some weak link in our previous conceptualization of the substantive area?

Summary

The research decisions of an investigator generate a strategy, such as that for studying societal problems. To students of personality and related fields, society presents many and diverse problems relevant to improving the welfare of persons and the effectiveness of institutions. Society states these problems in terms of its own concepts. The problems involve decisions between courses of actions. A problem may deal with decisions made within a single institution or agency; alternatively, it may refer to decisions applicable throughout a set of institutions.

Societal problems typically involve persons as they are perceived by others. One set of people makes evaluative judgments about other persons, and so research on societal problems has all the weaknesses associated with such attributions. Replicability is limited, reproducibility of findings is constrained, and little generalizability is present. Yet much can be done within these restrictions. Purely descriptive studies have practical utilities. Societal concepts can be analyzed, and the formulations of societal problems can be examined.

In particular, methodological studies can make important contributions to work on societal problems. Whatever the problem, optimal methods for collecting observations and optimal procedures for instructing observer-raters must be sought. It is essential that the investigator who chooses to work on a societal problem recognize the temporal and situational relativity of his observations and findings.

XI

The Strategy for
Studying Attributions

The last chapter considered the strategy for work on societal problems, a strategy identified primarily by the investigator's decision to choose a problem presented by society. This chapter examines another broadly defined strategy, Strategy 3 in Table 3 (Chapter Nine), which is formed by the investigator's decisions to identify his own problem (1b) and to study expressions about people (3a). These choices locate a large and heterogeneous area, including attitudes that people express about groups of people (as studied in social psychology and cultural anthropology) and opinions about political figures (as expressed in surveys and in voting behavior). For the investigator interested in the personality domain, the important

266

phenomena identified by these two decisions are the attributions that people make about individuals, including those they make about themselves. The latter will be mentioned in this chapter, but the stress will be placed on attributions that persons make about others.

These phenomena are clearly the products of interpretation and inference. As noted in the preceding chapters, however, there can be two or more observational stages for the production of data in the personality domain. The initial attributions are typically processed by another set of observers. The investigator may have his final observers make observations that are simple cognitions about those attributions (for example, he may ask them to identify the actual words used in the attributions), or he may have them make observations that interpret the attributions made by the initial actors (Decision 6 in Table 2, Chapter Eight). To illustrate, the investigator may want to determine the specific words most frequently used in spontaneous descriptions of friends, or he may wish to learn the proportion of attributions that refer to interpersonal actions as opposed to personal abilities and styles.

The investigator studying attributions need not be concerned with the accuracy of the attributing. His focus is on the attributing, with more emphasis on the person making the attributions than on the person described. He also is not necessarily concerned with how the attributor "really" perceives the other. Although usually expecting considerable similarity between what the attributor says and what he thinks to himself, the investigator's phenomena are the attributive statements.

What one person attributes to another is obviously of central importance to the understanding of phenomena in the domain of personality and in related domains. Attributing is of particular importance to relationships between people. A person's statement to us about her perceptions of someone can influence our own perceptions of both the person described and the person making the attributions. It is also possible that the attributor herself is affected by her overt statement of her perceptions. Even more important is the light that her statement throws on her impressions, perceptions, and construals of the person described—or, in other words, on that person's effects on her.

What a person overtly attributes to another and how she formulates her attribution is presumably influenced by the context of the attributing, including both the audience and the factors leading the person to make the attributions. Social norms may induce someone to say "You're looking well" to a sick person she wants to cheer up. In addition to such incongruence between inner impressions and what is spoken, there is a selective factor. In any one verbal statement about another, the attributor does not include everything she feels or perceives about that person. Finally, there is the subjective feeling of the inadequacy of words. After a subject has been asked to describe someone, either on a standardized instrument where choices are provided or in her own words, she can be asked how well her report captures her picture of that person. She will typically reply that her description is somehow not complete. The wealth of feelings, perceptions, and attitudes that the subject has about the other is never completely expressed in the subject's responses to the psychological task given her.

Since both the study of societal problems and the study of attributions involve interpretations, the distinction between them is not always sharp. The criterion resides in the mind of the investigator. It can be based on the investigator's stated perception of his choice. Other people, especially clinicians, may perceive his choice as having an unconscious determination (for example, see Devereux, 1967, p. 148). More important for the purposes of this book is whether the investigator sees himself as taking on a problem posed by society and couched in society's concepts, a problem whose solution would benefit some persons or some institution, or whether he sees himself as picking his own problem for its intrinsic interest or conceptual significance.

There is a major difference in emphasis between the societal and the attributional strategies. In research on societal problems, the emphasis is on the person as judged. Each datum is a judgment about a person, the stress being on that person and not on the judge. In research on attributions, the emphasis is on the attributing process as it occurs in the attributor. Each datum is an attribution made by a person, and the other person to whom the attribution is ascribed is part of the identification of the datum but of secondary interest. Within the attributional strategy, research can focus on individual differences among attributors or on the attribution process as it occurs in most people.

Brodbeck writes that "what people say (and what and how they mean by what they say) is part of the social scientist's subject matter" (1968, p. 5) although the scientist uses a different language in investigating it. That scientist is studying the social reality experienced by people in their everyday living, according to Schutz. "The constructs of the social sciences are, so to speak, constructs of the second degree, that is, constructs of the constructs made by the actors on the social scene, whose behavior the social scientist has to observe and explain in accordance with the procedural rules of his science" (Schutz, 1967, p. 59). People's construals as manifested in their attributions form one of the worlds that can be investigated by the behavioral scientist.

The Nature of Attributing

The way people view other people is crucial in their reactions to and interactions with others. Consequently, we need to know what goes on in everyday attributing. Some of this attributing seems to occur as an end in itself, as when we think back about an interaction and describe another person to ourselves. At other times, we may describe that other person to someone else because there was something unusual about the behavior we observed or because we simply want to share our interpretation and perhaps obtain some confirmation or support for our ascriptions. Often we are trying to find an explanation of the observed behavior that satisfies us, and so we have to make a judgment under conditions with considerable uncertainty —a judgment liable to biases (Tversky and Kahneman, 1974; Shweder, 1977). Then there is the attributing associated with making a decision whether to initiate a renewal of the interaction with the person or to avoid further interactions. Finally, there is the attributing that results in an evaluation for some practical decision about the other, as in a societal problem.

Although the understanding of everyday attributing is a primary concern, researchers must also examine the attributing that is done as part of their own investigations. What goes on in the production of the attributional data that are used in research studies, especially in the traditional kinds of personality research where the data are ratings of others or reports about one's own feelings and actions? As emphasized in Part One, most personality data have been attributional judgments, and it is essential that we understand how those judgments are made.

Leonard Rorer (unpublished remarks) has urged that we discover the ascription rules that people use in their everyday life and the rules they use in producing personality data for us. How do people integrate impressions from diverse situations? Against what norms do they compare a person? From what reference group are the norms derived? There is good reason to expect to find some consistent individuality in a person's attributions to others (Koltuv, 1962) and in judgmental styles (Ramanaiah and Goldberg, 1977). There are also consistencies in the attributions made by one social group as opposed to another, and probably by one culture when compared to other cultures. What are these consistencies? Can they be construed as implicit rules?

Since attributing is a complex process, it is likely that it does not have a universal form. It is a kind of problem solving, and we know that people go about solving problems in various ways, even for such standardized problems as items in a test of aptitude. So we must look for processes, not a single process. Depending on the occasion and the reasons for making an attribution, a person may follow a different process from one time to another, varying the cognitive style he uses.

Attributing is part of information processing and information reduction, as various writers have noted (for example, Bruner, 1958; Brown, 1965, Chap. 12; W. Mischel, 1977). Its chief feature is that it takes a large body of information—the multitude of perceptions while with another person—and reduces it to a few categorical statements. In this respect, it is much like the formation of attitudes, and it contrasts sharply with cognizing processes in which the stimulus is fixed and the person cognizes a word, a symbol, or a picture. For attributions, the stimuli are constantly changing as the person moves and talks. Yet the identity of the person remains the same, and hence the attributions are associated with the person and not with the stream of her behavior. In this aspect, the formation of an attribution differs from the more generalized formation of an attitude where the object of the attitude is often less clearly identified. Although that object may be a specific thing (my car) or a particular person (John Smith), the object for an attitude is commonly a concept (Marxism), a political issue (tax reform), or a class of people (environmentalists).

Attributing is a common, recurring, practiced process. It is not undertaken as a novel experience each time it occurs. Attributing draws on our prior attributing and on the labels we have used before. It invokes our preconceptions of the meanings of particular actions and sentences, the meanings of the stimuli the person is reacting to, and the meanings of the situations in which the person is behaving. Being a practiced activity, it should have some consistency over time, a matter that should make it easier to study. But since it involves personal meanings, it is difficult to analyze empirically.

Research on the Content of Attributions

Research directed at attributions can be roughly divided into research on the process of attributing and research on the products or contents of attributing—the attributions themselves. Since these products are directly available, the study of the contents is the easier type of investigation. These contents may be adverbial in form, labeling the way the person is doing something. Such attributing is typically momentary, characterizing the behavior at this time without necessarily implying any lasting attribute of the person. As Carr and Kingsbury (1938) suggested, the description of behaving persons probably starts with adverbs ("he acted impulsively") and then moves to adjectives ("he is impulsive"). The noun form ("impulsiveness") is the construct used by the professional in the field.

Although research on content can examine naturally occurring attributions, such research is comparatively rare. A classical instance is the *Letters from Jenny* (Allport, 1965) that were analyzed by Baldwin (1942). Investigators probably avoid the analysis of natural products in part because of the tremendous amount of effort entailed in determining categories from the material and in doing the coding. Other inhibiting factors are the difficulties encountered in obtaining comparable material about several persons and the limitations imposed on generalizing over persons, especially if the coding categories are formed separately for each person's protocol.

One fruitful type of research on attribution involves compiling
and analyzing attributive words. The earliest extensive catalogue is
that of Allport and Odbert (1936), who compiled about 18,000 trait
names identifying distinctive forms of personal behavior. Allport
(1961) notes that such a lexicon of trait names is influenced by our
desire to label, by cultural sources, and by evaluative purposes.

That list has been a resource for several later studies. For example, Norman drew on this pool in arriving at his *2800 Personality
Trait Descriptors* (1967). For each of his terms, Norman determined
the familiarity level, the specificity of connotative meaning, and such
operating characteristics as desirability and endorsement rates for
describing self and others, all within a university population.

The large contribution of evaluation to attributions, noted by
Allport and assessed by Norman, was critically examined by Peabody
(1967), who pointed out that extremes are evaluated negatively. Taking off from that work, Goldberg and others (1975) have developed a
paradigm involving the semantic categories of a term and its opposite, along with the desirability dimension, which can be dichoto-
mized as favorable-unfavorable. To illustrate the resulting two-
by-two table, *flexible* is favorable and *rigid* and *inflexible* are
unfavorable opposites diagonally away from *flexible; firm* and *deci-
sive*, though opposed to *flexible*, are in the other favorable category,
and diagonally away from them is *indecisive*, another unfavorable term.

Any study of content involves examination of meanings, and
the study of attributions is no exception. Of course, the several taxonomies organize attributive labels in terms of presumed common
meanings, and the study of covariations is also based on meanings.
But the meaning of an attribution can also be approached directly,
like the meaning of other concepts. A major framework for studying
meaning was developed by Osgood (Osgood, Suci, and Tannenbaum,
1957), who has identified three major dimensions that seem to pervade
meaning in most areas. His factors are evaluation, potency or
strength, and intensity or activity. About half of the common variance
in judgments about meanings is accounted for by the evaluative
factor. Osgood (1962) has offered considerable evidence for the generality of these factors across people and cultures. Other cross-cultural
studies are included in Snider and Osgood (1969). Shweder (1972) utilized Osgood's framework in his cross-cultural study of the semantic
structures in personality assessments.

Osgood (1962) also reports application of his approach to descriptions of persons. In this work, he found a number of factors, the major one again being evaluative. This factor took the form of terms like *moral* and *reputable;* activity became *excitable* and *emotional;* potency was expressed by the term *toughness (hard, masculine).* Osgood's basic instrument, the Semantic Differential Technique, has been used in a number of studies in the personality domain (see Wiggins, 1973, p. 349; Snider and Osgood, 1969, Pt. IX).

Among other questions about the meanings of attributions, we can ask how they develop ontogenetically. Ervin and Foster (1960) report a somewhat undifferentiated evaluative factor in the responses of first-grade children to drawings of a face. Yet Di Vesta (1966) found Osgood's three factors as early as the second grade. We can also ask about the immediate development of meanings in formulating attributions about a particular person. Does the evaluative component appear first in all attributing? Does it have consistent primacy for some attributors but not for others? Are there individual differences in the patterning of emerging components of meaning?

It does seem quite likely that, in forming an impression, the first quality to emerge is evaluative—positive-negative, liking-disliking. Although the evaluative factor has a central role in meanings in general, its relative importance seems even greater in attributions, and its primacy is fairly general, regardless of context. It is, of course, of particular significance in the attributions involved in the study of societal problems. One intriguing question is the basis for favorableness of attributions. In the Shrout study (1976) summarized in Chapter Eight, favorableness was associated with the amount of activity as scored independently for a number of acts. It would be interesting to know whether physical activity, the sheer frequency and duration of these acts, is related to attributed activity as assessed on the Semantic Differential.

Attributions can also be studied by analyzing the relationships among attributive terms. One tactic has been to look for opposites, as discussed above. Although judges can decide that one term is essentially the opposite of another, investigators do not find that judged opposites have an exact negative relationship when people apply these terms to others (Fiske, 1971, p. 100). After all, no one is always dominating and never submissive, or the reverse. Almost every attribute applies to every person's behavior to at least a minimal degree. Hence, the semantic structure in a set of attributive words is not completely reproduced in the empirical analysis of attributions applied to people. Other factors, such as response sets, also contribute to the discrepancies.

The prevailing approach has been to examine positive covariations among attributions, hoping not only to find redundancies but also to identify major dimensions so that the mass of attributions can be described systematically in terms of a relatively small number of dimensions. Some investigators would have us settle for just two or three bipolar dimensions; others find that five are sufficient; still others have identified two or three dozen. The investigator can make her choice as a function of the number of scales or dimensions she wishes to use and the level of abstraction she decides to emphasize. There is no compelling empirical evidence in favor of any one set of dimensions. A person can be described by very particular idiographic phrases, by very broad abstractions, or by terms at some intermediate level. And personality theories provide no guidance. No conceptualization of attributions has proved to be distinctly more fruitful than any other.

The major obstacle to the identification of primary dimensions among attributions is the simple fact that we cannot determine any dependable estimate of the covariation or relationship between two attributive terms. I examined several sets of obtained correlations that had been reported among a well-known list of personality variables, Murray's needs (Fiske, 1973). I found that the empirical relationship between two needs often varied with the instrument by which the attributions were obtained, even when the same people used these instruments in reporting their observations. (In this instance, most of the data were self-attributions. It seems almost certain that the same findings would occur if descriptions of others were made on several instruments.) Each obtained relationship was in part a function of the special content for the items created by each test constructor in building his own instrument. Further analyses by Ebbeson and Allen (1977) suggested that the structure of the relationship varies with the instrument.

In contrast, the covariation among particular attributive scales can be determined with fairly good reproducibility. For example, Norman (1963) has replicated a five-factor structure derived from the twenty scales developed by him. But the critical question is the locus of such dependable covariation. Using the same scales, Passini and Norman (1966) had subjects rate others who had been in the same room with them for a few minutes but with whom they had had no verbal communication. These ratings yielded the same structure. Of course, the raters agreed with each other poorly. Norman and Goldberg (1966) went on to show that the same structure is found with varying degrees of acquaintance even though the level of agreement between raters increased with acquaintanceship. The covariation among these scales appears to be based on meanings for the words and phrases in these scales, meanings that are shared by members of a given subculture.

But what do covariations among specific scales tell us? More than a decade ago, D'Andrade raised the question of whether studies presenting "correlations between two or more linguistic labels have been reporting about relations between real world events, or about how similar in meaning the labels are, or some complex interaction of meanings and external events" (1965, p. 228). The study of attributed terms is valuable in uncovering the patterns of association among such terms. Even when these patterns are reproducible, however, it is still uncertain whether they correspond to relationships among entities in the real world. The very fact that the reproducible relationships are associated with the words in a particular measuring instrument makes it difficult to imagine with what in the real world these relationships might correspond. More plausible is the view that these empirical relationships pertain to observers' perceptions and construing of their experiences with others when reported in the particular language of the given instrument.

For the labels used in instruments for recording observations, D'Andrade (1965, 1974) has demonstrated correspondence between patterns of relationships among observational reports and patterns of judged similarity between the terms themselves. Mulaik (1964) and Shweder (1972, 1975) have reported similar findings. There seems little reason to doubt that relationships among attributions do reflect semantic relationships among the words used to report those attributions.

D'Andrade's question cannot be answered in the form in

which he posed it. We have no standard procedures for observing any "real world events" to which our attributive terms can be applied. For a few personality variables, there is some single measuring operation for a given label. For the overwhelming majority, however, a particular variable is not linked to one or two standard measuring procedures consensually agreed on by workers in the personality field. Instead, we find that a variety of procedures have been used for each of these variables, other investigators tolerating these usages or accepting them with some reservations. But beyond the problem of lack of consensus on definitive procedures for measuring each variable is the very general finding that the several procedures used to measure any one variable covary only to a limited extent. When the procedures involve different modes (such as self-report and observations of current behavior), the agreement between procedures is typically very low (Fiske, 1971). Even when two procedures involve the same mode, the correlations are ordinarily quite modest.

As indicated in Part One, observers usually have little agreement with each other, even when using the same procedure. When they use different procedures, and especially when they are in different roles and are observing from different perspectives, the agreement is further reduced. The central fact of personality measurement is that the observations are attributive judgments, so that each datum is an observer-observed entity. Given this state of affairs, D'Andrade's question cannot be put to a direct empirical test. We can obtain information pertinent to most personality variables only through the use of observers, and the lack of congruence between their observations does not permit us to establish facts about any "real world" of personality phenomena.

If we note that attributive judgments are retrospective, some analyses by D'Andrade (1974) do throw light on the problem. He showed that scores obtained from recording each instance of a behavior (for example, laughs and jokes) when it occurred had only moderate correlations with ratings of these behaviors after the total period of observation. Particularly pertinent to the present discussion is the finding that the intercorrelations among the scores from immediate recordings were distinctly lower than those among the retrospective ratings. Analyses by Shweder (1975) had a similar result.

The difference between the immediate observations and the

retrospective ratings raises two major questions: How are the differences to be interpreted? To what does each set of data pertain? In considering the first question, we must note that data based on immediate observations are processed by the investigator in some standard way to obtain the final index. For example, she may use the number of occurrences of a particular behavior, or she may use the total time during which the behavior was manifested. When the ratings are made retrospectively, however, the rater may base his ratings on apparent frequency, apparent duration, or even on the recollection of one extreme manifestation of the behavior. Thus, even with perfect recollection of the entire behavioral segment being rated, a retrospective rater could easily use a process for integrating and summarizing the behavior that was different from the investigator's automatic or clerical one, and hence arrive at a different final index.

It also seems reasonable to assume that some processes within the observer have modified the informational input between the time of the initial observations and the time of the subsequent ratings. In processing the original input, the observer has brought to bear his set of semantic meanings for the several terms and his notions of their similarity in meaning. D'Andrade and Shweder have demonstrated the correspondence in patterning between correlations among retrospective ratings and perceived similarity in meanings for the rated variables. These perceived similarities in meanings have been labeled *implicit personality theories* (see Schneider, 1973), although a theory ordinarily asserts more than the pattern of covariation among construed elements.

We must be cautious, however, about concluding that the correspondence between patterns among ratings and patterns in judged similarity necessarily indicates that attributors somehow used perceived similarity among the attributes being rated when they made their retrospective judgments. Does a person make a few ratings and then determine his subsequent ratings by the degree of similarity that each item has to the several items he has already rated? That hypothetical process seems quite unlikely. It would mean that attributors would have to take much longer to make their last ratings than their earlier ones, and the opposite appears impressionistically to be more usual. As so often happens in psychology, the interpretation of data from a particular technique does not always mean what we tend at first to assume that it means. Each technique sets a particular task for the subject, and he responds to that task as he sees it. In studies of perceived similarity, the subject is literally asked to judge the similarity between the meanings of two words. This procedure is not the same as asking for a judgment about the extent to which the two terms covary over people or about the probability that the two words are applicable to the same person.

The close agreement between the patterns of relationships among ratings of personality traits and among judgments of semantic similarity probably stems from what happens when a person makes a rating. When a subject encounters a personality term or phrase on the rating form, she searches her impressions of the person being rated for relevant evidence, and she tries to retrieve from memory some relevant behaviors. When that subject later is faced with another term that has for her a fairly similar meaning, her scanning may identify evidence and her retrieving may yield memories with much the same contents as those used as the basis for her previous rating. In fact, the memories retrieved a few minutes earlier are especially likely to be available for recall again. The more the two sets of content overlap, the more probable is agreement between the ratings for the two terms—the subject endorses both or neither; or, on the two rating scales, she will check the same degree of applicability to the person described.

Shweder (1977) cites evidence that people have difficulty thinking in correlational terms. Hence, it is not likely that, in making ratings, they determine their ratings for one trait (such as gentle) by their prior ratings on another (good-natured) because they see the two as correlated. He goes on to show that a judgment about the extent to which two traits go together in the general population has very little correspondence with the correlation between those traits as computed from the same person's judgments of the relative frequencies of those traits and of their co-occurrence in the same persons. Different research tasks require different cognitive activity and yield different results. Even more important in the present context is Shweder's discussion of the erroneous inferences that subjects make about attributes and his speculation about the role of availability or accessibility of images in such cognizing processes. Although the study of cognitive processes in making attributional judgments is difficult because it must necessarily be indirect, it is a research area of great importance to the personality domain.

To what do direct observations and retrospective judgments pertain? The observations recorded as the pertinent behaviors occur are associated primarily with the perceived behaviors. Although a laugh is quite readily identified, behaviors like "shows solidarity" and "tends to be nervous" do involve some interpretation. The relatively high agreements between observers making direct observations indicate that their data are minimally influenced by individualistic processes in each observer.

In contrast, retrospective ratings are determined in part by the perceptions of the subjects' behavior and in part by the cognizing and interpreting processes of the observer. Some of these processes are similar in the several observers. There is considerable agreement, for example, on the perceived overlaps in semantic meanings among any set of personality variables. But insofar as the interobserver agreement on retrospective ratings is lower than the agreement on immediate observations, we must accept the conclusion that some of these processes within each observer take forms somewhat specific to that observer.

Another line of evidence has been furnished by Bowers (1973) in his analyses of published studies comparing the relative variance contributions of person and situational influences. Among seven studies in which the data were based on observations of behavior in specific situations, four report greater setting variance than person variance. In another group of findings, subjects were exposed to some one specific situation and, immediately afterward, rated their experiences. For only one of these four analyses was the setting variance greater than the person variance. A third set of studies utilized self-report instruments, like the S-R inventories of Endler and Hunt (1968), in which the subject reports his experiences, as imagined or as recalled, in each of several described situations. Three of these eight analyses had more setting variance than person variance. Since the several publications involved a variety of research methods and procedures and since the trend is only moderate, we must be cautious about interpreting the overall picture. The results do seem to suggest, however, that direct observation by an observer gives different findings than self-reports and that larger situational effects are found in direct observations than in retrospective judgments.

The contrast between direct observations and retrospective ratings should not lead us to the conclusion that direct observations are never influenced by the observers' implicit personality theories. Berman and Kenny (1976) have reported an experimental study indicating that immediate ratings (based on limited verbal material) can be influenced by correlational bias just as delayed ratings are. Berman (n.d.) has also found that behavioral descriptions pertinent to Bales' dimensions of interpersonal interaction were clustered by judges into categories yielding dimensions approximately those of Bales.

Common-Sense Psychology

We have been discussing the words that people apply to other people and the relationships among those words. These words constitute the language that people use in talking about people. In addition to attributions about individuals, people also make attributions about groups of people and about human nature. Whether or not they verbalize such attributions, people feel that they have some understanding about people and especially about interactions between people. This presumed knowledge about people has sometimes been labeled *common-sense psychology*. Since it is based on attributions about individuals, it falls within the attributional strategy we are examining. We must look at this knowledge in its own terms. It is knowledge that its possessors believe to be true. Its congruence with the knowledge that professional psychologists believe to be true is a separate question.

There are a number of arguments for looking at the content of common-sense psychology and for learning what people in general believe to be true about human beings. At the simplest level, an investigator can just say that he wants to study it because it is there. That content is a human product, and as such it has its own intrinsic value. Fairly obvious is the further argument that it is an interesting example of human cognizing and conceptualizing. More important is Eisenberg's (1972, p. 124) view that "what we choose to believe about the nature of man has social consequences" and so "what we believe of man affects the behavior of men, for it determines what each expects of the other." Eisenberg is emphasizing general knowledge and belief here, whether formal and scientific or popular.

It does seem reasonable to assume that a person's perception and construal of the human world determine in large part his reactions to it. We must, however, examine that assumption carefully. We should be careful about deciding that what a person says to an investigator or to a friend is a determining element. What a person says at any one moment is determined in part by the particular circumstances and almost certainly does not indicate everything that she believes about human nature. In addition, when a person is interacting with others in her everyday behavior, she does not ordinarily formulate statements to herself about people or even about the people she is with. Her intuitive knowledge is not systematically organized into propositions. In operating a car, the experienced driver acts rapidly, as if by reflex. If she is asked what she does in a given highway situation, she can put her pattern of actions into words, but we cannot be sure that her verbal description is entirely congruent with her modal pattern of action. She may put in features that are not generally present, and she may omit aspects that usually occur. There is, to be sure, merit to the assertion that we can expect some relationship between what a person says about people and how she acts. But it is dangerous to assume that her statements can be taken as expressing the determinants of her actions.

Still another argument for studying common-sense psychology is that it is the distillation of human experience over the centuries and hence should have some validity. Most of us would agree that common-sense assertions and many of the statements in folklore about human nature are true under some conditions. Perhaps one task for investigators is explicating those conditions.

Finally, it can be argued that we must understand clearly the knowledge with which we start as we go about our work as scientists. As Scriven has phrased it, "The ordinary procedures for explaining behavior that are embedded in our everyday language contain a considerable proportion of the low-level laws (albeit imprecisely formulated) obtained simply as a result of long experience" (1956, p. 332). The behavioral scientist begins his conceptualizing and his empirical studies with a wealth of basic generalizations about behavior; conse-

quently, he feels that he must direct his efforts to higher-order propositions. This argument holds that we must first systematize and for-
malize our primitive, intuitive knowledge in order to provide a firm
foundation for our next efforts. The argument is unconvincing, however, since history shows that established sciences abandoned
common-sense impressions and concepts at very early stages.

An opposed position is that, as behavioral scientists, we must
recognize the initial assumptions that we carry over from our experiences in everyday life, viewing these preconceptualizations as obstacles to be overcome. We must break away from seemingly natural
approaches and perceptions, starting afresh on the task of understanding people and their actions. Physical scientists have been able
to convince themselves (and, at an intellectual level, the rest of us)
that the earth is not flat and that the sun only appears to circle around
the earth. The consensus of popular experience may summarize phenomenal appearances that do not conform to the systematic constructions of science.

Baldwin (1960), for example, argues that our naive theories
may interfere with our scientific theories. He is uncertain whether our
prototheories are blocks to progress or steps toward more adequate
theory. "If the tacit theories of the man on the street are distillations of
generations of human interaction, then common sense is a good basis
for theory building. Psychology should first try to catch up with common sense by making these naive theories explicit before it tries to
forge ahead into new territory" (1960, p. 18). On the other hand, he
says, perhaps common sense is merely a projective system.

Common-sense psychology has many advocates. Heider has
written an extensive analytic monograph about common-sense psychology. His rationale is that, since psychology is still in an infantile
stage, it should not be weaned prematurely from intuitive thinking
about behavior. "Intuitive knowledge may be remarkably penetrat-
ing and can go a long way toward the understanding of human
behavior, whereas in the physical sciences, such common-sense
knowledge is relatively primitive" (Heider, 1958, p. 2). He goes on to
consider causal attribution and the way people react to the meaning
they attribute to the acts of others. He also discusses the perception of
dispositional properties in others. His influential book is a theoretical statement offering many propositions that could be subjected to

empirical investigation. He himself does not attempt to provide systematic empirical data to support the components in his rich formulations.

Peters (1969, 1974) has also argued for the value of studying common sense and using it as the basis for more systematic work. In understanding others, he writes, we have the advantage that "in learning to *behave* as human beings we are, ipso facto, being initiated into the concepts, rules, and assumptions [which] structure our own *behavior* as well as our *understanding* of the behavior of others" (1974, pp. 40–41). All types of understanding of others, he believes, are dependent on having personal relationships with people.

An extreme advocate of building on common sense is Madison. "Psychology has assumed," he says, "that its ultimate objective is to replace common sense" (1969, p. 253). Instead, "the proper aim of psychology is not to replace common sense and the everyday language but to refine and add to it as do poets, writers, physicists, social scientists, and the man on the street" (1969, p. 254). Theodore Mischel expresses a somewhat similar position, proposing that psychological theory can begin with the traditional view of behavior. "Psychological theories based on empirical research with human subjects might be regarded as important additions to our knowledge of human behavior that do not depart fundamentally from common sense" (1969a, pp. 268–269). He notes, however, that common sense fails to give a coherent account of how its variables combine to determine action.

In a provocative pair of articles, Horton (1967a, 1967b) has compared and contrasted African traditional thought and Western science. He argues that traditional African religious systems can be treated as theoretical models like those in science. In both, the theory puts things in a causal context wider than that of common sense. The differences are highly instructive. Traditional modes of thought are closed and have no developed awareness of alternatives to the established body of theoretical tenets. In a science-oriented culture, there is such awareness, at least among many scientists, and so the modes of thinking are open. In Horton's view, the Western lay person is rarely more open or scientific than an African villager.

Common sense also has its critics. Basically, common sense is a set of phenomena, not knowledge of the scientific sort. It is an unreliable guide for systematic classification (Harris, 1964, p. 10). Nagel (1961, Chap. 1) has compared and contrasted science and common sense. Among the differences important in the context of this book is his description of the language in which common-sense knowledge is formulated and communicated. Its terms are often quite vague with respect to the limits of the classes to which they refer, and they lack the specificity necessary for stating testable propositions. At the level of interrelationships, Nagel notes that "a well-recognized feature of common sense is that, though the knowledge it claims may be accurate, it seldom is aware of the limits within which its beliefs are valid or its practices successful" (1961, p. 5). Common sense overgeneralizes. It does not specify the conditions within which it holds. In an earlier discussion of attributions, we asserted that a person typically describes qualities in another with no reference to the conditions under which these qualities were observed or might be observed in the future. Psychologists have for years paid lip service to the principle that behavior is a function of the person and the setting, yet a systematic concern with the interaction between person and situation has become a focus of personality work only in recent years (for example, Endler and Magnusson, 1976a, 1976b; Magnusson and Endler, 1977).

The products of common sense have an inherent interest for all of us and merit investigation in their own right. Yet, given what we know about them and given the history of the established sciences, we cannot expect to build a science on them. And it is difficult to see how the investigation of common sense can make even an indirect contribution toward the development of behavioral science. We must differentiate clearly between what can be the subject matter for a science and what must be left for other disciplines.

Processes in Attributing

Within the scope of the strategy formed by the investigator's decision to study people's expressions about people, there is the challenging task of trying to understand the processes associated with those expressions. In an earlier discussion of research topics pertaining to the content of these expressions, some references were made to these processes. Although an investigator may choose to emphasize either content or process, it is not only difficult but also undesirable to try to maintain a sharp separation between them.

The processes in attributing occur at different times. First, there are the processes that produce the initial impressions of a person. These processes can be identified as those that occur *during* an interaction with that person. Second, *after* an interaction, there are the processes used in recalling the interaction and the impressions, in mulling them over, and in formulating attributions. Finally, there are the processes associated with the *subsequent effects* of those attributions on later behaviors of the person who formulated them and on other persons to whom they are communicated. These distinctions do not correspond to the common usages of the terms. Much of the literature not only on person perception but also on impression formation is based on response data that are attributions, largely neglecting the distinction between the first two of these kinds of process. Moreover, much of the recent research in this area has a particular direction, as indicated in this title: *Attribution: Perceiving the Causes of Behavior* (Jones and others, 1972).

Like the study of other mental processes, the study of how impressions are formed and developed is difficult. The forming of impressions during an interaction cannot be examined directly. We cannot dissect the organism anatomically or psychologically to isolate and manipulate the neural system producing these impressions. As a first step, we can introspect and try to recall the processes from our own experiences, and we can talk nondirectively to others about their recent experiences. For example, I recently began to wonder at what time the descriptive terms used by psychologists—such as the labels for traits—entered into laymen's natural processes. From introspection and from querying others, I have developed the tentative hypothesis that, in most interactions, each person is attending to the interaction and is not engaged in private internal thinking about attributes characterizing the behavior of the other person. My informants did not recall "thinking" any descriptive terms. There is an exception, however. When a person has some reason for evaluating the other person (for instance, in interviews related to some subsequent decision), she may make mental notes of characteristics pertinent to that objective.

To continue this speculation, the act of attributing seems to occur after an interaction. We may review our impressions, formed but not verbalized during the interaction, and begin to assign attributes to the behaviors observed earlier. When we tell someone else about the interaction, we typically do not repeat the actual words of the conversation but summarize our impressions in descriptive terms. Although an introspective examination of impression development is a fruitful first step in research, an investigator must be careful about assuming the veridicality of the protocols obtained. In discussing "impressions of personality" with a viewpoint rather similar to that being presented here, Brown issues a warning. "The surest principle in psychology is that whenever man first undertakes to conceive of his mental processes, to represent them to himself, he grotesquely distorts them" (1965, p. 621).

The development of impressions during interactions with other people probably involves much the same processes that occur in other experiences, both routine and unusual. The impressions seem to be related to what is out of the ordinary, to the unexpected, to what attracts attention. An unsatisfactory transaction involving the clerk in a store, or a difficulty in starting a car or in driving it to our destination will focus our attention on occurrences that normally are barely registered in memory.

The forming of impressions can be viewed as part of the natural processes of ordering experience. As Bruner describes it, we have a limited span of attention and a limited span of immediate memory. As a consequence, we must be selective. We attend to essentials, "we 'recode' into simpler form the diversity of events . . . so that our limited attention and memory span can be protected" (1958, p. 86). Bruner notes the economy of effort involved here. Harvey (1976) suggests that a similar principle of least effort is also involved in attributing dispositions to other persons rather than making attributions to situations or to person-situation interactions.

After impressions occur, attributions may be formulated for various reasons. Under some circumstances, we simply express our feelings by putting them into words. When an interaction generates strong affect, either positive or negative, we are likely to talk about it to ourselves or to others afterward. And we may even express it to the other person during the interaction—another exception to the speculative hypothesis that attributions are not made during an interaction. Such attributing is consummatory. The stating of our characterization of the other person or of his behavior may help us to work through our feelings, to get them out of our system—in technical terms, attributing involves a reduction of drive or arousal.

At other times, attributions may be instrumental. We may make them as a way of resolving our puzzlement about some behavior of another person. A person's behavior may be inconsistent with what we consider usual behavior, especially the modal behavior in the particular situation. We may then say "that person was upset about something," or we may simply say "that is the kind of person he is." In this connection, Simon's (1967) concept of "satisficing" is applicable. As Kanouse suggests, "individuals may be primarily motivated to seek a single sufficient or satisfactory explanation for any given event, rather than one that is the best of all possible explanations" (1972, p. 131). He goes on to say that "it is as if individuals in their attributional endeavors are satisfied with *sufficient* explanations and do not require explanations to be *necessary* as well" (1972, p. 134). In some way, we are content when we have attributed a verbal label to another person or to some behavior. We are not seeking a comprehensive explanation that is fully explicated and logically related to a body of consensual knowledge.

It follows that attributing is incomplete. We cast impressions into attributes for some reason, selecting those characterizations that accomplish our immediate purpose. Free descriptions of others have been shown to be oriented toward the purpose given by the investigator (S. T. Fiske and Cox, n.d.). If we accept the notion that our purpose guides our selection among potential attributions, we still need to determine how that selection is made.

This selectivity in attributing makes it necessary for those studying attributions to be careful about inferring from the absence of attributions. One attributor may say that a person is outgoing, warm, and interesting. Another may say that the person is dominating. These two descriptions may not indicate disagreement on the attributes the person is perceived to possess but only differences in salience for the two attributors. When asked whether the person is also dominating, the first attributor may agree, even though she did not produce that term in her own description.

Note also that a person will describe another in terms of her own vocabulary. In fact, persons tend to have a set of words they typically use in their descriptions. This individual preference, noted by Koltuv (1962), can readily be observed whenever subjects are asked to make attributions about more than one person (as in Bourne, 1977). A general preference for certain descriptive terms may indicate something about the attributor and her emphases in forming impressions. Although it is possible that these preferred labels may affect a person's perceptions and cognitions of the behavior of others, it seems more likely that both are products of some underlying feature of the attributor.

Attributions are the product of a complex process. The attributions made about a particular person are not repeated so frequently that they become practiced associations. In making attributions for an investigator, the subject is flexible and responds to the task given to her. In such a situation, her attributions are not spontaneous (Proposition 2a, Chapter One), and she tends to feel indifference about them. They do not particularly affect her, and they will be kept confidential by the investigator, so that they will not affect the person described. In a different kind of study, Fiske and Bourne (1977) obtained attributions on an adjective checklist. Compared to endorsements made under usual instructions, fewer endorsements were made under instructions to check only those adjectives that applied definitely and without question, and more were made under instructions to check those that might reasonably be applied, perhaps by someone else. A bit of evidence about the willingness of subjects to complete an attributive task, regardless of its nature, is furnished by Newcomb (1931), who included with other ratings a series of items on guessed behaviors that the subjects could not have observed. It is intriguing to note that he obtained as good agreement on these items as on items about observed behaviors.

An attribution, then, is a behavior associated with the attributor, the observed person, and the conditions. The investigator studying attributions and their development must see the attributions produced by his subjects as observer-observed entities. These products are affected by both the person described and the attributor. The investigator's task is to determine the contribution from each of these sources and from the interaction of observer and observed. Moreover, an attribution is made at a single moment in time under some set of conditions. We need to know what led to that attribution. Even when the attributor phrases his attributions as though he were describing some relatively permanent characteristics of the person, the investigator must keep in mind that the attributor may well make different attributions at another time or under different conditions. The investigator needs to determine the attributional process that produced the particular characterizations reported by the subject.

Since an attribution is determined not only by the observer's prior experience with the person described but also by the conditions under which the attribution is formulated, attributions can be expected to show some variation from setting to setting and from task to task. The requirements of a given attributive task may lead to the retrieval of a set of memories and impressions that are not exactly the same as those for some other task. For the same setting and task, attributions will also vary from time to time as a function of factors internal to the attributor. Hence, a set of reported attributions may well not be reproduced at a later time.

In contrast, the memory images and the impressions that an attributor has about a person may be relatively enduring, especially when the attributor has many interactions with that person and when his images and impressions have been spontaneously reviewed from time to time. Although a person's behavior when with an attributor may not be quite as stable as the functioning of one's automobile, it is consistent enough to provide considerable reinforcement of earlier impressions. This analysis suggests the hypothesis that there is more potential consistency in one's picture, one's memories, and one's unverbalized impressions of another person than there is in the particular terms with which one may describe the other on one occasion or another. It is not immediately obvious how this speculation can be tested empirically because all that the investigator can observe are the reported attributions. Experimental propositions derived from this speculative expectation, however, may hold empirically, offering indirect support for it.

Among the previously listed classes of processes involving attributions, the last is the utilization of attributions in subsequent behavior—the effects of attributions on the attributor, on persons hearing the attributions, and on the person described. There seems little reason to doubt that people are affected by the way other people describe them. Other people's evaluations can raise or lower our current self-esteem. Attributions made by others can affect the way we perceive ourselves, if only by leading us to wonder how it could happen that others see us as they tell us they do.

A somewhat similar situation, although ordinarily with much less involvement, occurs when we hear attributions made about another person. If we already know that person, we are likely to compare those attributions to our own impressions, looking for confirmations and wondering about discrepancies. Hearing such descriptions may lead us to see the person described in a different light and hence may affect our subsequently formed impressions of him. Of course, if we hear attributions about a person we have not met, they may affect the way in which we later enter into an interaction with that person.

Do our attributions about others affect our subsequent interactions with them because the attributions lead to expectations? A parallel in studies of memory might seem pertinent. In a classical study (Carmichael, Hogan, and Walter, 1932), an ambiguous figure was given one of two labels, such as bottle or stirrup. In later drawing of these figures from memory, the attributed label affected the direction in which the reproductions distorted the original figures. Does the analogy hold? Is the way we perceive subsequent behavior influenced by the attributive labels we have previously assigned to a person? Do the connotations of these labels have effects? These are questions for empirical study.

Even if empirical findings showed some congruence between earlier attributions and later attitudes and behaviors toward a person, we should be very cautious about interpreting the attributing as a determinant of the subsequent reactions. It is certainly not common for us to initiate a specific action consciously on the basis of our earlier verbal formulations about the other person. The course of interactions is ordinarily too rapid to permit much conscious planning of particular acts. In the viewpoint presented in this book, attributions are almost epiphenomena. More exactly, they are a separate set of phenomena paralleling the stream of other behaviors. On the one side, there are the immediate actions and reactions, occurring at a rapid rate. These lead to memories that may be stored directly as visual images or indirectly as summarizing impressions of the interaction. On the other side, there is the recall of some of these stored memories and the further cognitive activity processing them into attributions. These attributions themselves are stored.

We would have difficulty in determining whether subsequent behavior is more closely related to the original imagery and impressions or to the later attributions. There seems to be little reason to postulate that we have *specific* expectancies about the behaviors of persons we know. I grant that we can readily elicit from subjects some reported expectancies if we ask for them. But these are like attributive protocols—they are produced in response to the task given to the subjects. More likely is the parsimonious assumption that people have learned to expect consistency in the behavior of others. Such expectancies are soundly based in the relatively strong consistencies in psychomotor acts, in styles of moving, in patterns of handwriting, and in patterns of sound production in speaking. Our expectancies cannot be as specific as "She will frown" (under what conditions?). More general predictions may be involved: "She is likely to talk about her job." A generalized expectation of consistency over time is sufficient for our actual coping and adapting. If she acts as she has acted with us in the past, we can expect that she will probably not do anything that will greatly surprise us or that will upset us and make it difficult for us to handle the situation easily. This generalized expectation is a modification of the even more general modal expectation that we have for all of our associates as they behave in situations familiar to us.

In the preceding examination of directions for research on attributing processes, we have stayed close to the kind of approach that investigators have been taking. The orientation has been guided by an interest in how the process has led to the particular content of the resulting attribution. More might be learned by a different approach, that used in cognitive psychology. In much work on cognition, the investigator's dependent variables do not pertain to content but to other aspects of the subject's behavior, such as reaction time and time spent looking at a stimulus. The indirect study of attributing by using more objective variables might allow us to infer the process from more replicable data and more reproducible findings. It is certain that attempting to get at attributive processes from reports of attributors is dangerous. The severe limitations of verbal reports on mental processes have been well documented by Nisbett and Wilson

(1977). Between the work on attribution theory and the work of experimentalists on cognition is the topic of judgment under uncertainty. Fischhoff (1976) has critically examined attribution research by contrasting it with the study of judgment processes. Other descriptions of current research on attribution are available in Harvey, Ickes, and Kidd (1976).

Generalizability in Studies of Attribution

We turn now to a critique of the strategy for studying attribution in terms of generalizability and its aspects. It is difficult to see how a productive degree of generalizability can be achieved in studies of the content of attributions. We have noted that the meaning of an attribution depends in large part on the meanings that the words of the attributor have for him. Hence, replication over persons can be only limited. One possibility is to avoid reference to meanings by studying the words used by each attributor, each word being treated as a class by itself. For example, in studying the tendency of an attributor to use certain preferred words, the replication over persons has to do with individually preferred words, whatever they may be for each attributor. (Such analyses need not ask whether a given attributor used a word with the same meaning each time she applied it in various descriptions.) Findings from research on preferred words should be reproducible. The extent of generalizability beyond the conditions set by the task given the attributor would, of course, have to be established empirically. Given what we know from other areas of investigation, it is possible that generalizability over tasks might be limited and that, as a consequence, no useful generalizability to natural attributions would be warranted.

The study of common-sense psychology would have to be essentially an analysis of content. The investigator or other judges would have to determine what lay statements appeared to have the same meaning and therefore seemed to fall in the same class. The replicability of these beliefs and assertions about people would be an interesting topic in its own right. Alternatively, one might simply determine the kinds of propositions occurring in common-sense psychology. How many of them involve categorizations of people into types? ("You can always tell a Harvard man but you can't tell him much.") How many refer to motivations? ("The grass on the other side of the fence is greener.") How many to processes? ("Seeing is believing" but "The hand is quicker than the eye.") Such folk maxims, of course, constitute only a small portion of the content of common-sense psychology. The consistency of common-sense psychology would also be an interesting study. Familiar maxims are often almost diametrically opposed to each other, as in the example above. We could also investigate the frequency of inconsistent statements among the general beliefs of individuals.

Some replication and reproducibility might be found in studies of processes in attributing. Impression processes, the first of the classes proposed earlier, appear too difficult to study in any satisfactory way. Not only would the content and form be highly individual but gaining access to these internal processes without distorting them seriously in the very attempt to get reports about them would also be difficult. Processes in formulating attributions seem more accessible. Again, the replication and reproduction of data and findings is likely to be greater when the investigation centers on forms or styles rather than on content or meaning. Studies of the threshold or readiness to make attributions, of the rate of formulating descriptors, and of the number of different descriptors used could be made with reasonable replicability of observations. Consistency across time for the attributor would need to be determined.

Considerable research has been done on processes utilizing attributions. As indicated earlier, descriptions purportedly made by others seem to affect the momentary self-esteem of subjects, and prior information appears to generate sets toward persons one is about to meet. But given the variety of experimental conditions that have been used, it is not clear what general propositions can be taken as definitively established. And within what limits would such propositions hold? This research, along with research on the other processes and on the content of attributions, faces the major underlying difficulty of generalizability from the experimental setting to naturally occurring attribution, a matter to be examined below.

Methodological Considerations in the Strategy for Attributions

As in other parts of psychology, two basic approaches, two "scientific disciplines" (Cronbach, 1957), can be identified in the study of attributions. The investigator can seek to determine what holds for people in general when they are making attributions. Alternatively, she can direct her work toward identifying the factors associated with the differences in attributing from one attributor to another. Ultimately, for a more solid understanding of attributing, the two approaches must be integrated into a single conceptual system.

One obvious instance of individual differences is associated with the sex of the attributor. Among their experienced psychologist-judges in their longitudinal Oakland study, Haan and Livson (1973) found that male judges stressed unfavorable characteristics more than did females. In judging men, the male judges were more reactive to "unmasculine" characteristics, and the females seemed more reactive to hypermasculine excesses. In judging females, the female judges again seemed more concerned with excesses of traits stereotypical for women, while the males attended more to departures from stereotype. Some of the judges had interviewed some of the subjects; others saw only the transcripts of interviews. It is possible that subjects reacted differently to the male and female interviewers who later became judges. It is hard to see, however, how those facts would account for the differential attributing by the judges.

In studying individual differences and in studying general features of attributing, the central methodological obstacle is the major effects of the investigator's methods on the attributive responses of her subjects. As pointed out earlier, subjects will pretty much do what the investigator asks them to do. They will make attributions on the basis of little or no information about the persons they describe (Passini and Norman, 1966). They will endorse fewer or more descriptive terms (Fiske and Bourne, 1977), although there will still be much intersubject variability in the number of endorsements. They will use the investigator's choice of descriptive terms even though they are not sure exactly what these mean or whether they are applicable to the person described (see Kuncel, 1973). In fact, a wide range of meanings is typically assigned by attributors to each descriptive adjective presented by the investigator (Fiske and Barack, 1976). Hence, even when the investigator standardizes her protocols by providing subjects with the terms to be attributed, she does not avoid the problem that the same word has varying meanings for her several subjects (see Chapter Two).

A strong argument can be made for obtaining free-response descriptions, allowing the subjects to employ terms that come naturally to them. That argument is derived from the assumption that we are interested in understanding what happens in nature and from the assertion that attempts to study ideal instances in the laboratory do not work in the behavioral sciences as they do in the natural sciences (see Nagel, 1961). But even if we accept that argument, we are faced with the problem of coding the free responses. When are two attributions to be placed in the same class? If the same word has somewhat different meanings for two attributors, can we ever study the meanings of attributions with any precision? Here, again, as so often in this book, we are confronted with the conflict between high standards of objectivity (interobserver interchangeability) and the desire to understand the meanings in psychological content.

There are aspects of attributions that can be studied with high consensus on the data produced by the observers examining the descriptions. Although the length of the description may be of little interest, the style of attributing may be worth studying. Are the attributes qualified or stated dogmatically? What is the temporal pattern? For example, does the attributor make several attributions quickly and then slow down, or does he think awhile and then give a number of descriptors in some organized fashion? In another approach, Allen and Potkay (1973) have shown how one major characteristic of attributions, favorableness, can be coded from free responses. Can their method be refined to generate scores with high interobserver agreement? Their procedure did, of course, involve assigning a task to subjects, with the associated problems discussed earlier.

Ideally, an investigator should seek out attributions made by people in their daily life, away from psychology buildings. Obviously, that search will take time and energy. Where can he find naturally occurring attributions? We make attributions frequently in our daily conversations, although it must be granted that listening to such material would take time—the dross rate (Webb, Campbell, Schwartz, and Sechrest, 1966) would be high. There is the additional problem of ethics. How can an investigator obtain protocols of everyday talking without violating the principle of informed consent, such prior consent possibly affecting the nature of what is said? One source of material might be standard evaluation practices that produce

descriptions for a particular purpose, as in letters of recommendation. Although we are all aware of the influences of the conditions and
the writer's motivations on these letters, they are nevertheless natural
products uninfluenced by the methods of the investigators.

At several earlier points, I have expressed my conviction that
the study of the personality domain and related fields must move back
to, or close to, the study of naturally occurring behavior, using naturalistic observation. My belief stems in part from our failure to build a
body of consensually accepted findings and concepts in our previous
research efforts. It also is based on observation of research in other
parts of psychology, with its fashions and fads over the years. There
was a long period when the study of the rat in the maze preempted
experimental psychology. Then it was gradually recognized that the
laboratory rat was a different animal from the rat in nature and that
the laboratory rat's learning of mazes was not throwing any light on
human learning—on the child in the classroom or on the child
acquiring competence in his free play. Examples of fads can also be
found in social psychology—the risky shift effect and the prisoner's
dilemma game.

Many explanations can be offered for the decline in psychologists' interest and effort in these areas. Perhaps the single most comprehensive interpretation is simply that the actual phenomena that
were being empirically investigated in these areas came to be recognized as behaviors generated in large part by aspects of the experimental conditions. As such, their degree of resemblance to the natural
phenomena in which investigators were really interested was uncertain but clearly not high. In other words, experimental findings had
questionable external validity in terms of generalizability beyond the
experimental setting. Doubts can also be raised about the internal
validity of their interpretations.

Because of my bias in favor of naturalistic studies, I have said
little about attribution theory and its experimental literature.
Although this work clearly falls within the strategy examined in this
chapter, most of its investigations are not naturalistic in terms of two
or three of Tunnell's (1977) dimensions of naturalness—behavior,
setting, and treatment. The tasks given to a subject often seem highly
contrived. For example, the subject is given a statement about a person and is asked to react attributionally to it. The adequacy of such

research for illuminating general human functioning depends on the correspondence between the experimental tasks and everyday life. It is difficult to see much correspondence. How often does a person make an attribution on the basis of someone else's statement?

One useful product of research on attribution is the light it throws on what people will do, at least under some circumstances. None of these experimental studies have reported such striking effects as those of the well-known Milgram studies of compliance with the experimenter (and those of course were a pale shadow of the horrible behaviors that initially led Milgram to devise his experimental procedures). Yet the findings of studies of attribution do provide glimpses of human cognitive activity and of causal attributions that broaden our picture of the phenomena we would like to understand systematically.

It is true, of course, that much work under the egis of attribution theory has been concerned with the cognitive processes associated with perceptions of behavior, particularly with subjects' statements about the perceived causes of the behaviors described in the experimental stimuli. As such, the work involves broader questions than those pertaining to the attributions that one person makes about another. And there seems to be increasing concern with the problem of generalizing the empirical findings. Researchers are moving to field studies and to the use of role-playing subject-observers (Jones, 1976; West, Gunn, and Chernicky, 1975).

The best that can be done at this time is to search for courses of action that should, in principle, get around these obstacles to research on attributing. One possibility is to try to understand the differences between laboratory behavior and natural behavior, with the hope of determining how experimental findings must be qualified before being generalized in some way to behavior in the outside world. But I am not sure how we can pin down these differences without having a clearer idea about the natural behavior in which we are interested. When laboratory research in the natural sciences can demonstrate that a variable affects the phenomena of interest, it usually can keep that variable constant in the experiment. Research in the behavioral sciences has difficulty in establishing the effects of variables and also in devising procedures for controlling them. As a consequence, the replicability of findings is poor. Even more critical is the inescapable fact that the conditions for conducting laboratory research add variables that cannot be assessed readily; consequently, their effects cannot be partialed out with any precision. It would indeed be strange if it should develop that major progress in experimental research on human behavior can be made only after we have a more adequate understanding of behavior in the laboratory and of reactions to being in an experiment and after we have developed adequate procedures for assessing the effects of these reactions on our experimental observations of subjects' behavior.

The study of attributing may be viewed as a prime example of the general research problem confronted by those seeking to understand personality as it is conventionally construed. Attributive phenomena do show some loose regularities that cannot be precisely pinpointed. Since the phenomena involve persons perceiving, cognizing, and interpreting their experiences with other persons, major contributions to the data are made by the attributor, the person described, and their interaction (in both the psychological and the statistical senses). Although these major determinants often show some low degree of consistency, so that the data can be construed as containing pertinent information, a great deal of "noise" is also present.

Many people who have written about the contrast between the natural sciences and the behavioral or social sciences have argued that the nature of the objects and systems studied is different in these two areas and that, as a consequence, the methods of the behavioral scientist should be determined by the nature of the phenomena studied, rather than slavishly aping the methods of the natural scientist. As indicated in Chapter Eight, I certainly agree that the methods for making observations must be appropriate to the phenomena observed, whatever the discipline within which the investigator is working. I am also convinced, however, that the basic principles of scientific work must be the same for all science, in all areas. In between, the ideal methodology is not so clear. For the most part, those who urge that the design of scientific operations be tailored to the nature of the phenomena either have not proposed distinctive new methods or have proposed methods that are at variance with those basic principles for science.

This evaluation does not preclude the possibility that appropriate, distinctive methods can be developed for behavioral science. We should be on the lookout for any methods that might help us. For example, a new kind of systems analysis involves the intriguing concept of fuzzy sets (Negoita and Ralescu, 1975). Instead of the sharp boundaries demanded by the traditional concept of set, a fuzzy set has varying grades of membership, a more-or-less notion rather than the all-or-none, in-or-out quality of the set. The transition from membership to nonmembership is gradual. Zadeh has described this approach: "As the complexity of a system increases, our ability to make precise and yet significant statements about its behavior diminishes until a threshold is reached beyond which precision and significance (or relevance) become almost mutually exclusive characteristics. . . . Indeed, the pervasiveness of fuzziness in human thought processes suggests that much of the logic behind human reasoning is not the traditional two-valued or even multivalued logic, but a logic with fuzzy truths, fuzzy connectives, and fuzzy rules of inference. In our view, it is this fuzzy, and as yet not well-understood, logic that plays a basic role in what may well be one of the most important facets of human thinking, namely the ability to *summarize* information— to extract from the collections of masses of data impinging upon the human brain those and only those subcollections which are relevant to the performance of the task at hand" (1973, pp. 28–29).

Perhaps we can use some assistance from philosophers about how to reason with the loose concepts in personality and other areas in behavioral science. Disagreeing with the view that logic assumes precise symbols, and hence it is not possible to reason logically with loose concepts, Black (1970) argues that one can do so if one can identify clear cases of the concept as well as borderline cases and if one also recognizes that the line between the two sets is arbitrary. Somewhat similar is the notion of open concepts (Meehl and others, 1971).

A more formal contribution is the concept of polythetic classes, which Beckner (1959) proposed under the label *polytypic*. For such a class, each unit possesses a large number of the properties associated with the class, each property is possessed by a large number of the units, but no property is possessed by every unit; therefore, no property is a necessary condition for membership in the class. The concept has proved useful in the natural sciences, especially biology. Widely applicable in behavioral science, however, is an important point that Needham (1975) makes about the utility of polythetic classes in social anthropology: "In the natural sciences, the features by which polythetic classes are defined have generally a real, distinct, and independent character, and they can be clearly stipulated in advance" (p. 363). In contrast, "in social anthropology the determination of the constituent features of a polythetic class cannot be carried out by reference to discrete empirical particulars, but entails instead a reliance on further features of the same character which themselves are likewise polythetic" (p. 364). The major obstacle to systematic use of polythetic classes in personality and related fields, then, is the matter of defining and identifying the features of the things to be classified. In terms of the major theses of this book, the use of such classes may not be profitable if we cannot obtain high interobserver agreement on whether or not a person or a piece of behavior has a specific feature.

In trying to understand common-sense knowledge, however, it may prove fruitful to look for instances of loose concepts and of polythetic classes in the content being analyzed. Everyday thinking is characterized by much looseness in thinking and reasoning. For example, what do people mean when they say that two attributes "go together"? In recent papers, Shweder has considered the question of whether everyday personality theories are correlational (1976) and has examined the reasoning that underlies everyday judgments about personality (1977). His analyses investigate processes occurring when people make several attributions about another.

We may be able to learn something about attributing from studies of clinical judgments and other decisions about people. These attributions are of a specific, instrumental kind. They are ordinarily made for some practical, applied purpose. As such, this research would appear to belong to the strategy for studying societal problems (Chapter Ten). The investigators, however, have chosen their particular research problems, rather than directly addressing themselves to the related societal problems.

Some of the earlier work on attributions was based on the models of Brunswik and Hammond (discussed in Chapter Two). This work has thrown light on the weights that attributors give to specific bits of information available to them. Other kinds of models have been derived for specific diagnosticians or decision makers. One direction of effort has been to develop a model of the diagnostic process. Kleinmuntz (1967, Chap. 11), for example, identified empirically a diagnostician who was particularly successful in interpreting MMPI profiles. He then asked that person to think aloud as he went through the diagnostic task. From the verbalization, a series of decision rules was developed in the form of a flow chart that could be followed by a computer. Guided by the diagnostician's approach, the computer was rather successful, even when compared to the diagnostician's own performance.

Another technique is bootstrapping (for example, Dawes, 1971). The admissions decisions made by faculty members can be analyzed to determine the weights given to several kinds of information that are objective (test scores) or fairly easily scaled (letters of recommendation). A simple linear model applying these weights to a new sample can do as well or better than the judges themselves, the evaluation being made in terms of the subsequent performance in graduate school as rated by faculty members.

In the present context, what is important is not the success in modeling these predictive judgments but the suggestions that emerge from considering the outcome. Why should a statistical model do better than the judges? Although further work is necessary to identify the reasons, it seems probable that the judge does not go about her decision in a fixed way. Her momentary state or some individualistic feature of the information available to her may lead her to depart from weighting the information as she usually does. These departures are more likely to impair her performance than to improve it, when compared to what she would have done if she had determined her standard weights for the several bits of information and used them consistently.

It has often been argued that the complexity of a diagnostic or predictive decision requires a human judge because the criterion is not related to predictors in a simple linear fashion and that weighting of predictors should be a function of their contributions to optimal judgments. Experimental and analytical studies have destroyed these arguments. Models based on linear relationships hold up better than human judges in subsequent applications. Assigning unit weights to each empirically established predictor has been demonstrated to be the preferable general strategy (see Einhorn and Hogarth, 1975). Simpler procedures seem more generalizable.

Direct analytic work can also throw light on judgment processes. For instance, Einhorn and Schacht (1977) have examined "decisions based on fallible human judgment." Their analyses show that even when the correlation between judgment and criterion departs only a little from 1.00, serious practical consequences can occur. The obtained correlation is, of course, ordinarily of much lower magnitude. They also bring out important effects associated with the proportion of cases that receive treatment in a medical context or are accepted in personnel work. Their work adds to what has been known about the significance of the selection ratio (that is, the proportion of applicants accepted). In another analytic paper, Einhorn and Hogarth (1977) have made a valuable contribution by bringing out factors associated with the conviction, so prevalent in all of us, that our judgments are accurate. In some situations, when we act on the basis of our judgment, that action has effects making our judgment look better than it actually is. Perhaps their work applies to attributions. If I decide that you are friendly and hence act reciprocally in a friendly way toward you, I am likely to find that you express friendliness toward me.

The Psychologist as Attributor

The phenomena of attributing are obviously a central part of the domain of personality. As this lengthy chapter indicates, I find them intriguing, as do most of us. I would like to see a body of systematic knowledge established about these phenomena, and yet I cannot be optimistic about the likelihood of our achieving that objective. Like other mental contents, attributions are very difficult to study in their natural habitat. From attributions produced for our investigations, we can learn about what is possible, about what occurs under some circumstances, and probably little else. The area needs some insightful discovery that could reorient our approach to it.

The continuing investigation of these phenomena may have an important by-product. Kelley points out "that there are only a limited number of ways of making sense out of available data about the world and that the scientific procedures [used in the study of attribution] are merely refined and explicit versions of methods upon which the common man also comes to rely" (1972, p. 171). As we noted earlier, psychologists are human beings before they are psychologists, and they enter their study of people with the assumptions and preconceptions they have developed in everyday living (see Ross, Amabile, and Steinmetz, 1977). The study of attributing can tell us how psychologists perceive and construe their experiences with others in their daily lives. Insofar as we, psychologists and other behavioral scientists, derive our concepts from that experience, perhaps the study of attributing can give us information about how we make attributions and label people in our professional roles and about the concepts we use in our theorizing and in our instructions to observers. Psychologist, know thyself.

Summary

Selecting his own problem, the investigator may decide to study some aspect of attribution. This strategy, although closely related to that used for societal problems, differs from it in several ways, including its emphasis on the attributing process and on the attributor as opposed to the person described. The investigator can choose to examine the contents of attribution—the organization and covariation of attributive terms as people perceive and apply those labels. A related topic is common-sense psychology, the pictures of people and of human nature developed from the everyday experience of persons as social beings. Another important area within this general strategy is the study of the attributing processes in which impressions are formed, in which memories and impressions are transformed into explicit attributions, and in which attributions are utilized.

From the methodological viewpoint, the critical consideration in this strategy is the overwhelming contribution of the method of obtaining attributions and the resulting constriction of generalizability. An attribution is a behavior occurring at a moment in time in response to the given conditions; its replicability is poor. The study of attributive processes and responses entails the same difficulties as other investigations of perceiving and cognizing, the obstacles often being harder to overcome because the stimuli are immersed in the stream of behaving. Perhaps new techniques can be found. The empirical and analytic research on decision making have illuminated some aspects of attributing. More generally, the study of attributing may help the psychologist to understand his own attributing and construing as he goes about his scholarly and professional work.

XII

The Strategy for Studying Actions

The strategy for studying actions, Strategy 4 in Table 3 (Chapter Nine), is characterized primarily by the investigator's choice of motor and vocal actions as his phenomena (Choice 3b, Chapter Eight), by his choice of his own problem (Choice 1b), and by his decision to have his observers make observations involving identification and recognition rather than inference and interpretation (Choice 6b).

Frequent references to the action approach, contrasting it to the conventional approach to personality that concentrates on attributive judgments, were made in Part One, especially in Chapter Four, to clarify the assertions made in analyzing that standard approach. In that earlier discussion, the emphasis was on the nature of the observations used. It is now time to examine the strategy more completely.

The action strategy focuses on the phenomena of behaving, on observable actions. The process in the observer involves a minimum of inference as he identifies each occurrence of a pertinent action. The investigator's subsequent processing of the observer's judgments is mechanical. The investigator does not contribute any inference or interpretation in transforming these judgments into the data entered into his analyses. Like any other researcher, of course, once he has obtained his findings, he engages in interpretations of one kind or another. Up to that point, everything that he or his observer has done can be very closely (if not exactly) replicated by another person.

When defined solely by the three choices indicated above, the action strategy includes a very large range of psychological research. For the field of personality, it embraces all laboratory investigation where the dependent variable is derived from simple, highly replicable observations rather than interpretive judgments by the subject or the observers. Specific examples include pupillometrics, most of ethology, much of the research guided by behavior theory, and much work on nonverbal communication. Actions in interactions, as in Duncan's research (Duncan and Fiske, 1977, Pt. III), also fall within this strategy, although they form a distinct substrategy (to be examined more closely below). In this chapter, discussion of the action strategy will concentrate on a more restricted category, naturalistic research. The stress reflects my conviction that we should study phenomena under conditions that are as natural as possible. In terms of the dimensions identified by Tunnell (1977), the treatment (the stimuli) should be natural (Choice 10b), and the actions observed should be representative of the actor's ordinary behavior. Although it is very desirable that his third dimension, the setting, should also be as naturalistic as possible, that aspect appears less crucial than the others.

The action strategy deals with relatively concrete behavior. It is based on observation and analysis of discrete, typically brief, actions, with particular attention to their initiation and their termination. These actions are directly perceived by the observer as he carries out the instructions of the investigator. The three strategies— societal, attributional, and action—can be seen as successively more removed from the physical movements in moment-to-moment behaving. The action strategy focuses on the action, regardless of the specific person who is acting. The attributional strategy concentrates on the observer as he perceives and interprets the behavior of another. The societal strategy emphasizes the person being evaluated by others.

The term *action* is used because it is a common word with no restrictive connotations except that of physical movement. Our word should not be confused with the same term as used by philosophers (for example, T. Mischel, 1969b). In the latter usage, an action is often a large segment of behavior identified and interpreted by the observer, frequently construed as involving intention, and hence an essentially different construct.

Phenomena for the Action Strategy

The phenomena in the action strategy are actions—any movement of any part of the body is a potential unit of observation. More comprehensively, the phenomena of behaving can be seen as change in activity (Atkinson, 1969). The most obvious change is the initiation of an action, in which a person or a part of the body moves from no activity to activity. Almost as important is the termination of an action, in which a person or a part of the body moves from activity to no activity. These changes can be construed as occurring practically instantaneously, with an observer identifying a moment in time when the change occurs.

A continuing action may also be important. Such an action is typically a state of changing, which in principle could be analyzed more minutely as a series of shorter actions. For example, the ongoing activity of talking is composed of a flow of actions of the lips and also of the tongue and vocal cords. Gesturing can be construed either as an ongoing action or as a series of briefer acts characterized by direction and rate of movement. The presence of gesturing, rather than its onset or offset, has been found to be an important act in Duncan's analysis of the system for taking turns in a conversation.

The phenomena of actions also include steady states lasting for a brief period; for example, a steady gesture, such as holding the hand up, palm toward another person. Again, once a smile has started, its presence may be important even though it continues with little or no detectable change in the facial features. What appears to be important in gazing, a significant act in the interaction between people, is the direction of the gaze toward or away from the other person. In each of these instances, the onset and offset may prove more significant than the continuation of the action. It is, nevertheless, frequently desirable to construe the continuation itself as an action.

Perhaps the most inclusive characteristic of actions is muscular tension or effort that is observable by persons other than the actor. This criterion eliminates tonic contractions of antagonistic muscles that might make an arm or leg more rigid but that do not result in movement or in observable changes in the body surface. Although such muscular tension may be apparent to the actor, it would not be a unit of observation in the study of actions because it is not observable by others. We should also recognize that an actor may engage in several actions at the same time. A person may be smiling, gazing at the other, gesturing, and moving her foot, all while talking. This concurrence may even extend to two actions beginning or terminating simultaneously, as closely as anyone can tell from careful observation.

Although not essential to the viewpoint being taken here, it is worth recalling that sensory stimulation is associated with change in input at the receptors. Both the onset and the offset of a stimulus are reflected in neurosensory activity. A reaction to a perceptible change in a continuing stimulus resembles a reaction to an onset. Furthermore, since the neurosensory system reacts almost instantaneously to changes in stimulation, motor actions can occur very quickly after changes in sensory input. Hence, an action by one person can follow rapidly after an action by another person, approaching the classical laboratory reaction times of fractions of a second.

In Chapter One, we referred to the problem posed by Stent (1975): What is it exactly about human behavior that we want to explain? The answer of the action strategy is that the phenomena to be explained are human actions, with special attention to those actions that make a difference in the sense that they are related to other actions of the same actor or of other actors. Since the onset or offset of an action can be followed very closely by the onset or offset of another action, we must work at a comparatively molecular level of analysis.

Underlying this strategy is the assumption that actions convey information. Just as changes in sensory input convey potential information, so do changes in behaving. In effect, the action strategy involves empirical testing of the broad hypothesis that an action can make a difference to other persons present and to the actor. The conceptualization presented in Duncan and Fiske (1977), for example, views some actions as signals to the other participants in an interaction. As applied in that work, the strategy involved looking for the smallest units of behavior that could be shown to convey information. An action can be taken as conveying information whenever there is empirical evidence that its presence or absence is associated with a subsequent action.

There seems to be a lower limit to the duration of an action that can convey information. Some units of behavior may be too brief to be clearly perceived by others and may therefore not be useful in studying interactions. Others may be just detectable. Although the micromomentary facial expressions detected by Haggard and Isaacs (1966) may be expressive movements that can be shown to be related to hypothesized internal states, they may not have any function as signals conveying information. In support of this view is the fact that judges studying these changes as recorded on motion picture film agree with each other rather poorly (with average coefficients in the fifties). The quality of the film may not be good; still, if judges who are looking for these expressions do not agree well on whether or not they have occurred, it seems likely that, at best, these expressions are barely perceptible to other people present in an interaction.

In construing an action as a signal, the investigator does not need to assume that his conceptualizing exhausts the meaning of the action. Finding one relationship between an action and some subsequent action should not be taken as a complete account of that action. It may be found to be related to additional actions that follow it. Furthermore, the investigator has to look in both directions. What prior actions are related to the one he is examining? Although an action is an initiative, a change of activity related to subsequent changes, the action itself is a response, a reaction to preceding actions. A gesture may be related to the speaker's continuing to talk, to verbal emphasis, and also to "back channels" from the auditor. And of course the ges-

ture could be classified by its form—the hand and fingers may symbol-
ize something.

If nonverbal actions are taken as having meaning, what about
verbal actions? Why not apply the action strategy to the actual words
people use and not just to paralanguage and other types of actions?
There is no reason, in principle, why it should not be done. But what
unit can be used? The phoneme is unlikely to be related to anything
other than other linguistic variables, that is, to other aspects of the
language sequence of the speaker. The same appears to be true for the
syllable.

What about words as units? Much has been done in the study of
words, word frequencies, and redundancies (which can be viewed as
commonly occurring sequences of words). The study of words, however, is difficult because the number of classes, one for each word, is
enormous. In addition, we are unlikely to find many strong relationships between a specific word and subsequent words or actions by
other participants. If we move up to a longer unit, such as the sentence, the difficulties are increased. The number of classes is almost
infinite, and the frequency in each class is typically just one.

The obvious way around these obstacles is to develop classes of
words with the same or very similar meanings. But this solution is not
satisfactory in terms of the specifications for the action strategy.
Although it is possible to establish explicit categories for words, each
with a list of the terms to be placed within it, it would not be possible
to obtain high interjudge agreement on the appropriateness of these a
priori classifications. Furthermore, the investigator would have no
assurance that the meaning (class) he assigned a word was the one the
speaker would have used or the one the listener implicitly used.
Finally, the same word may have several meanings. From the listener's viewpoint, the particular meaning is to be gleaned from the
immediate verbal context and from the setting as a whole. From the
speaker's orientation, the sense in which she uses a word today may
not be the sense in which she uses it tomorrow.

For a person in an interaction, the meaning of what the other
person says is usually not a series of discrete bits of information but
rather a general sense conveyed by the whole complex of verbal content, paralanguage, and other actions. Thus, the words of a speaker
can be studied within the context of the other words she utters; in con-

trast, many actions can most profitably be studied in the context of actions by the other person. Nonverbal actions have the advantage that their meaning, as derived from their associations with other actions, appears to be relatively consistent across persons—the same relationships can be found in interactions involving different participants.

Underlying this examination is a fundamental distinction between words and actions. We take it for granted that words have meanings. We assume that the investigator's objective in studying words is to determine those meanings by making interpretive judgments about the words. Although such investigation may explicate the words as they are used, it does not bring out relationships and concepts that contribute to understanding human behavior. It seems unlikely that a word or a class of words identified a priori will be found to have strong relationships to other units of behavior of a kind that will help us to understand what is going on in an interaction. (A possible exception is the heterogeneous class of vocal back channels, composed of words like "yeah" and sounds like "m-hm.") In contrast, the action strategy makes no prior assumption about meanings of actions. It does assume that most actions convey information, that information becoming manifest to the investigator in the relationships uncovered by empirical work. Furthermore, the nonverbal actions of different people appear to be more interchangeable than their verbal actions. Nonverbal actions are characterized by a degree of regularity that offers promise for developing a systematic body of knowledge that is not dependent on the particular observer, the single investigator, or any one conceptualizer.

Verbal actions, words, are rich in meanings for each of us. When we read or listen, we engage in complex cognitive processes as the words call up connotations and person associations. We must use these riches to try to understand what people are saying. Moreover, we find it valuable to seek the meanings of recurring cultural activities, in both our own and other cultures. These efforts have led to a variety of conceptual systems, each of which makes sense to us and each of which adds something to our understanding. But no one such theoretical construction is ever accepted consensually, that is, by the great majority of students in a given discipline.

Critical to the study of actions is the identification of each kind of action to be examined. We must be able to specify each such action explicitly. Even when the action is labeled by a word familiar to everyone (such as *smile* or *gesture*), we should provide a brief verbal definition. Major reliance, however, should be placed on ostensive definition, indicating actions that fall within that class and actions that do not. I am taking the position here that the study of actions is not yet ready to use mechanical or electronic instruments that, by reacting to the purely physical properties of an action, would provide the basic data without involving any observer. Hence, the problem is to explicate the specifications of a class of actions so that observers can determine whether a given action falls within it or is to be excluded.

Although words may be needed to state recognition rules, any "verbal coding rules always fall back on undefined terms" (D'Andrade, 1974, p. 159). Insofar as possible, any undefined terms should be explicable ostensively, by pointing to instances in actual or recorded behavior. In this connection, it is worth noting a statement by Cannon and Jensen: "Time is a primitive element in the logical structure of science. Consequently physics does not explicitly define time but rather specifies operational procedures for its measurement in units of seconds" (1975, p. 317). The measurement of time can be done best by instruments. As long as people are used as measuring instruments, some definition is needed for our communication with observers and for our reports to our colleagues.

An essential requirement for defining an action is that its identification should require no inference, or very minimal inference, on the part of anyone wishing to use that definition in coding behavior. The use of common words, like *smile*, as labels is desirable because it is often just that class of actions which the investigator wishes to study. Of course, we all have rich connotations for the word *smile*. It is, nevertheless, possible to use such a category without regard for associations with the label. And these associations need not impede us in coding a stream of behavior to record the onset and offset of each smile. The designation of a class of actions should involve no implicit connotations of the label used.

In coding an action, the action is taken purely as an action. There need be no confounding contamination in the resulting datum. The particular action is not taken as a symbol or as conveying content or as indicating a choice or a judgment by the actor. No meaning is imputed to the action. Any meaning that the investigator may give to that action is determined by the empirical associations that he uncovers.

When observers are used in research on actions, an absolutely essential requirement is that the observers agree so closely that they are, for all practical purposes, interchangeable. The fundamental importance of interchangeable observers, of having data that are not determined by individualistic features of the observer, has been stressed interminably in this book. The first step for an investigator is to establish that her classes of actions can be coded with very high agreement between independent observations, that her data can be replicated across observers. If she finds that one class does not meet that requirement, she must modify her verbal and ostensive definitions until she obtains adequate agreement, or she must drop that class from her research.

Having determined her classes of actions, the investigator must then decide on her procedure for coding the actions. Since the natural sciences also study changes in objects or organisms, we can glean some suggestions from them. They have the advantage, frequently, that the change leaves an objective trace. Where it does not, the natural scientist can often set up an instrument that will record the occurrence of the change. In the behavioral sciences, traces can sometimes be utilized by an investigator, as pointed out by Webb, Campbell, Schwartz, and Sechrest (1966) in their monograph on *Unobtrusive Measures*. More generally, however, the investigator must arrange for her own traces.

It seems highly desirable to make a recording of the behavior one wishes to analyze. A recording device is often no more obtrusive than an observer, and the gain to the investigator is enormous. She can arrange for observations to be made with no time pressure, replaying the recording or stopping the action as needed. Furthermore, once she has a set of recordings, she can readily search for new classes of actions and can test her hunches and speculations fairly easily. Using a recording, an observer can concentrate on one person and on one class of actions at a time, scanning the tape for each instance of that class. When he has completed that coding, he can replay the tape and code the same class of action for another participant, or he can move to another class.

Each instance of the given class being coded is manifestly located in space since it refers to a part of the body of a specific person in the physical setting. The observer can also locate it in time, pinpointing both its onset and its offset. He can use a relative frame of reference, locating that action in terms of occurrences of other actions. It is easier to take as the reference frame such a continuous behavior as speech. Once the vocal productions of the participants have been transcribed completely, each action can be located with reference to the syllable being uttered when the action began or terminated. This procedure has been used by Duncan. An alternative procedure is to relate each change in activity to an absolute time line calibrated as finely as necessary (as in Kaye, 1977b; Brazelton, Koslowski, and Main, 1974; and Stern, 1974). Absolute time is also used in studies of intervals and durations (for example, Jaffe and Feldstein, 1970).

Precise location in time is not easy to achieve, especially when the observer is coding live behavior as opposed to a recording that can be replayed. It is particularly difficult when the observer is trying to code several actions in the same session. The investigator must take into account observer reaction time, which may be significant when the investigator is studying sequences where a change of one person's activity is followed in a second or less by some change for the other person. When studying sequential events, the investigator must check each instance to make certain that the order of the actions was as he believes it to be. If two nearly simultaneous actions have been recorded live, especially if they are recorded by two different observers, he may not be able to determine with confidence what the temporal order was.

Although the coding of actions does currently require the use of an observer's judgment, the observer's task can be aided by various devices. Instead of judging what speech sound is simultaneous with the change of activity to be recorded, the observer can simply press a button when the act starts and release it at the termination. These observer actions can be marked on a temporally oriented record that can be synthesized with the recording of the behavior being coded. Other automatic data generators can also be devised. A promising one is GALATEA, in which the recording of the phenomena is projected onto a table-top screen. Using an electronic pencil, the observer can simply touch the screen at the moment he wishes to record an event. The device can also record the place on the screen where the event occurred. These records are automatically transformed onto punched cards suitable for entry into statistical analysis. A brief description of GALATEA can be found in Duncan and Fiske (1977).

In this discussion, each class of actions has been treated as though it was coded on a nominal or categorical scale—the action is either present or absent. Such scales for actions can be applied with generally higher interobserver agreement than other types of scales. But, in addition, nods could be coded as slow or fast and smiles as slight, moderate, or broad, each of these ordinal scales requiring discriminations between adjacent steps. In some instances, a step might be identified by an additional criterion. For instance, a higher degree of smiling might specify changes around the eyes as well as the turning upward of the corners of the mouth. In the absence of such an explicit definition for the degree, it seems most probable that agreement on degree will be lower than agreement on presence or absence. Note, of course, that the ordinal scale is embedded in one category, presence of the action, of the nominal scale.

As a research tactic, it seems sensible to begin by studying actions as present or absent. Not only is that kind of scale easier to code and easier to think about, but it also seems likely that the critical matter is generally the occurrence of the action and not its qualities. To engage in speculation, we might start by presuming that the action itself is more likely to convey information than the quality of the action. Looking at the matter another way, it seems unlikely that a vigorous or rapid action conveys information when a gentle or slow action conveys no more information than the absence of that action. For instance, the relationships associated with a gentle smile seem more likely to resemble those for a broad smile than those for not smiling.

One inherent property of a classification for actions should be noted. Actions are located in parts of the actor's body. As a consequence, one action is not entirely independent of all other actions. If one action is occurring, it may not be physically possible for another action to occur. There may thus be mutual exclusions between two or more of the classes. One cannot gesture and touch oneself with the same hand at the same moment. To gaze at someone, the eyes must be open (eye closing longer than a blink is such a rare action that it is ordinarily not used in studies of actions). We must recognize that these are exclusions by our definitions. It would be possible to code a laugh as also a smile. And hand movement could be a class by itself, ignoring the distinctions among gesturing, self-adapting, and object-adapting. Alternatively, and less desirably, one could have categories for hand movements that were assigned on the basis of a judgment as to whether more or less than half of the time was spent in touching oneself, a rather unsatisfactory distinction that not only would be difficult to judge in many instances but also would employ a unit of activity that was not viewed as homogeneous throughout its duration. By definition, an act extended in time is construed as homogeneous; if there is sufficient change, the first action is coded as terminated and another action as started.

Actions and Concepts

We have considered the defining of a class of actions and the coding of actions. But what actions is the investigator to study? From the very large number of actions that can be identified, which should she select? No one can tell the investigator what actions to study—that is her choice. In Reichenbach's context of discovery, everything is up to the investigator. She must make her own decisions, that is, she must place her bets on classes of actions that she believes and hopes will prove important. The field is wide open. In addition to extensions of the relatively small amount of prior work, there are many new areas and topics that have not been subjected to systematic examination. There are many kinds of behaviors and many phases of interactions and other behavioral sequences that we need to try to understand.

In the framework of this volume, the investigator's selected classes of actions are the lowest order of concepts in her overall conceptual scheme. They are not subdivided in any way. As argued above, they should be simple concepts that can readily be grasped and applied by others. It does seem wise to follow the natural step of starting with some everyday classes familiar to all of us, such as gesturing and smiling. These are preferable to artificially contrived sets of classes. This recommendation need not exclude the formation of new labels for readily recognized actions that do not have a common label in everyday language. For example, the term *self-adaptor* (Ekman and Friesen, 1969) has been coined for actions involving touching oneself, one's clothes, or one's immediate possessions (such as facial tissue or pipe). Similarly, the term *back channel* has been proposed by Yngve (1970) for various kinds of feedback that one person (usually the auditor) gives the other person. This class includes nods and brief verbal interjections ("Yeah!"; "I see what you mean."). Back channel, however, is the concept for a class of classes of actions; each of its component categories can be coded separately. A third example is *filled pause*, the label for the sounds ("er . . .") that a speaker may make when continuing to vocalize in a gap between spoken words. These various new concepts are readily recognized and understood.

I am, of course, recommending the use of familiar terms for actions, not for broader categories like tendencies, dispositions, or traits. There is a vast difference between terms like *smile* and *sociable*, between *gesture* and *energetic*, and between *self-adaptor* and *introverted*. As discussed in Part One, the rating of the second term in each of these pairs is typically an integrated judgment summarizing in some way the observation of a segment of behavior extending over some interval—possibly a few minutes but, more often, many hours or even months.

In addition, empirical associations among actions are more likely to have good internal validity than are findings involving broader terms. When an investigator obtains indices for broad concepts, he has difficulty in establishing that observed relationships are attributable to those concepts and not to some other similar concepts or to determinants associated with the procedures for obtaining the indices. In contrast, it is very unlikely that some obtained relationship between two coded actions by different participants will turn out to reflect a stronger relationship involving other actions that closely covary with the particular actions he was analyzing.

The investigator is likely to choose relatively frequent actions so that he can obtain a sizable set of occurrences and so that his results will be more dependable than those based on a few isolated instances. As an additional advantage, more common actions are more likely to be perceived and reacted to by the other participants in an interaction, such reactions perhaps being more consistent over time for each participant and also for all participants. In a sense, common actions are more likely than uncommon actions to be used as information by other participants (an admittedly interpretive statement but one that could be checked by a review of empirical findings). Insofar as actions convey information to others (and perhaps to the actor), the study of actions is relevant to areas of personality.

A set of concepts for classes of actions is obviously not sufficient for developing knowledge and understanding of human behavior in interactions. From these low-order concepts, successive levels of more abstract concepts must be formulated in some kind of hierarchical scheme. The second level can include families of acts, such as the concept of back channel mentioned earlier. But that category was established on the basis of similarity in the presumed functioning of the classes it subsumes. Such a priori labels should be seen as tentative, being convenient for communication. Conceptually more significant are second-level classes bringing together first-order classes that have been found to have the same relationship with something else. For example, in Duncan's system, smooth exchanges of the speaking turn were found to be preceded by one or more of several distinct classes. Any one, or any set of two or more, might be found. In this context, the several classes appear to be interchangeable. Hence, Duncan called the six classes *turn cues* and labeled the second-order class of these classes the *turn signal.*

For an optimal conceptual hierarchy, the critical characteristic is that a concept at any level above the lowest one is defined in terms of one or more concepts at the next level below. Hence, the referent for each concept is explicit. The meaning of any concept comes from two sources—its relationships to concepts above and below it in the hierarchical scheme and its horizontal connections with concepts at the same level. We are considering here only substantive conceptualizations. One can have a metatheory—a theory for theories—that does not rigorously limit its concepts to ones with referents to lower concepts, ultimately resting on direct observations. Similarly, methodological conceptualizations often do not refer to particular observations; instead, their abstract concepts can be illustrated by a variety of specific applications.

The building of a hierarchy based on concepts for simple actions follows an inductive approach. That approach seems desirable in research on personality and related fields as a tactic for counteracting our natural tendency to start with everyday concepts that are broad and loose and that cannot be defined directly or indirectly by readily observable behaviors that exhaust the denotative meanings of the concepts. The process of science does involve a cycling of focus, moving from observations to concepts to new observations to modified concepts, and so on. In the present primitive state of the field, the use of the hypothetico-deductive approach, starting with concepts and propositions, has the serious limitation that one cannot fully explicate the referents for the broad concepts. In the other approach, as soon as we have some tentatively established propositions or hypotheses grounded on observed data, we can make deductions and test them. The investigator can formulate and test propositions at any time after the initial stages in which classes of simple actions have been set up and tried out, preliminary empirical relationships have been obtained, and concepts at one or two levels above the lowest order have been selected. Hunches and speculations fertilize research following the action strategy, just as they are the source of progress in any other systematic investigation. In selecting the actions to be studied, the investigator uses hunches based on unstructured observing; when he has coded some protocols, he examines them to get ideas as to what might be related to what. At later stages in his program, he formulates theories and hypotheses on the basis of his preceding work, together with the pertinent work of other investigators.

The concepts in a theory of actions cannot be limited to low-order concepts and higher-order concepts built on them. There must be concepts pertaining to the locus within which the actions occur. How many participants are involved? What is the nature of the physical circumstances in which the interaction occurs? Does the conceptualizer need concepts for classes of interaction defined in terms of the reasons why the people came together? It is to be hoped that these reasons can be classified in terms of observable precursors, such as a written communication received by all participants or the cook's call, "Come and get it!" Where such identification of a class of situations is not possible, the investigator must proceed cautiously. Any prior intuitive classification should be treated as highly tentative. A conservative tactic is to group together those interactions for which the same set of relationships has been empirically demonstrated.

In the preceding discussion, the illustrative concepts have been drawn largely from face-to-face interaction, a part of the diverse phenomena to which the action strategy can be applied. But even for work on interactions, the list of possible action classes is very long. Duncan and Fiske (1977) provide one such list (pp. 156–162). Closely related to the group of action classes are the many classes within paralanguage, such as intensity, pitch, pauses, and inhalations. A related group consists of haptics, body contact between people. There are also proxemics, involving the use of personal and social space. It is, however, not clear whether variables in these areas can be coded with as high interobserver agreement as those for the body motions noted earlier.

Certain other areas do not fit as neatly into the specifications for the action strategy. Within the topic of facial expressions, some variables do fit while others do not. For example, the judging of emotion, although using familiar labels, does require some interpretation by the observer. There are also areas where the variables do not ordinarily have such sharp boundaries in time, pertaining instead to relatively sustained time periods, such as a whole interaction. One such area is the role of natural and artificial scents, perhaps including detectable body heat. Another is the use of artifacts, such as dress and cosmetics. Some of these should be construed as variables pertinent to extended states. Variables pertinent to somewhat shorter states are those referring to bodily position or posture. (For another account of the range of actions that have been studied, see Weick, 1968.)

Like all classification, some decisions about categorization within the action strategy are rather arbitrary. As delineated here, the strategy deals with motor and vocal acts. But what is an act? There is really no theoretical reason why the action strategy or some close relative of it cannot include variables pertaining to extended states, such as scents and the use of artifacts. Certainly changes in posture can be treated as actions. In practice, the study of many of these variables will prove difficult because the investigator will have relatively few occurrences to observe—a person may wear a particular article of clothing only occasionally, each occasion providing one unit of measurement. There is the additional problem of comparing positive instances, where the variable is present, with other instances, where it is absent. With what group does the investigator compare a group of persons he has categorized on the basis of its members wearing a decorative item consistently?

Although this listing of actions and of variables resulting from actions may seem lengthy, it is by no means complete. Much good work in animal ethology fits within the action strategy, as does the careful work on human ethology. In fact, N. Blurton Jones (1972a) describes the ethological approach to child development with essentially the same emphases and general orientation as those of the action strategy presented in this volume. And the whole realm of actions related to objects, as opposed to organisms, needs to be considered. Many variables used in research guided by behavior theory are consistent with the preceding specifications for actions. Further examples will be given below.

Programs for Research on Actions

Given the possibility of establishing classes of actions that can be coded with very high interobserver agreement, what can the investigator do? Within the actional strategy, what tactics can she incorporate into her research plan? What kinds of research programs can she undertake?

The investigator can identify one or more actions that interest her and that she believes have some significance in behavior. She can then select some segments of behavior and simply study them with as open a mind as possible. What actions might be related to those she has selected? What are the various angles from which these segments can be viewed? George Kelly (1964) has suggested the phrase *invitational mood* for the preliminary thinking about possibilities and formulating speculations.

But what action or actions does an investigator choose for study? She will, of course, find it easier to focus on an action that occurs rather frequently. She can begin by selecting an action that has been described but not fully explicated in systematic work. Much remains to be learned, for example, about the eyes and eyebrows and about hands and touching. Whatever action she chooses, she can ask two questions: What actions or events preceded it? Do its relationships with other acts vary with the precise moment at which it occurs, as compared to a few moments before or after?

An investigator can focus her efforts on identifying the determinants for a single kind of action. One example is the research on pupil size reported in *The Tell-Tale Eyes* (Hess, 1975). Dilation or constriction of the pupil occurs in the absence of the usual source, a change in the brightness of the visual field. What changes in stimulation, that is, what kinds of introduced stimuli produce these changes in the diameter of the pupil? Very loosely, stimuli that evoke positive feelings, stimuli that are liked, tend to be followed by dilation. Dilation is also associated with effort. Stimuli that are disliked and evoke negative feelings tend to be followed by constriction. Although some stimuli produce almost universal reactions, others are associated with a range of individual reactions that can be linked to other characteristics of the subject.

In addition to the biological significance of changes in size of pupil, these effects appear to have importance in interpersonal interactions. Although we are not aware of changes in the size of our own pupils, we do react to the size of the pupils in other people (Hess, 1975, Chap. 7). Even though we may perceive and react to a change in size or to a relatively large or small size of pupil, we are generally not aware of noting such features. But when asked to complete a drawing of a face so that it expresses a given mood, subjects tend to draw pupils of the appropriate size for the particular instruction, without consciously knowing about the functioning of the pupil (Hess, 1975, pp. 214–219).

Pupillometric research is ordinarily done in the laboratory, with the subject's head in a fixed position so that the pupils can be photographed for later measurement. That measurement can be made with high objectivity; in fact, there is an automatic device for obtaining the measurements. Thus, although this area of research certainly fits the requirement that the data be objective, it is restricted to the conditions for laboratory experimentation. It is the study of the responses associated with physical stimuli provided by the investigator. The stimuli are constant. What precedes the response is the presentation of a stimulus that remains unchanged during its exposure.

Also involving the eyes is the pendulum-tracking research of Holzman (Holzman and others, 1974). In these investigations, the subject is instructed to keep his eyes on a swinging pendulum, while a recording is made of the path of his focus. The action here is a complex one continuing over the course of the observation period. The adequacy of the performance is judged from the total pattern and also in terms of such specific features as arrests of eye movements and overly rapid movements.

This research is included within the action strategy because it studies an ongoing action. Once the recording of the eye movements has been obtained, it can be examined on a moment-to-moment basis, considering whether each identified point is in the appropriate position relative to the point preceding it. (The correct position can be determined from knowledge of the physical locus of the pendulum at each instant.) The response is to a physical stimulus, not an interpersonal one. Also, unlike the pupil response, it is affected by the general motivation of the subject. It requires that he be willing to try to track the stimulus. It also requires a laboratory device for recording the eye movements. The fact that observations can be made in places other than the laboratory, as Holzman has done in studying schizophrenia in twins, does not invalidate the point that the actions studied are not occurring under naturalistic conditions.

In this, as in all research, data from a series of observations are reduced to indices that represent the array of separate measurements. In the pupillometric research, one measurement, or the average for a period of time following a stimulus presentation, is averaged together with measurements after other stimuli that the investigator believes to be of the same type. Similarly, the pendulum-tracking research generates one or more indices for each period of observation, each summarizing the subject's reactions at a number of times.

Much of the research on the actions studied in nonverbal communication has proceeded in a similar fashion. The investigator codes the occurrences of each class of action and then counts these events for some selected period. The index, then, is the frequency of actions in that class. This approach characterizes what has been called *external-variable* research (Duncan, 1969), in which nonverbal actions have been related to an outside variable that usually is not part of the immediate behavioral context in which the action occurs (for example, the sex of the subject or of the other participant or a personality test score). More completely, each index refers to actions during a more or less extended period of time. When its relationship to an external variable is examined, the index is presumed to estimate for the subject a general characteristic; its applicability is not restricted to the particular period of observation, and sometimes it is not restricted to the particular set of conditions under which the index was obtained.

A comprehensive example of external-variable research is given in Duncan and Fiske (1977, Pt. II). From five minutes of interaction, about fifty action variables were coded for each of the two participants, frequency or extent of time indices being obtained for the total period. Another set of indices was obtained for an immediately following interaction with a person of the opposite sex from that of the first partner. The indices for each interaction were correlated with each other, with all the indices from the other interaction, with indices for the partner, with self-report personality scores, and with reactions to the interaction as reported afterward. Although the results were interesting, they were not very informative. They threw little light on what was going on during the interaction.

Much other work in this area has been of the same general kind, though usually with fewer variables and fewer subjects. The emphasis has been on a single type of action, rather than on relationships between each kind of action and the actions of other people. An intriguing example is the account of the eyebrow flick given by Eibl-Eibesfeldt (1972). When greeting another person at a little distance and when very friendly with that person, some people smile, nod, and then manifest a rapid eyebrow flick upwards, the brows remaining maximally raised for about one-sixth of a second. Eibl-Eibesfeldt has noted this action in natural settings for widely different ethnic groups and has offered some general statements about his observations. He has related it to characteristics of the actor and of his relationship to the person being greeted, rather than to contemporary actions of that other person.

The action strategy has also been used in the extensive research under the general egis of behavior theory. Skinner has focused on the single action, defined objectively so that interobserver agreement in reading the recordings of the occurrence of the action is no problem. The primary index is the rate of occurrence of the selected action, that is, the total frequency for a set period of time. Thus, it is a summarizing index like those mentioned earlier. The investigator is less interested in understanding each occurrence of the action at a particular moment than in determining whether the rate has increased or decreased after some experimental manipulation.

The action studied is termed an *operant behavior* or *response*. In the operant conditioning paradigm, it is identified by its consequences. The reinforcement occurring after the action is seen as a stimulus for the organism, its occurrence affecting the likelihood of the organism making that action again under the same conditions. Thus, the rate of occurrence of an action is seen as governed by the prior history of reinforcement. Consequently, a major focus of research under behavior theory is on the linkage between an action and the environmental event that follows it with more or less regularity.

To be more precise, this work has been concerned with a three-event sequence: action, reinforcement, and subsequent repetition of the action. The action and its reinforcement is usually taken as a combined event, the history of the occurrence of that event being related to the later appearance of the action. Thus, the observed relationships are between aggregations of action-reinforcement events and aggregations (frequencies or rates) of subsequent actions. The single occurrence of the total sequence (one action, one reinforcement, and one subsequent occurrence of that action) has not been taken as a unit. In the laboratory, the complete sequence can occur within a short time span. Outside the laboratory, the time intervals between the components and especially between the reinforcement and a subsequent action may be fairly lengthy.

Although operants and reinforcements were first studied in the laboratory, they have been shown to be pertinent to the personality area, especially to the control of behavior (a major emphasis in behavior theory). One early application was to desensitization, as in the treatment of phobias. More recently, behavior modification has become a widespread type of treatment. The major effort has been on the elimination of undesirable behaviors, such as smoking and stuttering. Note, however, that in the treatment of stuttering, a desired action (smooth speaking) is increased as the undesired action of stuttering is reduced. In the elimination of smoking, no specific action replaces the smoking behavior. What is increased by the treatment is the occurrence of nonsmoking actions. This is not a matter of semantics; as we shall see later, the absence of an action at a particular time should, for some purposes, be construed in the same way as the occurrence of an action.

Behavior theory has proved fruitful in its contributions to the understanding of behavior in general and of personality phenomena in particular. One basis for its significance has been its emphasis on time, both in the notion of rate of occurrence of an action and in the temporal association between an action and its subsequent reinforcement. Another basis may well be its insistence on studying observable motor actions that can be coded with little or no disagreement. For the most part, these actions have been brief and relatively homogeneous, so that no further analysis of their components is needed. These characteristics are most evident in the use of bar-pressing and pecks on discs in the work with animals and birds. It may also be significant that much research following behavior theory studies organisms under conditions where a given action may occur at some time, rather than testing for the occurrence of a response after a stimulus manipulated by the investigator.

An Optimal Strategy for Studying Actions

In the preceding pages, some examples of the action strategy have come from psychological areas outside of personality. Within the phenomena of personality and similar domains, a particular form of the action strategy appears to be especially promising. The key feature is the study of each action in its behavioral context, that is, the study of the action as related to other actions occurring at more or less the same time, both before and after it. Behavior is action and reaction. A change in the sensory input leads to an action, which in turn changes the input for another person, who then engages in an action. Complex and interwoven chains or sequences of action are continually going on.

In this optimal strategy, the unit of analysis is the occurrence of two or more actions within a very brief interval of time, ordinarily involving two persons. The analysis compares the frequency of a given sequence with that of other sequences in which one or more of those actions does not occur. To return again to the exchange of speaking turns as an example, the frequency of a turn signal with a smooth exchange can be compared to the frequency of simultaneous claimings of the speaking turn by the two participants in the absence of that signal. Each of these units of analysis has similarities to the action-reinforcement sequence used in behavior theory but is quite different from the rate concept, which ignores the occurrences of any other actions by taking each occurrence of an action as a unit integrated into the rate index.

In terms of the research decisions considered in Chapter Eight, the general action strategy has been characterized by the investigator picking his own problem (Choice 1b), choosing to study motor and vocal actions (Choice 3b), and setting for his observers the task of recognizing and identifying those actions (Choice 6b). In the optimal strategy for studying actions, the setting is as natural and unobtrusive as possible, so that generalization to ordinary behavior can be done with considerable confidence. In addition, the stimuli presented to actors are naturally occurring ones (Choice 10b), the stimuli being the actions of other persons and of the actor. To be sure, the actions preceding a given action are identified by close examination rather than by manipulation by the investigator. Stressful situations and stimuli are not induced, although of course they may occur naturally.

To these specifications of an optimal strategy, one more should be added explicitly. The identification of each action class should, as discussed earlier, be complete within itself. No stated or unstated rules for coding the occurrence of an action should involve any other action preceding or following it or simultaneous with it. Similarly, the identification of the action class should not require any additional knowledge on the part of the observer. It is essential that the investigator and her observers take little or nothing for granted, that they make the minimal number of assumptions, and that these assumptions be explicit.

When the several actions have been identified, the investigator then looks for regularities among these actions, watching recordings of the phenomena being studied and perusing transcriptions coding such phenomena. In examining interactions, she can think of regularities as possible rules that are implicit in what she is studying. Just as we speak grammatically without necessarily being able to spell out the rules of grammar, so the investigator can conceive of rules for interacting that can be formulated and demonstrated empirically even though neither she nor the actors being studied have been aware of those rules. Although the rules have not been explicitly stated previously, they can be important to understanding these interactions, and they can be conceptually fruitful.

It seems wise to construe these rules as the investigator's constructions, her interpretation of what she is perceiving, just as any scientific conceptualization has its existence in the minds of scientists. The rules may have a long life if they are supported by replications of the observations and of the relationships in other protocols. When, however, they are not replicated, or when the investigator develops a more satisfying formulation of the rules, the previous construing can be abandoned. In any case, the rules are stated in terms of the explicit classes of actions so that their referents are clear and restricted.

The word *rules* should be reserved for relationships among actions that hold for most instances where they might be expected to be observed—that is, for consistent regularities. Once rules have been located, the complementary concept of violation of a rule can be brought in. If a pattern of actions is very common, the occasional occurrence of a pattern where one of the components, one action, does not occur or is replaced by a different action becomes an interesting topic for further study.

The analysis of an interaction will reveal instances where the action that usually occurs does not occur. Such a nonaction may be as important as an action. As examples, consider the situation in which two individuals come face to face at a distance of a few feet. Suppose one person extends his hand toward the other in the usual motion preceding the shaking of hands, and the other person makes no complementary motion. Even more striking would be an instance in which two people from the same subculture are facing each other; one says "How are you?" and the other continues to gaze at the speaker but stays silent. We may confidently anticipate that subsequent actions of the speaker will differ from those which occur when the speaker receives a verbal reply.

The notion of action sequence is central to the optimal action strategy proposed here and to the general orientation in Duncan and Fiske (1977). The idea is obviously not new. For example, Weick (1968, 1969) has used the concepts of *act, interact,* and *double interact* for an action by A, a subsequent action by B, and another action by A, respectively. Others have used these or similar terms in the preceding decade or two. In discussing her comprehensive compilation of ninety-four observation schemes, MacFadyen (1974) reports that about one-third did use two- or three-term contingencies similar to Weick's interact and double interact. Her review provides useful information on such matters as the frequency of using recordings and the large variety of procedures by which behavior has been assessed for purposes of evaluation and treatment. However, the actions involved in these contingencies are often much more interpretive than those discussed in this chapter.

A significant formal characteristic of the double interact or three-term contingency must be pointed out. Consider a sequence involving an action by person A immediately followed by an action by person B and then another action by A. In classical terms, the action of B is a response to the first action of A, and then it is a stimulus for A's subsequent action. This is typical of the stream of behavior —one action is both a reaction and a stimulus, depending on the investigator's unit of analysis. The striking implication of this point is that, in studying actions and their classification, we are concurrently identifying classes of behaviors and classes of events eliciting behaviors. The same classification can be used for both purposes.

Research studies of action sequences within the action strategy are reviewed in Lewis and Rosenblum (1974). To examine a specific instance, consider the turn system developed by Duncan. Here, the action patterns were observed and construed for conversational interactions between two persons. Figure 4 illustrates with three diagrams of sequences. In these diagrams, the presence of an action is indicated by a letter, the action continuing as long as the letters are there. Important periods where the action transcribed on that line does not occur are indicated by a series of dots. Section A in Figure 4 is a diagram for a smooth exchange of speaking turns. While he is speaking, X gives the turn signal at various times. This signal refers to one or more actions that are construed as cues subsumed under that signal. After one of these signals, Y starts talking and X no longer talks. The exchange of speaking turns has occurred smoothly. The moment of critical interest is marked by an arrow.

Section B in Figure 4 illustrates simultaneous turns or interruption. Again, X is talking and giving the turn signal intermittently.

Time ───▶

Person   Action

X   Talking   TTTTTTTTTT..TTTTTTTTTT.TTTTTTTT.........
X   Turn signal   SS   S   SSS
Y   Talking   TTT

A. Smooth Exchange of Speaking Turns   ↑

X   Talking   TTTTTTTTTT..TTTTTTTTTTTT.TTTTTTTTTTTT
X   Turn signal   SS   S   .....
Y   Talking   TTTT

B. Simultaneous Talking Turns   ↑

X   Talking   TTTTTTT..TTTTTTTT.TTTTTT...TTTTTT
X   Turn signal   SS   S   SSS   SS
X   Gesticulation
              signal   GGGGGG
Y   Talking   ?   TTT

C. One Signal Overriding Another   ↑

Figure 4. Action Sequences in Conversational Interaction.

But at some point where the signal does not appear, Y starts talking. Since X continues, they talk simultaneously for at least a few moments. These two illustrations involve two classes of action, speaking and the turn signal. The observer notes the occurrence and nonoccurrence of each class in each person. Here, we are concerned only with three actions, X talking or not, Y talking or not, and X giving the turn signal. There are actually four components in this analysis, since X's speaking or not speaking after the critical point marked by the arrow is treated as an element separate from her prior talking. (These patterns may remind some readers of those identified by Chapple, 1962. Chapple's patterns, however, are at a more molar level of analysis.)

The pattern of actions in exchanges of turns can also involve another signal by the speaker. This signal, the speaker gesticulation signal, is composed of two cues, the speaker either gesturing or holding a hand in a tensed position. This signal is construed as preemptive, as canceling any turn signal. See Section C in Figure 4. If Y started talking at the point marked "?," simultaneous turns would be likely (although few instances of such turn-claiming have been observed). In this pattern, there are four actions involved. The corres-

Time ⟶

Person	Action	
X	Talking	TTTTTTTT..TTTTT.TTTTTTTTTT...TTTTTTT
X	Continuation signal	
Y	Back channel	... BBB

A. On-Time Back Channel   ↑

Person	Action	
X	Talking	TTTTTTTTTT..TTTTT.TTTTTTTTTT...TTTTTTT
X	Continuation signal	CCC
Y	Back channel	BBB

B. Early Back Channel and Subsequent Continuation Signal   ↑

Figure 5. Back Channels in Conversational Interactions.

ponding case where Y does not start talking involves three actions and one nonaction.

In these illustrations of turn exchanges, the importance of timing is not directly apparent. If, however, Y starts talking at any point when the turn signal is absent, there would be an interruption and simultaneous turns. To bring out more clearly the significance of timing, Figure 5 presents two illustrations involving back channels—such actions of the auditor as nods, "Yeah!," "I see it." Section A in Figure 5 illustrates a back channel occurring on time, that is, at a moment that has been construed as appropriate on the basis of empirical findings. The important point is that the speaker continues to talk and nothing else happens. In contrast, Section B illustrates what can happen when the back channel occurs too early: the speaker not only continues to talk but also gives a continuation signal. (Patterns involving back channels are actually more complex than these diagrams may seem to imply. Other signals are involved, including those affecting the observed frequency of back channels. See Duncan and Fiske, 1977, Chap. 11.)

In addition to the notion of appropriate moments, time enters the turn system in the notion of an action providing a kind of standing condition. While the action is going on, it establishes a condition that must be taken into account in studying the relationships among other actions. One example is the gesticulation signal in Figure 4. Moreover, the occurrence of an action may have effects after its termination. Thus, it seems desirable to identify and conceptualize states of various kinds in the participants in an interaction. These states may be associated with particular actions that are construed as cues forming a signal.

In addition, further investigation is needed to identify states existing throughout an interaction. The actions selected as indicants of such states may be more varied than those for more temporary states and hence may be more difficult to discover. Their investigation will require a much larger and more diverse collection of protocols than any available today. I am referring here to states that are of shorter duration than that assumed for states in the trait-state conceptualizations that have emerged in recent years (Cattell, 1966; Spielberger and Lushene, 1971). What makes both shorter and longer states important is that they provide some specification of aspects of *situation* as that term enters into the contemporary discussions of person-situation interaction (see Endler and Magnusson, 1976a; Magnusson and Endler, 1977).

The importance of timing and of state or readiness is evident in other contexts. After a mother duck has been sitting on her eggs for most of the usual incubation period, a duckling still in its shell may emit distinct sounds consisting of bill clapping and vocalization. At that normal time, the mother duck responds by clucks, singly or in small bursts (Hess, 1973, p. 431). This pattern of vocal actions has been observed by microphones buried in nests used for field experimentation. It is also possible to place a small speaker unit in those nests. If the experimenter plays a recording of those duckling sounds during the first few days of the duck's brooding, an abnormal time for such sounds, she does not respond with the usual clucks. One mother duck flew away from the nest. "Two others gave a panting sound while fluffing their feathers, a behavior regarded by students of mallard behavior as being a threat response" (Hess, 1973, p. 434). The relative timing in this instance is a matter of days, a much larger order of magnitude than that examined in the earlier instances of conversational interactions between humans.

When searching for associations between actions, an investigator should not limit himself to examining an action and subsequent events. A fruitful tactic is to search for events that regularly precede the action of interest. There are, to be sure, relationships of the form: If A, then subsequent action B is very likely. But there are many where the picture is: If A, then B may or may not occur, as a function of other circumstances. In spite of that result, the investigator may find that: If B, then A preceded it with a very high relative frequency. Hence, if he had started with A, he might not discover the link with B. But if he starts his search with B, he will probably discover the link with A.

In conversational interactions, and presumably in other types of interaction, there are options available to a participant. For example, if the speaker gives a turn signal, the auditor may or may not start talking. A rule here would be permissive: If a speaker gives the turn signal (and no other signal), the auditor may start speaking without producing simultaneous turns. In a related case, the speaker's signal may be composed of one or more cues. The more cues, the more likely it is that the auditor will take over the speaking turn with a smooth exchange. An auditor may jump in when only one cue is given, or he may prefer to wait until several cues appear. Options and permissive rules permit the identification of consistent individual patterning beyond the obvious individual differences in the frequencies and extents of actions occurring during a conversation. Although indices for totals may not prove very informative (see Duncan and Fiske, 1977, Pt. II), there may be consistencies in the action patterns associated with a particular person. As suggested above, during one interaction, a given person may prefer to let the other keep talking, taking the speaking turn only occasionally when several cues have been given for the signal. In complementary fashion, by giving more turn cues, the speaker can encourage the auditor to take the turn. She can also encourage that action by turning her gaze toward the auditor. Thus, by choosing among the options open to her, a person can manifest a regular pattern that can be labeled her *strategy*. In another interaction, she may manifest a different strategy. But it may be found that a person tends to show a given strategy rather regularly in all her interactions.

Note that the regularities in the action patterns of one person are presumed to be of the same kind as those for other persons. For example, the general regularity may be that action B is almost invariably preceded by action A. For some persons, B is less frequent; for others, more so. But for all of them, when B occurs, A can be found to have preceded it. I shall not develop these conceptual speculations here because they are tentative. Almost nothing has been done empirically to explore optionality, strategies, or other generalized individual differences in actions embedded in the context of other actions (that is, where the unit of analysis is an action together with other actions by that person or by others). Of course, the elements in these patterns may be nonactions as well as actions.

By developing information about individual differences from the single interaction, from other interactions of the same kind, and from other kinds of interaction, the extent of individual consistencies can be determined empirically. Although this approach would greatly extend the number of potential individual difference variables, each would be specified in terms of a given kind of interaction as well as being located within explicit patterns of actions. This orientation avoids the serious difficulties in applying a general variable, such as talkativeness, to a group of persons, only to have to qualify the overall index for a person by saying that of course he talks more at some times than at others. Instead, a time-consuming assessment might determine explicitly that he takes the speaking turn almost every time his partner gives any turn cue or that, when with a partner of the opposite sex, he keeps talking for long periods with almost constant manifestations of the gesticulation signal.

The approach to individual differences as observed within the action strategy is quite different from the usual approach. It has been common to try to determine how one person as an entity differs from other persons or to demonstrate that there is dependable variation over persons along some postulated dimension. In contrast, the action strategy examines actions of people within a circumscribed context, locates regularities in the actions of all the persons, and then asks whether, within the bounds of those regularities, there are regularities associated with individuals. For instance, it may be found that when action B occurs, it is consistently preceded by action A. The rates of occurrence of A, of B, and of B given A can vary from person to person.

Summary

The action strategy examines motor and vocal actions as changes in activity that are readily observable and easily coded for times of onset and of offset. The strategy assumes that actions convey information, that they make a difference. That assumption should not be taken as indicating that anything that has meaning can be studied with the strategy. Although words are verbal actions, their content and meaning may require so much interpretation that high interobserver agreement cannot be established. In this strategy, simple action classes are identified, often using a label from everyday language. From these low-order concepts, a hierarchy of concepts can be developed, the higher-order concepts being defined in terms of concepts at the next lower-order level.

Studies of a single action class and of frequencies for action classes may be valuable in some areas. More profitable is the study of paired occurrences, in which an action is followed by another action. Work on behavior theory, one form of the action strategy, stresses the reinforcement occurring after an operant action.

An optimal action strategy concentrates on action sequences— that is, actions in the context of other actions, all occurring within a particular set of conditions. Some behaviors or products of behaviors may provide standing conditions for an entire interaction. The optimal action strategy studies all these phenomena in highly naturalistic settings with minimally obstrusive recording equipment or observational procedures. In this approach, both the occurrence of an action and the nonoccurrence of that action may prove to be significant. The total relationship may involve other actions in addition to the pair being examined. Since the observed regularities may provide options for a participant, consistent choices of particular options can be construed as a strategy that characterizes the individual in one interaction or in a series of similar interactions.

XIII

Critique of the Action Strategy

The presentations of the strategies for studying societal problems and for studying attributions included critical evaluation of them. It is now time to undertake a critique of the strategy for studying actions. What are its weaknesses and limitations? To what substantive areas can it be applied and to what areas is it not applicable? We shall begin by considering its generalizability.

We noted earlier that the action strategy permits a high degree of replicability of observations. By setting up action classes that are clearly defined and readily identified, the investigator can obtain a very high level of agreement among her observers when they are coding the same set of phenomena. In addition, there is little reason to

336

doubt that the findings from the action strategy will usually be highly reproducible. In empirical work following this strategy, the results from one set of phenomena have typically been very similar to those from independent sets studied at a different time.

The representativeness of the data and of the relationships among variables is, of course, crucial. In particular, there is the question of external validity, of generalizing the findings and interpretations from the sample to the population from which the sample is presumably drawn. The best basis for such generalizing is consistency across samples, especially diverse ones. In the absence of empirical evidence, the evaluation must be a considered judgment. Is there anything about the conditions for observing the phenomena that might well limit their representativeness? For most psychological research, this question must be asked because the investigator has generally established special conditions for her study, including the presentation of selected stimuli to the subjects. In other research, including much of ethology, the investigator is not obtrusive, and the organisms are observed as they interact with naturally occurring stimuli. As a consequence, the extent to which these observations and findings represent those for the populations from which they are drawn can be taken as high.

Representativeness is best determined on an empirical basis. Once certain relationships have been found in one set of phenomena and replicated in other sets, the investigator should then attempt to find out within what range of phenomena her findings and interpretations hold. In a sense, the population being sampled can only be guessed in advance. Although the investigator can select in advance some population from which she hopes to sample, she may well find that the population available to her is a subset of the larger population, a subset with specifiable characteristics, and hence her results do not generalize to the total population she had in mind originally. When an investigator chooses to study action, she may or may not find that her results have high generalizability. If she studies actions in a context with naturally occurring stimuli, she is more likely to find satisfactory generalizability.

The investigator must also determine within what range of contexts her findings and interpretations hold. Relationships among actions in an action sequence must be assumed to be associated with a

context or a class of contexts. The identification of the relevant context or class has to be established by extensive research. Some actions,
such as the eyebrow flick when a person is approached by another
who is liked, may be found in any culture. In contrast, a particular
form of handshake may be restricted to the members of a small group
within their clubhouse.

Although considerable attention has been paid to the context
or situation in which behavior is observed, the problem of conceptualizing situations has not been resolved. One reason is that situations
have been examined in a very general way. Various classifications of
psychological contexts have been proposed, but usually without
identifying a particular type of behavior for which the descriptive
scheme is pertinent. It seems quite likely that the labeling and categorizing of situations will have to be done separately for each major
type of action concept. Another reason is purely practical. Although
it is fairly easy to vary conditions within the general context of the
laboratory, it is difficult to make observations in many other places,
both in terms of getting observers or recording equipment to the
appropriate places and in terms of being unobtrusive and ethical.
The investigator must be ingenious. One example of resourcefulness
is Anderson's (1972) study of children's attachment behavior to their
mothers, as observed in a public park.

To What Behaviors Can the Action Strategy Be Applied?

The action strategy seems applicable to a wide range of behaving. In principle, any observable activity of a person can be coded
into action classes. The only requirement is that the action classes be
sufficiently identifiable to permit the observations of different observers to be essentially interchangeable. In practice, the potential value
of this strategy will depend on the investigator's success in having
hunches that lead to discovering classes of actions with interesting
regularities.

Even the optimal action strategy can, in principle, be extended
to a very wide range of activity. Wherever appropriate action classes
can be specified, it should be possible to examine each such action in
its behavioral context. The units of analysis can include sequences of
two actions and sequences involving a nonaction (an action and a

nonaction, a nonaction and an action, or two nonactions), each nonaction being a unit of observation where the corresponding action might have occurred. The additional feature of studying actions in natural settings with natural stimuli does not impose any major conceptual restriction. It does, however, impose a serious practical limitation that cannot be overcome for many areas of activity. It may simply not be possible, for ethical or social reasons, to obtain audiovisual recordings of some activity. If the majority of people are unwilling to have such recordings made in certain circumstances, the investigator may have difficulty in determining the generalizability of his findings from the atypical persons who are willing. The alternative of concealed recordings must be rejected on ethical grounds. (The only possible exception here is the recording of behavior in public places where the actors are under no risk of embarrassment or other psychological or psychosocial harm from the making and the analysis of the recordings. For example, the conditions might make it impossible to establish the identity of the actors.) In all instances where the recording is not concealed, the investigator must determine in some way the degree of obtrusiveness of his procedures: Does the observing or the recording affect the activity being studied?

The potentialities of studying actions in conversations between two persons look good on the basis of the small amount of research that has been completed in this area. Although most of the conversations studied by Duncan and Fiske (1977) were held for the purposes of the research, those that were held for other purposes appeared to yield highly comparable findings. There is a need for further study of interactions held for instrumental purposes, where the two people come together to get something done—to reach a decision, to make an evaluation, or to determine a joint course of action.

More complex interactions, among three or more persons, also need to be investigated. Other areas of investigation might include conversations being held while the participants are doing something together. (Duncan, for example, has videotaped two families eating dinner together, with repeated days of observation.) Another interesting area is that of the monologue: the lecture, the political speech, or the sermon.

A special type of interaction is nonverbal but not necessarily nonvocal. Kenneth Kaye has studied mother-infant interactions at different ages. In one study (Kaye, 1977a), he focused on the mothers' teaching strategies with their six-month-old infants, noting how the infant's actions were related to the mother's. In another study (1977b), he focused on the sucking behavior of infants at two and at fifteen days. He observed relationships among an infant's termination of a sucking period, an action of the mother, and the subsequent return to sucking, seeing them as possibly prototypic to dialogue. Also using the action strategy is other research with infants reported in the various chapters of Lewis and Rosenblum (1974). Applications of the action strategy to research on children can be found in *Ethological Studies of Child Behaviour,* edited by N. Blurton Jones (1972b). In these reports, child interactions, especially with the mother, are emphasized. Possibilities for cross-cultural investigations are also demonstrated.

A recent report (Truscott, Parmelee, and Werner, 1977) notes a regularity in human behavior that is possibly related to territorial behavior in animals. Persons in a restaurant touch their plate after being served by another much more often than after serving themselves. This is one of few studies of nonvocal, impersonal interactions. Other examples of impersonal interactions are walking through a crowd, shuffling along in a cafeteria line, and getting off a crowded bus. More significant is the area of haptics, body contact between two persons. This topic can be investigated along with simultaneous motor and verbal acts, as in greetings and leave-taking. More intimate touching will be very difficult to study unobtrusively for ethical reasons. Some enterprising investigator might see whether films produced for use in sex therapy are sufficiently natural to be of any value in research.

The strategy designated as optimal in Chapter Twelve has been used in some social psychological work. For example, some of the classical observations of passersby being affected by one person's behavior fall within that rubric. When a pedestrian stops at a red light even though there is no automobile traffic going by, does a following pedestrian also stop? Similar studies involve cars at stop signs. Most of the research on this topic, however, has used confederates in order to make more systematic observations in a shorter period of time. The dross rate in waiting for the desired events to occur naturally can be high.

Research on the involvement of bystanders present when a person needs help has had to be experimental, with simulated traumas. It is simply not possible to spend days waiting for the opportunity to observe a number of these unfortunate events. Moreover, the action classes employed in this research tend to be rather gross and interpretive. Did the bystander confront the situation or turn away? Did he actively help? Each of these judgments ordinarily has to be made in a short period of time, which has not been delineated sharply. And the judgments have been made by observers present during the event rather than from recordings.

There seems to be no reason why the action strategy cannot be applied to many other phenomena subsumed under the rubric of social psychology. The usual topics and chapter headings provide rough labels for types of phenomena that can be chosen for study. As in research on personality, the investigator must start with actions that can be observed with minimal interpretation and with very low-order concepts rather than with the loose general concepts that resemble the broad ones so prevalent in personality. Some field research projects represent steps in that direction. In the collection of studies presented by Bickman and Henchy (1972), many of the dependent variables require judgments involving little inference or interpretation.

Beyond social psychology, the action strategy can be used for investigating topics pertinent to more than one culture. A similar anthropological strategy has been proposed by Harris (1964). We have seen that the societal strategy studies a portion of a given subculture and that the attributional strategy examines attributions stated in a particular language and made by members of some subculture. Hence, although these strategies can be applied in a variety of cultures, the products of each application pertain to a given culture. But when the action strategy is applied to other cultures, some of its products may not be restricted to any one or a few cultures. It may well be that some empirical relationships among actions hold cross-culturally. In this context, the distinctive feature of this strategy is that the lowest level of concepts, those for actions, can be applied to behavior in all persons. As noted earlier, the definition of an action class can be communicated ostensively, indicating instances that fall within it and instances that do not. In principle, no language is necessary for communicating the nature of these classes. Insofar as the definitions of the classes do not refer to the meanings of words used in interactions, observers can code the behavior of persons in another culture. Therefore, not only can observers within a culture be interchangeable but also observers can be drawn from different cultures.

Does the cultural identity of the investigator make a difference? It should not. In fact, there may be an advantage in the investigator being from a different culture than that of the persons whose activity is being studied. He can look at that activity with fewer implicit preconceptions than he has for activity within his own culture. He is more like a man from Mars or some other extraterrestrial body. It is interesting to speculate about the science of earth-person behavior that would be developed by observers from another sphere, assuming that they could observe unobtrusively.

We must, nevertheless, grant that the investigator's selection of his action classes is likely to be determined in part by his prior professional or everyday experience. A scientist from an African country might well choose actions that differed from those that have been investigated by members of the Western European culture. And two investigators from the same culture may also select different actions. But regardless of the personal or cultural determinants of these preferences, the several investigators should be able to understand what the others are doing and should be able to make observations of the same actions, either in the same locale or elsewhere.

The culture-free aspect of the action strategy does not, of course, mean that the observed relationships cannot be specific to the subculture from which the persons come. It is very likely that many relationships among actions will hold for one or more cultural groups but not for others. Although such probable differentiations have nothing to do with the general methodology, they do imply that the observer should develop his categorization of actions from empirical protocols. There may well be classes of actions that are important in one culture but are rarely if ever observed in another culture.

In an entirely different direction, the action strategy can be applied to person-object interactions. There has been relatively little investigation of actions in such contexts. Although many observations have been made of children interacting with things, the usual coding classes have involved considerable inference and interpretation. We can readily observe people's manipulation of passive objects. Much of the older work on style and expressive movements is of that kind.

One fruitful application of the action strategy is the study of artistic production by Getzels and Csikszentmihalyi (1976) discussed in Part One. They observed student artists producing a still life. A few of their categories for coding this activity resembled action sequences; for example, switching from one sheet of paper to another or from one medium to another. Here, one could construe the unit of analysis to be one action followed by a different action. More realistically, these are changes in activity, shifts in the objects being dealt with. In that research, some indices were based on counts of actions from a period of time—number of available objects touched, for example. Others, including the extent of manipulation of the objects, were judgments requiring some interpretation. Thus, their procedures did not fit neatly into the specifications for the action strategy. These authors did, however, show ways in which such an elusive concept as artistic creativity can be analyzed in terms of concrete actions. Whether the use of action classes requiring less interpretation and inference would yield further understanding of creative activity remains to be demonstrated empirically. The important lesson from their research is that there are fruitful ways of studying interactions between persons and objects by the use of action classes requiring little or no interpretation and inference by observers.

The preceding example suggests possibilities for studying other cognitive processes where there are observable actions accompanying them. There are, unfortunately, few opportunities to study these processes as they occur naturally. In principle, the balancing of one's checkbook against a bank statement could be studied. In contrast, it is unlikely that the choice of a paperback to read on a plane trip would be worth trying to analyze. It has been possible to study problem solving with physical objects, although the subject's actions have usually not been observed at a molecular level, and this research has been done in the laboratory with artificial tasks.

As the action strategy is applied in various areas, increasing emphasis must be placed on the immediate, continuing conditions within which actions and action sequences occur. For example, some variables presumably important in interpersonal interactions are more or less constant throughout the interaction. In the last chapter, reference was made to dress and cosmetics. Such artifacts may well affect actions and action sequences. One might speculate that they are more likely to be related to actions near the beginning of an interaction than to later ones. Similar comments apply to scents, both artificial perfumes and naturally occurring body odors.

In principle, these aspects of a person can be studied in essentially the same way as actions occurring within the interaction. They can be identified and coded just as actions are studied, using low-order concepts and specifying instances of what falls within the class and what is excluded, so that very high interobserver agreement can be obtained. We must recognize, however, the practical limitations on the study of such variables. Although an observer can readily note the dress of a person, he may be too far away to detect scents or body warmth. Information available through sensory channels other than vision and audition thus may not be available to observers and cannot be part of standard recordings. Special recording devices would be needed.

More generally, although these variables for standing conditions are not like the action classes emphasized earlier, investigators do need to take them into account. Once an investigator has located regularities within an interaction, she will want to determine whether they are present in other interactions. The interactions themselves must be classified in terms of their characteristics. Interactions differ not only in obvious variables, such as the number of persons present and the presumed reason for their being together, but also in terms of more subtle features, and the investigator must find out which of these are necessary for the appearance of the relationships among actions and which are associated with the absence of those associations. Both the physical characteristics surrounding an interaction and the psychological features can be viewed as standing conditions.

It is difficult enough to study actions in a set of interactions taking place under similar and presumably neutral conditions. It will be much more difficult to study the effects of standing conditions, and many investigators will want to manipulate these conditions rather than studying them in naturally occurring interactions. Perhaps a feasible tactic is to begin by studying events occurring as the interaction begins, trying to identify actions or other occurrences that somehow set the stage for what follows. For example, aspects of the action sequence, action A followed by action B, may be found to be different when action A is given by one person rather than the other. If so, is the form of the action sequence related to the identification of one person as the first to speak or the first to gesture at the onset of the interaction?

As our discussion illustrates, there are many possible topics to which the action strategy can be applied. Some are more interesting than others, and, unfortunately, there may be a negative relationship between our general interest in a topic and the ease with which it can be investigated under conditions that are likely to produce representative findings with high generalizability. These extensions will test the ingenuity of investigators. They will have to break away from their usual ways of gathering protocols and making observations.

It would be foolhardy and a disservice to the field to state categorically and in advance that the action strategy can be fruitful in some particular areas and not in others. Only at some future time, after reviewing what has been done, are such assertions appropriate. I grant that there are limits to its applicability. For example, muscle tonus has been studied profitably, but tonus in most muscles cannot be judged adequately by observers. Hence, such studies must be done in the laboratory where appropriate instrumentation can be used.

The reader has undoubtedly noted that much of experimental personality research appears to pursue the action strategy. The investigators in this research have chosen their own problem and frequently have studied motor or vocal acts of their subjects in the laboratory, using as their data the judgments of observers who were recognizing and identifying the pertinent actions. Little space in this book has been devoted to such research because these investigators ordinarily are not concerned with those actions themselves but rather with those actions as presumed indicants of broad and abstract concepts. The problems in generalizing from such experiments have been examined earlier. Furthermore, personality research in the laboratory obviously has little resemblance to the optimal action strategy, with its focus on naturalness of stimuli, setting, and behavior.

Is the Optimal Action Strategy Method-Free?

A major argument of this book concerns the intrusive and limiting effects of methods that bias the data so that they are not exactly what the investigator would like to obtain. Many of our observations seem to be specific to the methods by which they were obtained (see Fiske, 1971, Chap. 11). It is therefore appropriate to ask whether the action strategy is confounded by method. Certainly, there is plenty of room for such distortion. One clear example is the laboratory investigation of imprinting (see Hess, 1973). To study this phenomenon under controlled conditions, it was brought into the laboratory, and much systematic work was carried out. It was eventually realized, however, that the experimental method changed the phenomena. What was studied in the laboratory was not exactly the same as what went on in nature. In particular, the hatching of eggs in an incubator did not allow the natural interaction between the brooding duck and the ducklings about to hatch from their shells, the interactions among newly hatched ducklings, and the interactions between them and their parent.

The action strategy obviously involves methods, and each investigator must determine whether her methods are intrusive and distorting. The optimal action strategy is formulated to minimize the possible effects of many aspects of method. For example, the use of naturally occurring stimuli eliminates the possible influences of experimentally neat but unrepresentative types of stimuli designed and presented by the investigator.

The optimal action strategy is not method-free. Some means must be developed to obtain the basic protocol of behavior to be studied. In the work by Duncan and Fiske (1977) on actions in conversational interactions, part of the method involved asking people to come in and talk with a stranger. Although the surroundings and the videocamera and microphones were as unobtrusive as possible, they were nevertheless present. The participants were aware of these constant stimuli and of the circumstances that brought them there. These aspects of method did exert some influence on the frequencies of the actions studied. In terms of the mean values for total interactions, there were occasional changes from the first to the second interaction. Such changes need not, however, affect the regularity with which one action—when it does occur—is preceded by another. Whatever the investigator is studying by this strategy, she must make every effort to minimize effects associated with her particular method of obtaining her basic protocols. In many instances, the only way in which she can identify such effects is by using two or more methods and determining whether each yields highly comparable, generalizable findings.

Even with protocols minimally biased by the method used to obtain them, there is still room for other unwanted contributions from methods. Part of method is the framework used for observing and coding behavior. What conceptual scheme provides the basis for the action classes selected for investigation? Does that scheme bias the observations made and the resulting data? Certainly it determines what will be transcribed and coded. These considerations have already been discussed in Part One, especially in Chapter Three. One major advantage of studying recorded protocols of behavior is that the investigator can modify her conceptual scheme or even replace it and then reanalyze her protocols to see whether she has improved her scheme.

Among the several steps in the optimal action strategy, the place where method influences are most likely to enter—and enter unrecognized as such by the investigator—is in the delineation of the action classes and of the rules for applying them in the coding of behavior. The classes are chosen because the investigator believes them to be more promising than those she excludes. She is not entirely dispassionate or neutral in her selection and possibly not in her instructions to observers about recognizing and identifying instances of the classes. The comment of Kuhn (1970a) that, like Popper, he is skeptical of efforts to produce any neutral data language seems pertinent here, if *neutral* means unrelated to any prior ideas, speculations, or hunches.

Questions About the Action Strategy

Several questions about the action strategy may have occurred to the reader (as they have to people who have heard about it before). The reader may feel that the criterion of interchangeability among observations of different observers is excessively strict. Is not *substantial* agreement between observers sufficient for our present state of knowledge? One argument for working with essentially interchangeable judgments can be made on a somewhat indirect basis. In the world of decision making, Einhorn (1978; Einhorn and Schacht, 1977) has shown that even when evaluative judgments have substantial predictive validity, the proportion of erroneous decisions (false positives and false negatives) will be surprisingly high. Although we cannot ordinarily determine the validity of the observers' judgments examined in this book, we can reasonably infer, from the correlation between judges, the maximum possible average validity. The value can be taken as the square root of the reliability correlation. The argument, then, is that unless observers agree very closely, their observations cannot have very high validity and, as a consequence, a substantial proportion of their judgments will be erroneous to a smaller or a larger degree.

Are actions trivial? Skeptics may argue that the action strategy studies trivial things, like muscle twitches. Such skeptics obviously construe the phenomena of personality in terms of longer time periods—at least sentences and episodes in an interaction, if not the entire interaction or one's whole set of impressions about a person. Note, however, that we have worked with the standard approaches to these phenomena for decades without achieving much in the way of positive results; hence, we should reexamine that conventional orientation and consider trying other approaches, such as the action strategy and the reorientations in the other two strategies proposed here.

Labeling actions as trivial can also imply that they are too small to be significant. In weighing that objection, consider the progress that has been made when established sciences have studied the smallest units possible to study. Particle physics is an obvious example. At a more gross level, we are beginning to learn about the moon and other astronomical bodies by going beyond the global views from telescopes to examination of the finer structures—their geological topography and even down to the mineralogical composition of their soil. Analogously, the action strategy attempts to identify the smallest units of behavior that convey information to other persons who are present.

Another objective may be that the action strategy will not pay off—small motor acts are just not very important. But what is the evidence for that assertion? From the work that has been done, it is clear that actions do play a major role in the structure and process of interactions. The actions of one person do make a difference for the actions of the other person, and hence the study of actions seems likely to contribute to our understanding of what happens in those significant phenomena, interpersonal interactions. Although we cannot predict what will be found, at least there is reason to believe that reproducible, positive results can be established.

Perhaps these skeptics are really saying "Show me how the action strategy can help me study the significant topic that I am working on." Such a demand might be made by those dealing with societal problems stated in terms of loosely defined concepts. The reply must be that we cannot tell yet whether research using the action strategy will contribute to the desired solutions of such problems. Little has been done to find out. There do, however, seem to be possibilities for exploring some societal areas, such as the process of psychotherapy, in terms of this strategy (Fiske, 1978). In more general terms, higher-order concepts developed within the action strategy from explicit lower-order concepts will probably not correspond to those that are in current use. Nevertheless, they might well provide a fruitful reconstrual of the same set of perceived phenomena from which the conventional concepts were formulated.

An alternative phrasing of the objection might be that actions are not the phenomena in which the skeptic is interested. One reply to that is to ask the skeptic to make explicit the phenomena with which he is concerned. Such an examination is likely to bring out an interest in what people say or do (the action strategy is, of course, concerned with what people do). Even more intensive scrutiny is likely to reveal that the skeptic is really concerned with how he interprets the behavior of persons and how he construes people (recall Proposition 1, Chapter One). If his target phenomena are actually his own interpretations, it seems unlikely that his empirical work will prove to be replicable by others. If those targets are how people interpret and evaluate other people and their behavior, then the strategy for societal problems or the strategy for the study of attributions may be more appropriate for him. But there is a possibility that the study of actions will throw light on the usual data of personality research, attributive judgments. We may find that actions contribute to attributions and that some common concepts are empirically linked to a set of actions (see Shrout, 1976).

Clearly, there are no grounds for holding that the action strategy is trivial in the sense that it cannot lead to theory. Low-order concepts for actions provide a firm foundation for developing a hierarchy of concepts at successively more abstract levels, along with conceptual propositions about their interrelationships. The application of this strategy in animal ethology has generated theoretical statements. In the familiar example of actions in interactions, theoretical propositions concerning rules in interactions have been formulated from Duncan's work. Extending that conceptual work, Duncan and Fiske (1977, Chap. 12) outline a metatheory for face-to-face interactions.

Some reactions to the action strategy can be viewed as the natural unwillingness of investigators to consider dropping their long-practiced modes of thinking and methods of research and taking up new ones. Such a radical shift is unlikely to occur unless the investigator is becoming doubtful about the fruitfulness of her own efforts, a doubt that is not reinforced when she sees others doing as she does and, like her, publishing papers on their findings. To be realistic, one cannot expect a revolution in most people's thinking and modes of work. More probable is a gradual shift as people learn about what has been discovered by new approaches, with new entrants into the discipline leading the way.

Another factor is that the action strategy is a new and difficult empirical approach. It cannot be adopted easily. One cannot try it out effectively in a week or two, as one can a new paper and pencil procedure or a new experimental paradigm for use in social psychological research. Even the use of direct observation requires considerable preparation in identifying action classes and in practicing their application. And the use of recorded protocols necessitates an investment in expensive equipment.

Once the investigator has developed her observational procedures, the task of coding the protocols and of examining the codings takes time and personal effort. The search for the actions related to a particular action class requires the testing of numerous hunches, especially when the relationship ultimately established is of the form:

action B is preceded by action A in most instances when action C has also occurred. Of course, a relationship of that kind will not be discovered unless the investigator, having guessed that all three actions are pertinent, has included them among the actions to be coded. When she has found a relationship in one protocol, she must determine its generality by looking for it in other protocols. If she has already obtained and coded a number of protocols, this step is not difficult. The prior painstaking coding of the actions is the laborious stage in this work.

Those who want to investigate behavior should not expect to have an easy time. Psychologists have found it relatively simple to obtain responses to paper and pencil tests and to get people to make judgments about other people. We have not had much difficulty in devising experimental conditions for observing behaviors of special interest to us. In contrast, research in the natural sciences is often extremely slow. Consider how long it took, after the initial decision to do so, to study the composition of the moon by landing a man on it. Look at the work involved in making observations of cosmic particles by installing a tank at the bottom of a deep mine. And once such an installation is completed, the rate of obtaining pertinent data may be very slow—taking days or months. Setting up an experiment on a particle accelerator may take months of advance work. In the nearer fields of biology and biopsychology, devising and producing a biological preparation can be a long process. Where the goal is important, however, the lengthy effort is worth the costs.

Is the action strategy simply the operationist approach? Is it merely the insistence on operational definitions for its lowest-order concepts? The action strategy is not a strict operationist position because it has become evident that such a position is sterile. If every particular operation must be taken as a distinctive concept, there can be no fruitful generalization across sets of observations obtained by independent applications of measuring procedures. What the action strategy does require is minimizing the contributions from single observers to the resulting data. If the observers are essentially interchangeable, their data are treated as equivalent and interchangeable, contrary to what a strict operationalism would require.

In addition, the meaning of the label for an action class is not taken as restricted to the operation for observing an instance of it. The action strategy searches for the meanings of an action in terms of its associations with other variables and especially its relationships to other actions. The resemblance of the action strategy to operationalism comes from the strategy's insistence that the investigator not presume the significance of his observational variables on the basis of folklore or prior conceptualization by the investigator.

Is the action strategy the same as behaviorism? Some people may interpret the action strategy as essentially the same as behaviorism. They would be correct in perceiving similarities to the behavioristic viewpoint, especially when contrasted to other orientations. The insistence on minimizing the role of the observer, on using the observer as a special type of recording instrument, is roughly similar to the behavioristic view. Behaviorism is, however, a total theoretical system that is not limited to a particular methodological orientation. The action strategy is essentially a methodological position based on the assertion that, to replace our preparadigmatic (Kuhn, 1970b) science of human activity with a science resembling the established sciences, we must start with low-order concepts that are labels for simple observations.

The action strategy is clearly not the classical respondent conditioning or the subsequent operant conditioning, both of which emphasize the acquisition or elimination of responses (more strictly speaking, the change in the probabilities of responses). It is not behavior theory because it makes no substantive statements. It is a methodological orientation under which most research stimulated by behavior theory is a special case. It is not the same as behaviorism in any of its several forms. From the early statement of Watson (1913) to the recent formulations of Skinner (1974), behaviorists have set as their goal the prediction and control of behavior. They have focused on learning, on the acquisition and the elimination of responses. In contrast, the action strategy is simply aimed at understanding by careful observation. In the optimal form, the strategy is not manipulative; it uses observations of naturally occurring phenomena rather than observations of responses to events controlled by the experimenter. The strategy does, of course, resemble behaviorism in excluding as data the products of introspection and in ruling out consciousness as an object for study. In this connection, it is interesting to note that Skinner (1974) appears to be willing to ask subjects questions such as

"What are you doing?" and "Why are you doing that?" although not necessarily taking these reports at face value.

Behaviorism and the action strategy are similar in taking as the basic datum the action of an individual. Skinner stresses the study of the individual as he interacts with his environment, rather than dealing with the average response for a group. Skinner's unit of analysis, as we have been using the phrase, is often the action of an organism together with a subsequent change in the environment; that change may be an action by another or a change in the physical world. The general unit of analysis in the action strategy is rather similar—an action and some other event, usually another action. (The unit may, however, include nonoccurrences of an action.) When the strategy is applied to the study of interpersonal interactions, each of the actions is ordinarily identified with a separate actor, although two concurrent or successive actions by the same actor may be studied. What is common to behaviorism and the action strategy is the collection of data for the single person in a particular setting, the analysis of the relationships detectable in those data, and the subsequent comparison with sets of data for other persons and for other settings.

In Skinner (1974), the emphasis is on the action and what follows it, not only at the moment but also in a larger temporal framework. The action is to be understood in terms of its history—what followed prior emissions of that action. Behaviorism also looks ahead in time and, from the environmental events that followed this particular instance and prior instances of an action, predicts the future probability of the action in that setting. The optimal action strategy, however, looks for relationships between actions at the present time. Although it can examine changes in those relationships, its first concern is identifying consistent regularities. Again, it looks both ways. For example, Duncan has found it profitable to study an action in terms of the actions that preceded it more or less immediately. Although not all occurrences of one action are followed by a second action, almost every instance of that second action may be found to have been preceded by the first one. (This oversimplification leaves out the necessary qualifications about the presence of other actions that can affect the observed relationship and about the defining of some events in terms of actions or nonactions by the other. See Chapter Twelve for illustrations.)

One interesting parallel exists between the behavioristic approach and Duncan's work on actions. Neither attempts to account for everything about the actions studied. Skinner (1974) pays limited attention to what determines the moment at which an operant appears, and Duncan does not try to account for the appearance of cues on the basis of the person's prior history. Even more important, both incorporate probabilistic conceptualizations. A reinforcement for an operant may occur only occasionally. In Duncan's formulation for some signals, the signal need not be followed by an action of the other; that other person has the option of acting or not acting, but whenever he does manifest that action, the signal has preceded it.

The first words in *About Behaviorism* are "Behaviorism is not the science of human behavior; it is the philosophy of that science" (Skinner, 1974, p. 3); a similar identification of behaviorism is made in the closing pages of that book. If the content between these references is what Skinner means by philosophy, then behaviorism is quite distinct from the action strategy. That strategy may be closer to what Skinner calls *methodological behaviorism*.

We may conclude, then, that although the action strategy is fairly compatible with a behavioristic orientation, it should not be taken as involving many aspects of behaviorism. In particular, the optimal action strategy differs from the research strategies used in most empirical investigations made from the behavioristic viewpoint. The latter have generally studied reactions to stimuli manipulated by the experimenter (Choice 10a, Chapter Eight), whereas the action strategy emphasizes natural behavior in the presence of naturally occurring stimuli.

Summary

The action strategy has many desirable features, especially its potentialities for generalization. It has wide applicability, even in the more restricted form designated the *optimal action strategy*. There is a broad range of interpersonal interactions to which it can be applied, including nonvocal interactions and topics in social psychology. Person-object interactions, which have scarcely been looked at, could be studied using the action strategy. Another kind of needed investigation is the relationship between conditions holding for an entire interaction and the actions and action sequences during it. Although broadly applicable, the action strategy is not method-free. As in any other approach, the investigator must determine whether aspects of his methods are biasing his findings and interpretations. Unlike some other methods, however, it does seem to be relatively culture-free.

Objections to the action strategy include assertions that actions are trivial or are not as significant as other construals of behavior. We must grant that this strategy may not solve problems posed in societal or attributional form. It is also clear that the strategy requires a major shift of orientation and an enormous amount of work. In comparing it with familiar viewpoints, we hold that the action strategy is not strict operationalism. It does resemble behavioristic approaches in its focus on simple observations and on the intersubjective nature of its data. As opposed to behaviorism, however, it emphasizes naturalistic observations without experimental interventions, and it is not concerned with attempts to control behavior. In addition, it takes a broader approach to linkages between one action and other events that precede or follow it.

XIV

Strategies Proposed
by Others

Concern for the unsatisfactory state of personality as a discipline has been expressed by a number of persons. In 1964, Holtzman posed a set of "recurring dilemmas in personality assessment," including these: "How can one separate personality variance from method variance?" (p. 147); "Can we ever develop a personality theory that is systematic, comprehensive, and closely linked with empirical data?" (p. 148). He was too wise to propose any solutions to his dilemmas. A few years later, W. Mischel (1968) published his comprehensive critique. He pointed out that trait ratings reflect the constructs of observers and that trait factors can be seen as the constructs of researchers. A major impact of his work came from his compilation of evidence that empirical data on personality did not support the presumption, so prevalent in personality theories, of behavioral consistency across situations.

Cronbach (1975) has expressed deep pessimism in his sweeping evaluation of the state of social science, emphasizing psychology in particular. He asked, "Should social science aspire to reduce behavior to laws?" (p. 116) and concluded that "enduring systematic theories about man in society are not likely to be achieved" (p. 126). Although he was not examining the specific field of personality, he did not seem to be granting any exception for it. Explicit focus on personality research is a recent negative evaluation by Sechrest (1976).

Yet skepticism and criticism alone are unlikely to produce changes in institutionalized ways of scientific investigation. Although critiques may reduce confidence in scientific theories or paradigms, the critiques by themselves rarely lead to abandoning any theory or paradigm. Historians of science have noted that old and deficient theories are retained until a replacement comes along. The same is probably true for a paradigm. Only after a new approach has been demonstrated to be more fruitful than the prior one is it likely to be generally adopted.

In more advanced fields of science, progress is sometimes made by "strong inference" (Platt, 1964). When there are competing theories aimed at accounting for a set of phenomena, a powerful strategy is to demonstrate empirically that each alternative theory does not hold, thereby increasing the acceptability of the one advocated by the investigator. The strategy has been proposed because a theory cannot be proved. It can only be shown to be more congruent with empirical findings than any other theory. Unfortunately, personality theories cannot be effectively evaluated in this manner because they cannot be falsified (see Popper, 1959). It is not possible to demonstrate empirically that any one of them is not sustained by research findings because it is never clear what empirical results would invalidate the theory.

I will not attempt here to review the many efforts to defend the current view of personality. Wiggins has written "in defense of traits" (1974). Hirschberg has developed "a correct treatment of traits" (forthcoming). On the empirical side, the well-known study of Bem and Allen (1974) suggests that trait concepts may fit some people better than others, and Sorrentino and Short (1977) indicate that trait strength may be more complex than has been believed, since there is evidence for discontinuities in that presumed dimension. But modifications of contemporary construals of trait do not meet the objections to such broad concepts.

I have the impression that many people are dissatisfied with the current state of the personality field but do not say so, probably because they do not know what to do about the situation. Yet some writers expressing negative evaluations of the domain have proposed remedies. In this chapter, some of these proposals will be considered, although the evidence necessary to evaluate them definitively is not yet available. The analyses will not be cast into the decision framework of Chapter Eight because such translation would sometimes involve debatable interpretations of those proposals and would distract us from examining each proposal in its author's terms. For the reader who accepts much or all of the critique in Part One but is skeptical about the strategies proposed in Chapters Ten through Thirteen, this chapter will permit a comparison with other possibilities and thus provide a perspective on the whole problem.

Some Alternative Strategies

Some writers have urged us to shape up, to mend our ways. In their view, we will make progress if we will just be more scientific. One form of this proposal urges us to try the scientific method thoroughly before giving it up. Levine (1974) argues that the scientific enterprise follows an adversary model, each side trying to make the best possible case for its position. Hence, any field or clinical research team should include an adversary assigned the task of cross-examining the evidence and developing a rebuttal for every bit of evidence used by the investigator. Levine recognizes that "the adversary and investigator will both require a great deal of personal maturity in order to function in a task-oriented fashion" (p. 675). His proposal reminds one of Békésy's statement (1960) that a good way of dealing with errors in design is to have a really capable enemy who will go to the trouble of uncovering one's errors. Unfortunately, he adds, such enemies are all too scarce; besides, they sometimes develop into friends and lose their zeal. In the field of social psychology,

McGuire (1973, 1975) urges a return to an emphasis on behavior as behavior and not as an indicant of abstract concepts. Social psychology should "search for interrelations among naturally varying factors in the world outside the laboratory" (1973, p. 449). Like Levine, he is dissatisfied with the effectiveness of the laboratory experiment for the study of human behavior.

In contrast, an argument could be made for restricting our efforts to the study of optimal functioning. Much of the success of aptitude measurement has come from its focus on performance under the most favorable conditions. In administering an intelligence test, the examiner tries to minimize distractions and anxiety because both he and the examinee want the examinee to do as well as possible. Personality is not measured under those conditions (see Fiske and Butler, 1963). One demonstration of the value in studying maximal performance can be found in Guilford (1967). Developing and expanding his structure-of-intellect model, he has not only provided an analysis of facets to be considered in analyzing intellectual tasks but also has brought intelligence back into the mainstream of general psychological theory. Going from these analyses to an operational-informational type of psychology, he is able to point out applications for many fields of psychology that are usually seen as separate from the topic of intelligence per se.

The direct parallel in personality would involve the study of persons as they behaved under what were judged to be the most favorable conditions. Wallace (1966, 1967) proposes that we develop an abilities conception of personality, testing for capacities. How extreme are the most extreme responses the person is capable of making? He has asked subjects to tell a Thematic Apperception story that was as hostile and cruel or as sexual as possible. Coming at the problem from the viewpoint of behavior theory, Wallace emphasizes the properties of the situation—its reinforcement conditions and the subject's expectancies. This proposal obviously involves considerable manipulation of instructions and setting by the investigator, rather than simply observing the subject as he responds to naturally occurring stimuli (Decision 10 in Table 2, Chapter Eight). Wallace's proposal does not seem to have been taken up by others. One reason may be that the observed behavior would depend primarily on the subject's willingness to cooperate, to attempt what the investigator asked. Although subjects are willing to try to do their best on a test of aptitude, it does seem likely that instructions to maximize the expression of socially constrained material would not elicit full cooperation from many persons.

Wallace's proposal is a particular form of the strategy of studying persons under the controlled conditions of the testing room or the laboratory. That strategy has the great advantage of standardized conditions permitting ready comparisons between the responses of different subjects. Another advantage is economy of investigator effort—by producing the stimuli to which she wants the subjects to react, she can obtain a number of pertinent responses in a short time. As suggested by Wallace, the stimuli and conditions can be ones that occur rarely in everyday life.

The crucial issue with respect to findings from testing rooms or laboratories, the predominant locus for research observations today, is whether they can be generalized to conditions in other settings. As argued in Chapter Eleven, there is little evidence that such generalization can be made with confidence. The primary obstacle limiting generalizability does not stem from standardizing the setting and minimizing the contributions of potentially confounding variables; instead, it comes from the effects of variables introduced or maximized by the investigator's manipulations. In particular, the subject is responding to the investigator, to her instructions, and to the atypical nature of the entire setting. We know that these factors can affect behavior, but how can we assess their contributions to what we observe and to what we subsequently conclude from the findings?

Try a Different Theoretical View. Proposals that we take a different view of the phenomena to be explained have been frequently stated and extensively worked out. Endler and Magnusson (1976a, 1976b; Magnusson and Endler, 1977) have marshalled a considerable body of work supporting their view that personality must be construed as interaction between person and situation. The phenomena in the field of personality, as they see it, are determined not by the person and not by the situation but by the person as he interacts with the situation. Their position is compatible with the views of most conceptualizers working in the field today, since few if any writers claim that behavior is solely a function of either the person or the situation. Yet the emphasis of Magnusson and Endler on the need to study the continuing interaction between person and situation is valuable because most empirical studies concentrate on just the person or just the situation, neglecting the other component.

Emphasis on interaction makes it necessary for us to confront the question: What exactly is the situation with which the person is interacting? Although psychology has had great difficulties in studying people, at least the identification of the actor who is performing the actions presents no problem. But what is the situation? What are its boundaries? What is its nature? Pervin's (in press) thoughtful review points out the inadequate efforts that have been devoted to defining situations, environments, and even stimuli, along with problems of measuring them.

There are two major difficulties. First, the important aspect of a situation is how it is perceived and interpreted by the person interacting with it. The investigator's conceptualization of the situation may not agree with that of the person. Second, when one is studying interacting, both actions and reactions are occurring. An action of an actor is followed by an action or a change in the situation surrounding the actor. A change in the situation is followed by an action of the actor. At any one point in this interchange, just what is the situation?

It is obviously necessary to view behavior as stemming from the interaction between the person and the external world surrounding him. The question is, where do we go from there? Within a clearly interactional orientation, the thesis of this book is that one needs to pick one's strategy explicitly and to identify one's decisions in selecting the type of problem and the kind of observational data. Pervin himself has chosen to define and study personality as "the individual's pattern of stability and change in relation to defined situational characteristics" (1977, p. 372). In his work, he relies heavily on self-reports identifying situations and their characteristics.

Another theoretical position is behavior theory. Certainly Skinner (for example, 1971) has presented a particular view of human nature and therefore of personality. Although the statements in that book are compatible with the empirical generalizations that have emerged from research, they are clearly a considerable extension beyond the conditions under which the research observations were made. Many people would not accept the degree of generalizability that has been given to those empirical findings. In fact, one wonders whether the overall view of human nature in Skinner's writings is a product of his empirical work or is a statement, in terms of his current concepts, of a general perspective that he has held for many years.

Since behaviorism and behavior theory were considered in Chapter Thirteen, they will not be discussed further. From them, however, a movement has emerged that is pertinent to our examination of proposed new directions. Starting with desensitization as a treatment for phobias, behavior modification has developed as a major form of therapy. Associated with that treatment is "assessment of the specific behaviors in need of change and the variables maintaining these behaviors" (Goldfried and Kent, 1972, p. 409). Among the measurement procedures used by behavior assessors, some (such as the Fear Survey Schedule) rely on self-report and therefore tend to have several problems associated with conventional questionnaires. Others have been much more direct—the Behavioral Avoidance Test assesses a person's fearfulness when confronted with specific objects, such as a live snake. Also direct are the measures of physiological arousal.

Another class of behavioral assessment techniques relies more heavily on observers. With observers present, persons can be asked to imagine that they are in a particular situation and to enact what they would do, playing out the situation with the aid of other persons present. In addition, direct observations of everyday behavior have been used. (Details about all of these methods are given in reviews by Goldfried and Sprafkin, 1974, and by Ciminero, Calhoun, and Adams, 1977.) These observational procedures encounter the usual problems in this kind of observation: reactivity of the subject to being observed, rater drift, and biases from expectancies. Yet all of these procedures represent steps toward more adequate measurement than is obtained from conventional procedures. The self-report measures ask more specific questions. The observational techniques have been carefully developed so that high levels of interobserver agreement are obtained. In some instances, unusually high correlations with external measures (even ratings by others) have been reported.

The comparative success of behavioral assessment stems from several features. The phenomena being observed are often dramatic and vivid, as in reactions to a live snake. Much of behavioral assessment has restricted itself to variables reflecting strong reactions and high involvement. Another source of effectiveness is the concern of the investigators with methodological problems in terms of maximizing objectivity and directness. These workers have tried to stay as close as possible to the values and standards of behaviorists.

As the nature of the behavioral problem being studied has changed, however, behavioral assessment looks more and more like traditional measurement. Fear of a live snake can be readily quantified in a standard stimulus situation, using distance between person and snake and latency of approach as indices. In contrast, when Goldfried and D'Zurilla (1969) measure competence, they resort to self-observations and self-report. Their work is distinctive because they explicitly bring the situation into the picture; they are, for example, concerned with effectiveness in a particular setting. More generally, much of behavioral assessment involves judgments about fairly broad variables, the judgments being based on such segments of behavior as the total course of a role-playing incident. Nevertheless, behavioral assessment has generally used constructs that are somewhat narrower than those in more traditional assessment, some constructs being limited to behavior in a particular situation. Behavioral assessors' restriction of target variables includes a restriction of the domain to which they want to generalize. As a consequence, it seems very likely that they can generalize with more confidence than assessors who are aiming at more global variables.

Closely related to behavioral assessment with its origins in behavior theory are the social learning approaches emphasizing the acquisition of behaviors from interactions with the environment, especially the social environment. In one of the earliest systematic formulations, Rotter (1954) sees the field of personality as the study of learned behavior, and so the investigation of personality requires the study of prior experience and of the conditions preceding the observed behaviors. A later statement says that "The occurrence of a behavior of a person is determined not only by the nature or importance of goals or reinforcements but also by the person's anticipation or expectancy that these goals will occur. Such expectations are determined by previous experience and can be quantified" (Rotter, Chance, and Phares, 1972, p. 11). Here again, there is a strong emphasis on the situation in which the behavior occurs. Rotter's conceptualization has led to new instruments, the best know of which is his I-E

Scale for assessing "generalized expectancies for internal versus external control of reinforcement" (Rotter, 1966). These procedures involve content appropriate to the theory. In their formal characteristics, they resemble familiar kinds of self-report instruments.

W. Mischel (1973b) has provided a major reconceptualization of personality from a cognitive social learning viewpoint. In this framework, the central person variables include construction competencies (referring to what the person knows and can do), encoding strategies and personal constructs, expectancies about behavior outcome and stimulus outcome in particular situations, subjective stimulus values, and self-regulatory systems and plans. Perhaps because these variables are so oriented toward the individual person, Mischel gives little explicit guidance on how they are to be assessed. He states a position (W. Mischel, 1973a) close to that of behavioral assessors considered above, arguing that assessors should "look more at what people do and say, not as these events serve as indirect signs underlying dispositions, but rather as direct samples of their behavior. Such a focus . . . requires a different theoretical paradigm for studying behavior in relation to the conditions in which it occurs" (p. 323).

Although Mischel's proposals are advances beyond the traditional approaches, he seems still to be pursuing the classical objective of understanding personality as what we perceive and construe. For instance, he has recently noted that an individual's self-assessment and self-prediction may be empirically more accurate than judgments made by others (W. Mischel, 1977). Like other social learning people and like behavioral assessors, he is still dealing with broad concepts that generally must be assessed by observers making inferences or interpretations in arriving at their judgments. On the one hand, Mischel and others have correctly recognized the specificity of behavior as a function of the conditions under which it is observed, together with the importance of setting and of interaction between person and situation. On the other hand, they are continuing the traditional focus on explaining behavior as it is construed by observers. Their reconceptualizations depend heavily on prior conceptions and on concepts that are not explicitly linked to simple observations.

Construe the Objective in a Different Way. The preceding discussion has considered proposals to reorient our efforts or to take a new theoretical position. All of them have taken for granted that the study of people should be scientific and that we should make every effort to be as scientific as possible. Although these adherents recognize the difference between the phenomena involved in studying people and the phenomena of the natural sciences, they implicitly assume that most norms of natural science are just as applicable to their domain of investigation.

Another set of proposals argues that we cannot produce a science of human nature parallel to the sciences of things and of biological organisms. The argument appears to require a reconceptualization of that which we are trying to understand. At first thought, this position seems compatible with one thesis of this book, namely, that we cannot hope to develop a science of people as their behavior is perceived and interpreted by other people. As long as these construals of behavior and people have a major component associated with the observer-construer, as long as the mental processes involved in arriving at these interpretations are individualistic and unobservable, and as long as we must rely for our data on what these observers tell us, we cannot make scientific progress. Quite at variance with the viewpoint of this book, however, the recommendations in this set of proposals urge us to give up the futile effort to be scientific and to adopt an approach close to that found in the humanities. I have no quarrel with those who wish to follow that route. What is critical, however, is that each professional worker explicitly identify her position, recognizing and stating publicly her choice of norms and objective.

Harré and Secord (1972; see also Harré, 1974) would take exception to the previous paragraphs. They argue for a realistic view of science rather than a positivistic one and hence would claim that they are being scientific in their own way. Their book develops "the naturalistic conceptions of a human being as a rule-following agent" (1972, p. v). This and other lines of thought "converge on the model that people have of themselves, and that is embedded in much of the logic of ordinary language" (p. v). They insist that, for scientific purposes, we must treat people as human beings. In their model, personal reports are accepted as a crucial element in psychological study. A person is capable of saying what he is up to. Moreover, "lay explanations of behaviour provide the best model for scientific theory" (p. 29). Peters (1974) takes a somewhat similar position. He believes that, in our efforts to understand others, we have an advantage that we lack in trying to understand the natural world. In our development, we acquire concepts and ways of thinking that help us to understand the behavior of people. Furthermore, that understanding requires our having had personal relationships with people.

Part of this general viewpoint is the assertion that people should be seen as responsible social beings. Armistead, the editor of *Reconstructing Social Psychology* (1974b), says that it is a product of the several authors' dissatisfaction with much of psychology and especially with social psychology, which currently is not making sense of people's experience. In his own chapter, he has "argued that asking people is the crucial methodology; that people's accounts constitute public evidence; that classification, generalization and explanation will involve some interpretation of meaning, albeit with the suggested checks and safeguards; and that explanation of experience should move in a societal direction" (1974a, p. 128).

Note that these authors are claiming that an understanding of people and their behavior can be built on people's accounts. Consequently, their view is distinct from the attributional strategy, which studies such accounts as indicating perceptions that are not necessarily congruent with perceptions of other persons and that may not reflect the way things really are. Harré and Secord (1972) call for developing a conceptual system for analyzing people's accounts that can be tested by determining "how far it makes overt behaviour intelligible" (p. 125). Although they recognize that accounts can be questioned, they argue that if several accounts form a coherent whole, without one contradicting or discounting an item in another account, the accounts are authentic.

The book by Harré and Secord does contribute a systematic statement of their orientation. Although they state their philosophical position as realistic, their claim that their approach is scientific does not seem realistic in the everyday sense of that term. Certainly they cannot hope to achieve sufficient interobserver agreement to make their observers interchangeable. And clearly their constructs cannot readily be tied to observations of simple actions. In reviewing their book, Shaw (1974) sees them as using new terms for old concepts and claiming a new methodology for the old standby, self-report. Shaw himself argues "that social psychologists have never followed the methodology inherent in their professed philosophy of science. . . . The accepted philosophy of science should be tried before we conclude that it is inadequate and begin frantically looking for a substitute" (1974, p. 97).

Pertinent to the argument of Harré and Secord is a recent paper by Nisbett and Wilson (1977) about verbal reports on cognitive processes. They amass considerable evidence that subjects do not have introspective access to their cognitive processes and cannot usually tell why they did what they did or came to the judgment they had reported. They also discuss the reasons for prevalent beliefs to the contrary. Much of their evidence concerns laboratory experiments. If, however, people cannot report accurately on their cognitive activity in rather simple interactions with stimuli in the laboratory, it is unlikely that they can perceive, cognize, and understand correctly their processes in the more complex domain of naturally occurring interactions with people.

Although Harré, Secord, Peters, and similar authors are writing about social behavior, their work is pertinent to personality because they are talking about understanding people and behavior. Their topic does seem to include most of the phenomena usually subsumed under the rubric of personality. In my reading, I have found that there are more critiques of social psychology than of personality. If that is generally true, why should it be so? Is it easier for social psychologists to distance themselves from their discipline, or are they simply more dissatisfied with the contributions of their field to societal problems?

The views of Harré and Secord seem close to the position that we should begin our efforts to study personality and related areas by examining common-sense views of human nature. Since that approach was examined in Chapter Eleven, it will not be discussed further. Still, we can appropriately call attention here to a general questioning about the progress of psychology, especially about its failure to contribute a basis for determining how people should live, along with a plea for considering the value of what human beings have learned over the centuries. D. T. Campbell points out "our need to be modest about the scientific validity of our present conclusions. *Psychology could be wrong* even on issues on which we now seem to have scientific consensus" (1976, p. 381). He urges us to consider "the possible sources of validity in recipes for living that have been evolved, tested, and winnowed through hundreds of generations of human social history. On purely scientific grounds, these recipes for living might be regarded as better tested than the best of psychology's and psychiatry's speculations on how lives should be lived" (1975, p. 1103). The implicitly humanistic nature of these recipes becomes apparent if we ask where these recipes are. Recipes differ over epochs and cultures. Is there one standard set of recipes in a general cookbook? Do the recipes specify the ingredients and operations in a form that can be applied universally and unambiguously?

Abandon the Impossible in Favor of the Possible. Other proposals urge a more distinct shift in our norms and objectives than that required by the views just discussed. One recommendation is that we limit ourselves to description and in particular to description of events as a function of their time in history. As we noted earlier, Gergen (1973) argues that "social psychology is primarily an historical inquiry. Unlike the natural sciences, it deals with facts that are largely nonrepeatable and which fluctuate markedly over time" (p. 310). As "the systematic study of contemporary history" (p. 319), social psychology should not be detached from history and such historically bound sciences as sociology, political science, and economics. "The study of history, both past and present, should be undertaken in the broadest possible framework. Political, economic, and institutional factors are all necessary inputs to understanding in an integrated way. A concentration on psychology alone provides a distorted understanding of our present condition" (p. 319). The enterprise he proposes is obviously different from that of current social psychology. He is emphasizing the particular, the persons and the peoples living at a certain time and the attributions made about them. He points out the implicit or explicit evaluative component in psychological conceptualizations, both in personality and in social psychology. As indicated in Chapters One and Two, those concepts are generally broad and loosely defined, even the stated definitions varying with the individual author.

It is certainly true that a historical fact often describes a social phenomenon observed in a particular social group at a given time. An understanding of historical events cannot be based on a science built painstakingly on observations where the observers are completely interchangeable. A visiting scientist from a different culture would not make the same observations as one raised in the culture being examined. At the very least, the concepts employed by the two scientists in making their judgments would not be identical.

Gergen's proposal has not gone unchallenged. For example, Manis (1975) points out that the contents of social behavior may vary over time and place, even when the processes underlying social behavior are relatively stable. Other rejoinders can be found in *Personality and Social Psychology Bulletin* (1976) and Sherif (1977). From the view developed in this book, the task of a science is to find regularities in phenomena and to determine the range of conditions within which these regularities occur. Just as the imprinting of birds can be observed in both Europe and America, so other behavioral regularities may be found to hold for human beings in varied places and in different decades.

Cronbach (1975) holds a pessimistic view. He came to his conclusions after studying aptitude-treatment interactions, especially in the educational context, in which the characteristics of individuals are measured and treatments are specified. Complete generalizability would require that all persons, wherever they are, who have been assigned the same test score be taken as interchangeable and that a complex treatment applied in one school or laboratory by one investigator be taken as interchangeable with the treatment as applied elsewhere. Dependable, replicable generalizations are rare when they involve complex variables and methods of estimating them, especially when they involve interactions between such variables. At the level of analysis with which Cronbach is concerned, generalizability will be very difficult to attain. Cronbach urges us to observe and to describe what we see. "The special task of the social scientist is to pin down the contemporary facts. Beyond that, he shares with the humanistic scholar and the artist in the effort to gain insight into contemporary relationships, and to realign the culture's view of man with present realities. To know man as he is is no mean aspiration" (p. 126). If Cronbach's final sentence can be restated as "To know men and women as other people perceive and construe them is no mean aspiration," I would wholeheartedly agree. I see that goal as falling within the attributional strategy sketched in Chapter Eleven. It is an important objective, but not the most essential one. Cronbach's negative view is not a solitary position. Thorngate (1976) has made a related argument concerning "possible limits on a science of social behavior."

Psychology has also been critically evaluated by Smedslund, who refers to its "hopeless struggle to become a respectable natural science" (1972, p. 235). He has a "growing suspicion that we have been too afraid to explore systematically the gold mines of our unreflected common sense for subtle and efficient ideas about how to *help,* how to *educate,* and how to *liberate* people" (p. 235). Psychology must be primarily a study of the other person, of his subjective world as known through communication with him. More recently, Smedslund (1976) has argued that, although psychologists have for years tried to develop generally valid, testable theories that were supported by empirical research, they have failed because of the nature of the phenomena. As an alternative, he proposes that we construct a rational formulation. Analogous to the work of Euclides in making explicit the structure of our concepts of space, we should make explicit the structure of our conception of psychological phenomena. For him, empirical work is not necessary for establishing general laws, although he grants that we may want to arrive at empirical generalizations that hold for particular groups of persons at particular times.

These several writers are arguing that an empirical science is not possible for the domain they wish to understand. Examination of their arguments and proposals indicates that their target phenomenon is the world as they and other people perceive and construe it. If that interpretation is correct, then I agree with them. The phenomena of people's judgments and concepts about the behavior of themselves and of others cannot be studied and understood with as rigorous methodology as that used for the content of the natural sciences. Yet they can be, and have been, examined—social commentary and social philosophizing have gone on for centuries. Perhaps contemporary writers can add to the wealth of insight that has been accumulated over the ages. The work in that domain, however, must be sharply differentiated from work on the actions of persons. The study of behaving has only begun. We have no definitive evidence indicating the boundaries to the understanding that may be achieved in that laborious empirical endeavor.

Change Our Method. Many of the preceding alternatives urge the adoption of a different conceptualization of the pertinent phenomena involving a change in the way in which the phenomena are to be seen. We do observe and record within some conceptual framework, that framework consisting of concepts for the things or events to be attended to. Those concepts can be fairly abstract or they can be simple, fairly direct variables tied closely to the various phenomena. The investigator's preference among types of conceptualization tends to constrain her choice of methods to be used in her empirical studies. In a similar fashion, a change in objective is also likely to involve a change in method. And the descriptive study of the human world as it is today calls for a method appropriate to that end.

Some proposals have concentrated more explicitly on method. Several have urged us to bring the scientist more directly into the picture, instead of trying to minimize the personal contribution of the individual scientist to his work. Rather than having the investigator, in the context of justification (Reichenbach, 1938) or confirmation, seek to carry out his research operations and his observations in a way that other investigators can replicate, these proposals advocate an emphasis on the scientist as a distinct individual.

One proposal has been for abandoning method (Phillips, 1973). Although Phillips' argument is directed toward sociology, much of it seems quite applicable to social psychology and to personality. It is foolish, Phillips argues, to believe that we can collect objective data. Responses to questionnaires are biased. People's reports, even for the census, are inaccurate. Yet the sociologist uses procedures and goes about his work within the perspective and rules of the scientific community of sociologists. Sociological knowledge is created or constructed by the members of that community. Its decision and its consensus determine sociological truth and knowledge.

"The alternative to this dependence on method and demonstration . . . is to employ and rely on reasoning and argumentation" (Phillips, 1973, p. 169). "I want to suggest that human behavior is explained by presenting arguments which justify the behavior in question" (p. 172). Argumentation "sees truth entirely as a social construction, as something resulting (if at all) from the confrontation of *opinions*" (p. 177). He would have us rely more on our "tacit awareness" of our experiences, but he also feels that there must be proce-

dural rules for accepting a proposition or statement as a fact. In particular, any statement, any argument must be capable of falsification.
The criteria for refutation must be established beforehand.

It is difficult to appraise Phillips' position. He argues that the
present method of sociology has not paid off because of the professional community's slavish adherence to scientific method. What he
is attacking is a blind reliance on observations and verbal statements
when these must be taken as biased or inaccurate because they are
produced by individuals in terms of their personal perspectives. What
he advocates is that the scientist free himself from his professional
socialization and try to see things as they really are. Thus, although
he is urging the abandoning of method, his argument seems to be for
a more fruitful conceptualization of the phenomena.

Phillips draws on Feyerabend, who has written *Against
Method: Outline of an Anarchistic Theory of Knowledge* (1975).
Feyerabend argues that no rule in scientific method can or should be
applied without exception. "All methodologies, even the most obvious ones, have their limits" (p. 32; original italics omitted). "Una-
nimity of opinion may be fitting for a church. . . . Variety of opinion
is necessary for objective knowledge" (p. 32; original italics omitted).
Successful scientific inquiry, he says, does not proceed by rational
methods. Progress requires emphasis on the creativitiy of the individual scientist. Anything goes. We should proliferate theories play-
fully. Thus, like Phillips, Feyerabend urges the individual scientist to
speculate, hypothesize, and theorize as freely as possible. Although he
may correctly perceive that scientists have not been sufficiently unfet-
tered in their thinking, the plethora of theories and speculations in
personality and many fields of behavioral science has not led to the
progress that one might expect from Feyerabend's perspective.

Approaching the problem from a psychoanalytic position,
Devereux proposes that we bring the scientist as observer directly into
the scientific process. He notes that "behavioral science data arouse
anxieties, which are warded off by a countertransference-inspired
pseudomethodology; this maneuver is responsible for nearly all the
defects of behavioral science" (1967, p. xvii). The observer, her observational activities, and her anxieties produce distortions that must be
treated "as the most significant and characteristic data of behavioral
science research" (p. xvii). Moreover, the subjectivity inherent in all

observation must be used as the way to an authentic objectivity. There is, however, a fatal flaw in his argument. He takes for granted that a truly objective picture of the scientist's character structure can be obtained and that a valid knowledge of the scientist's distortions can be achieved. Since the interpretations of psychoanalysts do not seem to show any better consensus than the interpretive judgments about people made by other observers, how can his proposed program be carried out?

Somewhat similar is the proposal of Gadlin and Ingle that "psychological knowledge should be reflexive. Conducting research means entering into relationships with people, and these relationships significantly affect the outcome of the research. . . . Reflexivity can be created by acknowledging that the study of human behavior necessarily includes the behavior of psychologists. . . . The knowledge that derives from such reflexivity is a tripartite knowledge—about the subject, about the researcher, and about the knowledge itself" (1975, p. 1008).

Other writers are not willing to give up the scientific model but urge the integration of the scientific with the humanistic. For example, Smith argues for a humanized social psychology, one that is concerned with social problems without being "muscle-bound methodologically" (1974, p. 6). Addressing himself to much the same issue, Kelman says that "the humanization of social research, for me, cannot take the form of abandoning scientific method or of washing out the distinctions between scientific and humanistic approaches to the study of man" (1968, p. 109). We should "move toward a definition of social science as an activity that is necessarily and deliberately embedded in a value-oriented and policy-relevant process" (p. 111).

Overview

One reason for presenting these alternative proposals of others is to help make apparent the orientations available to an investigator. If he does not like the structure of the several strategies advocated in earlier chapters, what other position might he take? The several proposals sketched above were not selected to strengthen the argument of this book but to offer a reasonably representative sample of alternative proposals. I sympathize with the values underlying the objectives of these formulations, and I will follow with much interest the efforts made in these directions to see whether they produce any new insights that enrich our personal and humanistic understanding of human beings. I have, nevertheless, come to the conclusion that none of these proposals provides a satisfactory framework for scientific work. Pervading many of these proposals is the study of expressions about people by interpretive and inferential observations, an orientation contrasting sharply with the major thesis of this book that such judgmental observations cannot form the foundation for a science of human behavior.

We are not in a position to make final and definitive evaluations of the proposals described in this chapter. Many are incomplete. For the most part, these authors do not fully explicate their program. Frequently, these writers provide few or no illustrations of how their proposals could be implemented. None of the programs have been used sufficiently to permit an evaluation of their long-range fruitfulness. I freely grant that many of my arguments cannot yet be supported by an extensive and compelling body of evidence. Each of us must, however, decide on the ultimate values that will govern the direction and nature of our scientific work. Each choice between two values rules out one or more of the investigative strategies that have been proposed.

Summary

Many writers share my view that personality and other fields in behavioral science are in an unacceptable, unsatisfactory state. This condition is not just a function of the immature developmental stage of social science. The history of these fields does not reveal successive steps in growth toward mature status.

Many prescriptions have been offered. Some would have us take a different approach, one that alters to some degree our present orientation. Others argue that a different theoretical position will enable us to overcome the apparently insuperable obstacles now blocking our path. Interactionism, behavior theory, and social learning theory have their strong adherents. More radical are the proposals that we give up the effort to understand people by standard scientific practices and turn toward the understanding of our own experience and the understanding that people in general seem to have. Many of the recommendations involve setting a different task for the investigator in behavioral science. Changes in methods accompany these proposed changes in approach and orientation. A common theme is a focus on the observer and interpreter. Some authors argue that, instead of being scientific, we have been pseudoscientific. Each scientist must determine the values that will guide and restrict his activities.

XV

Extensions to
Other Fields

The impregnable obstacles to progress toward a science of personality phenomena are of vital significance for that field as it is currently identified. These impediments, however, are not limited to that area. In parts of social psychology and cultural anthropology, the phenomena investigated are essentially similar to those in personality. Hence, even if the critique presented in this volume applied only to the study of these various phenomena, it raises important questions and points to major problems.

The focus of the book has been on personality because that is the area I know best. Yet my acquaintance with related fields has led me to the strong belief that some, if not all, of the difficulties confronting the investigation of personality can also be found in other parts of psychology and in other behavioral sciences. Two purposes of this chapter are to suggest the fields beyond personality to which the critique can be extended and to indicate what components of the argument might apply there. The chapter will also consider whether analogues to the reorientations and strategies proposed for personality may be found in other areas.

The Generalizability of the Argument

Let us look back at the critique as outlined in Chapter One. Proposition 1 states that, probably unwittingly, investigators have been trying to understand their own impressions about people as they behave. Their phenomena have been their own cognitions and construals of what they have perceived. This statement seems applicable to investigators studying persons in clinical settings, in their social environments, and in other cultures. The investigator in many behavioral sciences uses concepts derived from everyday experience, as Proposition 1a asserts. These concepts cast into words impressions from all of the investigator's experience, not just from his research observations, data, and findings.

The use of observers' explicit judgments as research data (Proposition 2) is very common in the behavioral sciences. Made in accordance with the investigator's instructions, these judgments ordinarily require interpretation or inference both when the data refer to designated individuals and when they refer to institutions or things. These judgments may also be made by the investigator himself in the role of observer. As in the personality domain, these observer judgments are appendages to natural processes, as Proposition 2a states. They are made for the purposes of the research and otherwise would not have occurred, at least in that particular form. Whatever the judgments are about, they are typically made without restriction as to time or situation (Proposition 2b). And as in personality, Proposition 2c holds in other fields; there is considerable individuality in the perceiving, cognizing, judging, and hence in the stated attributions. Furthermore, the meanings of the words used by the observers, along with those for the words used to elicit the judgments and to conceptualize them, are somewhat specific to each user (Proposition 2d). So the

consequence stated in Proposition 2e holds—the judgments of individual observers have significant degrees of specificity and are not
interchangeable. Note that, for these propositions to apply to parts of
other disciplines, the only necessary change is in the objects being
observed and interpreted.

The synthesizing of data, scores, and descriptive statistics from
heterogeneous elements (Proposition 3) is also prevalent elsewhere.
The assertion that the elements cannot always be specified seems to
hold as well. As an outsider I am diffident about claiming that Proposition 4 can be applied beyond the personality domain, and yet I do
see what appear to be unwarranted extrapolations and unsystematic
generalizations. Similarly, I am hesitant about generalizing Proposition 5, which notes the failure to locate conceptually useful units.
Some other fields do not need to unitize behavior. Their units are the
person, the dollar or other monetary unit, the geographical area, or
the vote cast. Although investigators in personality have neglected
the status of time in the flow of behaving (Proposition 6), time is fundamental to investigations in several other fields. In particular, economics is concerned with trends over time. Of course, the temporal
framework in that field—as in history, sociology, and anthropology
—involves periods on the order of years, decades, or larger. This
proposition appears to be the one that is least applicable to these
related fields.

From this review, the critique of research in the domain of personality phenomena seems fully applicable to investigations in those
related fields where the phenomena are the behavior of people and the
data are recorded judgments about those behaviors. It is especially
applicable where each judgment is based on a segment of behavior in
which sequential actions occur over some period of time, that is,
where the unit of observation is a temporal segment (such as several
minutes) rather than a single action. More generally, it is pertinent
when the observational datum is identified with a designated person
about whom other classificatory information is available. When a
datum is attributed to an individual, other specifications of the datum
tend to be neglected. The investigator acts as though each datum
could be viewed as referring to an attribute of that person, even
though the unit of measurement is a composite product of the
observer, the observed person, a segment of the latter's behavior, and

the several interactions among these determinants. Finally, the critique is also pertinent to fields in which the interpretive judgments producing the data are made about content other than persons. The objects of the judgments may be institutions, cultural objects, or the respondent's feelings and preferences. In such instances, a distinction must be drawn between using judgments as descriptions of those objects and obtaining judgments to study the perceptions and cognitions of the respondents. The critique applies to the use of observers as instruments for studying persons and other objects.

From another viewpoint, the critique is pertinent whenever the investigator has decided in advance on the meanings of his variables, assigning meanings that are not based on prior systematic research. It is also applicable in so-called empirical studies (such as content analysis) where no variables have been specified beforehand and where the investigator identifies categories or scales in terms of the meanings he assigns to segments of the protocols he is examining. One practical criterion of applicability may be the level of agreement between independent observers. When that agreement is limited and the observations are not essentially interchangeable, the prevailing case, the individual observer is adding his specific component to the variation among observations, and the obtained data have a serious if not crippling degree of fallibility.

Applicability of the Critique to Particular Fields

Let us consider the question of applicability for one field at a time. It is evident that the critique of research in personality also applies to the overlapping domain of diagnosis and assessment in clinical psychology. The identification and treatment of psychopathology are based on interpretive and inferential judgments. The portion of clinical psychology that falls outside of personality (if one chooses to make such a categorization) is investigated and conceptualized in essentially the same way as the domain of personality.

In the terms of this critique, most investigation in psychiatry seems indistinguishable from research in personality. The appraisal of psychiatric status and the practical decisions to commit or release from a hospital involve interpretive and inferential judgments. Biological psychiatry might appear to be outside the realm to which the critique applies. The determination of neurological and neuropsychological conditions can often be established by observations on which expert clinicians can agree, even before any postmortem examination. Similarly, the study of drugs involves objective identifications of the drugs and of the procedures in administering them. We must not overlook, however, the role of judgment in biological psychiatry. A pattern of objective neurological signs may be used as the basis for a diagnostic judgment, and this categorization of the patient may involve interpretive processes on which other experts may disagree. In studying the effects of drugs, the dependent variable is often judgments about the subsequent behavior of the patient. Thus, it seems reasonable to conclude that little if any psychiatric investigation is entirely free from the difficulties pointed out in the critique of personality.

Personality overlaps with clinical fields on one side and with social psychology on another side. Frequently, it is difficult to decide whether an investigation belongs under the rubric of personality or that of social psychology. The two can be distinguished by the implicit interpretation of the data—are they seen as attributions to particular individuals or as attributions to behavior under particular social conditions? Many studies of the latter kind involve interpretive judgments based on a segment of behaving during a period of several minutes or more. Classical social psychology dealt with such broad questions as the effects of the leader and of other group members on a single member. More recent work has examined behavior in one situation as opposed to another, the behavioral indices using judgments based on a sustained sequence of actions within each situation.

Many social psychologists have expressed dissatisfaction with the state of their discipline. Some have been cited in the previous chapter. Elms (1975) notes that self-doubts have also been expressed by those working in other parts of psychology and in sociology, economics, and anthropology. After stating that he left social psychology because of his dissatisfaction, Proshansky (1976) sets out, for research on environmental problems, a series of methodological requirements that are related to aspects of the critique of personality presented in this book. In an analysis of the "crisis" in social psychology, Triandis (1975) also has propositions pertinent to the critique. Again, strong criticisms of social psychology have been voiced by Alex Bavelas (1973) in terms indicating the relevance of the critique. I am in general agreement with his prescriptions. The proposals of most other critics of social psychology, however, differ in direction from the orientations outlined in this book.

In 1940, Blumer wrote about the ill-defined and ambiguous concepts in social psychology. How many of the concepts prevalent today are subject to the same criticism? The fact that Blumer published his paper in the *American Journal of Sociology* is indicative of the overlap between sociology and social psychology. From this outsider's viewpoint, it seems likely that other aspects of the critique of personality, especially those pertinent to social psychology, also apply to some parts of sociology.

"Sociologists are primarily interested in human beings as they appear in *social interaction,* that is, as actors taking account of one another in their behavior" (Reiss, 1968, p. 1). If these are the phenomena studied in sociology, the critique in Part One seems largely applicable to that domain. The appropriate degree of extension depends of course on the data used by sociologists to study social aggregates and groups. Insofar as these data require interpretation and inference on the part of the investigator or other observer, the argument of this volume is highly relevant.

The study of organizations appears to be a prime example of the applicability of the critique in Part One. An analysis of organizational research by Roberts, Hulin, and Rousseau (forthcoming) stresses many points similar to those considered in this book. Diesing (1971) notes that the effort of March and Simon (1958) to organize empirical laws about organizations yielded results that were "suggestive rather than precise because of the shifting meanings of the central variables" (p. 4). Very close to the argument in this book and not incompatible with its recommendations is the viewpoint expressed by Weick (1969) in his *Social Psychology of Organizing.* He states that the crucial events to be explained are processes. Moreover, "too little attention has been paid to actions and too much to cognitions, plans, and beliefs. Cognitions may well summarize previous actions rather than determine future events, yet this possibility has not been considered seriously" (p. 30). He goes on to assert that "once a concept is anchored in something that other people can observe for themselves, the investigator is free to construct whatever explanation he wants. First, he has to establish a consensual starting point, a point that others can duplicate" (p. 32). But, for him, it is not enough to observe acts. What are crucial are interacts and double interacts, action sequences in which the action of one person is followed by an action of another person, which may in turn precede another action by the first person.

Let us turn to other extensions of the critique. Research on personality usually studies adults, the modal subject being a young adult in college. Developmental psychology is concerned with younger persons. The large part of its research that investigates their personalities faces the major difficulties that have been considered in the critique presented in Part One. Questionnaires and peer ratings completed by children are methodologically the same as those by adults. Developmental psychology uses observations by raters to study other topics pertaining to children. For the most part, these ratings are judgments requiring interpretation or inference, and the agreement between such judgments is at much the same modest level as that for adult subjects. Hence, the argument of this book can be extended to large areas in developmental psychology.

The work of the leading figure in developmental psychology, Piaget, has involved a methodology somewhat different than the one we have been examining for the personality domain. Piaget presents many descriptive protocols of his observations of children. These protocols are basically qualitative. They describe small actions of the infant or child, along with the activity of the observing adult: "I place the rattle in her mouth, the handle lying on her chest: she immediately brings her hand to it and grasps it. The experiment is repeated three times: same reactions" (1963, p. 100). These observations certainly seem to involve identification and recognition on the part of the observer, rather than interpretation and inference. Other reported observations do not specify the actions as concretely: "Dal . . . after examining the ten vases, took nine flowers, thinking he had seen the exact number he needed. When he came to the seventh vase, he saw that he wouldn't have enough, and took another. When the flowers had been put in the vases, they were taken out and bunched together" (1965, p. 52). Although this account seems to give us a good idea about what happened, it would be difficult to reconstruct the various actions of the child and the observer with precision. Moreover, interpretation is entering; the observer is inferring what is going on within the child.

Aside from the interpretive statements of this observer, it does seem likely that, if a second observer had been present and had given an independent account, most of his statements describing the child's activity would correspond to statements in the preceding protocol. We cannot tell with any confidence, however, since Piaget neglects the question of the possible agreement between observers. Moreover, his descriptions are freestyle, without systematic nomothetic categories. Strictly speaking, the critique in this book appears to apply to these materials. Yet it seems likely that these phenomena can be studied by using observations on which very good interobserver agreement can be obtained. Researchers after Piaget have set up standardized testing procedures for investigating his concepts, procedures that permit observations relying on identification and recognition.

A major difficulty in Piaget's work lies in the links between his protocols and his conceptual contributions. Thus, he often writes that several examples confirm the presence of a state identified by broad, abstract concepts. He does not attempt to determine systematically the empirical relationship between a given class of observer actions and a subsequent class of actions by the child. Instead, he states generalizations about relationships among his concepts and supports his argument with his descriptive accounts. An intensive analysis of Piaget's writing reveals much vagueness and ambiguity in his central concepts as he uses them (Haroutunian, 1976).

In the related field of education, many of the concerns are societal problems. Education as a discipline draws on other fields of behavioral science, not only developmental psychology but also social psychology and sociology. Insofar as these fields are brought into the educational domain, the comments about applying the critique of personality to those fields are relevant. Educational evaluation often involves complex interpretive judgments, as in grading students. But most measurements of educational aptitude and achievement are relatively free of the difficulties confronting personality. The testing assesses maximum performance and yields indices that are generally consistent and stable. Judgments do enter in determining whether the contents of achievement tests are appropriate and in determining the objectives to be sought. Many of the objectives listed in the two taxonomies of educational objectives (Bloom, 1956; Krathwohl, Bloom, and Masia, 1964) are difficult to assess without using interpretive or inferential judgments made by the student.

In those parts of developmental psychology and social psychology where attributes are ascribed to a particular individual, the critique of personality research is applicable. Much of the rest of psychology has avoided the difficulties in these fields. In the study of sensation and perception, there is ordinarily a definite response by the subject on which observers can agree with ease. Even in cognitive work concerned with the accuracy of the subject's response, observations are made with a minimum of interpretation or inference. The same is true for studies of conditioning and learning. One problem does enter, however, in the field of learning. It is well known that experimentally independent measures of learning are not interchangeable. There is evidence of method variance and behavioral specificity associated with particular experimental procedures.

For some psychological topics, the critique of personality applies to only part of the area but not elsewhere. For example, studies of motivation in animals are ordinarily free of the problems indicated in the critique. On the other hand, much work on human motivation utilizes procedures similar to those in personality studies. Even in laboratory studies of people's motives, the observational data often require interpretation and inference.

A pervasive problem in most of psychology is the linkage between concepts and observational data. The concepts are usually a priori, rather than constructed to refer to phenomena that can be observed consensually by observers. As a consequence, when studies seeking to establish the relationships between these broad concepts utilize different procedures, they all too often obtain findings that do not replicate each other. Even when the findings from several similar experiments show some agreement, the domain to which the common results can be generalized is unclear. Moreover, behavior is a function of the conditions surrounding the organism at any moment, and experimental controls cannot eliminate the subject's awareness of these conditions and his reactions to them. McNeill (forthcoming) makes a similar point in his arguing for the study of speech production, where the output is known and observable, rather than the study of speech comprehension, which requires responses that are not part of the normal perceptual process. His fine-grained analysis of naturally occurring speech is generally compatible with the action strategy proposed in Chapters Twelve and Thirteen.

Psychology grew out of human experience. Much psychological work today is still trying to understand the experience of human beings. Insofar as psychology relies on reports of personal experience or on observers' reports that summarize and synthesize large segments of their experience while observing, it will make little progress toward becoming a science like any of the established sciences. Psychology as a science must be based on data that are not influenced by the individuality of the observer.

Anthropology. Let us now turn from psychology to anthropology, the one science bridging the gap between the hard and the soft sciences, according to Arensberg (1972). Although he believes anthropology cannot rely on analogies from other sciences, he does point out the need for operational definitions. The peculiar position of anthropology is in part a function of its diverse subfields and their phenomena. Physical anthropology seems clearly beyond the realm of the subject matter to which the critique in this book might be extended. Archeology also should be excluded, since it studies objects that are stable through time, especially recent time, and that are therefore available for repeated observations and judgments about them by different investigators.

The subfield closest to personality is cultural anthropology. Indeed, work in that area often uses techniques developed for studying the personality phenomena of our own culture. Campbell and Naroll write about "the mutual methodological relevance of anthropology and psychology" (1972). Discussing descriptive-humanistic and abstractive types of science, they state: "It goes without saying that a science of either type cannot be built without intersubjective verifiability of observations. . . . The greater the direct accessibility of the referents to sense perception, the greater the intersubjective verifiability of the observations" (pp. 443–444). Their stress on degree of interobserver agreement reflects their concern about observational judgments that contain too much interpretation and inference to permit observer interchangeability.

The problems of subjectivity and bias in ethnographic reports have been intensively examined by Naroll (1962), who proposes bases for estimating the reliability or trustworthiness of such reports. He suggests comparing reports obtained under more and under less favorable bases as a way of determining their acceptability. A more direct attack on the personal equation in field work is urged by Lewis (1953). He argues that there should be more than one observer in the ethnographic party. Although the ideal is independent studies of the same community at about the same time, very few such restudies have been done. Writing more than two decades ago, Lewis says that he knows of no instance of a restudy aimed at reevaluating a predecessor's work.

It is of course necessary to distinguish the judgments of the ethnographer from those of his informants. Campbell and LeVine note that "current trends in ethnographic data collection would seem to recommend treating ethnographic observation in a given behavioral domain, and the recording of informants' views of behavior patterns in that domain, as separate tasks and independent data source[s] to be checked against one another" (1973, p. 383). The cultural anthropologist, to be sure, is interested in the culture and the patterns observed within it, not in the members of that culture as particular individuals. He works as a scientist rather than as a practitioner providing service to individuals.

LeVine (1973) has proposed alternatives to the ethnographer's reports about the personality variables differentiating one group from another. As a check on the ethnographer's bias, he urges the collection of judgments about a group from various outsiders having different perspectives. The use of such sources avoids the potential limitations of judgments based on in-group informants. Among the outside observers from whom information can be gathered are foreign visitors, immigrants, and neighboring groups. Convergent validation would have to be demonstrated for estimates of each personality variable obtained from these sources and from psychodiagnostic methods. The problem, of course, is to estimate the modal strength of the variable in that group, a task that may be more feasible than obtaining convergence on diverse indices for the strength of a disposition in an individual.

At the conceptual level, cultural anthropology appears to be at about the same primitive level as personality. Tatje notes that "many terms are used in different ways by different theorists, and often without any clear definition to indicate which usage is intended. . . . Often the meanings of the terms used by ethnographers are altered by the cultural context in which they are used" (1973, p. 691). And a given writer may use several definitions—Geertz (1973, pp. 4–5) notes that, in a chapter on culture in *Mirror for Man*, Kluckhohn defines culture in eleven ways, besides using several similes. Although Murdock believes that independent ethnographic accounts usually corroborate each other to a very satisfactory extent, he is dissatisfied with anthropological theory. "I have come to the conclusion that most of the principles we have advanced to order our data bear little resemblance in kind to the systems of theory that have been developed in the older physical and biological sciences. They have far more in common with the equally complex, but unverified and often unverifiable, systems outside the realm of science which we know as mythology, or perhaps as philosophy or even theology. It is for this reason that I have chosen to designate them in this paper as 'anthropology's mythology'" (1972, p. 18). He goes on to argue that the focus of investigation should be "on the actual behaviour of real people" (p. 20).

A viewpoint similar to that advocated in this book has been detailed by Harris (1964), who argues that "cultural things" should be studied in the same way as entities in the physical sciences. He urges the use of categories that are culture-free and that can be used with intersubjective agreement by trained observers. For him, the cultural field of inquiry is behavior, taken as gross changes in the state of bodily parts together with internal responses that have direct effects on external parts of the body or on the immediate environment. His unit is motion with an environmental effect, a somewhat broader unit than the action proposed in Chapters Twelve and Thirteen of this book.

On the basis of the preceding discussion, there is good reason to believe that, in general, the critique of personality applies to the field of cultural anthropology. Although the cultural anthropologist is not particularly concerned with the covariation of individual differences within a culture, her focus on the distribution of personality variables in single cultures and on comparisons between cultures requires the same kinds of judgments that pervade the investigation of personality.

Some anthropologists see cultural anthropology as interpretive. They point out that the informant interprets, and the ethnographer interprets the informant's interpretations. "In short, anthropological writings are interpretations, and second and third order ones to boot" (Geertz, 1973, p. 15). "Anthropology, or at least interpretive anthropology, is a science whose progress is marked less by a perfection of consensus than by a refinement of debate. What gets better is the precision with which we vex each other" (Geertz, 1973, p. 29). Another anthropologist argues that the simple observations stressed in the preceding chapters of this book are not necessary and may not be particularly pertinent for the work of the student of culture. Referring to examples he has been discussing, Schneider asserts that "the cultural rule or the cultural unit exists at a cultural level of observation and without regard to the level of specific instances and concrete occurrences. No amount of direct observation of the behavior of ghosts themselves will yield any information about how the cultural construct of the ghost is formulated. Direct visual observation can certainly yield *hypotheses*, but only hypotheses, about the units and the rules of traffic lights as cultural constructs, but even in such a case it is a moot question whether this manner of producing hypotheses about the cultural constructs is very useful" (1968, pp. 6–7).

For those who construe the objectives of cultural anthropology more or less as these writers do, much of the critique of personality in Part One is not relevant because their norms are different from the ones on which this book is based. Similarly, the proposed reorientations of strategies in Part Two are not appropriate for their concerns.

Economics. The phenomena and data of economics depart in several important respects from those of the other social sciences mentioned above. From the viewpoint of this book, one primary difference is that most of the data are not in themselves judgments made by individuals about persons. The purchase of an automobile by a consumer is a datum, not the consumer's judgment leading to her decision to buy the car or her subsequent actions in concluding the purchase—matters that the economist might study although they are less readily accessible. Moreover, the economist is concerned with what people judge and do about the objects, not what people judge and do in interactions with other people. For the most part, people's judgments about people do not enter into economics.

A brief consideration of economics, nevertheless, is pertinent because the field utilizes naturally occurring events as its phenomena. There is essentially no manipulation for research purposes (the negative income experiment is a rare exception). As a consequence, economists must specify carefully the conditions under which each observation is made. For example, a study may relate the total United States production of automobiles to estimated personal income over a series of years. Each datum on auto production for one year refers to an observation made under the particular set of conditions holding for that year. The values indexing those conditions may fall within ranges that are relatively normal, and yet the specific pattern of those values is probably unique. Although this individuality of temporal pattern may not be important for a descriptive study, it is clearly crucial to the matter of generalizability of a study's findings. Econometricians do take into account the values for pertinent conditions. They use statistical controls in place of experimental manipulations.

Much of the data in economics—for example, the number of units manufactured and the number of dollars spent or saved—is objective. Yet this apparent objectivity is deceptive because it is typically not possible to obtain figures that are fully accurate and complete, and so estimates must be made. Morgenstern (1963) has called attention to many problems of accuracy in economic observations. He shows that data are often not internally consistent and that complementary data may not agree as they presumably should. For example, data on gold shipments from Country X to Country Y may not agree with data on gold shipments received by Y from X. He notes the occurrence of false representation in data, the presence of instrument errors (some from human sources), and the difficulties with definitions and classifications.

Many of the data of economics are, however, indirect indicators of central concepts. Economics "deals with the ways in which men and societies seek to satisfy their material needs and desires" (Rees, 1968, p. 472). Rees goes on to say that "the goals of economic activity are often subsumed under the heading 'utility,' a construct embracing all of the satisfactions to be obtained through consumption, production, and related behavior" (1968, p. 473). Like colleagues in other social sciences, the economist is faced with the problem of identifying and using naturally occurring events or records that can serve as appropriate indices for his concepts. How are satisfaction and utility to be assessed? When the economist goes beyond the Gross National Product to a composite Measure of Economic Welfare (or Net Economic Welfare), he must estimate values for component variables that have a highly subjective character.

Some data used in economic investigations are strictly judgmental, although not judgmental about people. Surveys are conducted to determine consumer purchasing dispositions and whether consumers are optimistic or pessimistic about the economic outlook. Studies of consumers' plans provide data for a particular time, the data being used to make a more informed estimate about subsequent consumer behaviors. At a more microeconomic level, surveys are used to learn about consumer preferences regarding the appearance and other attributes of brand-name products. These investigations of preferences are specific to one or more manufactured products and cannot be generalized with confidence beyond the population of respondents that was sampled.

Fortunately for him, the research economist is interested in aggregates, in what applies to a country's population or to an industry. He can therefore accumulate data from a variety of sources. Insofar as errors in those data are random, his aggregate figures can be very good estimates of the quantities he wishes to study. As in most measurement, however, systematic errors can enter to bias the data.

More than other social sciences, economics is oriented toward application and especially toward prediction. These are the features of economics that make the matter of generalizability so critical. The economist wants to predict from observations made under complex and not fully understood conditions to future observations to be made under conditions that cannot now be estimated accurately, to say nothing of being fully understood after they have occurred. Writing in the context of prediction, Samuelson concludes: "Events of the last half dozen years have shown us how much economics remains an art rather than a science" (1974, p. 77).

An interesting new discipline, labeled *cliometrics*, is concerned with quantitative historical data. Some work in this field involves data that can be used to make judgments about social and economic history. Instead of relying on the historian's further interpretations of contemporary interpretive descriptions produced during the period studied, the cliometrician seeks out historical records that he believes will provide a firmer basis for inferences and conclusions. In terms of the argument in this volume, the historian uses reports of personal cognitions, attributions, and generalizations, while the cliometrician uses relatively objective records. The latter must grant the fragmentary nature of his records and the possibility of bias in what is recorded—for example, the plantation owner's records on whippings of slaves in *Time on the Cross* (Fogel and Engerman, 1974). Furthermore, each of these investigators must make interpretations and draw inferences from whichever kind of protocols he examines. The cliometrician, however, does seem to be building on firmer ground when he uses records of relatively specific events. Once again, the records being used may be objective in the sense that different observers will agree in their perceptions of the contents (as with a subject's answer sheet for a personality questionnaire). Although the objectivity of the records is very important, it does not affect the question of the interchangeability of the investigator's judgments interpreting these materials. Cliometrics is a distinct advance over traditional historical work that relies on interpretations of prior interpretive accounts. It is too soon to determine whether enough objective records can be uncovered to reduce substantially the degree of individuality in investigators' comprehensive judgments based on such records.

Applicability of the Research Decisions and Strategies

As we have seen, insofar as the data used in other fields have characteristics that are the same as or similar to those for the data studied in personality, the critique of Part One is applicable. Let us now examine the research decisions and the strategies proposed in Chapters Eight through Thirteen to determine their pertinence to these other fields. That framework of decisions and choices made by investigators (Table 2, Chapter Eight), as stated in fairly general terms, seems applicable to other parts of psychology and to related fields of behavioral science. In particular, two of the choices stressed earlier in

Part Two have broad relevance: whether the problem is presented by society or invented by the investigator (Decision 1) and whether the observers' task will require interpretation and inference or recognition and identification (Decision 6). The decision whether the behavior to be studied will be expressions about people or moving and speaking (Decision 3) has to be broadened to include expressions about things and institutions in the first alternative.

Since this framework of choices was developed for research in personality, some of the decisions are less relevant elsewhere. For example, many behavioral scientists would not consider it pertinent to study the behavior of their observers (Choice 5a), and few would use professional observers (Choice 4a). Furthermore, there may well be additional research decisions that are made by investigators in these other fields but not by those studying personality.

The scheme for research decisions has the valuable function of permitting the delineation of many research strategies. No attempt will be made here to identify the strategies predominant in each of the related fields. Instead, we can briefly consider whether the three main strategies proposed for personality research have relevance outside that domain.

Many investigators in behavioral science are applying the societal strategy, having chosen to work on a problem presented to them by society. Much of economic research deals with such problems. Many subfields of sociology, such as criminology and intergroup relations, fall within that category. In investigations of societal problems, the data are often expressions about people. That research choice must be generalized, however, in this context. The data are expressions about groups of people, rather than about individuals, and also expressions about larger aggregates, such as community and national needs. Also involved are judgments about broad topics, including conservation and sources of energy.

Thus, the general concept of societal problems is certainly applicable to many areas of behavioral science. The societal strategy proposed for work within the personality domain was portrayed in terms of that area and does not apply exactly to other areas. It is apparent, nevertheless, that appropriate societal strategies that would be analogous to that for personality could be developed for these related fields. Furthermore, it seems very likely that much of the discussion of generalizability and other implications of the societal strategy considered in Chapter Ten would be pertinent to these analogous strategies.

Even more than in the case of the societal strategy, the attributional strategy was formulated specifically for the field of personality, with its concerns for how people construe their experience of the behavior of others. Hence, the attributional strategy in its pure form has little applicability elsewhere. Yet when an investigator chooses expressions about things and problems as his phenomena, he works with a strategy much like the attributional. When a person is making decisions, his motives, utilities, and attitudes enter the process, much as they do for a person making attributions. Even psychophysical judgments are affected by these personal factors. There are also clear analogues for those behavioral sciences that are concerned with attributions made about groups, institutions, policies, and objects. Important research topics include how people develop their attitudinal attributions about other ethnic groups, how they determine their utilities, and how they acquire their political attitudes and values (as in political socialization, for example). Investigators can focus either on attributions showing wide individual differences or on concepts and values shared by most members of a designated group. Thus, the etiology of the phenomena in each field can be studied as a critical aspect of understanding those phenomena. We may conclude that the general ideas underlying the attributional strategy presented in Chapter Eleven are applicable to other fields.

Some extensions of the action strategy have already been considered in Chapter Thirteen. Outside of psychology, few fields concentrate their attention on the activity of an individual organism. One exception, ethology, is concerned with regularities in the interactions of various organisms with other organisms and with objects. Most of the behavioral sciences are concerned with the consequences of actions of individuals, such as decisions leading to an extended course of activity. And their focus is on the central tendencies of aggregates of people, treating as secondary the variation around those averages.

The action strategy attends to the ongoing process of interaction, studied at a relatively molecular level. Most behavioral scientists are interested in much more molar processes—such as the institutionalization of value orientations and the decline of demand following a rise in price. Construing their research problems at broad conceptual levels, they do not attempt to determine what is happening in the individual child or what occurs when a potential customer reads the price tag that has just been revised upward. For many of their purposes, it is sufficient to count such molar events as cars leaving the assembly line of a factory.

One clear exception is the sister field, cultural anthropology. One might say that cultural anthropologists include among their concerns the typical personality of each group they observe. They arrive at formulations of that topic by observing the behaviors of members, without noting separate actions and action sequences. The proposal of Harris (1964), mentioned earlier in this chapter, would, however, lead to an approach very similar to the action strategy.

More generally, it is unlikely that the action strategy can be directly applied by workers in most other areas of behavioral science. These workers formulate their problems at levels of abstraction several steps removed from such low-order concepts as actions. For example, we should not expect that research on minute actions can ever contribute to solving the problems now central to economics and especially to economic policy.

There may, however, be some similarity between difficulties faced by investigators of personality and those confronting workers in other behavioral fields. Earlier in this book, I argued that one source of the handicaps impeding personality research was the prior conceptualizations, derived from personal experience and from the formulations of others, that the investigator brings to her scientific work. In other behavioral disciplines, the investigator enters with a similar burden of preconceptions. Just as the investigator of personality can start afresh by simply observing what actions take place and determining their sequential relationships, so investigators in other fields could try to observe what is going on, using observational categories carrying a minimal load of connotations.

It would be presumptuous to try to indicate what all the categories should be. Some obvious examples can be taken from current research in these fields: the casting of a vote, the purchase of an automobile, the joining of a church. These are substantial molar actions. But what can the investigator do with such observations? Can he identify other molar events that typically precede each of these occurrences? And are there such events? Perhaps the analogy breaks down at this point. The casting of a vote may be preceded regularly not by molar actions of the voter or of others but by various sequences of less molar actions, the sequence not being the same for every voter. Naturally occurring decisions leading to molar actions may be so complexly determined that it is not feasible to identify consistent precursors. Moreover, the temporal magnitudes separating prior influences from the explicit decision and its behavioral manifestation may be too large and too variable to permit systematic investigation at this time.

In addition to the investigator decisions and the resulting research strategies presented in Chapters Eight and Nine, those chapters delineated the notions of research roles and behaviors. Much other behavioral research involves the three distinct roles found in personality investigations—investigator, observer, and actor. Each role is associated with a particular set of behaviors. Just as paradigms were developed for the research process in each of the strategies proposed for personality research, paradigms could be formulated for the processes in related disciplines. These formulations could explicate the complexities involved and could make clear to the investigator the locations of influences possibly confounding his assumptions about his data.

Summary

The critique of personality research in Part One is applicable to other parts of psychology and to other behavioral sciences, especially in areas where the research data are interpretive judgments. Extensions can be made to clinical psychology and psychiatry, social and organizational psychology, developmental psychology, education, sociology, anthropology, economics, and cliometrics. In some extensions, the phenomena are expressions about groups, institutions, and objects, rather than expressions about persons.

Several of the decisions made by the investigator, identified early in Part Two, are very widely applicable. Although the three strategies—societal, attributional, and action—formed from those decisions were developed for the personality domain, analogous strategies can be developed for other areas. Progress in behavioral sci-

ence will increase when each investigator identifies explicitly to himself and others the approach he is taking in his research and
scholarship.

Epilogue

"Several times during its career the science of psychology has
changed its mind about fundamental notions. Psychologists have
taken pleasure in proving, at regular intervals, that psychology has
gone so far astray as to require drastic revision, repudiation of the
past, and the organization of some new school equipped to lay hold of
the future. Revolution occurs easily when government is weak, and
the notable instability of psychology may arise from its lack of rigor
in the formulation of fundamental concepts, for into its most fundamental notions there has seeped a variable mixture of initiation, *a
priori* postulations, reified entities, and empirical fact" (Stevens, 1935,
p. 323). In many parts of psychology, considerable progress has been
made in the four decades since Stevens wrote, and there is less instability and revolution. In personality, some new schools have appeared
and there have been some shifts of emphasis, but no major revolution
has taken place. When will there be a revolution?

This book is based on the assertion that personality has made
little or no positive progress toward becoming a science. In Part One,
I have identified some reasons for that lack of progress; in Part Two, I
have proposed reorientations that can change that situation. Since
the two parts have different theses, the argument in Part One can
stand by itself, independent of the proposals in Part Two. After making oral presentations of the critique as developed in Part One, I have
heard no direct statements rebutting my position. What have been
expressed are claims by individual investigators that their research
program is making progress or that there are instances of better agreement among observers than I have stated.

In contrast, listeners have raised objections to the proposed
strategies, especially the action strategy. Some of these objections
were discussed in Chapter Thirteen. These objections make sense
when one looks at personality in traditional ways or ways that apply
in one's everyday interactions with people. In my scientific work, it
has taken me several years to come to the conviction that people do

not inherently carry around with them the traits and the personality that I attribute so naturally to them. But when I find that the attributions made by others do not coincide with those I have made, I realize that attributions of traits are in large part a function of the attributor.

I recognize that these strategies may not be the only routes to progress toward becoming a science. One of my major reasons for making these proposals is my strong belief that criticism by itself changes little in a science. Theories are given up not just because they are soundly criticized but because more promising theories are developed. The same holds true for methodologies—scientists continue to use methodologies with known weaknesses until more acceptable ones are invented. The strategies were formulated and presented in the hope that fellow-investigators would see that there are alternatives to the way they have been going about their business, and hence they can permit themselves to entertain the possibility of construing the field and their research programs in some different way.

Debate about the issues raised in this book is unlikely to change the minds of many colleagues. All too often, public debate results in separating the debaters even more widely, each retreating to a more extreme position that seems easier to defend, regardless of its veridicality. What debate and discussion can do is sharpen the issues and explicate the assumptions and implications of the contrasting positions. The purpose of this book is to get some colleagues in personality and related fields to examine carefully what they are doing. In particular, I hope that younger colleagues, especially those just entering one of these fields, will give these matters some careful thought. Each investigator must reflect on what she is actually doing in her research. She must ask herself what her data are and how her data were produced. Are her constructs derived from systematic empirical observation or from her everyday experience? She can consider these matters in the privacy of her office. She should not try to resolve these issues in an hour or two. She can take weeks or months to mull them over.

Perhaps our mores need to be changed. Instead of the usual curt introduction to publications reporting empirical investigations, a more discursive and personal statement would be valuable. Suppose each author indicated his view of his research area and the long-range objectives of his personal research program. Suppose he delineated the phenomena he was trying to understand. Suppose he discussed his constructs and made clear the linkages between his constructs and his observational data. That kind of public statement would not only make evident the reasons for incongruities between studies that looked similar in terms of the general concepts used but also would help the reader decide the appropriate directions and extents for any generalizing that he might want to do with the particular findings.

As indicated earlier in this book, there obviously are many kinds of knowledge and many approaches to the understanding of human behavior. Although a person may pursue more than one of these approaches, each of us decides which approach we wish to adopt as our primary orientation. Some of us take the position of the humanistic commentator or the social philosopher. Many people with that perspective have enriched our lives. Others of us are applied social engineers, trying to do what we can to improve the psychological welfare and well-being of our fellows. Still others of us are intrigued by the challenge in trying to develop a scientific understanding of human behavior. When we take up that challenge, we must make a personal decision about the requirements involved in a commitment to the scientific enterprise. Some of those requirements lead to abandoning ways of thinking that seem completely natural and eminently plausible.

In Hans Christian Anderson's fairy tale, everyone talks about the emperor's new clothes as if they actually existed. Only when a child naively says "But he has nothing on!" do the people openly recognize the fact, but the emperor and his chamberlains are still unable to face reality. If we investigators form an aristocracy, let us guard against shared illusions about the garments that have been created for the Emperor Personality. A scientist must think for himself and not merely conform to the perceptions prevailing among the fellow-members of his professional club.

Scientists and other people have had to face disillusionments. Writing in 1917, Freud noted that people's narcissism has "been three times severely wounded by the researches of science" (1957, p. 350). The cosmological blow came when Copernicus showed that the abode of the human race, the earth, did not have a special position in the universe, an earlier view that accorded well with the proclivity of the human race to regard itself as "lord of the world" (p. 351). Darwin was responsible for the biological blow when he demonstrated that the human race was not different from animals, contrary to the prior view that only human beings possess reason, an immortal soul, and divine descent. The psychological blow, credited by Freud to Schopenhauer, came with the idea that a person does not know everything that goes on in his mind. Each of these blows displaced the human race from an illusory pinnacle on which it had placed itself.

In all three instances, the blow forced people to recognize that they could not give special status to themselves and to their construals of the world and of their experience. All of us working in the domain of personality or in a related field must realize that we construct our interpretations of people and of their behavior from our personal perceptions and individual perspective. My construction is not exactly the same as yours. My interpretive judgments differ in some degree and often in kind from yours. If we are to build a science, our data must come from observations that are not relative to the particular observer. As long as we rely on observers, we should use them as a special kind of recording instrument, and the several instances of that device should produce interchangeable observations.

The methods that have been developed in the established sciences are aimed at overcoming the human limitations of the investigator—for example, his potentialities for misperceiving and for leaping to premature conclusions. What is blocking progress in personality and behavioral sciences can be construed in terms of the psychology of investigators. In their scientific work, as in everyone's daily lives, they perceive in terms of preconceptions and they make interpretations in terms of their assumptions. It is very difficult to examine one's preconceptions and assumptions, and almost impossible to alter them, and yet that is exactly what must be done.

As early as 1903, Pavlov found that attempts to imagine the subjective condition of his animals were unsuccessful, and so he had "to abandon entirely the natural inclination to transpose our own subjective condition upon the mechanism of the reaction of the experimental animal, and, instead, to concentrate our whole attention upon the investigation of the correlation between the external phenomena and the reaction of the organism" (1928, p. 50). Although the extrapolation is smaller when human beings are the animals being studied, the dangers in judgmental interpretations are equally critical. To understand human behavior, we must get outside ourselves and gain a better perspective. Although interpretive human judgments are useful for many purposes and appear reasonably effective in our everyday interactions with people, those judgments are not an adequate basis for a science, as the history of personality has amply demonstrated. A corpus of scientific knowledge about human behavior cannot be developed from unsystematic observations or even from systematic interpretive judgments. It can be built only by studying specifiable actions and by relying on observations made by interchangeable observers.

Glossary

Absolute Agreement. The degree of congruence between observations. (*Compare* relative agreement.)

Act, Action. These terms are used essentially as synonyms. Each refers to a brief section of a person's behavior—a section that, throughout its duration, is homogeneous in terms of the definition of the category to which an observer assigns it. Examples include a nod, a smile, a gesture. (*Compare* behavior, segment of behavior.) *Act* is often used to emphasize the momentary nature of the behavior; *action* is used to emphasize the process, the behaving. (*Action* as used in this book should not be confused with the way the term is used in philosophy, where it sometimes denotes voluntary behavior, behavior with an intention, or with an end in view.)

401

Act Approach. The study of behavior by identifying and coding brief, specific acts. The phrase is somewhat more general than the explicitly defined term, action strategy.

Action Sequence. A pair of actions, usually by different persons, occurring close together in time and analyzed as a unit. One member of the pair may be a nonaction, a moment when an action might occur but does not. The term may also refer to linked pairs.

Action Strategy. The research strategy studying motor and vocal actions and using observations requiring recognition and identification, rather than interpretation and inference.

Actor. The person who carries out an act, an action, or a sequence of behavior; the person who is observed. He may or may not be a subject, in the usual sense of that term. (*See* subject.)

Agreement. Correspondence. The term usually refers to correspondence between observational judgments of two or more persons but is also applied to correspondence between other cognitive products, such as the meanings given to words and concepts, and to similarity between beliefs, values, and evaluations.

Association. A type of statistical relationship (for example, the Pearson r) that assesses extent of covariance of relative position within an array. (*Compare* congruence.)

Attribution. (a) A word or statement used to represent how one perceives a person's behavior or the person herself; (b) the cognitive act of describing behavior or a person in this way.

Attributional Strategy. The research strategy studying the attributions made about people and the process of doing so. Emphasis is on the observer who makes these interpretive judgments.

Behavior. This term is used essentially in its familiar sense. It refers to any activities of one person that can be perceived by another person—primarily those perceived visually in the case of physical movements or auditorially in the case of speech or other vocalizations. Usually, it refers to activity extending over time and activity that includes one or more actions at any single moment. (*Compare* action, segment of behavior.)

Congruence. A type of statistical relationship that assesses the extent to which observations in one array are identical with corresponding observations in another array. (*Compare* association.)

Congruence of Observations. Two observations that are identical in form and content, even though made at different times or by different observers.

Datum. A systematic observation that is utilized in an investigator's analysis: (a) it may be identified or labeled and entered directly into a statistical analysis; (b) it may be operated on by the investigator (for example, it may be combined mathematically with other data) before being entered into a statistical analysis. A *datum* is an index to an aspect of phenomena.

Environment. The locus of any concurrent thing, event, or condition that might affect behavior. The *external environment* includes whatever is outside the person. The *internal environment* refers to inferred psychological or physiological states of the person.

Event. A phenomenon occurring in the outside world. The term emphasizes a change in what is going on.

External Validity. The extent to which an investigator can generalize from his particular empirical data and findings. Originally applied to generalizing obtained findings to populations of persons, types of settings, sets of treatment variables, and sets of measurement variables, the term is now also applied to generalizing the interpretations and inferences made about the investigator's particular data. (*See also* generalizability. *Compare* internal validity.)

Generalizability. The extent to which an investigator can confidently generalize or induce from the particular observations or findings in his empirical research. (*See also* external validity, representativeness, replicability, and reproducibility.)

Impressions. The content about another person that is stored in memory and is retrieved when attention is directed toward that person in his absence. *Impressions* include images and feelings. The term refers to the content before it has been cast into words.

Interpretation of Behavior.   Going beyond the manifest activity in behavior to apply labels to segments of a person's behavior or to the person himself—a process typically involving an inference from the activity perceived. This book postulates that the interpreter contributes individualistically to his interpretive process.

Judgment.   The product of the cognitive activity of an observer. In this book, it is usually used to imply an extended cognitive process involving interpretation or inference and resulting in attributing a general characteristic to the person observed.

Observation.   A cognitive act applied to some phenomena. The term is applied to what people do in their natural behavior as well as to the more systematic cognitive acts performed by observers selected by investigators. An *observation* always involves both an observer and some phenomena being observed, though the exact nature of the latter may not be known or knowable by the investigator. The term is also used to refer to the product of the cognizing behavior, as reported to the investigator. When contrasted with interpretation, *observation* refers to relatively simple, replicable cognitions involving just recognition and identification.

Observer.   A person who makes observations, usually as instructed by an investigator in a research context.

Optimal Action Strategy.   A particular form of action strategy stressing the study of an action in its behavioral context of other actions, as in action sequences. It also emphasizes naturalness of stimuli and of setting.

Personality.   (a) The way a person is construed as interacting with her external environment and with her intrapsychic world; (b) the discipline concerned with the study of such construals of persons and attributional judgments about persons and their behavior.

Phenomena.   The raw material under consideration, taken as it is, with only minimal and colloquial construing or interpreting—that is, before any systematic analysis, labeling, or construing takes place. *Phenomena* are taken as occurring in the outside world.

Place.   *See* situation.

Population. A subset, of a world or of a universe, that is potentially accessible to an investigator.

Relative Agreement. The extent to which the position of one observation in an array of observations corresponds to the position of another observation in a separate array. (*Compare* absolute agreement.)

Replicability. The degree to which one thing can be made congruent with another. The term as used here refers primarily to the degree to which one observation or set of observations, carried out independently, can be made congruent with another observation or set of observations of the same phenomena, usually by a separate observer.

Representativeness. Similarity between the values, on one or more variables, for a sample and those for the population from which it is considered to have been drawn.

Reproducibility. The degree to which the findings from the study of one set of phenomena can be approximated by those from studying another set of phenomena.

Sample. The subset from a population that is used in a specific investigation.

Segment of Behavior. A sequence of behavior that is arbitrarily bounded at both ends by the arrival or departure of the observer, by initiating and terminating a recording (or the replaying of a recording), by the instructions given to the observer, or by the observer as he interprets those instructions.

Setting. *See* situation.

Situation. The immediate physical conditions surrounding the person, together with the psychological meaning of these conditions for the person. The term has a slightly more restricted meaning than external environment. Situation, setting, and place are used in this book almost interchangeably.

Societal Problem. A problem, formulated in the everyday world, that concerns the welfare of persons, institutions, or a part of society.

Societal Strategy. The research strategy studying problems presented to the investigator by society—problems typically involving interpretive, evaluative judgments about people.

Strategy.   The set of choices selected by the investigator, one for each of the several implicit or explicit decisions that are made in determining a research program and in planning an empirical study.

Subject.   The term is used in its usual sense to refer to a person observed in an investigation, especially in an experimental study. (*See* actor.)

Trait.   A characteristic that is assumed to be lasting and is attributed to persons in varying amounts or strengths. Sometimes *trait* is used loosely to refer to any variable by which a personality is described.

Unit of Analysis.   The pairing of one value for an object or event, as assigned by a unit of measurement, with a value or values from a separate measuring process. In simple correlational or contingency analyses, just two values are paired. In other analyses, one value for the object or event may be paired simultaneously with each of several other values, often ones that had been determined earlier by the investigator.

Unit of Measurement.   The product of a cognitive action in the measuring process, stated as a quantity or quality by the observer and used by the investigator in his analysis. The very general term *response* has often been used in this sense.

Unit of Observation.   The segment of behavior that is utilized for a given observation.

Universe.   All instances of something that is of interest to the investigator—all persons or all instances of a class of phenomena or of behaviors.

World.   A major subset of a universe.

References

Abelson, R. P. "Script Processing in Attitude Formation and Decision-Making." In J. S. Carroll and J. W. Payne (Eds.), *Cognition and Social Behavior*. New York: Halsted Press, 1976.

Allen, B. P., and Potkay, C. R. "Variability of Self-Description on a Day-to-Day Basis: Longitudinal Use of the Adjective Generation Technique." *Journal of Personality*, 1973, *41*, 638-652.

Allport, G. W. *Personality: A Psychological Interpretation*. New York: Holt, Rinehart and Winston, 1937.

Allport, G. W. *Pattern and Growth in Personality*. New York: Holt, Rinehart and Winston, 1961.

Allport, G. W. (Ed.). *Letters from Jenny*. New York: Harcourt Brace Jovanovich, 1965.

Allport, G. W., and Odbert, H. S. "Trait-Names: A Psycho-

Lexical Study." *Psychological Monographs*, 1936, *47*, 1 (whole issue).

Altman, I. "Environmental Psychology and Social Psychology." *Personality and Social Psychology Bulletin*, 1976, *2*, 96-113.

Anderson, J. W. "Attachment Behaviour Out of Doors." In N. Blurton Jones (Ed.), *Ethological Studies of Child Behaviours*. Cambridge, England: Cambridge University Press, 1972.

Anderson, N. H. "Functional Measurement and Psychophysical Judgment." *Psychological Review*, 1970, *77*, 153-170.

Anderson, N. H. "How Functional Measurement Can Yield Validated Interval Scales of Mental Qualities." *Journal of Applied Psychology*, 1976, *61*, 677-692.

Anderson, N. H. "Note on Functional Measurement and Data Analysis." *Perception and Psychophysics*, 1977, *21*, 201-215.

Arensberg, C. M. "Culture as Behavior: Structure and Emergence." In B. J. Siegel (Ed.), *Annual Review of Anthropology*. Vol. 1. Palo Alto, Calif.: Annual Reviews, 1972.

Armistead, N. "Experience in Everyday Life." In N. Armistead (Ed.), *Reconstructing Social Psychology*. New York: Penguin, 1974a.

Armistead, N. (Ed.). *Reconstructing Social Psychology*. New York: Penguin, 1974b.

Aronson, E. "The Need for Achievement as Measured by Graphic Expression." In J. W. Atkinson (Ed.), *Motives in Fantasy, Action, and Society: A Method of Assessment and Study*. New York: Van Nostrand, 1958.

Aronson, E., and Carlsmith, J. M. "Experimentation in Social Psychology." In G. Lindzey and E. Aronson (Eds.), *Handbook of Social Psychology*. Vol. 2. (2nd ed.) Reading, Mass.: Addison-Wesley, 1968.

Arrington, R. E. "Time Sampling in Studies of Social Behavior: A Critical Review of Techniques and Results with Research Suggestions." *Psychological Bulletin*, 1943, *40*, 81-124.

Ashton, S. G., and Goldberg, L. R. "In Response to Jackson's Challenge: The Comparative Validity of Personality Scales Constructed by the External (Empirical) Strategy and Scales Developed Intuitively by Experts, Novices, and Laymen." *Journal of Research in Personality*, 1973, *7*, 1-20.

Atkinson, J. "Change in Activity." In T. Mischel (Ed.), *Human*

Action: Conceptual and Empirical Issues. New York: Academic Press, 1969.

Baldwin, A. L. "Personal Structure Analysis: A Statistical Method for Investigating the Single Personality." *Journal of Abnormal and Social Psychology,* 1942, *37,* 163-183.

Baldwin, A. L. "The Study of Child Behavior and Development." In P. H. Mussen (Ed.), *Handbook of Research Methods in Child Development.* New York: Wiley, 1960.

Bandura, A. *Aggression: A Social Learning Analysis.* Englewood Cliffs, N.J.: Prentice-Hall, 1973.

Barker, R. G. (Ed.). *The Stream of Behavior: Explorations of Its Structure and Content.* New York: Appleton-Century-Crofts, 1963.

Bavelas, A. "Social Psychology—What the Hell." Paper presented to the Department of Psychology, University of Victoria, British Columbia, November 16, 1973.

Beckner, M. *The Biological Way of Thought.* New York: Columbia University Press, 1959.

Beekman, S. J. "Nonverbal Behaviors in Dyadic Conversations in Relation to Subject Sex and Partner Sex." Unpublished doctoral dissertation, University of Chicago, 1973.

Békésy, G. von. *Experiments in Hearing.* New York: McGraw-Hill, 1960.

Bem, D. J., and Allen, A. "On Predicting Some of the People Some of the Time: The Search for Cross-Situational Consistencies in Behavior." *Psychological Review,* 1974, *81,* 506-520.

Bennett, C. A., and Lumsdaine, A. A. (Eds.). *Evaluation and Experiment: Some Critical Issues in Assessing Social Programs.* New York: Academic Press, 1975.

Benton, A. L. "The Interpretation of Questionnaire Items in a Personality Schedule." *Archives of Psychology (New York),* 1935, *190.*

Bergman, G., and Spence, K. W. "The Logic of Psychophysical Measurement." *Psychological Review,* 1944, *51,* 1-24.

Berman, J. S. "A Comparison between Formal and Implicit Theories of Personality." Cambridge, Mass.: Department of Psychology and Social Relations, Harvard University, n.d.

Berman, J. S., and Kenny, D. A. "Correlational Bias in Observer Ratings." *Journal of Personality and Social Psychology,* 1976, *34,* 263-273.

Bickman, L., and Henchy, T. *Beyond the Laboratory: Field Research in Social Psychology.* New York: McGraw-Hill, 1972.

Bieri, J. "Complexity-Simplicity as a Personality Variable in Cognitive and Preferential Behavior." In D. Fiske and S. Maddi (Eds.), *Functions of Varied Experience.* Homewood, Ill.: Dorsey, 1961.

Bieri, J. "Cognitive Structures in Personality." In H. M. Schroder and P. Suedfeld (Eds.), *Personality Theory and Information Processing.* New York: Ronald Press, 1971.

Bishop, Y. M. M., Fienberg, S. E., and Holland, P. M. *Discrete Multivariate Analysis: Theory and Practice.* Cambridge, Mass.: M.I.T. Press, 1975.

Black, M. *Margins of Precision: Essays in Logic and Language.* Ithaca, N.Y.: Cornell University Press, 1970.

Bloom, B. S. (Ed.). *Taxonomy of Educational Objectives: The Classification of Educational Goals.* Handbook I: *Cognitive Domain.* New York: McKay, 1956.

Blumer, H. "The Problem of the Concept in Social Psychology." *American Journal of Sociology,* 1940, *45,* 707-719.

Boen, J. R. "Will Evaluation Outgrow the Game Stage?" *Evaluation: A Forum for Human Service Decision-Makers,* 1975, *2*(2), 9-10.

Botein, B. "The Manhattan Bail Project: Its Impact on Criminology and the Criminal Law Processes." *Texas Law Review,* 1964-65, *43,* 319-331.

Bourne, E. "Can We Describe an Individual's Personality? Agreement on Stereotype Versus Individual Attributes." *Journal of Personality and Social Psychology,* 1977, *35,* 863-872.

Bowers, K. S. "Situationism in Psychology: An Analysis and a Critique." *Psychological Review,* 1973, *80,* 307-336.

Bradburn, N. *The Structure of Psychological Well-Being.* Chicago: Aldine, 1969.

Bradburn, N., and Caplovitz, D. *Reports on Happiness: A Pilot Study of Behavior Related to Mental Health.* Chicago: Aldine, 1965.

Brazelton, T. B., Koslowski, B., and Main, M. "The Origins of Reciprocity: The Early Mother-Infant Interaction." In M. Lewis and L. A. Rosenblum (Eds.), *The Effect of the Infant on Its Caregiver.* New York: Wiley, 1974.

Brodbeck, M. "General Introduction." In M. Brodbeck (Ed.), *Readings in the Philosophy of the Social Sciences.* New York: Macmillan, 1968.

Brown, R. *Social Psychology.* New York: Free Press, 1965.

Bruner, J. S. "Social Psychology and Perception." In E. E. Maccoby, T. M. Newcomb, and E. L. Hartley (Eds.), *Readings in Social Psychology.* (3rd ed.) New York: Holt, Rinehart and Winston, 1958.

Brunswik, E. "Thing Constancy as Measured by Correlation Coefficients." *Psychological Review,* 1940, *47,* 69-78.

Brunswik, E. *Systematic and Representative Design in Psychological Experiments.* Berkeley: University of California Press, 1947.

Brunswik, E. "Representative Design and Probabilistic Theory." *Psychological Review,* 1955, *62,* 193-217.

Brunswik, E. *Perception and the Representative Design of Psychological Experiments.* Berkeley: University of California Press, 1956.

Butt, D. S., and Fiske, D. W. "Differential Correlates of Dominance Scales." *Journal of Personality,* 1969, *37,* 415-428.

Byrne, D. "The Repression-Sensitization Scale: Rationale, Reliability, and Validity." *Journal of Personality,* 1961, *29,* 334-349.

Campbell, A. "Subjective Measures of Well-Being." *American Psychologist,* 1976, *31,* 117-124.

Campbell, A., Converse, P. E., and Rodgers, W. L. *The Quality of American Life: Perceptions, Evaluations, and Satisfactions.* New York: Russell Sage, 1976.

Campbell, D. T. "The Mutual Methodological Relevance of Anthropology and Psychology." In F. L. K. Hsu (Ed.), *Psychological Anthropology.* Homewood, Ill.: Dorsey, 1961.

Campbell, D. T. "On the Conflicts Between Biological and Social Evolution and Between Psychology and Moral Tradition." *American Psychologist,* 1975, *30,* 1103-1126.

Campbell, D. T. "Reprise." *American Psychologist,* 1976, *31,* 381-384.

Campbell, D. T., and Fiske, D. W. "Convergent and Discriminant Validation by the Multitrait-Multimethod Matrix." *Psychological Bulletin,* 1959, *56,* 81-105.

Campbell, D. T., and LeVine, R. A. "Field-Manual Anthropology." In R. Naroll and R. Cohen (Eds.), *A Handbook of Method in Cultural Anthropology.* New York: Columbia University Press, 1973.

Campbell, D. T., and Naroll, R. "The Mutual Methodological Relevance of Anthropology and Psychology." In F. L. K. Hsu (Ed.), *Psychological Anthropology.* (rev. ed.) Cambridge, Mass.: Schenkman, 1972.

Campbell, D. T., and Stanley, J. C. "Experimental and Quasi-Experimental Designs for Research on Teaching." In N. L. Gage (Ed.), *Handbook of Research on Teaching.* Chicago: Rand McNally, 1963.

Campbell, N. R. *What is Science?* New York: Dover, 1952. (Originally published 1921.)

Cannon, W. H., and Jensen, O. G. "Terrestrial Timekeeping and General Relativity—A Discovery." *Science,* 1975, *188* (4186), 317-328.

Caplan, N., and Nelson, S. D. "On Being Useful: The Nature and Consequences of Psychological Research on Social Problems." *American Psychologist,* 1973, *28,* 199-211.

Carmichael, L., Hogan, H. P., and Walter, A. A. "An Experimental Study of the Effect of Language on the Reproduction of Visually Perceived Form." *Journal of Experimental Psychology,* 1932, *15,* 73-86.

Carr, H. A., and Kingsbury, F. A. "The Concept of Traits," *Psychological Review,* 1938, *45,* 497-524.

Cartwright, D. S. "Success in Psychotherapy as a Function of Certain Actuarial Variables." *Journal of Consulting Psychology,* 1955, *19,* 357-363.

Cartwright, D. S., Kirtner, W. L., and Fiske, D. W. "Method Factors in Changes Associated with Psychotherapy." *Journal of Abnormal and Social Psychology,* 1963, *66,* 164-175.

Cary, M. S. "Nonverbal Openings to Conversation." Paper presented at the 45th annual convention of the Eastern Psychological Association, Philadelphia, Pa., April 18, 1974.

Cattell, R. B. *Description and Measurement of Personality.* Yonkers-on-Hudson, N.Y.: World Book, 1946.

Cattell, R. B. "The Data Box: Its Ordering of Total Resources in Terms of Possible Relational Systems." In R. B. Cattell (Ed.), *Handbook of Multivariate Experimental Psychology.* Chicago: Rand McNally, 1966.

Chapple, E. D. "Quantitative Analysis of Complex Organizational Systems." *Human Organization,* 1962, *21,* 67-87.

Chun, K-T., and others. "Selection of Psychological Measures: Quality or Convenience." *Proceedings, 80th Annual Convention, American Psychological Association,* 1972, pp. 15-16.

Churchman, C. W. "Why Measure?" In C. W. Churchman and P. Ratoosh (Eds.), *Measurement: Definitions and Theories*. New York: Wiley, 1959.

Ciminero, A. R., Calhoun, K. S., and Adams, H. A. (Eds.). *Handbook of Behavioral Assessment*. New York: Wiley, 1977.

Cohen, J. "A Coefficient of Agreement for Nominal Scales." *Educational and Psychological Measurement*, 1960, *20*, 37-46.

Coleman, J. S. *Policy Research in the Social Sciences*. Morristown, N.J.: General Learning Press, 1972.

Cook, T. D., and Campbell, D. T. "The Design and Conduct of Quasi-Experiments and True Experiments in Field Settings." In M. D. Dunnette (Ed.), *Handbook of Industrial and Organizational Research*. New York: Rand McNally, 1976.

Coombs, C. H. *A Theory of Data*. New York: Wiley, 1964.

Coombs, C. H., Dawes, R. M., and Tversky, A. *Mathematical Psychology: An Elementary Introduction*. Englewood Cliffs, N.J.: Prentice-Hall, 1970.

Cronbach, L. J. "The Two Disciplines of Scientific Psychology." *American Psychologist*, 1957, *12*, 671-684.

Cronbach, L. J. "Beyond the Two Disciplines of Scientific Psychology." *American Psychologist*, 1975, *30*, 116-127.

Cronbach, L. J., and Furby, L. "How We Should Measure 'Change'— or Should We?" *Psychological Bulletin*, 1970, *74*, 68-80.

Cronbach, L. J., Gleser, G. C., Nanda, H., and Rajaratnam, N. *The Dependability of Behavioral Measurements: Theory of Generalizability for Scores and Profiles*. New York: Wiley, 1972.

Cronbach, L. J., and Snow, R. E. *Aptitudes and Instructional Methods: A Handbook for Research on Interaction*. New York: Halsted Press, 1977.

D'Andrade, R. G. "Trait Psychology and Componential Analysis." *American Anthropologist*, 1965, *67*, 215-228.

D'Andrade, R. G. "Memory and the Assessment of Behavior." In H. M. Blalock, Jr. (Ed.), *Measurement in the Social Sciences: Theories and Strategies*. Chicago: Aldine, 1974.

Dawes, R. M. "A Case Study of Graduate Admissions: Application of Three Principles of Human Decision Making." *American Psychologist*, 1971, *26*, 180-188.

Dawes, R. M., and Corrigan, B. "Linear Models in Decision Making." *Psychological Bulletin,* 1974, *81,* 95-106.

Devereux, G. *From Anxiety to Method in the Behavioral Sciences.* The Hague, Netherlands: Mouton, 1967.

Di Vesta, F. J. "A Developmental Study of the Semantic Structures of Children." *Journal of Verbal Learning and Verbal Behavior,* 1966, *5,* 249-259.

Dickman, H. R. "The Perception of Behavioral Units." In R. G. Barker (Ed.), *The Stream of Behavior.* New York: Appleton-Century-Crofts, 1963.

Diesing, P. *Patterns of Discovery in the Social Sciences.* Chicago: Aldine, 1971.

Dollard, J., and Auld, F., Jr. *Scoring Human Motives: A Manual.* New Haven, Conn.: Yale University Press, 1959.

Duncan, S., Jr. "Nonverbal Communication." *Psychological Bulletin,* 1969, *72,* 118-137.

Duncan, S., Jr. "Some Signals and Rules for Taking Speaking Turns in Conversations." *Journal of Personality and Social Psychology,* 1972, *23,* 283-292.

Duncan, S., Jr., and Fiske, D. W. *Face-to-Face Interaction: Research, Methods, and Theory.* New York: Halsted Press, 1977.

Ebbesen, E. B., and Allen, R. B. "Further Evidence Concerning Fiske's Question: 'Can Personality Constructs Ever be Empirically Validated?' " La Jolla: Psychology Department, University of California, San Diego, 1977.

Ebbesen, E. B., Cohen, C. E., and Lane, J. L. "Encoding and Construction Processes in Person Perception." Paper presented at the 83rd annual convention of the American Psychological Association, Chicago, 1975.

Edwards, A. L. *Edwards Personality Inventory: Manual.* Chicago: Science Research Associates, 1967.

Eibl-Eibesfeldt, I. *Ethology: The Biology of Behavior.* New York: Holt, Rinehart and Winston, 1970.

Eibl-Eibesfeldt, I. "Similarities and Differences Between Cultures in Expressive Movements." In R. A. Hinde (Ed.), *Non-Verbal Communication.* Cambridge, England: Cambridge University Press, 1972.

Einhorn, H. J. "Decision Errors and Fallible Judgment: Implications for Social Policy." In K. Hammond (Ed.), *Judgment and Decision in Public Policy.* Boulder, Colo.: Westview Press, 1978.

Einhorn, H. J., and Hogarth, R. M. "Unit Weighting Schemes for Decision Making." *Organizational Behavior and Human Performance*, 1975, *13*, 171-192.

Einhorn, H. J., and Hogarth, R. M. "Judging Our Own Judgment." Working paper, Graduate School of Business, University of Chicago, 1977.

Einhorn, H. J., and Schacht, S. "Decisions Based on Fallible Clinical Judgment." In M. Kaplan and S. Schwartz (Eds.), *Human Judgment and Decision Processes: Applications in Practical Settings*. New York: Academic Press, 1977.

Eisenberg, L. "The *Human* Nature of Human Nature." *Science*, 1972, *176*, 123-128.

Eisenberg, P. "Individual Interpretation of Psychoneurotic Inventory Items." *Journal of General Psychology*, 1941, *25*, 19-40.

Eisenberg, P., and Wesman, A. G. "Consistency in Response and Logical Interpretation of Psychoneurotic Inventory Items." *Journal of Educational Psychology*, 1941, *32*, 321-338.

Ekman, P., and Friesen, W. V. "The Repertoire of Nonverbal Behavior: Categories, Origins, Usage, and Coding." *Semiotica*, 1969, *1*, 49-98.

Elkind, D. "Piaget's Conservation Problems." *Child Development*, 1967, *38*, 15-27.

Elms, A. C. "The Crisis of Confidence in Social Psychology." *American Psychologist*, 1975, *30*, 967-976.

Endler, N. S., and Hunt, J. McV. "S-R Inventories of Hostility and Comparisons of the Proportions of Variance from Persons, Responses, and Situations for Hostility and Anxiousness." *Journal of Personality and Social Psychology*, 1968, *9*, 309-315.

Endler, N. S., and Magnusson, D. (Eds.). *Interactional Psychology and Personality*. Washington, D.C.: Hemisphere, 1976a.

Endler, N. S., and Magnusson, D. "Toward an Interactional Psychology of Personality." *Psychological Bulletin*, 1976b, *83*, 956-974.

Ervin, S. M., and Foster, G. "The Development of Children's Terms." *Journal of Abnormal and Social Psychology*, 1960, *61*, 271-275.

Feigl, H. "The 'Orthodox' View of Theories: Remarks in Defense as Well as Critique." In M. Radner and S. Winokur (Eds.), *Analyses of Theories and Methods of Physics and Psy-*

chology. Minneapolis: University of Minnesota Press, 1970.

Feyerabend, P. *Against Method: Outline of an Anarchistic Theory of Knowledge*. Atlantic Highlands, N.J.: Humanities Press, 1975.

Fischhoff, B. "Attribution Theory and Judgment Under Uncertainty." In J. H. Harvey, W. J. Ickes, and R. F. Kidd (Eds.), *New Directions in Attribution Research*. Vol. 1. New York: Halsted Press, 1976.

Fiske, D. W. "Values, Theory, and the Criterion Problem." *Personnel Psychology*, 1951, *4*, 93-98.

Fiske, D. W. "Some Hypotheses Concerning Test Adequacy." *Educational and Psychological Measurement*, 1966, *26*, 69-88.

Fiske, D. W. "The Subject Reacts to Tests." *American Psychologist*, 1967, *22*, 287-296.

Fiske, D. W. *Measuring the Concepts of Personality*. Chicago: Aldine, 1971.

Fiske, D. W. "Can a Personality Construct Be Validated Empirically?" *Psychological Bulletin*, 1973, *80*, 89-92.

Fiske, D. W. "The Use of Significant Others in Assessing the Outcome of Psychotherapy." In I. E. Waskow and M. B. Parloff (Eds.), *Psychotherapy Change Measures: Report of the Clinical Research Branch Outcome Measures Project*. (DHEW Publication No. [ADM] 74-120.) Washington, D.C.: U.S. Government Printing Office, 1975.

Fiske, D. W. "Methodological Issues in Research on the Psychotherapist." In A. S. Gurman and A. M. Razin (Eds.), *Effective Psychotherapy: A Handbook of Research*. Elmsford, N.Y.: Pergamon, 1978.

Fiske, D. W., and Barack, L. I. "Individuality of Item Interpretation in Interchangeable ACL Scales." *Educational and Psychological Measurement*, 1976, *36*, 339-345.

Fiske, D. W., and Bourne, E. "Thresholds for Attributing Can Affect Factorial Structure." *Educational and Psychological Measurement*, 1977, *37*, 713-723.

Fiske, D. W., and Butler, J. M. "The Experimental Conditions for Measuring Individual Differences." *Educational and Psychological Measurement*, 1963, *23*, 249-266.

Fiske, D. W., and Cox, J. A., Jr. "The Consistency of Ratings by Peers." *Journal of Applied Psychology*, 1960, *44*, 11-17.

Fiske, D. W., Hunt, H. F., Luborsky, L., Orne, M. T., Parloff, M. B., Reiser, M. F., and Tuma, A. H. "Planning of Research on Effectiveness of Psychotherapy." *Archives of General Psychiatry*, 1970, *22*, 22-32.

Fiske, S. T., and Cox, M. G. "Describing Others: There's More to Person Perception than Trait Lists." Cambridge, Mass.: Department of Psychology and Social Relations, Harvard University, n.d.

Fogel, R. W., and Engerman, S. L. *Time on the Cross*. Boston: Little, Brown, 1974.

Fox, K. A. *Social Indicators and Social Theory: Elements of an Operational System*. New York: Wiley, 1974.

Freud, S. "A Difficulty of Psycho-Analysis." In E. Jones (Ed.), *Collected Papers*. Vol. 4. (J. Riviere, Trans.) London: Hogarth, 1957.

Gadlin, H., and Ingle, G. "Through the One-Way Mirror: The Limits of Experimental Self-Reflection." *American Psychologist*, 1975, *30*, 1003-1009.

Gardner, R., Holzman, P. S., Klein, G. S., Linton, H., and Spence, D. P. "Cognitive Control: A Study of Individual Consistencies in Cognitive Behavior." *Psychological Issues*, 1959, *1*, 4 (whole issue).

Garner, W. R. *The Processing of Information and Structure*. New York: Halsted Press, 1974.

Geertz, C. *The Interpretation of Cultures*. New York: Basic Books, 1973.

Gergen, K. J. "Social Psychology as History." *Journal of Personality and Social Psychology*, 1973, *26*, 309-320.

Getzels, J. W. "Creative Thinking, Problem-Solving, and Instruction." In E. R. Hilgard (Ed.), *Theories of Learning and Instruction*. 63rd Yearbook of the National Society for the Study of Education, Part 1. Chicago: University of Chicago Press, 1964.

Getzels, J. W., and Csikszentmihalyi, M. *The Creative Vision: A Longitudinal Study of Problem Finding in Art*. New York: Wiley, 1976.

Glass, B. "The Ethical Basis of Science." *Science*, 1965, *150*, 1254-1261.

Glass, G. V. "The Wisdom of Scientific Inquiry on Education." *Journal of Research in Science Teaching*, 1972, *9*, 3-18.

Goldberg, L. R., Norman, W. T., Peabody, D., Rorer, L., and

Wiggins, J. S. *A Description of the O.R.I. Taxonomy Project.* Technical Report, Vol. 15, no. 2. Eugene: Oregon Research Institute, 1975.

Goldfried, M. R., and Kent, R. N. "Traditional Versus Behavioral Personality Assessment: A Comparison of Methodological and Theoretical Assumptions." *Psychological Bulletin,* 1972, 77, 409-420.

Goldfried, M. R., and Sprafkin, J. N. *Behavioral Personality Assessment.* Morristown, N.J.: General Learning Press, 1974.

Goldfried, M. R., and D'Zurilla, T. J. "A Behavioral-Analytic Model for Assessing Competence." In C. D. Spielberger (Ed.), *Current Topics in Clinical and Community Psychology.* Vol. 1. New York: Academic Press, 1969.

Goodenough, F. *Mental Testing: Its History, Principles, and Applications.* New York: Holt, Rinehart and Winston, 1949.

Goodman, L., and Kruskal, W. "Measures of Association for Cross Classifications." *Journal of the American Statistical Association,* 1954, *49,* 732-764.

Gottschalk, L. A., and Gleser, G. C. *The Measurement of Psychological States Through the Content Analysis of Verbal Behavior.* Berkeley: University of California Press, 1969.

Gough, H. G., and Heilbrun, A. B. *The Adjective Check List—Manual.* Palo Alto, Calif.: Consulting Psychologists Press, 1965.

Guilford, J. P. *Psychometric Methods.* New York: McGraw-Hill, 1936.

Guilford, J. P. *The Nature of Human Intelligence.* New York: McGraw-Hill, 1967.

Gurwitz, S. B., and Panciera, L. "Attributions of Freedom by Actors and Observers." *Journal of Personality and Social Psychology,* 1975, *32,* 531-539.

Haan, N., and Livson, N. "Sex Differences in the Eyes of Expert Personality Assessors: Blind Spots?" *Journal of Personality Assessment,* 1973, *37,* 486-492.

Haggard, E. A. *Intraclass Correlation and the Analysis of Variance.* New York: Dryden, 1958.

Haggard, E. A., and Isaacs, K. S. "Micromomentary Facial Expressions as Indicators of Ego Mechanisms in Psychotherapy." In L. A. Gottschalk and A. H. Auerbach (Eds.), *Methods of Research in Psychotherapy.* New York: Appleton-Century-Crofts, 1966.

Hakel, M. D. "How Often Is Often?" *American Psychologist,* 1968, *23,* 533-534.

Hammond, K. R., Hursch, C. J., and Todd, F. J. "Analyzing the Components of Clinical Inference." *Psychological Review,* 1964, *71,* 438-456.

Hannan, M. T. *Aggregation and Disaggregation in Sociology.* Lexington, Mass.: Heath, 1971a.

Hannan, M. T. "Problems of Aggregation." In H. M. Blalock, Jr. (Ed.), *Causal Models in the Social Sciences.* Chicago: Aldine, 1971b.

Hanson, N. R. *Patterns of Discovery.* Cambridge, England: Cambridge University Press, 1958.

Hargreaves, W. A. "Longitudinal Measurement of Depressive Symptoms." In T. A. Williams, M. M. Katz, and J. A. Shields (Eds.), *Recent Advances in the Psychobiology of the Depressive Illnesses.* (DHEW Publication No. [HSM] 70-9053.) Rockville, Md.: National Institute of Mental Health, 1972.

Haroutunian, S. "Some Problems with Piaget's Explanation of Stage Transition." Unpublished doctoral dissertation, University of Chicago, 1976.

Harré, R. *The Principles of Scientific Thinking.* Chicago: University of Chicago Press, 1970.

Harré, R. "Blueprint for a New Science." In N. Armistead (Ed.), *Reconstructing Social Psychology.* New York: Penguin, 1974.

Harré, R., and Secord, P. F. *The Explanation of Social Behaviour.* Oxford, England: Basil Blackwell, 1972.

Harris, M. *The Nature of Cultural Things.* New York: Random House, 1964.

Harvey, J. H. "Dispositional Attributions: A Manifestation of the Principle of Least Effort?" Paper presented at the meeting of the Midwestern Psychological Association, Chicago, May, 1976.

Harvey, J. H., Ickes, W. J., and Kidd, R. F. (Eds.), *New Directions in Attribution Research.* Vol. 1. New York: Halsted Press, 1976.

Hayden, T. "Person Perception." In L. Berkowitz, *A Survey of Social Psychology.* Hinsdale, Ill.: Dryden Press, 1975.

Heider, F. *The Psychology of Interpersonal Relations.* New York: Wiley, 1958.

Hess, E. H. *Imprinting*. New York: D. Van Nostrand, 1973.

Hess, E. H. *The Tell-Tale Eye: How Your Eyes Reveal Hidden Thoughts and Emotions*. New York: Van Nostrand Reinhold, 1975.

Hirschberg, N. "A Correct Treatment of Traits." In H. London (Ed.), *Strategies of Personality Research*. Washington, D. C.: Hemisphere, forthcoming.

Holly, J. W., and Linert, G. A. "The G Index of Agreement in Multiple Ratings." *Educational and Psychological Measurement*, 1974, *34*, 817-822.

Holtzman, W. H. "Recurring Dilemmas in Personality Assessment." *Journal of Projective Techniques and Personality Assessment*, 1964, *28*, 144-150.

Holzman, P. S., and Klein, G. S. "Motive and Style in Reality Contact." *Bulletin of the Menninger Clinic*, 1956, *20*, 181-191.

Holzman, P. S., and others. "Eye-Tracking Dysfunctions in Schizophrenic Patients and Their Relatives." *Archives of General Psychiatry*, 1974, *31*, 143-151.

Horton, R. "African Traditional Thought and Western Science. Part 1: From Tradition to Science." *Africa*, 1967a, *37*, 50-71.

Horton, R. "African Traditional Thought and Western Science. Part 2: The 'Closed' and 'Open' Predicaments." *Africa*, 1967b, *37*, 155-187.

Hoyt, W. G. *Lowell and Mars*. Tuscon: University of Arizona Press, 1976.

Hyman, R. *The Nature of Psychological Inquiry*. Englewood Cliffs, N.J.: Prentice-Hall, 1964.

Ittelson, W. H., and others. *An Introduction to Environmental Psychology*. New York: Holt, Rinehart and Winston, 1974.

Jackson, D. N. *Personality Research Form Manual*. Goshen, N.Y.: Research Psychologists Press, 1967.

Jackson, D. N. "The Relative Validity of Scales Prepared by Naive Item Writers and Those Based on Empirical Methods of Personality Scale Construction." *Educational and Psychological Measurement*, 1975, *35*, 361-370.

Jackson, D. N., Ahmed, S. A., and Heapy, N. A. "Is Achievement a Unitary Construct?" *Journal of Research in Personality*, 1976, *10*, 1-21.

Jackson, D. N., and Messick, S. (Eds.). *Problems in Human Assessment.* New York: McGraw-Hill, 1967.

Jackson, D. N., Neill, J. A., and Bevan, A. R. "An Evaluation of Forced-Choice and True-False Item Formats in Personality Assessment." *Journal of Research in Personality,* 1973, 7, 21-30.

Jaffe, J., and Feldstein, S. *Rhythms of Dialogue.* New York: Academic Press, 1970.

Jahoda, M. *Current Conceptions of Positive Mental Health.* New York: Basic Books, 1958.

James, W. *The Principles of Psychology.* Vol. 2. New York: Holt, Rinehart and Winston, 1890.

Jones, E. E. "How Do People Perceive the Causes of Behavior?" *American Scientist,* 1976, *64,* 300-305.

Jones, E. E., and Davis, K. E. "From Acts to Dispositions: The Attribution Process in Person Perception." In L. Berkowitz (Ed.), *Advances in Experimental Social Psychology.* Vol. 2. New York: Academic Press, 1965.

Jones, E. E., and others. *Attribution: Perceiving the Causes of Behavior.* Morristown, N.J.: General Learning Press, 1972.

Jones, M. B., and Fennell, R. S. "Runway Performance in Two Strains of Rats." *Quarterly Journal of the Florida Academy of Sciences,* 1965, *28,* 289-296.

Jones, N. Blurton. "Characteristics of Ethological Studies of Human Behaviour." In N. Blurton Jones (Ed.), *Ethological Studies of Child Behaviour.* Cambridge, England: Cambridge University Press, 1972a.

Jones, N. Blurton (Ed.). *Ethological Studies of Child Behaviour.* Cambridge, England: Cambridge University Press, 1972b.

Jones, R. R. "Conceptual Versus Analytic Uses of Generalizability Theory in Behavioral Assessment." In J. D. Cone and R. P. Hawkins (Eds.), *Behavioral Assessment: New Directions in Clinical Psychology.* New York: Brunner/Mazel, 1977.

Kanouse, D. E. "Language, Labeling, and Attribution." In E. E. Jones and others, *Attribution: Perceiving the Causes of Behavior.* Morristown, N.J.: General Learning Press, 1972.

Kaye, K. "Infants' Effects Upon Their Mothers' Teaching Strategies." In J. C. Glidewell (Ed.), *The Social Context of Learning and Development.* New York: Gardner Press, 1977a.

Kaye, K. "Toward the Origins of Dialogue." In H. R. Schaffer (Ed.), *Interaction in Infancy: The Loch Lomond Symposium.* London: Academic Press, 1977b.

Kellam, S. G., Branch, J. D., Agrawal, K. C., and Ensminger, M. E. *Mental Health and Going to School: The Woodlawn Program of Assessment, Early Intervention, and Evaluation.* Chicago: University of Chicago Press, 1975.

Kelley, H. H. "Causal Schemata and the Attribution Process." In E. E. Jones and others, *Attribution: Perceiving the Causes of Behavior.* Morristown, N.J.: General Learning Press, 1972.

Kelly, E. L., and Fiske, D. W. *The Prediction of Performance in Clinical Psychology.* Ann Arbor: University of Michigan Press, 1951. (Reprinted by Greenwood Press, New York, 1969.)

Kelly, G. A. *The Psychology of Personal Constructs.* Vol. 1: *A Theory of Personality.* New York: Norton, 1955.

Kelly, G. A. "The Language of Hypothesis: Man's Psychological Instrument." *Journal of Individual Psychology,* 1964, *20,* 137-152.

Kelman, H. C. *A Time to Speak: On Human Values and Social Research.* San Francisco: Jossey-Bass, 1968.

Kendon, A. "Introduction." In A. Kendon, R. M. Harris, and M. R. Kay (Eds.), *The Organization of Behavior in Face-to-Face Interaction.* The Hague, Netherlands: Mouton, 1975.

Kendon, A., and Ferber, A. "A Description of Some Human Greetings." In R. P. Michael and J. H. Crook (Eds.), *Comparative Ecology and Behaviour of Primates.* New York: Academic Press, 1973.

Kleinmuntz, B. *Personality Measurement: An Introduction.* Homewood, Ill.: Dorsey Press, 1967.

Klinger, E., Barta, S. G., Mahoney, T. W., and others. "Motivation, Mood, and Mental Events: Patterns and Implications for Adaptive Processes." In G. Serban (Ed.), *Psychopathology of Human Adaptation.* New York: Plenum, 1976.

Klüver, H. "The Study of Personality and the Method of Equivalent and Non-Equivalent Stimuli." *Character and Personality,* 1936, *5,* 91-112.

Koch, S. "Psychology as Science." In S. C. Brown (Ed.), *Philosophy of Psychology.* London: Macmillan, 1974.

Koltuv, B. B. "Some Characteristics of Intrajudge Trait Intercorrelations." *Psychological Monographs,* 1962, *76,* 33 (whole issue).

Krathwohl, D. R., Bloom, B. S., and Masia, B. B. *Taxonomy of Educational Objectives: The Classification of Educational Goals.* Handbook 2: *Affective Domain.* New York: McKay, 1964.

Krippendorff, K. "Bivariate Agreement Coefficients for Reliability of Data." In E. F. Borgatta and G. W. Bohrnstedt (Eds.), *Sociological Methodology: 1970.* San Francisco: Jossey-Bass, 1970.

Kroeber, A. L., and Kluckhohn, C. *Culture: A Critical Review of Concepts and Definitions.* New York: Random House, 1952.

Kuhn, T. S. "Logic of Discovery or Psychology of Research?" In I. Lakatos and A. Musgrave (Eds.), *Criterion and the Growth of Knowledge.* Cambridge, England: Cambridge University Press, 1970a.

Kuhn, T. S. *The Structure of Scientific Revolutions.* (2nd ed.) Chicago: University of Chicago Press, 1970b.

Kuhn, T. S. "Second Thoughts on Paradigms." In F. Suppe (Ed.), *The Structure of Scientific Theories.* Urbana: University of Illinois Press, 1974.

Kuncel, R. B. "Response Processes and Relative Location of Subject and Item." *Educational and Psychological Measurement,* 1973, *33,* 545-563.

Kuncel, R. B., and Fiske, D. W. "Stability of Response Process and Response." *Educational and Psychological Measurement,* 1974, *34,* 743-755.

LaBarre, W. "Preface." In G. Devereux, *From Anxiety to Method in the Behavioral Sciences.* The Hague, Netherlands: Mouton, 1967.

Lachenmeyer, C. W. "The Subject Matter of Social Science." *Journal of General Psychology,* 1972, *87,* 277-293.

Lachenmeyer, C. W. *The Essence of Social Research: A Copernican Revolution.* New York: Free Press, 1973.

Lambert, M. J., Bergin, A. E., and Collins, J. L. "Therapist Induced Deterioration in Psychotherapy." In A. S. Gurman and A. M. Razin (Eds.), *Effective Psychotherapy: A Handbook of Research.* Elmsford, N.Y.: Pergamon, 1978.

Levine, M. "Scientific Method and the Adversary Model: Some Preliminary Thoughts." *American Psychologist,* 1974, *29,* 661-677.

LeVine, R. A. "Outsiders' Judgments: An Ethnographic Approach to Group Differences in Personality." In R. Naroll and R. Cohen

(Eds.), *A Handbook of Method in Cultural Anthropology*. New York: Columbia University Press, 1973.

Lewis, M., and Rosenblum, L. A. (Eds.), *The Effect of the Infant on Its Caregiver*. New York: Wiley, 1974.

Lewis, O. "Controls and Experiments in Field Work." In A. L. Kroeber (Ed.), *Anthropology Today: An Encyclopedic Inventory*. Chicago: University of Chicago Press, 1953.

Lipsey, M. W. "Research and Relevance: A Survey of Graduate Students and Faculty in Psychology." *American Psychologist*, 1974, *29*, 541-553.

Loevinger, J., and Wessler, R. *Measuring Ego Development*. Vol. 1: *Construction and Use of a Sentence Completion Test*. San Francisco: Jossey-Bass, 1970.

Lorenz, K. Z. *Studies in Human and Animal Behaviour*. 2 vols. (R. Martin, Trans.) Cambridge, Mass.: Harvard University Press, 1970–1971.

Luborsky, L., Singer, B., and Luborsky, L. "Comparative Studies of Psychotherapies: Is It True that 'Everyone Has Won and All Must Have Prizes?'" *Archives of General Psychiatry*, 1975, *32*, 995-1008.

Luborsky, L., and others. "Factors Influencing the Outcome of Psychotherapy: A Review of Quantitative Research." *Psychological Bulletin*, 1971, *75*, 145-185.

Luce, R. D. "What Sort of Measurement is Psychophysical Measurement?" *American Psychologist*, 1972, *27*, 96-106.

McClelland, D. C. *Personality*. New York: William Sloane, 1951.

McClelland, D. C. "Methods of Measuring Human Motivation." In J. W. Atkinson (Ed.), *Motives in Fantasy, Action, and Society*. New York: D. Van Nostrand, 1958.

McClelland, D. C. "Opinions Predict Opinions: So What Else Is New?" *Journal of Consulting and Clinical Psychology*, 1972, *38*, 325-326.

McClelland, D. C., Atkinson, J. W., Clark, R. A., and Lowell, E. L. "A Scoring Manual for the Achievement Motive." In J. W. Atkinson (Ed.), *Motives in Fantasy, Action, and Society*. New York: D. Van Nostrand, 1958.

MacFadyen, H. W. "Evaluative-Observational Schemes for Behavior Assessment and Therapy: A Review." Alberta, Canada: Department of Educational Psychology, University of Calgary, 1974.

McFall, R. M., and Lillesand, D. B. "Behavioral Rehearsal with Modeling and Coaching in Assertion Training." *Journal of Abnormal Psychology,* 1971, 77, 313-323.

McGuire, W. J. "The Yin and Yang of Progress in Social Psychology: Seven Koan." *Journal of Personality and Social Psychology,* 1973, 26, 446-456.

McGuire, W. J. "The Concepts of Attitudes and Their Relations to Behaviors." In *Perspectives on Attitude Assessment: Surveys and Their Alternatives.* Washington, D.C.: Smithsonian Institution, 1975.

McNeill, G. D. *Conceptual Basis of Language.* New York: Halsted Press, forthcoming.

MacRae, D., Jr. *The Social Functions of Social Science.* New Haven, Conn.: Yale University Press, 1976.

McReynolds, P. "The Assessment of Anxiety: A Survey of Available Techniques." In P. McReynolds (Ed.), *Advances in Psychological Assessment.* Vol. 1. Palo Alto, Calif.: Science and Behavior Books, 1968.

Madison, P. "Complex Behavior in Natural Settings." In T. Mischel (Ed.), *Human Action: Conceptual and Empirical Issues.* New York: Academic Press, 1969.

Magnusson, D., and Endler, N. S. (Eds.). *Personality at the Crossroads: Issues in Interactional Psychology.* New York: Halsted Press, 1977.

Magnusson, D., and Heffler, B. "The Generality of Behavioral Data III: Generalization Potential as a Function of the Number of Observation Instances." *Multivariate Behavioral Research,* 1969, 4, 29-42.

Mandler, G., and Kessen, W. *The Language of Psychology.* New York: Wiley, 1959.

Manis, M. "Comment on Gergen's 'Social Psychology as History.'" *Personality and Social Psychology Bulletin,* 1975, 1, 450-455.

March, J., and Simon, H. *Organizations.* New York: Wiley, 1958.

Mash, E. J., and McElwee, J. D. "Situational Effects on Observer Accuracy: Behavioral Predictability, Prior Experience, and Complexity of Coding Categories." *Child Development,* 1974, 45(2), 367-377.

Masterman, M. "The Nature of a Paradigm." In I. Lakatos and A.

Musgrave (Eds.), *Criticism and the Growth of Knowledge.* Cambridge, England: Cambridge University Press, 1970.

Meehl, P. E. *Clinical Versus Statistical Prediction: A Theoretical Analysis and a Review of the Evidence.* Minneapolis: University of Minnesota Press, 1954.

Meehl, P. E., and others. "Recaptured-Item Technique (RIT): A Method for Reducing Somewhat the Subjective Element in Factor-Naming." *Journal of Experimental Research in Personality,* 1971, *5,* 171-190.

Miller, A. G. (Ed.). *The Social Psychology of Psychological Research.* New York: Free Press, 1972.

Miller, G. A. "Psychology as a Means of Promoting Human Welfare." *American Psychologist,* 1969, *24,* 1063-1075.

Minor, M. J., and Fiske, D. W. "Response Processes During the Description of Others." *Educational and Psychological Measurement,* 1976, *36,* 829-833.

Mischel, T. "Epilogue." In T. Mischel (Ed.), *Human Action: Conceptual and Empirical Issues.* New York: Academic Press, 1969a.

Mischel, T. (Ed.). *Human Action: Conceptual and Empirical Issues.* New York: Academic Press, 1969b.

Mischel, W. *Personality and Assessment.* New York: Wiley, 1968.

Mischel, W. "On the Empirical Dilemmas of Psychodynamic Approaches: Issues and Alternatives." *Journal of Abnormal Psychology,* 1973a, *82,* 335-344.

Mischel, W. "Toward a Cognitive Social Learning Reconceptualization of Personality." *Psychological Review,* 1973b, *80,* 252-283.

Mischel, W. "On the Future of Personality Measurement." *American Psychologist,* 1977, *32,* 246-254.

Mitroff, I. I. *The Subjective Side of Science: A Philosophical Inquiry into the Psychology of the Apollo Moon Scientists.* New York: American Elsevier, 1974.

Morgenstern, O. *On the Accuracy of Economic Observations.* (2nd ed.) Princeton, N.J.: Princeton University Press, 1963.

Mulaik, S. A. "Are Personality Factors Raters' Conceptual Factors?" *Journal of Consulting Psychology,* 1964, *28,* 506-511.

Murdock, G. P. "Anthropology's Mythology: The Huxley Memorial Lecture 1971." In *Proceedings of the Royal Anthropological Insti-*

tute of Great Britain and Ireland for 1971. London: Royal Anthropological Institute, 1972.

Nagel, E. *The Structure of Science*. New York: Harcourt Brace Jovanovich, 1961.

Naroll, R. *Data Quality Control—A New Research Technique*. New York: Free Press, 1962.

Needham, R. "Polythetic Classification: Convergence and Consequences." *Man*, 1975, *10*, 349-369.

Negoita, C. V., and Ralescu, D. A. *Applications of Fuzzy Sets to Systems Analysis*. New York: Wiley, 1975.

Newcomb, T. "Experiment Designed to Test the Validity of a Rating Technique." *Journal of Educational Psychology*, 1931, *22*, 279-289.

Newtson, D. "Attribution and the Unit of Perception of Ongoing Behavior." *Journal of Personality and Social Psychology*, 1973, *28*, 28-38.

Newtson, D. "Foundations of Attribution: The Unit of Perception of Ongoing Behavior." In J. Harvey, W. Ickes, and R. Kidd (Eds.), *New Directions in Attribution Research*. New York: Halsted Press, 1976.

Newtson, D., and Engquist, G. "The Perceptual Organization of Ongoing Behavior." *Journal of Experimental Social Psychology*, 1976, *12*, 436-450.

Nisbett, R. E., and Wilson, T. DeC. "Telling More Than We Can Know: Verbal Reports on Mental Processes." *Psychological Review*, 1977, *84*, 231-259.

Norman, W. T. "Toward an Adequate Taxonomy of Personality Attributes: Replicated Factor Structure in Peer Nomination Personality Ratings." *Journal of Abnormal and Social Psychology*, 1963, *66*, 574-583.

Norman, W. T. *2800 Personality Trait Descriptors: Normative Operating Characteristics for a University Population*. Ann Arbor: Department of Psychology, University of Michigan, 1967.

Norman, W. T., and Goldberg, L. R. "Raters, Ratees, and Randomness in Personality Structure." *Journal of Personality and Social Psychology*, 1966, *4*, 681-691.

O'Leary, K. D., and Kent, R. N. "Behavior Modification for Social

Action: Research Tactics and Problems." In L. A. Hamerlynck, L. C. Handy, and E. J. Mash (Eds.), *Behavior Change: Methodology, Concepts, and Practice*. Champaign, Ill.: Research Press, 1973.

Orne, M. T., and Wender, P. H. "Anticipatory Socialization for Psychotherapy: Method and Rationale." *American Journal of Psychiatry*, 1968, *124*, 88-98.

Osgood, C. E. "Studies on the Generality of Affective Meaning Systems." *American Psychologist*, 1962, *17*, 10-28.

Osgood, C. E., Suci, G. J., and Tannenbaum, P. H. *The Measurement of Meaning*. Urbana: University of Illinois Press, 1957.

Passini, F. T., and Norman, W. T. "A Universal Conception of Personality Structure?" *Journal of Personality and Social Psychology*, 1966, *4*, 44-49.

Pavlov, I. P. *Lectures on Conditioned Reflexes*. (W. H. Gantt, Trans.) New York: International Publishers, 1928.

Peabody, D. "Trait Inferences: Evaluative and Descriptive Aspects." *Journal of Personality and Social Psychology Monograph*, 1967, *7*, 4 (whole issue).

Pepper, S., and Prytulak, L. S. "Sometimes Frequently Means Seldom: Context Effects in the Interpretation of Quantitative Expressions." *Journal of Research in Personality*, 1974, *8*, 95-101.

Personality and Social Psychology Bulletin, 1976, *2*, 371-465.

Pervin, L. A. "The Representative Design of Person-Situation Research." In D. Magnusson and N. S. Endler (Eds.), *Personality at the Crossroads: Current Issues in Interactional Psychology*. New York: Halsted Press, 1977.

Pervin, L. A. "Definitions, Measurements, and Classifications of Stimuli, Situations, and Environments." *Human Ecology*, in press.

Peters, R. S. "Motivation, Emotion, and the Conceptual Schemes of Common Sense." In T. Mischel (Ed.), *Human Action: Conceptual and Empirical Issues*. New York: Academic Press, 1969.

Peters, R. S. "Personal Understanding and Personal Relationships." In T. Mischel (Ed.), *Understanding Other Persons*. Totowa, N.J.: Rowman and Littlefield, 1974.

Phillips, D. L. *Abandoning Method: Sociological Studies in Methodology*. San Francisco: Jossey-Bass, 1973.

Piaget, J. *The Origins of Intelligence in Children.* (M. Cook, Trans.) New York: Norton, 1963.

Piaget, J. *The Child's Conception of Number.* New York: Norton, 1965.

Piaget, J. *Biology and Knowledge: An Essay on the Relations Between Organic Regulations and Cognitive Processes.* Chicago: University of Chicago Press, 1971.

Platt, J. R. "Strong Inference." *Science,* 1964, *146,* 347-353.

Popper, K. R. *The Logic of Scientific Discovery.* New York: Basic Books, 1959.

Proshansky, H. M. "Environmental Psychology and the Real World." *American Psychologist,* 1976, *31,* 303-310.

Rabkin, J. G. "Opinions About Mental Illness: A Review of the Literature." *Psychological Bulletin,* 1972, 77, 153-171.

Ramanaiah, N. V., and Goldberg, L. R. "Stylistic Components of Human Judgment: The Generality of Individual Differences." *Applied Psychological Measurement,* 1977, *1,* 23-39.

Rees, A. "Economics." In D. L. Sills (Ed.), *International Encyclopedia of the Social Sciences.* Vol. 4. New York: Macmillan and Free Press, 1968.

Reichenbach, H. *Experience and Prediction: An Analysis of the Foundations and the Structure of Knowledge.* Chicago: University of Chicago Press, 1938.

Reid, J. B. "Reliability Assessment of Observational Data: A Possible Methodological Problem." *Child Development,* 1970, *41,* 1143-1150.

Reiss, A. J., Jr. "Sociology." In D. L. Sills (Ed.), *International Encyclopedia of the Social Sciences.* Vol. 15. New York: Macmillan and Free Press, 1968.

Riecken, H. W., and Boruch, R. F. (Eds.). *Social Experimentation: A Method for Planning and Evaluating Social Intervention.* New York: Academic Press, 1974.

Roberts, K. H., Hulin, C. L., and Rousseau, D. *An Approach to Understanding Organizational Research.* San Francisco: Jossey-Bass, forthcoming.

Rosenberg, M. J. "The Conditions and Consequences of Evaluation Apprehension." In R. Rosenthal and R. L. Rosnow (Eds.), *Artifact in Behavioral Research.* New York: Academic Press, 1969.

Rosenfeld, H. M. "Approval-Seeking and Approval-Inducing Functions of Verbal and Nonverbal Responses in the Dyad." *Journal of Personality and Social Psychology*, 1966, *4*, 597-605.

Rosenthal, R. *Experimenter Effects in Behavioral Research.* New York: Appleton-Century-Crofts, 1966.

Ross, L. D., Amabile, T. M., and Steinmetz, J. L. "Social Roles, Social Control, and Biases in Social-Perception Process." *Journal of Personality and Social Psychology*, 1977, *35*, 485-494.

Rotter, J. B. *Social Learning and Clinical Psychology.* Englewood Cliffs, N.J.: Prentice-Hall, 1954.

Rotter, J. B. "Generalized Expectancies for Internal Versus External Control of Reinforcement." *Psychological Monographs*, 1966, *80*, 1 (whole issue).

Rotter, J. B., Chance, J. E., and Phares, E. J. *Applications of a Social Learning Theory of Personality.* New York: Holt, Rinehart and Winston, 1972.

Runkel, P. J., and McGrath, J. E. *Research on Human Behavior: A Systematic Guide to Method.* New York: Holt, Rinehart and Winston, 1972.

Saks, M. J. "Social Scientists Can't Rig Juries." *Psychology Today*, 1976, *9*(8), 48-50, 55-57.

Samuelson, P. A. "Lessons from the Current Economic Expansion." *American Economic Review*, 1974, *64*(2), 75-77.

Sawyer, J. "Measurement *and* Prediction, Clinical *and* Statistical." *Psychological Bulletin*, 1966, *66*, 178-200.

Schachter, S. *The Psychology of Affiliation.* Stanford, Calif.: Stanford University Press, 1959.

Scheffler, I. *Science and Subjectivity.* New York: Bobbs-Merrill, 1967.

Schneider, D. J. "Implicit Personality Theory: A Review." *Psychological Bulletin*, 1973, *79*, 294-309.

Schneider, D. M. *American Kinship: A Cultural Account.* Englewood Cliffs, N.J.: Prentice-Hall, 1968.

Schoenfeld, W. N., and Farmer, J. "Reinforcement Schedules and the 'Behavior Stream.'" In W. N. Schoenfeld (Ed.), *The Theory of Reinforcement Schedules.* New York: Appleton-Century-Crofts, 1970.

Schroder, H. M. "Conceptual Complexity and Personality Organization." In H. M. Schroder and P. Suedfeld (Eds.), *Personality*

Theory and Information Processing. New York: Ronald Press, 1971.

Schulman, J., and others. "Recipe for a Jury." *Psychology Today,* 1973, *6*(12), 37-44, 77-84.

Schultz, D. P. "The Human Subject in Psychological Research." *Psychological Bulletin,* 1969, *72,* 214-218.

Schutz, A. "Common Sense and Scientific Interpretation of Human Action." *Philosophy and Phenomenological Research,* 1953, *14* (September), 1-38.

Schutz, A. *Collected Papers.* Vol. 1: *The Problem of Social Reality.* The Hague, Netherlands: Martinus Nijhoff, 1967.

Scott, W. A. "Reliability of Content Analysis: The Case of Nominal Scale Coding." *Public Opinion Quarterly,* 1955, *19,* 321-325.

Scriven, M. "A Possible Distinction Between Traditional Scientific Disciplines and the Study of Human Behavior." In H. Feigl and M. Scriven (Eds.), *The Foundations of Science and the Concepts of Psychology and Psychoanalysis.* Minnesota Studies in the Philosophy of Science, Vol. 1. Minneapolis: University of Minnesota Press, 1956.

Sechrest, L. "Personality." *Annual Review of Psychology,* 1976, *27,* 1-27.

Secord, P. F., and Backman, C. W. *Social Psychology.* New York: McGraw-Hill, 1964.

Sells, S. B., Demaree, R. G., and Will, D. P., Jr. "Dimensions of Personality: I. Conjoint Factor Structure of Guilford and Cattell Trait Markers." *Multivariate Behavioral Research,* 1970, *5,* 391-422.

Sells, S. B., Demaree, R. G., and Will, D. P., Jr. "Dimensions of Personality: II. Separate Factor Structures in Guilford and Cattell Trait Markers." *Multivariate Behavioral Research,* 1971, *6,* 135-185.

Shaw, M. E. "New Science or Non-Science? Review of Harré and Secord, *The Explanation of Social Behaviour.*" *Contemporary Psychology,* 1974, *19,* 96-97.

Sherif, M. "Crisis in Social Psychology: Some Remarks Toward Breaking Through the Crisis." *Personality and Social Psychology Bulletin,* 1977, *3,* 368-382.

Shrout, P. E. "Impression Formation and Nonverbal Behaviors as a

Function of Sex of Observer and of Target." Unpublished doctoral dissertation, University of Chicago, 1976.

Shweder, R. A. "Semantic Structures and Personality Assessment." Unpublished doctoral dissertation, Harvard University, 1972.

Shweder, R. A. "How Relevant Is an Individual Difference Theory of Personality?" *Journal of Personality*, 1975, *43*, 455-484.

Shweder, R. A. "Are Everyday Personality Theories Correlational?" Chicago: Committee on Human Development, University of Chicago, 1976.

Shweder, R. A. "Likeness and Likelihood in Everyday Thought: Magical Thinking and Everyday Judgments about Personality." *Current Anthropology*, 1977, *18*(4), 637-648, 652-658.

Silverman, I. *The Human Subject in the Psychological Laboratory*. Elmsford, N.Y.: Pergamon, 1977.

Silverman, L. H. "Psychoanalytic Theory: 'The Reports of My Death Are Greatly Exaggerated.'" *American Psychologist*, 1976, *31*, 621-637.

Simon, H. A. "A Behavioral Model of Rational Choice." *Quarterly Journal of Economics*, 1955, *69*, 99-118.

Simon, H. A. "Motivational and Emotional Controls of Cognition." *Psychological Review*, 1967, *74*, 29-39.

Simpson, R. H. "The Specific Meanings of Certain Terms Indicating Differing Degrees of Frequency." *Quarterly Journal of Speech*, 1944, *30*, 328-330.

Skinner, B. F. "Are Theories of Learning Necessary?" *Psychological Review*, 1950, *57*, 193-216.

Skinner, B. F. *Beyond Freedom and Dignity*. New York: Knopf, 1971.

Skinner, B. F. *About Behaviorism*. New York: Knopf, 1974.

Smedslund, J. *Becoming a Psychologist: Theoretical Foundations for a Humanistic Psychology*. Oslo: Universitetsforlaget, 1972. (New York: Halsted Press, 1973.)

Smedslund, J. "A Reexamination of the Role of Theory in Psychology." Paper presented at the 21st International Congress of Psychology, Paris, 1976.

Smith, M. B. *Humanizing Social Psychology*. San Francisco: Jossey-Bass, 1974.

Snider, J. G., and Osgood, C. E. (Eds.). *The Semantic Differential Technique*. Chicago: Aldine, 1969.

Snyder, M. "Attribution and Behavior: Social Perception and Social Causation." In J. H. Harvey, W. J. Ickes, and R. F. Kidd (Eds.), *New Directions in Attribution Research*. New York: Halsted Press, 1976.

Sorrentino, R. M., and Short, J-A. C. "The Case of the Mysterious Moderates: Why Motives Sometimes Fail to Predict Behavior." *Journal of Personality and Social Psychology*, 1977, *35*, 478-484.

Spence, K. W. *Behavior Theory and Conditioning*. New Haven, Conn.: Yale University Press, 1956.

Spielberger, C. D., and Lushene, R. E. "Theory and Measurement of Anxiety States." In R. B. Cattell (Ed.), *Handbook of Modern Personality Theory*. Chicago: Aldine, 1971.

Spiro, M. "Discussion." In R. F. Spencer (Ed.), *Forms of Symbolic Action: Proceedings of the 1969 Annual Spring Meeting of the American Ethnological Society*, 1969.

Stanton, H. R., and Litwak, E. "Toward the Development of a Short Form Test of Interpersonal Competence." *American Sociological Review*, 1955, *20*, 668-674.

Stent, G. S. "Limits to the Scientific Understanding of Man." *Science*, 1975, *187*, 1052-1057.

Stern, D. N. "Mother and Infant at Play: The Dyadic Interaction Involving Facial, Vocal, and Gaze Behaviors." In M. Lewis and L. A. Rosenblum (Eds.), *The Effect of the Infant on Its Caregiver*. New York: Wiley, 1974.

Stern, G. G., Stein, M. I., and Bloom, B. S. *Methods in Personality Assessment*. New York: Free Press, 1956.

Stevens, S. S. "The Operational Basis of Psychology." *American Journal of Psychology*, 1935, *47*, 323-330.

Stricker, L. J., Messick, S., and Jackson, D. N. "Conformity, Anticonformity, and Independence: Their Dimensionality and Generality." *Journal of Personality and Social Psychology*, 1970, *16*, 494-507.

Strupp, H. H., and Hadley, S. W. "A Tripartite Model of Mental Health and Therapeutic Outcomes: With Special Reference to Negative Effects in Psychotherapy." *American Psychologist*, 1977, *32*, 187-196.

Strupp, H. H., Hadley, S. W., and Gomes-Schwartz, B. *Psychotherapy for Better or Worse: An Analysis of the Problem of Negative Effects*. New York: Aronson, 1977.

Sturz, H. "The Manhattan Bail Project." *Legal Aid Briefcase*, 1962, *21*, 21-27.

Sturz, H. "Experiments in the Criminal Justice System." *Legal Aid Briefcase*, 1967, *25*, 111-115.

Taplin, P. S., and Reid, J. B. "Effects of Instructional Set and Experimenter Influence on Observer Reliability." *Child Development*, 1973, *44*, 547-554.

Tatje, T. A. "Problems of Concept Definition for Comparative Studies." In R. Naroll and R. Cohen (Eds.), *A Handbook of Method in Cultural Anthropology*. New York: Columbia University Press, 1973.

Taylor, J. S. "A Personality Scale of Manifest Anxiety." *Journal of Abnormal and Social Psychology*, 1953, *48*, 285-290.

Thorngate, W. "Possible Limits on a Science of Social Behavior." In L. Strickland, F. Aboud, and K. Gergen (Eds.), *Social Psychology in Transition*. New York: Plenum, 1976.

Triandis, H. "Social Psychology and Cultural Analysis." *Journal for the Theory of Social Behaviour*, 1975, *5*, 81-106.

Truscott, J. C., Parmelee, P., and Werner, C. "Plate-Touching in Restaurants: Preliminary Observations of a Food-Related Marking Behavior in Humans." *Personality and Social Psychology Bulletin*, 1977, *3*, 425-428.

Tunnell, G. B. "Three Dimensions of Naturalness: An Expanded Definition of Field Research." *Psychological Bulletin*, 1977, *84*, 426-437.

Tversky, A., and Kahneman, D. "Judgment Under Uncertainty: Heuristics and Biases." *Science*, 1974, *185*, 1124-1131.

Vernon, P. E. *Personality Tests and Assessments*. London: Methuen, 1953.

Waern, Y., Hecht, U., and Johansson, B. "How do Children Interpret Others' Behavior? A Developmental Description." *Reports from the Psychological Laboratories*, no. 437. Stockholm: University of Stockholm, 1974.

Wallace, J. "An Abilities Conception of Personality: Some Implications for Personality Measurement." *American Psychologist*, 1966, *21*, 132-138.

Wallace, J. "What Units Shall We Employ? Allport's Question Revisited." *Journal of Consulting Psychology*, 1967, *31*, 56-64.

Walster, E., and others. "Effectiveness of Debriefing Following

Deception Experiments." *Journal of Personality and Social Psychology*, 1967, *6*, 371-380.

Watson, J. B. "Psychology as the Behaviorist Sees It." *Psychological Review*, 1913, *20*, 158-177.

Webb, E. J., Campbell, D. T., Schwartz, R. D., and Sechrest, L. *Unobtrusive Measures: Nonreactive Research in the Social Sciences.* Chicago: Rand McNally, 1966.

Weick, K. E. "Systematic Observational Methods." In G. Lindzey and E. Aronson (Eds.), *Handbook of Social Psychology.* Vol. 2. (2nd ed.) Reading, Mass.: Addison-Wesley, 1968.

Weick, K. E. *The Social Psychology of Organizing.* Reading, Mass.: Addison-Wesley, 1969.

West, S. G., Gunn, S. P., and Chernicky, P. "Ubiquitous Watergate: An Attributional Analysis." *Journal of Personality and Social Psychology*, 1975, *32*, 55-65.

White, R. W. *The Enterprise of Living: Growth and Organization in Personality.* New York: Holt, Rinehart and Winston, 1972.

Wiggins, J. S. *Personality and Prediction: Principles of Personality Assessment.* Reading, Mass.: Addison-Wesley, 1973.

Wiggins, J. S. "In Defense of Traits." Paper presented at the 9th annual symposium on the Use of the MMPI, Los Angeles, February 28, 1974. (Available from Department of Psychology, University of British Columbia, Vancouver, British Columbia, Canada.)

Wigner, E. P. "Events, Laws of Nature, and Invariance Principles." *Science*, 1964, *145*, 995-999.

Wolfle, D. "Increased Pay, Diminished Stature." *Science*, 1973, *179*, 131.

Yngve, V. H. "On Getting a Word in Edgewise." In *Papers from the Sixth Regional Meeting, Chicago Linguistic Society.* Chicago: Chicago Linguistic Society, 1970.

Zadeh, L. A. "Outline of a New Approach to the Analysis of Complex Systems and Decision Processes." In J. L. Cochrane and M. Zeleny (Eds.), *Multiple Criteria Decision Making.* Columbia: University of South Carolina Press, 1973.

Zeisel, H., and Diamond, S. S. "The Jury Selection in the Mitchell-Stans Conspiracy Trial." *American Bar Foundation Research Journal*, 1976, *1*, 151-174.

Ziman, J. M. *Public Knowledge: An Essay Concerning the Social Dimensions of Science.* Cambridge, England: Cambridge University Press, 1968.

Index